Dungeons, Dragons, and Digital Denizens

Approaches to Digital Game Studies

Volume 1

**Series Review Board
(Alphabetically)**

Mia Consalvo, Massachusetts Institute of Technology
James Paul Gee, Arizona State University
Helen Kennedy, University of the West of England
Frans Mäyrä, University of Tampere
Toby Miller, University of California, Riverside
Torill Mortensen, IT University Copenhagen
Lisa Nakamura, University of Illinois
Gareth Schott, University of Waikato
Mark J. P. Wolf, Concordia University

Series Editors

Gerald Voorhees, Oregon State University
Josh Call, Grand View University
Katie Whitlock, California State University, Chico

Dungeons, Dragons, and Digital Denizens

The Digital Role-Playing Game

**EDITED BY
GERALD VOORHEES,
JOSH CALL, AND
KATIE WHITLOCK**

The Continuum International Publishing Group
80 Maiden Lane, New York, NY 10038
The Tower Building, 11 York Road, London SE1 7NX

www.continuumbooks.com

© Gerald Voorhees, Josh Call, and Katie Whitlock, 2012

All rights reserved. No part of this book may be reproduced, stored in a retrieval system, or transmitted, in any form or by any means, electronic, mechanical, photocopying, recording, or otherwise, without the written permission of the publishers.

Library of Congress Cataloging-in-Publication Data
Dungeons, dragons, and digital denizens : the digital role-playing game / edited by Gerald Voorhees, Josh Call and Katie Whitlock.
p. cm.
Includes bibliographical references and index.
ISBN-13: 978-1-4411-9189-2 (hardcover : alk. paper)
ISBN-10: 1-4411-9189-5 (hardcover : alk. paper)
ISBN-13: 978-1-4411-9518-0 (pbk. : alk. paper)
ISBN-10: 1-4411-9518-1 (pbk. : alk. paper)
1. Fantasy games. 2. Electronic games. 3. Role playing. 4. Games. 5. Role playing. 6. Fantasy games. I. Voorhees, Gerald. II. Call, Josh. III. Whitlock, Katie.
GV1469.6.D86 2012
793.93—dc23

2011037483

ISBN: HB: 978-1-4411-9189-2
PB: 978-1-4411-9518-0

Typeset by Fakenham Prepress Solutions, Fakenham, Norfolk NR21 8NN

```
LIBRARY AND LEARNING RESOURCES
CITY COLLEGE PLYMOUTH
CLASS NO.  006.69 CAL
ACCESS NO. 010367 9
```

Contents

Acknowledgments ix

Series Introduction – Genre and Disciplinarity in the Study of Games 1
Gerald Voorhees, Josh Call, and Katie Whitlock

Introduction – From Dungeons to Digital Denizens 11
Josh Call, Katie Whitlock, and Gerald Voorhees

SECTION ONE Game Master 25

1 Eco-Performance in the Digital RPG Gamescape 27
Adele H. Bealer

2 The Pathways of Time: Temporality and Procedures in MMORPGs 48
Joshua Abboud

3 Game and Narrative in *Dragon Age: Origins:* Playing the Archive in Digital RPGs 66
Alice Henton

4 When Language Goes Bad: Localization's Effect on the Gameplay of Japanese RPGs 88
Douglas Schules

5   *The Lord of the Rings Online*: Issues in the Adaptation of MMORPGs   113
    Neil Randall, Kathleen Murphy

SECTION TWO In-Character   133

6   Traumatic Origins: Memory, Crisis, and Identity in Digital RPGs   135
    Katie Whitlock

7   Risky Business: Neo-liberal Rationality and the Computer RPG   153
    Andrew Baerg

8   Postcards from the Other Side: Interactive Revelation in Post-Apocalyptic RPGs   174
    Zachary McDowell

9   Constructing a Powerful Identity in *World of Warcraft*: A Sociolinguistic Approach to MMORPGs   194
    Benjamin E. Friedline, Lauren B. Collister

10 In the Blood of *Dragon Age: Origins*: Metaphor and Identity in Digital RPGs   219
    Karen Zook

11 Epic Style: Re-compositional Performance in the BioWare Digital RPG   235
    Roger Travis

SECTION THREE Out-of-Character 257

12 Neo-liberal Multiculturalism in *Mass Effect*: The Government of Difference in Digital RPGs 259
Gerald Voorhees

13 'Simply Fighting to Preserve Their Way of Life': Multiculturalism in *World of Warcraft* 278
Christopher Douglas

14 From Meaning to Experience: Teaching Fiction Writing With Digital RPGs 304
Trent Hergenrader

15 Gaming the Meta: Metagame Culture and Player Motivation in RPGs 324
Josh Call

16 The Generalization of Configurable Being: From RPGs to Facebook 343
Chuk Moran

About the Contributors 363
Author Index 369
Game Index 372
Subject Index 374

Acknowledgments

Like most collaborative works, this book is a product of the open sharing of insight, fearless pursuit of curiosity, and bold willingness to engage with, and embrace as essential, the differences of perspective, approach, and opinion that brought together the editors. The contributors, intrepid and earnest, assembled their own voices, as well as those from the disciplines in which they are located, together in a chorus more profound than any one register could aspire to. The Series Review Board (Mia Consalvo, Massachusetts Institute of Technology; James Paul Gee, Arizona State University; Helen Kennedy, University of the West of England; Frans Mäyrä, University of Tampere; Toby Miller, University of California, Riverside; Torill Mortensen, IT University Copenhagen; Lisa Nakamura, University of Illinois; Gareth Schott, University of Waikato; Mark J. P. Wolf, Concordia University) helped shaped the content and coherence of this collection. Their intellectual labor and guidance was, and continues to be, an invaluable resource for the editors.

That said, this book was made possible by the work of many more people, most of whom are not credited elsewhere in this volume. Four anonymous reviewers gave this project the green light when it was little more than a well-conceived and researched proposal. They also raised questions about game studies, genre, and disciplinarity that have helped give shape to this series and volume. David Depew, Bruce Gronbeck, David Hingstman, and Robert Brooke provided some valuable insights about the process of putting together a scholarly anthology. Colleagues at High Point University, Grand View University and California State University, Chico offered moral and material support. Kim Nguyen sacrificed time and more interesting dialogue options to converse about the composition of this volume and provide scholarly perspective completely disinterested toward game studies. Nikki, Kairie, and Colin Call gave up valuable family time and willingly let the television be used for game research, while steadfastly remaining both encouraging and supportive. At Continuum, Katie Gallof has been a steadfast advocate of this project, shepherding the editors through the sometimes confounding process of publishing a scholarly anthology. Her patience, support, and interest have been invaluable.

Genre and Disciplinarity in the Study of Games

GERALD VOORHEES, JOSH CALL, AND KATIE WHITLOCK

This book series, *Approaches to Game Studies*, is organized around two premises, one of which is widely accepted among games researchers while the second – though not contentious – is ambivalent enough to elude consensus.

The first, uncontroversial premise is that the study of digital games is an interdisciplinary endeavor that synthesizes theories and methods from a broad swath of the humanities but nevertheless benefits from multidisciplinary approaches that bring new perspectives to the table. Arguably, this is the founding premise of game studies as an academic discipline. In the inaugural issue of the journal *Game Studies*, Espen Aarseth notes both that we have all come to the field from 'somewhere else' to make game studies the integrated discipline that it has become, and that existing fields should continue to study games as well. This interdisciplinarity is continually reaffirmed, most notably by Jesper Juul, Gonzalo Frasca, and Ian Bogost, who, respectively, convinced us that games are half-real hybrids of fiction and rules, reminded us that ludologists love stories too, and encouraged what may be the biggest paradigm shift in the field to date by blending the language and insight of informatics with humanistic methods.

This premise parallels, in some important regards, the process through which this project came into being. In 2007, we (Gerald, Katie, and Josh) were asked to serve as area chairs for the Game Studies area – then called the Digital Games area – of the Popular Culture Association/American Culture Association (hereafter, PCA/ACA)[1]. Being the geeky games people that we are, we all jumped at the opportunity. Usually, there are only one or two people chairing an area, but given that few academic organizations will ever turn away eager volunteer help, it was suggested that we co-chair the area along with Tony Avruch, making us the first four-person area chair team.

Our first priority was to grow the area. Our 'blue sky' dream was to create a fixed and recognizable location for game studies scholarship in America that would invite the kind of serious work that we saw happening elsewhere in the world. Over the past four years, we have made steady progress on both fronts. The year before we took over from Nathan Garrelts, who was visionary to start the Video Game Studies area in 2003, the Digital Games area featured eight panels consisting of twenty-eight presenters. At the April 2011 conference in San Antonio, Texas, the Game Studies area featured twelve panels consisting of forty-eight unique presentations. This is relatively modest growth over a four-year period and it parallels the growth of the field in general, but it also reflects our concerted effort to invite scholars from our respective disciplinary homes to join in an interdisciplinary conversation. In the past few years, several disciplinary organizations, including the Society for Cinema and Media Studies and the International Communication Association, have organized interest group and areas devoted to digital games, but the Game Studies area of the PCA/ACA has the most enduring footprint of any North American academic organization that gives serious attention to the social and cultural impact of games and gaming. Building from the same legacy that helped germinate Garrelts' two anthologies – one on players (2005) and one focused on the *Grand Theft Auto* series (2006) – it is our hope that *Approaches to Game Studies* will help broaden this footprint.

Along the way, we discovered two very significant details. First – and this corresponds with the first premise of the series – is that each of us came to this work from very different academic locations. While we all certainly shared that social tag of 'gamer', our intellectual and academic investments in this material drew from varied traditions: rhetoric and digital media, theatre performance and gender studies, and visual culture and literacy education. Our positions, both perspectival and institutional, rooted in these various locations and commitments has nurtured the overarching belief that one of the prime virtues of working in game studies is the inevitable likelihood of hybrid theorization and scholarship; it demands a commitment to inviting multiple, and often disparate, voices together in conversation.

To that end, and with respect for beginnings, the volumes in this series contribute both interdisciplinary and multidisciplinary insights. Each volume features scholarship that, for the most part, reflect the interdisciplinary blending of theories and methods characteristic of game studies in general. Works that reflect a more multidisciplinary orientation remain acutely sensitive to the imperative that scholars from neighboring fields be able to access, make sense of, and, ultimately, make use of their conclusions and implications.

Part of our conversation is drawn from the need to find touchstones that connect us despite our different disciplines. We each enter the gaming experience with a shared goal of pleasure and scholarship but with differing lenses to explore the nature of the experience. Genre was one of our entry points that allowed for common ground as we each openly label ourselves as being a fan of role-playing games and/or other genres. It provided the opening for our own conversation, much like the tired pick-up line 'What's your sign?' replaced with the genre of choice as our first marker of gamer identity. All three of us gravitate towards role-playing games, making it a natural point of exploration for the first collection in the series.

The second significant point we discovered after a couple of years of working together reviewing paper proposals and attending more panels than we imagined possible – and this corresponds with the second premise of the series – was that the idea of games belonging to genres seemed to be a significant but nonetheless ambiguous element of many of the conversations we were having. Clearly, this is related to the first premise of the series, in that the language which scholars bring to games as a way of highlighting the distinctions between artifacts are rooted in field-specific perspectives.

There are, for instance, some obvious differences between *Super Mario Brothers* (Nintendo 1985) and *God of War* (SCE 2005). The tricky business, as we have discovered, concerns how we locate and interpret those differences.

While both *Super Mario Brothers* and *God of War* are clearly different games with their own mechanics, representational styles and audiences, it is possible to classify them both as platform games that, as designed artifacts, share a core mechanic (Salen and Zimmerman 2003). Essentially, the games involve linear progression from point-A to point-B through a series of environmental obstacles and hostile entities which the avatar-character is uniquely capable of traversing (by running, jumping, swimming, etc.) and defeating (with fireballs and chain swords). In some very real ways, we might identify these as genre tropes shared in common, meaning that in many respects they are both the same *kind* of platform game. More specifically, we might say that their differences are by degree, rather than by kind.

Alternately, we could argue that these represent radically different types of game. One is a linear side-scrolling, non-filled narrative, while the other works with variable camera angles and more established narrative structures and themes. One is defined by a fixed perspective and fundamentally simple game interface (consisting of one four-axis directional pad and two buttons), while the other offers a malleable third-person perspective manipulated by the interplay of two analog sticks and poly-ludic input wherein a series of button and directional combinations determine the output. Seen in the light of these aesthetic, kinetic, and technological considerations, *Super Mario Brothers* and *God of War* are radically distinct artifacts that do not exist in the same continuum.

In short, the matter of genre cannot be divorced from the various disciplinary voices participating in the conversation. Arsenault's notion of the Great Genre Illusion is informative. Drawing from film scholar Rick Altman and literature scholar Northrop Frye, Arsenault observes that genre means different things in different contexts, and the means of distinguishing genre vary from object to object, field to field, and perspective to perspective (2009, 156–8). Arsenault ends up discussing genre not as a fixed set of characteristics but rather, borrowing from German composer Joseph Haydn, 'variations on a theme' (162). This is much akin to Wittgenstein's famous thought experiment endeavoring to define games; he ultimately rejects a succinct definition and argues instead for understanding the concept as a family of resemblances.

Others have been less willing to compromise what they construe as the most essentially gamic qualities of digital games: their ludicity. Apperley, for instance, constructs the dispute over game genres in terms of the very identity of the field of game studies (2006). In his analysis, failing to define game genres in terms of interactivity, or ergodicity, relegates games to the status of remediations (Boltner and Grusin 2000). Newman also expresses concern that conventional genres reflect a 'text-centered' bias that obfuscates the social, cultural, historical, and experiential aspects of gameplay (2004). This is an idea at least twenty years in the making. David Myers also asks critics to rethink popular genres in terms of the experience of gameplay (1990). Specifically, Myers attempts to re-examine popular genres in terms of the type of interaction they engender. However, Myers is not looking to mechanics but rather to interaction styles or sensibilities: discovering, learning, manipulating, and testing. More recently, Elverdam and Aarseth have decried the 'arbitrary, contradictory, or overlapping genres' that have proliferated as a result of the lack of formal conventions pertaining to the creation of game genres (2007, 4). In response, they offer a multidimensional, open-ended typology – which is based on and revises an earlier effort (Aarseth, Smedstad, Sunnana 2003) – that consists of eight 'metacategories', seventeen dimensions, and forty-two classifications. Once recombined to encompass each metacategory, this schema offers three million, nine hundred eighty-one thousand, three hundred twelve unique game types. Thankfully, Elverdam and Aarseth see this typology as more of an analytical tool for game designers than a viable system of genres.

Wolf, another notable advocate of defining game genres by the type of interactivity they facilitate (2002, 112), offers a compelling jumping-off point for the way *Approaches to Game Studies* takes up the question of genre. While all of the forty-two genres Wolf discusses do enable distinct styles of interaction, some are nonetheless more remarkable for their intended purpose (demos and diagnostics, for example) or their representational style (abstract games and adaptations, for example) than for the type of interactivity they engender. In this light, Wolf's genres highlight the core problem with efforts to define games based only on interactivity; games are formal structures, but they are also no less significantly socially and culturally meaningful artifacts.

In what appears to be the first effort to create a typology of games, in 1982 game designer Chris Crawford argued for two primary categories: skill and action games, and strategy games (1997). This distinction is essentially that between mind and body. Skill and action games – which include the subcategories of combat, maze, sports, paddle and race games – require physical exertion, the exercise of motor skills, and even the strenuous effort of repetitive button-pushing, but they substitute reacting for planning. Strategy games – which include the subcategories of adventure, *D&D*, wargames, games of chance, educational, and interpersonal games – require thinking about the short and long term; they 'emphasize cognition rather than manipulation' (1997, 29). Two points can be derived from this early effort to distinguish game types. First, different types rise to prominence and fall to obscurity with the passage of time and the progress of technologies. They are not fixed but instead rely on an increasingly complex history of experiences that draws not only on the multiple theories that inform the work of game studies, but also on an increasingly large, diverse, and evolving body of games. Where it made sense, in 1982, to talk about paddle games as a distinct genus of game worthy of its own type, this seems silly by contemporary standards. Similarly, the first-person shooter, arguably the most pervasive type of game in the contemporary commercial market, did not yet exist as a kind in 1982. The second observation that can be drawn from Crawford's types is that different logics of classification are unavoidably in play. While the broad categories are defined by styles of interaction (mental or physical), the subcategories are distinguished, variously, by game structures (*D&D*, paddle, racing, and games of chance), theme (combat, wargames, sports, and interpersonal games) and function (educational).

This resonates strongly with one of the starting points of Wolf's taxonomy – film scholar Ed Buscombe's observation that literary and film genres are commonly differentiated by form, iconography, and use (2004, 194). With Burn and Carr (2006, 17–18), we maintain that all three of these elements are relevant to efforts to distinguish game genres. And while these criteria enable the construction of competing, even contradictory genres, they are not – and need not be – construed as mutually exclusive. After all, the operative and defining characteristics of games, the qualities that allow them to be grouped by kind, will be identified differently when looked upon from different perspectives.

The idea is not that the issues discussed here are invisible, unimportant, or arbitrary. Quite the opposite. These are the kinds of conversations and issues we see contributors raising, implying, or invoking as they bring their multidisciplinary approaches to bear on an interdisciplinary field of study. And while we recognize that, as a field, the idea of genre is complicated past the point of difficulty, we resist answers that shut down conversations, regardless of the complexity of the question. So, we invite hybrid disciplinarity into the conversation with the idea of game genres, knowing that we will not produce consensus. And to be clear, we don't want consensus. We don't imagine this as a single voice speaking an idea. Instead, we want the poly-vocal barrage – a kind of euphonic dissonance that will both test existing genre categories and open spaces for competing genres to coexist. To that end, *Approaches to Game Studies*, as a series, is open to works organized around the examination of ludic, thematic, or functional genres. We offer very brief sketches of these notions of genre below.

Functional genres, defined by the use or purpose of the game, can be grouped into the broad categories of either entertainment or serious games. Entertainment games can be further distinguished between hardcore and causal, while serious games can be distinguished by an increasing diversity of types: edugames, advergames, health games, persuasive games, and games for change, to name a few. This notion of genre is problematic, however, because it privileges the intentions of the game designer or publisher and ignores the possible reception of the game.

Thematic genres, defined by representational characteristics, include science-fiction, fantasy, military, and crime-themed games. This means of categorizing genres is problematic to the extent that these narrative discourses and styles of visual representational do not point to the gamic quality of the games. On the other hand, as Burn and Carr argue (2006), these elements do structure gameplay by providing a meaningful framework for interaction. *Ludic genres*, defined by the 'the internal organization of game form' (Mäyrä 2008, 47), the systems of rules that structure gameplay, have been defined in a multitude of ways, including the categories of role-playing games, first-person shooters, platformers, etc. As Elverdam and Aarseth's taxonomy demonstrates – and Whalen (2004) and Apperley (2006) lend weight to this position too – ludic genres are defined by multiple registers. The first-person shooter is a great example: the classification refers to both a perspective and a core mechanic, differentiating it from side-scrolling shooters and other games that employ a first-person perspective but require stealth or puzzle-solving.

This series is intended to serve as a gathering of distinctive voices around the touchstone of genre. Drawing from ludic, thematic, and functional groupings, we hope to encourage a broad and complex conversation among scholars and players who feel drawn to the games they love and recognize in this manner. Rather than limiting the dialogue, this should serve to aid in deepening the conversation about the nature of genre in games as well as providing an entrée for those who want to enter game studies through the lens of the gameplay they recognize and feel kinship towards. The interdisciplinary nature of this series also allows us to position scholars alongside one another in new ways, exploring how the reading/playing of games when seen through varying disciplines can be challenging, thought-provoking, contradictory, and engaging.

Note

1 The Popular Culture Association/American Culture Association, founded in the 1960s as a result of an academic movement aimed to address the increasingly ubiquitous but nevertheless marginalized phenomena of popular culture, is a comfortable fit for those who would study games. For more about the organization and its pioneering work in the study of popular culture, see Browne's *Against Academia* (1989).

References

Aarseth, Espen. 2001. 'Computer Game Studies, Year One.' *Game Studies* 1, no.1 Accessed June 2, 2011. http://www.gamestudies.org/0101/

Aarseth, Espen, Solveig Marie Smedstad, and Lise Sunnanå. 'A Multidimensional Typology of Games.' In *Level Up: Digital Games Research Conference Proceedings*, edited by M. Copier & J. Raessens, 48–53. Utrecht, The Netherlands: Universteit Utrecht.

Apperley, Thomas. 2006. 'Genre and Game Studies: Towards a Critical Approach to Videogame Genres.' *Simulation & Gaming: An International Journal of Theory Practice and Research* 37(1): 6–23.

Arsenault, Dominic. 2009. 'Videogame Genre, Evolution and Innovation.' *Eludamos: Journal for Computer Game Culture* 3(2): 149–76.

Bogost, Ian. 2006. *Unit Operations: An Approach to Videogame Criticism*. Cambridge, MA: MIT Press.

Boltner, Jay and Grusin, Richard. 2000. *Remediation: Understanding New Media*. Cambridge, MA: MIT Press.

Browne, Ray. 1989. *Against Academia*. Madison, WI: Popular Press.

Burn, Andrew and Diane Carr. 2006. 'Defining Game Genres.' In *Computer Games: Text, Narrative and Play*, edited by Diane Carr, David Buckingham, Andrew Burn, and Gareth Schott, 14–29. Cambridge, UK: Polity Press.

Crawford, Chris. 1982. *Art of Computer Game Design*. Washington State University Vancouver. Accessed November 11, 2010. http://library.vancouver.wsu.edu/art-computer-game-design

Elverdam, Christian and Espen Aarseth. 2007. 'Game Classification and Game Design: Construction through Critical Analysis.' *Games and Culture* 2(1): 3–22.

Frasca, Gonzalo. 2003. 'Ludologists Love Stories Too: Notes from a Debate that Never Took Place.' Ludology.org. Accessed June 2, 2011. http://www.ludology.org/articles/Frasca_LevelUp2003.pdf

Garrelts, Nathan. 2005. *Digital Gameplay: Essays on the Nexus of Game and Gamer*. Jefferson, NC: MacFarland.

—2006. *The Meaning and Culture of Grand Theft Auto: Critical Essays*. Jefferson, NC: MacFarland.

Juul, Jesper. 2005. *Half-Real: Video Games between Real Rules and Fictional Worlds*. Cambridge, MA: MIT Press.

Myers, David. 1990. 'Computer Game Genres.' *Play & Culture* 3: 286–301.

Mäyrä, Franz. 2008. *Introduction to Game Studies*. Thousand Oaks, CA: Sage.

Nintendo. 1985. *Super Mario Bros*. [NES]. Redmond, WA: Nintendo.

Salen, Katie and Zimmerman, Eric. 2003. *Rules of Play: Game Design Fundamentals*. Cambridge, MA: MIT Press.
SCE Studios Santa Monica. 2005. *God of War*. [PlayStation 2]. Foster City, CA: Sony Computer Entertainment.
Whalen, Zach. 2004. 'Game/Genre: A Critique of Generic Formulas in Video Games in the Context of "The Real".' *Works and Days* 43/44(1/2): 289–303.
Wolf, Mark J. P. 2004. 'Genre and the Videogame.' In *The Handbook of Computer Game Studies*, edited by Joost Raessens and Jeffery Goldstein, 193–204. Cambridge, MA: MIT Press.

From Dungeons to Digital Denizens

JOSH CALL, KATIE WHITLOCK, AND GERALD VOORHEES

You mean you do not wish to share in a grand adventure?
GANDALF, THE HOBBIT

It's dangerous to go alone! Take this.
OLD HERMIT, THE LEGEND OF ZELDA

'You're sitting around a tavern table…'

It is a line familiar to anyone who has ever played *Dungeons & Dragons* (Gygax and Arneson 1974). One of the most-used plot hooks in recent gaming history, it represents something both familiar and welcoming. An adventure is about to begin. Players have a general idea what to expect next. There will likely be some small initial quest or task to be completed immediately. Keeping with the canonical *Dungeons & Dragons* (hereafter *D&D*) taxonomy, the quest will likely be to exterminate a small horde of rats in the cellar of the very tavern you are currently staying in. Whether or not the group of adventurers knows each other is immaterial, because after this quest they all will. And they will all have something in common; they will be rat-killers extraordinaire. Thus we have the beginning of a role-playing game (hereafter RPG).

The familiarity of this example is rooted in its reproducibility as an RPG trope. It has been constructed, presented and re-presented in multiple ways across several gaming contexts. Baudrillard (2006) and Benjamin (1999) remind us that recognition is rooted in reproduction; that to disseminate an idea fully we need only reproduce it repeatedly until it becomes a commonplace. We can see evidence of this in several notable digital role-playing games (hereafter DRPGs). For example, Black Isle's *Icewind Dale* (Bethesda 2000) opens with this exact quest (which is not surprising as it is a digital *D&D* adventure). Still other games have used this very trope in multiple ways. Bethesda's second installment in the *Elder Scrolls* series, *Daggerfall* (Bethesda 1996), regularly requires players to remove rat infestations from inns all over the many towns and cities of High Rock province, coincidentally offering the exact fee for staying in a room at that same inn as payment. More recently, BioWare's blockbuster *Dragon Age: Origins* (BioWare 2009) employed this trope as a part of the human noble origin story, a way of introducing the player to their history and their Mabari hound companion. In similar fashion, Bethesda's blockbuster *Fallout 3* (2008) teaches players about the game's combat mechanics by inviting the adolescent avatar into an early career removing radiated rats and roaches from the lower bowels of your post-nuclear vault home. It would seem that to play RPGs is to be forever saddled with the unenviable task of culling the rodent population of whatever world we happen to be adventuring in.

The reproduction of these tropes is expected of RPGs. They represent formal elements that serve to signify the status of the game artifact. Their re-presentation invites comparison to other games that share in their likeness. This is, in some way, what it means to work within an idea of genre. Of course, as the series introduction acknowledges, the very idea of genre is contested. But even when we can decide the criteria for parsing one genre from another, as Mortensen argues, genre is still often elusive (2009). Examining the game genres identified by the Norwegian Media Authority, Mortensen explains that that the problem with these genres, derived from categories prevalent within the game industry, becomes apparent when brought out of the abstract and into the game store. Many games have elements of each genre, making classification an exercise in prioritizing one or other aspect of each game. Still, role-playing games can be an intelligible type and, as such, can be used as a way of framing (and thus containing) a conversation about particular dynamics and modes of engagement.

As a genre, the RPG has a relatively well-established history. Its early origins are fairly well-known. Brad King and John Borland discuss this in their early history of computer role-playing games, claiming that 'scratch almost any game developer who worked from 1970s to today and you're likely to find a vein of role-playing experience' (2003, 4). This idea of locating DRPGs in relationship to *D&D,* as well as miniature wargaming, has been echoed in other scholarly histories (Barton 2006; Wolf 2005). Still, while its origins may clearly be established, the DRPG has developed its own unique history. We have progressed to a point where multiple DRPG franchises have established themselves as recognizable hallmarks. A player need only mention series such as *Final Fantasy*, *Dragon Quest*, *Knights of the Old Republic*, or *Baldur's Gate* to invoke not only a litany of signifiers but also the anticipation of gameplay conventions, both ludic and narrative.

Each generation of consoles and computer hardware has titles that serve to further establish the existing tropes of the genre and push those conventions with new developments. For years, console RPGs were defined by active-time battle menus (a kind of nod to the turn-based systems of pen and paper). As hardware became more advanced, the battle systems and mechanics became increasingly advanced, allowing DRPGs to become increasingly seamless and operate in 'real-time.' One has only to look at titles such as *Eternal Sonata* (Tri-Crescendo 2007) or *Tales of Vesperia* (Namco Tales Studio 2008) to see various evolutions of the battle system. Even *Final Fantasy XIII* (Square Enix 2010), the most recent iteration in the franchise, has pushed our concept of game mechanics in its ability to shift character role/archetype at will during combat.

In similar fashion, we have seen the evolution of the DRPG through the representation of perspective and narrative. While older iterations relied on either a top-down or side-scrolling view, incremental increases in graphics processing allowed RPGs to work with a first-person perspective. Early work by SSI on *Eye of the Beholder* (1990), as well as *Dungeon Hack* (1993), encouraged other projects like Bethesda's *Elder Scrolls* franchise. DRPGs developed new ways to immerse players, inviting them to participate in fictional worlds by inhabiting the gaze of characters. Along with this, games increasingly incorporated the complex interweaving of subplots that supported the central narrative of the game. Early titles such as Origin Studios' *Ultima* series had parties of characters, but often these characters were skeletal in nature, serving less as a part of the embedded narrative and more as recognizable plot markers. Later installments in the franchise introduced more complex elements to these characters, giving them history, personality, even individual motivations. Likewise, console games develop similar patterns. Square's DRPG epic *Final Fantasy VI* (1994) carries a cast of fourteen playable characters (although some can be missed in the gameplay), many of which have lengthy story arcs and side quests. This idea, once an anomaly, has become an expectation in current DRPGs.

There is no question that the tropes that signify a DRPG have evolved and even branched off in different directions. Still, some remain relatively unchanged, like the persistent, pesky rat problem with which we began.

Representation and Ludicity in Role-playing Games

What, then, to make of all the rat killing? It is a part of the same inevitability as 'You're sitting around a tavern table'. We know that an adventure is beginning. The trope is reproduced with enough frequency that these tasks serve as a familiar, identifiable introduction to what is to come. The tricky bit here is that in this very act of identification we see the groundwork for a possible schism to follow, one that explores the multiple and seemingly disparate parts of RPGs. These early quests, while often understood as a narrative introduction, also serve as a kind of 'tutorial' to the games mechanics. They not only bring together a disparate band of adventurers in some rising action, but also establish the base set of rules and conditions that players will be working with throughout the game. While our characters are learning their world through the introductory work of killing rats, the player is learning the gameworld through the introduction of playing this experience. This highlights the dual nature of what it means to engage in an RPG. On the one hand, play means to give over to a character and explore those depths in a diegetic space. On another, we are asked to engage with a system of mechanics and rules that govern the operation of reality in the game's contexts. This is a synergy noted by Burn and Carr (2006). They discuss DRPGs as relatively non-linear games that emphasize 'exploration, storytelling and characterization'; however, they further specify that the DRPG is defined by the ability to configure a character (and often a party of characters) through the management of attributes, skills, and equipment (17–18). And, ultimately, it is the narrative and ludic interplay of 'character management' that engenders the sensibility typical of RPGs, the emphasis on 'reflection, reading and strategy over pace and spectacle' (21).

If we begin with a focus on the character and the narrative, the rodent-infested humble beginnings represent something particular for the RPG as a whole. While rat killing is certainly a familiar example, what really makes the trope resonate with players is that these rudimentary tasks only serve to herald the unavoidable fact that there are larger, more arduous, and (hopefully) more rewarding tasks to come. Rarely do we jump into the game a full-blown epic-level character (though titles such as BioWare's *Mass Effect* [2007] have made interesting moves coupling narratives concerning the hero's status with low-level game mechanics). In many ways we could read these examples using traditional plot devices. If we applied some notion of Freytag's pyramid here, we might see these as a kind of exposition moving us towards the inciting incident of the narrative. There is much truth to that, as rarely do RPGs ask players to solely focus on the task of rodent removal, which instead often opens doors – sometimes literally, but more often figuratively – to some other intrigue. We might further push this narrative example and say that this exposition is simply a way of moving characters together towards an inciting incident that serves as (to borrow Joseph Campbell's language) 'the call to adventure' – a moment that heralds a larger, more involved story with stakes greater than the constituent characters (1972). The trouble is that this only foregrounds particular aspects of the RPG. To focus on these things alone would mean to ignore the not-inconsiderable scope of issues and ideas related to the construction of images and representations in RPGs. Much like the forerunner, *D&D*, in general DRPGs owe something to the texts that came before them. We can see elements of these character-driven events in the works of Tolkien, Verne, Scott, Wells, and a litany of other writers who locate their characters in relation to particular stories as a means to *tell us* something – about ourselves, our world, or our ideas. These presentations are rarely simply experienced as 'story', but instead operate with rhetorical purpose.

To play a 'role' in an RPG is to take up an ideology located in some relationship to the narrative and context surrounding it. During an interview for the *New York Times*, Gary Gygax remarked:

> The essence of a role-playing game is that it is a group, cooperative experience. There is no winning or losing, but rather the value is in the experience of imagining yourself as a character in whatever genre you're involved in, whether it's a fantasy game, the Wild West, secret agents or whatever else. You get to sort of vicariously experience those things. (Schiesel 2008)

Gygax's claim to 'vicarious experience' opens up several possible avenues for inquiry. What do the actions of our characters say about us (if anything), given that we (often) control them? Even the very language of that question is loaded. Are they, in fact, 'our characters'? What is the relationship between the player, the avatar, the gamespace, the narrative, and the constituent actions of play? Should we really be killing all these rats? What does it suggest about the quality of our characters and the worlds they inhabit if the first thing we do in these games is embark on a bloodletting of animal cruelty? Does it matter that our characters never bother to stop, dispose of the rat carcasses properly, and at least clean the blood off of the floor? Does the adventurer's handbook even cover how to remove blood from cobblestone? Do these issues even matter? What about the goblins and trolls we raid for loot and experience? Sure, they attacked the caravan, but this land was theirs for a thousand years before our traders began to exploit its wealth. Did we just exterminate a nuisance or participate in genocide? And does that reflect some historical or even hypothetical circumstance, or the contemporary moment? How we experience these issues both speaks to the RPG we are playing and speaks for us as players. These are the larger implications of working in and with role-playing games, and digital role-playing games in particular.

We run into similar issues of depth if we consider the mechanics of gameplay. To play a role means more than (and for some players has nothing to do with) being invested in the narrative events impacting a series of characters. There is, necessarily, attention to the less storied elements that define the capacities that characters bring into play. These capacities, governed by the game's mechanics and procedures, are mediated through the game but controlled by the player. These, too, are RPG commonplaces. We expect to see and use these conventions to flesh out 'who' these characters are by deciding – limited as those decisions may sometimes be in a DRPG – what they do in response to the events and entities they encounter. In a sense, these are simultaneously mechanical and ontological issues. Does the player-character have a high enough level to succeed? Or the requisite alignment or reputation to be granted access? Have the necessary skills and gear been acquired? Is the party composed to suit the task at hand? These issues function at a managerial level, but are no less ontological. They help establish the sense of 'being' for the character as rooted in the actions of the player. These identity markers are made manifest and negotiated through the ludological elements of play. King and Krzywinska argue that the bond between player and player-character is more strongly developed in RPGs than other game types because typically the player determines the character's attributes as well as 'the manner in which these are strengthened as the game proceeds' (2006, 42).

At the same time, the scaling of gear and items is a traditional RPG trope that connects strongly with the notion of the epic in fiction (for instance, when Bilbo obtains 'Sting' in *The Hobbit*.) Inevitably, players sometimes seek to acquire more and better items and equipment to modify their capacity to act, and just as often to maintain the construct of the fantasy.

It is an act of arrogation for theorists and critics, no matter how well-intentioned, to claim one or the other motivation supersedes or obviates the other. Thankfully, the RPG genre makes no demands that we do any such thing.

If this introduction has made one point clear we hope it is that, as a ludic genre defined by the game rules that structure gameplay, RPGs call for both dramatistic and mechanistic engagement. The structural and mechanical dimensions of playing a fighter are meaningless – or at best arbitrary – if absent from the conventional, representational construction of the fighter in relation to the gameworld and the other playable characters. The game's thematic – whether it is fantasy, science-fiction, steampunk, or historical – will undoubtedly influence the discursive framing of game structures (consider party versus squad), but the tropes that circulate across RPGs, and DRPGs in particular, are ludic. For this reason, RPG describes a kind to the extent that titles given the label share gamic structures.

Mapping the Adventure

Given the complexity of RPG history and contemporary forms of DRPG, we invested some effort into the internal taxonomy of this collection. Operating from the notion that RPGs involve both ludic and dramatistic (or narrativist, if you must) management of characters, and drawing from the vernacular of RPG player communities, we imagined a sectional taxonomy accordingly. The three sections, Game Master, In-Character, and Out-of-Character, refer to distinct modes of engaging with RPGs, but they also – imported into this alien, academic context – signify something more. We imagine Game Master, In-Character, and Out-of-Character as shorthand for, respectively, concerns about how RPGs are designed, played, and ultimately made relevant to contemporary society and culture. Of course, most of the essays in this anthology address the design, play, and impact of RPGs, but the various authors coming from distinct perspectives and applying different approaches tend to emphasize one of these dimensions more than others. As such, the organization of this collection reflects both the content of the chapters and the approaches applied in them.

The Game Master

The Game Master is, in table-top RPGs, a special role. Playing as the Game Master means running the game by determining – within the structure of the game's rules, though there is room for rules to be modified at the Game Master's discretion as well – the campaign setting, the non-player characters, items, and creatures that populate it, and the events occurring around and in response to player activity. Chapters in the section *Game Master* tend to focus on the processes and products of game production as a means of exploring the dynamics that make these particular games function as they do.

The first several contributors take designed elements of RPG games – gamescape, temporality, and narrative-quest structure – as starting points for exploring how players make gameplay meaningful. Bealer offers an eco-critical analysis of *Arc the Lad* that focuses on the relationship between gamescape, as it is narratively and visually constructed, and the performance of gameplay. In this sophisticated reading of the dialectic between gamescape and gameplay, Bealer breaks new ground by encouraging critics to give credence to the ecological antagonism underwriting of so many RPGs. Abboud's Derridian analysis of temporality in *World of Warcraft* demonstrates how 'time is out of joint' in Massively Multiplayer Online Role-playing Games (hereafter, MMORPGs). Focusing on the design and implementation of temporal relations, Abboud is able to offer a nuanced reading of the integral importance of player activity to virtual worlds that claim persistence, narrowing the gap between player and game by forcing the two constructs into relief. Henton takes a different tack to examine the creation of meaning in *Dragon Age: Origins*, focusing on the homologous relation between RPG quest structures and the organization of narrative fragments. Considering the archive as both a ludic and discursive structure, Henton makes a strong case for the RPG's ability to unmask the ways in which archival practices of organizing knowledge and experience permeate everyday life as well.

The last two works in this section consider what happens when DRPGs move through different linguistic and media contexts. Schules looks at the semantic quagmire created by the North American localization of *Lux-Pain*, highlighting circumstances in which discursive representation is absolutely essential to meaningful play. However, he also recovers, from these breakdowns in representation and painfully deficient processes of game production, the potential to demystify the discursive attribution of meaning to otherwise aimless and anomie phenomena. Randall and Murphy draw from adaptation studies in order to navigate the tension between the need for both fidelity to, and expansion upon, the source material of *The Lord of the Rings Online*. Randall and Murphy not only lay the groundwork for further adaptation studies of games, they also produce insights that might help the game industry move beyond the (typically) terrible games adapted from films and books.

Playing In-Character

Playing In-Character refers to the practice of playing from the subjective viewpoint of the game character. In this most literal 'role-playing' mode of engagement, the player acts as if they are the character, charging fists-first into overwhelming odds if that is something the character is brave enough, or more often dumb enough, to likely do. Chapters in the section *In-Character* tend to view the relationship between the player and player-character, or avatar, as the locus of inquiry and explore the relationship between that center and the game that surrounds it.

The first two contributions in this area take the player-character, or avatar, as the jumping-off point for examining the experience of play. Whitlock's consideration of memory, and the traumas that seem to disproportionately impinge upon RPG characters' abilities to remember, examines how different theories of memory impact the development of narrative and player engagement. Memory is explored in *Final Fantasy VII*, *Final Fantasy X*, and *Lost Odyssey*, exposing the use of memory as recollection, involuntary, ghosting, and body as developed in these games. This suggests the power and flexibility of the use of memory beyond the simplistic convention of amnesia. Baerg brings Foucault's critique of neo-liberal rationality to bear on the RPG character in order to help explicate and situate the DRPG in relation to the contemporary political and economic landscape. Looking at the *Neverwinter Nights* series of RPGs, Baerg highlights how playable characters serve as loci for the minimization of risk and the maximization of rewards and in this way enable the enactment and performance of neo-liberal subjectivity.

Additional chapters consider the performance of identity in RPGs and the contexts and conditions that make such performances psychologically and socially meaningful. McDowell looks at the *Fallout* series as an exemplar of the post-apocalyptic RPG and a jumping-off point for considering how playing RPGs means not only taking on a role but also taking on one's self. Applying Briankle Chang's Derridian theorization of postal communication, McDowell asks us to contemplate how playing a character is a process of self-discovery and self-construction – both the apocalyptic end and the continuing revelation heralding the new. Friedline and Collister employ a linguistic approach to examine how player communication styles enact distinct power roles within the speech community of *World of Warcraft*. Friedline and Collister's participant-observation in the *World of Warcraft* yields patterns of talk both determined by and determinate of players' power within the community. Zook performs a close reading of *Dragon Age: Origins* in order to uncover how the narrative and visual representation of blood constitute a metaphorical theme that provides meaning and context for the activity of gameplay. Zook's analysis is readily articulated to Travis's classical approach and highlights how compositional performance becomes consequential by linking gamic action to symbolic meaning. Travis examines how BioWare RPGs facilitate composition by theme as a means of enabling identification between player and character as well as the performance of the player's identity. Bringing insights from classical theory to bear on this most contemporary of media, Travis attends closely to the game narrative as a context that gives meaning and imparts social and psychological significance to the variable performances made possible by BioWare RPGs.

Playing Out-of Character

Playing Out-of-Character refers to a mode of engagement that utilizes the subjective knowledge of the game player. Here, the simple-minded fighter might refrain from barreling down a darkened dungeon corridor because the player recognizes that it might save the party much frustration to send a rouge first to check for traps. Chapters in the section *Out-of-Character* tend to focus primarily on the social and cultural consequentiality of RPGs and the practices of playing RPGs.

The first two offerings in this section consider the social and cultural construction of RPG characters as the point of contact for the significance of the experience of play. Voorhees examines the dynamics of squad management in the *Mass Effect* series as a truth game in which neo-liberal multiculturalism always wins. Employing Foucault's notion of governmentality, Voorhees argues that the nexus of narrative representation and procedural operation in *Mass Effect* encourage valuation of cultural difference to the extent that it yields tangible benefits. Douglas looks at the representation and performance of race and culture in *World of Warcraft,* focusing especially on how race and culture are conflated at the intersection of (back)story and character configuration. Bringing the lessons of postcolonialism to bear, Douglas's insightful critique of *World of Warcraft* takes aim at how RPGs, in the main, recirculate and reify this literary multiculturalism.

The last three pieces in this section quite literally take the analysis out-of-character. Hergenrader takes *Fallout 3* into new territory in his essay exploring the possibilities and pitfalls of using RPGs to help teach creative writing. Reflecting on his own experiences in the classroom, Hergenrader offers an example of how RPGs – simultaneously objects of analysis and exemplars of practice – can be utilized as serious games capable of nurturing understanding and building concrete skills. Call explores notions of metagaming rooted in the tensions between in-game and out-of-game logics to challenge the either/or dichotomy of player location. Drawing on notions of metagame as informed by game strategy and pen and paper culture, this argument relocates the issue as a matter of player literacy by examining the complex player decisions involved in *Suikoden II*. Moran reflects on the character of RPG characters, and their diffusion and dissemination through digital culture more generally. Viewing the RPG character as, essentially, one that is configurable, Moran shows how this trait is taken up in other types of games as well as the applications and services that constitute web 2.0.

These three areas will hopefully provide as much variety and lively discussion for readers as we experienced conceptualizing this text. The approach we chose is a reflection of the interdisciplinary nature of this collection, which builds off differences in language choice and perspective, and should provide access to a new range of theoretical approaches that are strengthened by working alongside disparate disciplines. Other organizational logics were available, and, plainly, several chapters (arguably all of them) could have been located in more than one area. We have opted for this arrangement in an effort to provide a more open and reflexive collection that engages rather than stifles discussion, but certainly this arrangement will highlight certain conversations and obscure others. So be it. Other narratives will undoubtedly emerge from, and in spite of, the one we have attempted to embed here.

We hope that you engage this text in this way and take away your own story and your own sense of the experience. You will likely find some familiar ground here (thankfully, no rat-killing). Some of these ideas are novel while others will resonate with your sense of what has come before. It is our hope that the material here will also present to you many of the ideas, arguments and issues in and around RPGs, and DRPGs in particular, in a manner that helps generate new ways of seeing these ideas as our characters grow and develop in the undertaking of this 'grand adventure.'

References

Barton, Matt. 2007. 'The History of Computer Role-Playing Games Part 1: The Early Years 1980–1983.' Gamasutra.com. Accessed June 1, 2011. http://www.gamasutra.com/features/20070223a/barton_01.shtml.

Baudrillard, Jean. 2006. *The System of Objects*. NYC: Verso.

Benjamin, Walter. 1999. 'The Work of Art in the Age of Mechanical Reproduction.' In *Illuminations*, 211–44. London: Pimlico

Bethesda Softworks. 1996. *Elder Scrolls II: Daggerfall*. [PC Game]. Bethesda Softworks.

—2008. *Fallout 3*. [Multiplatform]. Bethesda Softworks.

BioWare. 2007. *Mass Effect*. [Xbox 360]. Microsoft Game Studios.

—2009. *Dragon Age: Origins*. [Multiplatform]. Electronic Arts.

Black Isle Studios. 2000. *Icewind Dale*. [PC Game]. Interplay Entertainment.
Burn, Andrew and Diane Carr. 2006. 'Defining Game Genres.' In *Computer Games: Text, Narrative and Play*, ed. Diane Carr, David Buckingham, Andrew Burn, and Gareth Schott, 14–29. Cambridge, UK: Polity Press.
Campbell, Joseph. 1972. *The Hero With a Thousand Faces*. Princeton, NJ: Princeton UP.
Dreamforge Intertainment. 1993. *Dungeon Hack*. [PC Game]. Strategic Simulations, Inc.
Gygax, Gary and David Arneson. 1974. *Dungeons & Dragons*. [Game]. Tactical Studies Rules.
King, Brad and John Borland. 2003. *Dungeons and Dreamers: The Rise of Computer Game Culture, From Geek to Chic*. NY: McGraw-Hill.
King, Geoff and Tanya Krzywinska. 2006. *Tomb Raiders and Space Invaders: Videogame Forms and Contexts*. NY: Plagrave-McMillan.
Mortensen, Torill Elvira. 2009. *Perceiving Play: The Art and Study of Computer Games*. NY: Peter Lang.
Namco Tales Studio. 2008. *Tales of Vesperia*. [Xbox 360 and PlayStation 3]. Namco Bandai.
Schiesel, Seth. 2008. 'Gary Gygax, Game Pioneer, Dies at 69.' *The New York Times*. Accessed June 1, 2011. http://www.nytimes.com/2008/03/05/arts/05gygax.html?_r=1&ref=arts&oref=slogin.
Square Co. Ltd. 1994. *Final Fantasy VI*. [Super Nintendo Entertainment System]. Sony Computer Entertainment America.
Square Enix. 2010. *Final Fantasy XIII*. [Multiplatform]. El Segundo, CA: Square Enix.
Tri-Crescendo. 2007. *Eternal Sonata*. [Xbox 360]. Namco Bandai.
Westwoods Studios. 1990. *Eye of the Beholder*. [PC Game]. Strategic Simulations, Inc.

SECTION ONE

Game Master

1

Eco-Performance in the Digital RPG Gamescape

ADELE H. BEALER

Performance Studies encompasses a wide range of embodied behaviors, and its concerns about agency and event lead naturally to a consideration of the spaces of performance, since practices always *take place* somewhere. Cultural critics are charged with examining not just what is spoken, but also *who* is speaking (and more importantly, who is *not*) in the environment of a text or artifact. Landscape, like language, is not simply a passive medium facilitating the interactions between active and animate agents; landscape often determines actions and is determined by them in a recursive process that is evidenced in material and consequential ways. The spatial turn in both performance and cultural studies has prompted a resurgence of interest in the various ways that landscape performs, raising questions that probe both inclusive and exclusive ways of being and seeing in any cultural medium. Ecocriticism must also make this critical analytical commitment, asking how politics and economics shape the environments they inhabit, and considering how the materials and *matériel* of those environments are sedimented in the political and economic choices they produce[1]. More specifically, a radical ecocriticism should interrogate the performances in, and of, the RPG gamescape.

Arjun Appadurai proposed extending the traditional place-based concept of the landscape, whether natural or built, to encompass contemporary spatial categories such as financescape, mediascape, and ethnoscape (1996, 33). I would suggest an equivalent need for a critical examination of the gamescape, defined here as the multidimensional space within and against which the process of video-gameplay evolves. That gamescape contributes to what has been described as the 'creation of presence', the immersive experience in which videogame player/participants go beyond entertainment to experience a vividly affective engagement with the world of the game (Schieffelin 1998, 194). Conjoining place and performance in the notion of the gamescape stresses the natural and social relationships that inevitably develop between actors and contexts – relationships that are improvisational and contingent rather than predictable and fixed. The gamescape is simultaneously performance space and performative place, and it interrogates the identities that traverse its contexts even as it interpellates them. Successful gameplay demands that players read the gamescape as an active and critical component of RPG gameplay – and that same gamescape deserves to be read critically for its social constructions and cultural assumptions, especially those related to environmental issues. Revisiting the operations of the gamescape as performance encourages the growth of new dialogues between multiple disciplines, and unlocks new critical environments for exploration. Gamescapes are particularly ripe for a closer ecocritical consideration.

The term *gamescape* is not new to videogame criticism. Shoshana Magnet usefully proposed the term to serve as 'a way of thinking about the implications of the way in which landscape in videogames is actively constructed' and to foreground 'how the gamespace works to shape a player's particular understanding of a larger set of spatial ideologies' (2006, 143). Magnet duly notes that landscape theory has expanded its traditionally more narrow aesthetic definition to include conceptual vistas such as the playing fields of the videogame, and she rightfully considers the critical consequences of failing to examine the ideological implications of the gamescape (centering her argument on the popular computer game, *Tropico*). Similarly, both Baerg and Voorhees in this volume actively examine the political valences in game design and gameplay. I would add, however, that videogame critics must also interrogate the gamescape as something more than simply 'a thing to think with'; beyond providing the mise en scène of a staged political agenda, it must also be understood as a collection of performances that take place (and make space) with real consequences[2]. As I will demonstrate, the videogame *Arc the Lad: Twilight of the Spirits* (Sony 2003) provides a multifaceted example of the variable performances present in, and presented by, the RPG videogame genre.

The Gamescape is Thoroughly Mediate

Calling for a new definition of landscape that acknowledges its multiform identity and variable performance, John Brinckerhoff Jackson suggests that, understood as 'an environment modified by the permanent presence of a group', landscape is produced when two different aspects of human existence interact (1984, 12). Jackson describes those desiring aspects metaphorically, figuratively embodied as a 'political animal' and an 'inhabitant'. Landscape – and for my purposes, the gamescape – is produced in the dialectic exchange between these competing desires, making meaning out of the space between them while also delimiting the shape of each (see also Moran's chapter in this volume, specifically with regard to his comments regarding 'configurable being' as they might be extended to the gamescape).

The political aspect refers to the human need for community; like all creatures, we can neither thrive nor perpetuate our species alone. There is more to this social dimension than a simple desire for 'the mere presence of other bodies'; we have 'the need for sustained discourse, for the exchange of ideas ... and for disagreement, since both kinds of communication lead to a sharpened sense of our identity' (Jackson 1984, 11). Landscape evidences this social sensibility in multiple ways, marked by territorial borderlines, roads, cities, and towns – public spaces and domestic places that reflect the ingress and egress of multiple actors, incised by their constitutive and transgressive interplay. These emergent spaces have a clearly performative dimension as well as a material one, often ignoring natural boundaries in the construction and identification of political and social domains. Spatial outlines serve as performance scripts, directing certain kinds of social behaviors (and certain types of social actors) while rendering other performances impractical or impossible. RPG gamescapes are therefore informed and conformed by a variety of political/community elements. There are spaces to explore and places to visit, towns or cities teeming with creatures of every age and description, and pathways and roadways that must be traversed in order to connect with those other bodies. Players typically maneuver their avatars through a network of domestic and public spaces, homes and businesses and town squares and church ruins, around and across the gamescape, soliciting conversations with other avatars, building alliances, forging connections and negotiating and renegotiating both contracts and contexts in order to forward gameplay. In the process, the instinct for community constructs a social space, and players participate in the political construction of their avatar (including its environmental consciousness) within the confines and contours of the gamescape.

Alternatively, however, player and avatar also experience the environment of the game in a second way: as inhabitants. If the need for community modifies the kinds of interaction from which social identity emerges, then the natural landscape also influences and shapes both the actors and their interactions with other characters/avatars/elements in their performances. In turn, those performed behaviors can, and do, impact the surrounding environment, creating a kind of inhabited cyber-ecology in which every element ultimately inter*acts* and inter*faces* with every other element. Inhabiting the role of an avatar in the gamescape demands that, as actors, we 'are also inhabitants of the [world of the game], involved in the natural order and in a sense even part of it' (Jackson 1984, 11). Everyday activities, such as seeking food and shelter and locating safe spots to restore vitality or to memorialize performance, are characteristic behaviors prescribed and proscribed by environmental conditions – whether in the natural landscape of the real world or in the virtual gamescape of the RPG. Responding to the pressure to survive and thrive within the natural order of the gamescape, avatars must successfully adapt to conditions and evolve a variety of defensive behaviors that shape their performance identities (or as Moran describes in this same volume, their 'capacities') just as actively as the political pressures forge a social aspect; in the RPG, the progressive leveling up of individual avatars literally signifies the ongoing construction of identity in response to the pressures of inhabiting the gamescape.

In 1836, Ralph Waldo Emerson suggested that 'nature is thoroughly mediate', available for the production of an image of the world that is no more than 'a realized will – the double of man' (1991, 35). In the context of the RPG, the gamescape is equally and eerily so. Successfully performed gameplay is doubly 'ergodic', requiring a 'nontrivial effort' on the part of both player and avatar to negotiate the gamescape successfully (Aarseth 1997, 1)[3]. This video-gamescape is both naturally virtual and virtually political; it is at once an immaterial cyberspace without physical location or extension, and, at the same time, an imaginative place of performance and presence where behaviors generate immediate and material consequences. Here, in the gamescape, player/agents willingly and willfully merge their analog selves with the digital identities of their avatars, doubling themselves in conjoined performance (rather than simply exchanging identities, one for one). This gamescape is neither as broadly undefined as the game-space, nor as specifically local as any one game-place; instead, the gamescape resonates between them, 'a mediating term' that is 'more grounded and available to visual experience than space' and yet 'more environmental and constitutive of the imaginative order than place' (Chaudhuri and Fuchs 2002, 3)[4]. Gamescape is at once manifestly 'there', some *place* where performances can be *seen*, and then again diaphanously 'here', an imaginative *space* suffused with the potential of the virtual, where some other/Other *scene* might appear. While it is tempting to reductively read the natural order of the game environment as little more than the projection of design code, such a reading fails to grasp the multiple ways in which gameplay and gamescape are implicated in each other.

Conceived and constructed by game designers, the gamescape depends on its underlying game engine to provide what might be thought of as the natural laws that govern the potential manifestations of the world of the game itself (Bogost 2006, ch. 5). Not every option is available, not every outcome is possible in the gamescape; just as the laws of gravity and thermodynamics delimit how natural phenomena can behave in the material world, the game engine dictates the limit behaviors of objects and avatars within the game. Yet within the constraints of any game's coded parameters, multiple performances take place, performances that vary individually even as they ultimately coalesce around a desired end. In most RPG gameplay, there is a final outcome that is the goal of every player. Certain permutations of behaviors must be accomplished in order for gameplay to come to a successful conclusion; yet within the game, the specific order of that performance is not dictated either by the terms of the narrative or by the constraints of the game mechanics. Performance is both repetitive and yet non-iterative; players learn to negotiate the gamescape through a combination of repeated, patterned behaviors while also expecting to be rewarded with new opportunities for enhanced play. 'This balance of predictability with randomness of theme and variation', as Mark Wolf notes, 'is necessary to most video games' (2001, 82), and it is this same sense of video-gameplay as a rehearsed, repetitive performance, both inside the world of the avatar and outside in the world of the player, that suggests the doubling that is at the heart of performance studies. The gamescape, mediating between political spaces and inhabited places, also serves as a performance medium: a field of play for performance studies.

The Gamescape is Twice Performed

Richard Schechner describes performances as *restored behaviors* or *twice-behaved behaviors* – activities that are rehearsed and repeated over the course of many occasions and multiple lifetimes (2006, 28). Whether formalized onstage or acted out daily, these are practiced performances, behaviors that repeat and recall past performances and that are 'marked, framed, or heightened' by our consciousness that we are, in fact, performing: 'restored behavior can be worked on, stored and recalled, played with, made into something else, transmitted and transformed' (2006, 35). Video-gameplay, with its emphasis on pattern and repetition, is clearly restored behavior, doubled again by the simultaneous activities of player and avatar as each executes a series of learned, repetitive moves. Successful inhabitation requires that behaviors be rehearsed and repeated in order to render them readily available in the appropriate setting as conditions demand. Successful negotiation of a political space demands that traditional behaviors must be storable, recallable, and easily transmitted from one set of actors to another according to custom and tradition. Schechner reminds us that anthropologist Erving Goffman defined a performance as 'all the activity of a given participant on a given occasion which serves to influence in any way any of the other participants' (1959, 15–16). Those repeated performances he described as a 'part' or 'routine'; in the context of the gamescape, such restored behaviors correspond to the *roles* we play in the RPG videogame genre. These roles represent the accumulation of various bits of behavior, of skills and accessories, of items of equipment and magical abilities, all chosen by the player from a menu or earned through successful play; this improvisatory production of an identity, even limited by a finite set of options, further contributes to a sense of player agency and to a sense of avatar singularity. Battle performances, a significant set of rehearsed and repeated behaviors, are choreographed to respond to external threats and to maximize the performances of multiple avatars, often in synchronized performances together. Players must shift avatars to tactically defeat enemies that emerge in the gamescape, influenced by each character's specific skills and talents; at some moments, the battle performance of one avatar may be enhanced by the performance of another.

Significantly, Goffman elaborated on his definition of performance by adding: 'When an individual or performer plays the same part to the same audience on different occasions, a social relationship is likely to arise' (1959, 15–16). In the RPG gamescape, narrative development and environmental elements conspire to produce behaviors that are repeated, again and again, for audiences re-encountered throughout gameplay. Avatars hold conversations over and over again with a variety of non-playable characters (NPCs) in order to produce new information, and they frequently revisit locations in order to discover new objects or to uncover information not available during a previous episode. Sometimes, even previous battles must be re-fought when avatars retrace their footsteps through unstable segments of the gamescape. Inevitably, relationships between avatars and between players and places within the game emerge; moments of confusion often dictate a return to a likely safe place, typically a town or domestic space, where information is readily available and where NPCs have demonstrated a pattern of providing usable, reliable information. Knowing those audiences also enables better role-playing choices: skilled players use those encounters to better select weapons, skills, and restoratives based on previous experiences in the same place, with the same space. The pressures of inhabitation and the expectations of community (that together shape the inner world of the game) dictate these specific nuances of behavior, culminating in a performance that enacts a further doubling. Jackson notes that the inhabited and political aspects of landscape are always found together in the real world of the player 'out there'. 'In here', in the gamescape of the avatar, these same aspects continue to contribute in turn to the development of the identities that emerge in the mediated interface between them (Jackson 1984, 42).

The Gamescape is a System

Schechner points to the ubiquity of restored behaviors across time and space, but he also identifies a paradox at the heart of performance – a paradox he describes in language that returns us to the digital context of the gamescape. 'Performances are made from bits of restored behavior,' he writes, 'but every performance is different from every other', and the idea that 'bits of behavior' can be recombined in exponential ways adds yet another layer of variability to this non-iterative repetition (2006, 30). Jackson points out that while the political landscape is the product of some 'coherent design inspired by philosophy or religion', structured with 'a distinct purpose in view', the inhabited landscape is 'an existential landscape: it achieves its identity only in the course of existence' as it responds to changes in needs and wants in an adaptive evolutionary dialogue with its mediate and immediate surroundings (1984, 43). The virtual gamescape, mediating between bytes of information and bits of behavior, is simultaneously produced by the same Darwinian tension and is made productive by the same paradox. It emerges between the structured order of computational system operations and the improvisatory randomness of unit operations, between the linear, goal-directed narrative of the game and the episodic performances that traverse it.

Ian Bogost's creative engagement with a similar paradox in information systems can be useful here as well. Bogost critically compares system operations, which operate in a top-down fashion to ensure an orderly flow of information supporting the primary goal of a teleological system, to unit operations, creative 'modes of meaning-making that privilege discrete, disconnected actions'[5]. Bogost makes a fundamental distinction between the effects of these two types of operations: system operations actually '*regulate* meaning *for* their components', while the existential nature of unit operations, like that of inhabited landscape, suggests that any meaning that can be attached to these episodic and distinctive activities will be 'derive[d] ... from the *interrelations of* their components' (2006, 4, my italics). The political landscape of the videogame expresses an organizing system that is conveyed by narrative, particularly in the often extensive narrative typical of the RPG. This aspect of the gamescape is therefore filled with what Jackson identifies as visible political elements: roads and highways, monuments, ruins, and public spaces, which also 'have a definite role to play ... [t]hey exist to insure order and security and continuity', reminding players and avatars of the official history of the diegetic community and of the rights and responsibilities that its members are heirs to – a function that is clearly regulatory and prescriptive[6]. On the other hand, the episodic performances of the player/avatar are often driven by the immediate demands made by the inhabited landscape. Avatars are first concerned with their own survival, functioning primarily to secure health, rest, safety, and financial means, and to defeat external threats to their ability to continue to perform in the game. In these unit operations, avatar identity is always contingent upon the other components of the singular situation: on the skill of the player, on an accumulated inventory of weapons and spells, and on the rays of relation (a phrase I deliberately borrow from Emerson's *Nature*) between the primary avatar and the secondary playable characters who accompany him or her. Indeed, those relationships are generally invisible during narrative inter*ludes*, when their separate representations are often collapsed into the solitary figure of the playable avatar[7]. The individual identities of the assemblage that supports the primary avatar (masked during system operations by merging them into the single figure of the primary in order to simplify narrative in the service of the game's end) become visible components at the moment that narrative pauses and battle operations begin.

This paradoxical ambiguity at the heart of both performance and operations produces yet another doubling in our examination of the gamescape, and radically underscores the need for an eco-performative videogame criticism that interrogates the production of both space and performance. The multiple tensions between the political landscape and the inhabited landscape, between system operations and unit operations, between the mission and the moment, serve to highlight why a more expansive (and more ecological) videogame criticism must consider all these performances, rather than focus exclusively on the ideological script that is but one active aspect of the gamescape as a whole. Few games illustrate the potency of this creative and contradictory tension better than the PlayStation 2 RPG game, *Arc the Lad: Twilight of the Spirits* (Sony 2003)[8].

Restored Behaviors in *Arc the Lad*

From its opening sequence, Sony Computer Entertainment America's 2003 videogame *Arc the Lad: Twilight of the Spirits* visually and verbally presents a world characterized by dual performance, by a conflicted doubling that will recur across multiple aspects of character and story. We are presented with a gamescape in which nature and culture are simultaneously at odds and at one, where nature figures simultaneously as a spiritual resource and as a depleted energy source in a world populated by two vociferously opposed categories of inhabitants, Humans and Deimos. The story narrative replicates the shape of the world it describes, dividing play action between two concurrent yet non-iterative storylines, those of Kharg and Darc, twin offspring of a Deimos father and a human mother, separated at birth, each unaware of the existence of the other. The system operation is overcoded with the story of separate quests with the same goal – the successful recovery of a collection of original and elemental Great Spirit Stones whose possession endows the holder with great power that may be used for good or evil. In narrative sections that follow Kharg and Darc by turns, we are invited to experience a gamespace delimited by both its political and inhabited aspects, ostensibly moving to the same conclusion, but experienced very differently by its protagonists.

Indeed, *Arc the Lad*'s perspective is only one of the unique aspects of its system operations, an aspect that emphasizes a unique spatial orientation as a way to interrogate its own political gamescape. Using the third-person perspective that characterizes RPG play, *Arc* provides its own mechanism for challenging this univocal and homogeneous narrative viewpoint. Because gameplay is antiphonal (we play alternately as the Kharg avatar and then as Darc), our player's-eye view is not restricted to a single standpoint. This has the effect of doubling the ideological valence of the gamescape; as I noted earlier, we cannot remain unaware that the political elements of the gamescape are variably constructed depending on whose perspective controls the view. Jackson emphasized that the continuous tension between the political and the inhabited aspects of landscape means that 'no landscape can be exclusively devoted to the fostering of only one identity' (1984, 12); in *Arc the Lad*, this twofold identity is made visible in the twin avatars, Kharg and Darc. As Kharg, we perform in a human-centric gamescape, where extractive activities are justified ('The most important thing is to develop the country') and where the stated victory conditions for each early battle is '*defeat all enemies*'. Thus the gamescape's performative effect is to delimit a human-only community for which every non-human entity is excluded as enemy and to demand a centripetal performance that can only produce a utilitarian environmental practice. As Darc, we are Deimos, despising the greed of humans who 'steal' the spirit stones necessary for Deimos magic and demanding nothing less than genocide; victory conditions here are to '*defeat every last human*'! According to the master narrative, Darc's purpose, like Kharg's, is to locate and retrieve the lost Great Spirit Stones, but each avatar assumes that the power of the stones will be his to use exclusively for the benefit of his race and for the eradication of the other. An invasion force of human mercenaries dismissively responds to charges of trespass with the quip, 'This is Deimos territory ... therefore, it doesn't belong to *anyone*'. Neither race is willing to acknowledge the rights of the other to life, liberty, or property.

In primitive cultures, territorial boundaries worked like a protective container, preserving the purity of the cultural territory within from contamination by all that was outside that 'envelope' or 'packaging' (Jackson 1984, 14). In modern nations, however, those borderlines perform more 'like a skin: a thin surface which is in fact part of the body, part of space which it protects' (Jackson 1984, 12). *Arc the Lad*'s twin avatars perform like embodied social spaces, and these social behaviors are doubly framed, marked, and emphasized, since they are literally twice-performed, once in one skin and again in the other. In this fashion, the gamescape mediates the player's experience and that of each avatar. As Kharg, we experience life as the only son of a prominent political figure in a modestly successful urban setting. Kharg's narrative reflects the performances expected from a young person of means, with an emphasis on his responsibility to his social community and not to the environment that supports it ('Your time has come to give something back'). The presence and pressure of an audience – a key component of any performance – is also registered repeatedly across the gamescape. NPCs emphasize the safety and security of town life compared with the dangers reputed to be lurking outside the city walls. 'Once you leave town,' a non-playable character comments, 'you may come across monsters.' Townspeople offer Kharg advice on appropriate conduct, and all agree that the monstrous Deimos, 'just creatures that can talk and use tools', can never be reconciled to the human need for progress.

Once the narrative shifts to Darc's story, however, we are subjected to an entirely different interpretation of the events just experienced as Kharg. The performances in, and of, Darc's gamescape are manifestly different in tone and detail. While Kharg appears fully human, with only a secret mark to show his Deimos half, Darc has survived as an orphan slave, visibly marked as half human. He lives among the Orcon, one of many Deimos populations; we quickly realize that while all Deimos may look alike to humans, there are actually many species of Deimos, living in communities with their own social networks and conflicts. Just as Kharg understands his identity in terms of the performances expected of him in the social space he inhabits, Darc performs an identity conditioned on slavery and discrimination. In Orcoth, he is dismissed repeatedly as 'a Deimos wannabe', disqualified from full membership even in the restricted social sphere he initially inhabits. His constant query, 'Which path should I walk?', interrogates the instability of his identity, and his social status measurably limits his potential audience and retards his character's opportunities for growth.

Even when they walk separate paths, however, Kharg and Darc's separate identities follow similar developmental trajectories, noticeably in relation to their battle companions. Each assembles a supporting cast of confederates who make up the components of their singular battle units. Kharg and Darc are both literally and metaphorically non-identical twins, near doubles of each other, and those characters that encounter both of them remark on their similarity of gesture. The same near mirroring of non-iterative likeness can be observed between their battle companions – yet another example of parallel performance that resonates across this doubled and redoubled gamescape (Whitlock 2004, 181–3). Recalling Bogost's description of unit operations, we can see that these battle groups perform in a singular yet similar way. Neither Kharg nor Darc remains solitary for long; each needs other avatars in order to maximize survival in the inhabited gamescape, particularly when faced with battle conditions. Each is also constantly practicing his behaviors with and for this increasingly important cohort of companions. Out of these repeated performances, relationships emerge – relationships that become critical to survival. NPCs provide social density in every urban setting in the gamescape, but inhabitation demands more than the presence of other bodies and more than the critical exchange present in community. Inhabitation demands uniquely cooperative interrelationships, such as those made visible in the battle units. Those relationships are not born of the static conditions preset by narrative or historically determined by community standards; instead, they develop out of adaptive and improvisatory performances – both Kharg and Darc are at one time or another betrayed by one or more of their companions (which subsequently calls for a renegotiated relationship between them), and their battle units periodically reconfigure and recombine to produce variations on their original themes.

The twin narratives ultimately collapse into one as the game nears its conclusion, responding to a teleological system operation that condenses an otherwise unruly narrative into a single admirable story. United against a final enemy whose strength requires that they combine forces, Kharg and Darc perform a collapse of their doubling into a single identity. We also choose here, electing to play as either Kharg or Darc while the remaining half shadows the active avatar. As the game concludes, a final cinematic sequence allows us to step back, returning to our analog body while both avatars return. We see their handshake, a symbolic performance of a totalizing narrative that suggests a cooperative future for both human and Deimos, one that foregrounds a collaborative assimilation as pervasively seductive as the ideology of colonization that Magnet argues is so insidious in *Tropico*. The narrative subsumes the action of the game, and smoothly elides the doubled difference we have experienced in the course of gameplay. Magnet's critique would surrender the gamescape to the narrative at this point; Bogost's argument would assert that videogame criticism should emphasize the unit operations of gameplay, the discrete microperformances that inhabit the gamescape and that emphasize not narrative coherence but operative repetition. An ecocritical videogame criticism cannot settle for either alternative, but instead should consider the relation of each to all of the behaviors informing the expanse of the gamescape. Performances, as Schechner insists, 'exist only as actions, interactions, and relationships', and it is as multiple performances that *Arc the Lad* ought to be interrogated (2006, 30).

The Environment of the Gamescape

In his monumental ode to the production and representation of social space, Henri LeFebvre notes that social space emerges as a sort of by-product of the extension and acceleration of human traffic, in the growth and development of economic and information networks. Like the virtual gamescape of the videogame, social spaces are immaterial and yet real; we perceive them in the *spatial practices* that emerge out of the interaction between conceptual representations of space (like political maps or engineers' diagrams, these are maps or outlines rather than territories) and those lived spaces of representation where we act out our individual lives (Lefebvre 1991, 38–40). Social spaces/spatial practices are no more materially extensive than cyberspaces, yet they are real in the sense that they have consequences – they effect changes in the political and inhabited aspects of the gamescape, which mediates between them. These practices conform, transform, and perform social spaces; social spaces manifest a particular shape as a result of our repeated and rehearsed behaviors, and performance practices and performed spaces co-evolve over time. While not separable like physical spaces, social spaces are readily recognizable and they 'may be [...] superimposed' on one another so that they exist simultaneously rather than one simply absorbing or eradicating another (Lefebvre 1991, 86–8). The gamescape, as I have argued throughout this chapter, is a social space, marked by the spatial practices of both playable and non-playable characters whose comings and goings are lived and mapped within it. *Arc the Lad*'s gamescape contains a multitude of overlapping spatial practices: both human and Deimos avatars move from place to place, from simple dwelling to major plaza, from country to city, and from one nation to another. As the avatars traverse the worlds of *Arc the Lad*, the gamescape materializes around them, expanding the field of play as peripheral areas become more central, and as new centers of action redefine what is consequently peripheral. Movement and performance *make room* in the game; performances construct or produce the social spaces within which the avatars subsequently perform again.

Those performances that comprise the gamescape represent the collision of system narrative and unit operations in a repertoire of repeated behaviors. Bogost endorses unit analysis as a critical methodology for reading a variety of cultural artifacts, a 'general practice of criticism' that relies on 'the discovery and exposition of unit operations at work in one or many source texts', and he demonstrates his method by focusing on Steven Spielberg's 2004 film *The Terminal* (2006, 15). Arguing that the film's narrative is an unruly and undisciplined tangle of weak plotlines that thinly links discrete events together, Bogost instead examines its unit operations to discern their thematic motif. Like Magnet's recovery of the ideological narrative that overdetermines the action in *Tropico*, Bogost's approach is useful in its conclusions, but privileges only one aspect of the gamescape in its critique.

A more holistic approach to the analysis of the gamescape would be to embrace the paradigm of the *scenario* as a more nuanced tool for videogame criticism. As Diana Taylor defines it, a scenario is a rough schematic of plot and place that recalls Schechner's notion of a restored behavior; it is 'never for the first time', but is always already performed; it 'makes visible, yet again, what is already there [...] Simultaneously *setup* and *action*, scenarios frame and activate social dramas' (2003, 28). Instead of limiting analysis to a single plane of interpretation, applying this critical lens to videogame criticism acknowledges the episodic, rehearsed, and repetitious operations of gameplay while retaining a sense of the narrative's contribution to the tensions between the demands of community and individual survival that produce the gamescape. Taylor argues that scenarios are 'repeatable and transferable' and that they 'may appear stereotypical'; they are also adaptable, potentially subversive, and they may also be multiple, just like the systems that manifest them (2003, 31). In this same volume, Roger Travis's emphasis on the 'modularity of content' and the 're-compositional system' evidenced in videogameplay suggests the usefulness of the scenario as an analytical tool. Several scenarios traverse the gamescape of *Arc the Lad*, including story/map lines of conquest and colonization, racial discrimination, and the traditional *bildungsroman*. Importantly, however, each minor scenario is informed and inflected by the gamescape's always prior and present master scenario – the scenario of environmental damage.

Concerns about resource use, abuse, and acquisition ground both narrative and action in *Arc the Lad*. The presence of industrial waste and abandoned machinery littering the landscape of Kharg and Darc's domains is often experienced before it is explained, and episode behaviors are often linked to environmental issues. The search for the Great Spirit Stones and the contestation over the acquisition and use of lesser spirit stones is grounded in environmental crisis. Humans have depleted all of the gameworld's available natural resources, necessary to power their technology – including their weapons, which are vital to their ability to keep the stronger Deimos at bay. Early in the narrative, we are told that 'when two groups want the same resource, fighting is inevitable', and every narrative episode is framed by a battle that in some way performs the struggle for power which activates every environmental standoff. Humans recognize that the spirit stones they mine are not an infinite resource: 'It may run out, and when it does, we don't have any other resource to fall back on.' Even the knowledge that their last and only resource is not renewable, however, does not alter performances or practices. Instead, the humans propose a version of environmental wise use ('We just have to make sure we use the spirit stones we have wisely') and continue to justify their extractive mining practices on human and Orcon lands ('We'll probably find another deposit of spirit stones in the meantime' and 'At the moment, everything's looking all right'). Territorial invasion and colonization are resource-related, as is much of the genocidal race hatred that pervades the gamescape. Both humans and Deimos demand the total eradication of the other race in order to ensure access to, and control of, the only remaining source of literal and metaphorical power on the planet.

If humans repeatedly refuse to grasp the reality of their energy crisis, Deimos, whose cultural organization is demonstrably less technological and more primitive than that of the humans, are also contributors to the planet's environmental decline. One Deimos literally consumes the only living resource available to him. In a display of unthinking gluttony and lack of self-control, the Orcon leader Densimo eats a Firble, a harmless and rare creature that, if protected, will mature into a flying monster. Since Deimos lack any form of technology, and since the wingless Orcon are unable to travel other than on foot, a winged monster might enable an expansion of their social and political space, but Densimo eats the Firble because he believes it will make him stronger. Orcon social space is ruled by one mantra: 'Deimos only understands strength' – a solipsistic world view that threatens to lead ultimately to a Deimos tragedy of the commons. Deimos battle in order to destroy humans, while humans battle in order to destroy monsters. Both races are threatened by a global energy crisis that potentially will return them 'to the time of destruction … the endless night of despair', but it is not until the final battle that human and Deimos, Kharg and Darc unite. The primary environmental message in *Arc the Lad* is performed as a repeated failure to act responsibly in the face of dwindling resources and as an endless expenditure of energy against the one ally each side needs to combat the real threat to survival. In these repeated performances of their differences, Kharg and Darc, human and Deimos, double their past failures and forecast an identical future. It is only when those performances shed difference and embrace the common good – the shared survival of both races – that a potentially successful future outcome (predicated on repeated performances of cooperation) is activated in the gamescape.

Performing Ecocriticism

Ecocriticism has not traditionally focused on the videogame as a significant representation of popular engagement with environmental issues – an omission that should be addressed. *Arc the Lad*'s gamescape mediates between a system narrative gesturing towards a more sustainable future and microperformances more concerned with power struggles than with the ecological threat that will ultimately overrun both. The gamescape is shaped by the tensions of that eco-dialogue between doing and saying, between the inhabited landscape and its political doppelgänger. At the intersection of presence and performance, the gamescape echoes with the effects of past performances even as it models contemporary behaviors. Indeed, *Twilight of the Spirits* represents the first installment of this series available for the PlayStation 2, but it was preceded by older games, *Arc the Lad I, II,* and *III,* which also feature environmental scenarios that resurface in the present story. The landscapes of *Arc the Lad* are multiply haunted: by the debris of abandoned technology, by the corrosive effect of racial prejudice, and by the Spirits themselves, the elemental anima of this world now symbolized by the Great Spirit Stones. The restored nature of all scenarios result in this sense of what Taylor (citing Derrida before her) calls *hauntology*. For Taylor, the real power of performance 'rests on the notion of ghosting, that visualization that continues to act politically even as it exceeds the live' (2003, 143). Reminders that we have passed this way before, the sights and cites of these residual specters of our past behaviors can adjure us to change – and that is the plea of every contemporary environmental text. Performances summon those ghostly actors of the past, but the efficacy of those specters to move us is contingent on yet another doubling. 'Performance', Taylor notes, 'becomes visible, meaningful, within the context of a phantasmagoric repertoire of repeats', but 'we see only what we have been conditioned to see' (2003, 144). An ecocritical videogame criticism needs to point to both aspects of environmental visibility, so powerfully figured in this installment of the *Arc the Lad* series of RPGs. This is the *Twilight of the Spirits*, after all, where we are admonished by the fading manifestations of the Spirits to mend our ways in order to mend our world. If the narrative of *Arc the Lad* suggests that change is in the wind for this gamescape, our rehearsed and repetitive performances suggest otherwise. In a real world threatened daily with global climate changes, diminishing resources, and species extinction, the notion that we are always haunted by our past performances (whether or not we choose to see them) is the message for which the gamescape can be a powerful medium. LeFebvre asserts that 'to change life [...] we must first change space' (1991, 190). In the gamescape, we find ourselves interacting with the ghosts of our performances past, even as we improvise a new scenario with those performances we intend for the future. Performing ecocriticism within the gamescape of the RPG demands that we engage with both aspects of the gamescape. We must continue to challenge the sites of systemic narrative and claims of political community, while insisting that our rehearsed and restored individual behaviors remain clearly and honestly in sight. Videogame criticism, in dialogue with ecocriticism, doubles our chances of successfully reading the environmental nuances of the gamescape – speaking in unison, they can be a real game-changer.

Notes

1 Lefebvre 1991, 105. Lefebvre distinguishes between durable components/materials (stone, brick, cement) and the more disposable tools and instructions for their use, *matériel* that is

quickly replaced as those uses change over time. His distinction seems particularly appropriate in the context of the gamescape, where programming capabilities rapidly change to produce new representations with what are essentially the same bits of data, and in terms of environmental conflict over dwindling resources and extractive techniques.

2 Brown 2010, 187, 183–215. Brown's provocative phrase refers to artist Brian Jungen's unconventional 'misuse' of contemporary cultural artifacts, and his point underscores Magnet's claims for considering the gamescape as a useful artifact for the deconstruction of ideologies underlying representations. My point, however, is that to use the gamescape in this way also objectifies it, potentially occluding its active and evolutionary performance.

3 Aarseth's definition applies to any literature or text that demands substantial reader participation and response.

4 While Chaudhuri and Fuchs's intent is to consider how rethinking the tensions between theatre and the landscapes it represents can invigorate theatre criticism, the benefits they identify are also available to performance studies and to traditional ecocriticism.

5 Bogost 2006, 3. Bogost's thinking, which draws from cybernetics, informatics, and his 'home discipline', literary criticism, is an ambitious and notable effort to clearly connect the concept of unit operations with multiplicity as used by French philosopher Alain Badiou, about whom I have written elsewhere. While well beyond the scope of this article, the potential for generative thought made available in Bogost's text is well worth pursuing. See also Moran and Travis in this volume for other applications of Bogost's arguments to RPG analysis.

6 Jackson 1984, 12. I will return to the question of what constitutes an 'official' history, and whose version is therefore disqualified or suppressed altogether.

7 Emerson uses the phrase 'a ray of relation' to describe the interconnection between man and every other creature in *Nature*, 24. Note too that these connections between the various components of the gamescape, whether natural objects or other actors, are often not visible during those narrative stretches that interrupt, or come between, episodes of ludic performance.

8 From hereon I will refer to this game alternately as *Arc the Lad* or simply *Arc*, but the reader should be aware that there are multiple titles in the *Arc the Lad* series, of which this game, *Twilight of the Spirits*, is only one.

References

Aarseth, Espen J. 1997. *Cybertext: Perspectives on Ergodic Literature*. Baltimore: Johns Hopkins University Press.

Appadurai, Arjun. 1996. *Modernity at Large: Cultural Dimensions of Globalization*. Minneapolis: University of Minnesota Press.

Bealer, Adele Haverty. 2008. 'Interface: Connecting the Work of Gregory Bateson, Deleuze and Guattari, and Alain Badiou.' MA thesis, The University of Utah.

Bogost, Ian. 2006. *Unit Operations: An Approach to Videogame Criticism*. Cambridge, MA: MIT Press.

Brown, Bill. 2010. 'Objects, Others, and Us: The Refabrication of Things.' *Critical Inquiry* 36: 183–215. Accessed March 4, 2010. doi: 10.1086/648523.

Chaudhuri, Una and Elinor Fuchs. 2002. 'Introduction: Land/Scape/Theater and the New Spatial Paradigm.' In *Land/Scape/Theater*, ed. Elinor Fuchs and Una Chaudhuri, 1–7. Ann Arbor: University of Michigan Press.

Emerson, Ralph Waldo and Henry David Thoreau. 1991. *Nature/Walking*. Boston: Beacon Press.

Goffman, Erving. 1959. *The Presentation of Self in Everyday Life*. Garden City, NY: Doubleday. Quoted in Richard Schechner, 2006, *Performance Studies: An Introduction*. 2nd ed. New York: Routledge.

Jackson, John Brinckerhoff. 1984. *Discovering the Vernacular Landscape*. New Haven: Yale University Press.

Layton, Thomas. 2003. *Arc the Lad: Twilight of the Spirits – The Official Strategy Guide*. Indianapolis: Pearson Education.

LeFebvre, Henri. 1991. *The Production of Space*. Translated by Donald Nicholson-Smith. Malden, MA: Blackwell Publishing.

Magnet, Shoshana. 2006. 'Playing at Colonization: Interpreting Imaginary Landscapes in the Video Game Tropico.' *Journal of Communication Inquiry* 30, no(2): 142–62.

Schechner, Richard. 2006. *Performance Studies: An Introduction*. 2nd ed. New York: Routledge.

Schieffelin, Edward L.1998. 'Problematizing Performance.' In *Ritual, Performance, Media*, ed. Felicia Hughes-Freeland, 194–207. London: Routledge.

Sony. *Arc the Lad: Twilight of the Spirits*. [PlayStation 2]. Sony Computer Entertainment America: Foster City, CA, 2003.

Taylor, Diana. 2003. *The Archive and the Repertoire: Performing Cultural Memory in the Americas*. Durham: Duke University Press.

Whitlock, Katherine Lynne. 2004. 'Theatre and the Video Game: Beauty and the Beast.' PhD diss., The Ohio State University.

Wolf, Mark J. P. 2001. 'Time in the Video Game.' In *The Medium of the Video Game*, edited by Mark J. P. Wolf. 77–91. Austin: University of Texas Press.

2

The Pathways of Time: Temporality and Procedures in MMORPGs

JOSHUA ABBOUD

Always returning upon the paths of time, we are neither ahead nor behind: late is early, near far.

MAURICE BLANCHOT, *THE WRITING OF THE DISASTER*

In sketching a theory of computer and videogame time, Jesper Juul asserts that his article is based on three considerations: '(1) plain curiosity; (2) theoretical lack; and (3) [that it] serve as an analytical tool for opening other discussions in game studies and game design' (Juul 2001). While the first two concerns are the more elegant motives for theorizing time in digital games, it is the third that suggests that time can somehow articulate new understandings for the analysis of digital games. Juul's interest is not simply in prompting more discussion, but in activating other discussions. Time cannot be thought of as the grounding for theories of game design; there is no universal temporal theory for games to fall back on. In other words, to engage in discussions of time in game studies is to sever ties with binary structures (virtual/real) and identity which produce digital subjectivities; the digital subject is lost in the pathways of time.

The concepts of space and world have been an important part of game studies because of what space signifies in terms of game design: videogames present players with a distinct space, a unique world, a site of virtual interaction. For example, Espen Aarseth has done work on how videogames in general 'tend to incorporate a coherent, accessible space; a continuous, reliant area or set of areas for the players to explore, conquer, and inhabit' (Aarseth 2008, 131). What is at stake in this definition is the capacity of videogames to maintain a limited and consistent virtual space onto which can be organized game elements and events. This is a decidedly utopian vision that ignores the disparate temporal systems with which players navigate their virtual worlds. The disclosure of a gameworld is dependent on multiple temporal systems emerging out of both in-game instantiations of time (determined by narrative elements and game events) and direct individual player input, offering the player an illusion of control. Narrative and descriptive systems can project a sense of time through mimetic game conventions that quantify time units, such as timers, clocks, calendars, etc. Player-input experience responds to narrative and descriptive functions, and forms relays with these functions; however, the intersections of these temporal systems cannot be reduced to any consistent or coherent structure.

The radical flow of temporal relays between virtual and player spaces reveal the instability of coherent and continuous gamespaces. It also questions notions of player subjectivity based on identity and recasts the status of player and avatar as part of the same fluid relay. Massively Multiplayer Role-Playing Games (MMORPGs), large-scale deployments of DRPGs, present narrative and descriptive events that are programmed into the game, and yet lack a 'proper' order. These events emerge from MMORPGs revealing their worlds as a cyclical present (a present or presence of the past as future – a future anterior) constructed of sequences of instances that continuously recur. The events of these temporal pathways are predetermined instantiations of code that offer the appearance of choice and consequence. These instantiations are themselves affected by player-input and narrative elements that continually become unhinged from their proper places. In other words, in the online RPG community, time is 'out of joint'.

Disjointed Time of Narration and Description

Generally speaking, in game design it is genre that dictates the embodiment of time in any particular game. Sport games are regulated by the length of a match or event, some puzzle games use time clocks to challenge players, and even some action games restrict the amount of time players can spend in certain areas. Most MMORPGs vary time intervals based on gameplay situations. These interval variations are dependent on the fusion of what we could call simulation and representation, or the continuous movement that players experience between narrative and dramatic modes of time and descriptive and event modes of time.

I borrow the terms *narration* and *description* from Gérard Genette, who differentiates between narration as 'the representations of actions and events' and description as 'representations of objects and characters'. (Simons 2007). In his study of Genette's story schema, Jan Simons remarks that while temporal elements are most often attributed to narration, description 'suspends time'. By suspending time, description does not negate time, but 'displays the story spatially'. Simons explains that even Genette sees the distinction problematic: 'there are no clearly marked boundaries between narration and description, but the distinction at least has the merit of reminding that narratives are too complex to be subsumed under a single label' (Simons 2007). Not only do narrative and descriptive modes blur the boundaries of temporal experience, but time itself, at least in the descriptive mode, is sometimes represented in terms of space.

The finite possibilities of gameplay reveal the 'impossibility of perfect access control' that Friedrich Kittler perceived in programmable machines (Kittler 1997, 163). According to Kittler, access control to hardware is prohibited by the increasing gap between programmable machines and users through the proliferation of computer language in software (operating systems, etc.). More than anything, Kittler is concerned with the ethical significance of this discourse of impenetrability in the interaction between man and machine. What is important here is that, in order for the interaction to function, there must be open connections both ways. Games both restrict player possibilities through electronic procedures, and are, in turn, limited by player input.

The reciprocal movement of temporal relays in MMORPGs works as a feedback loop between game and player, on both the procedural level and player-input level. This simultaneous expression of power is an experience that Laurie Taylor terms 'telepresence' – a state which positions players in various capacities 'to be able to effect change in that (or those) other areas while also being able to effect change in the subject's physical space' (Taylor 2003). In telepresence, 'Videogame players must [...] simultaneously function on differing spatial planes' (Taylor 2003). And I would add that the performance of telepresence necessarily occurs within temporal planes as well.

The correspondence of telepresence and time falls short in its isolation of a uniform direction of effective movement from an active subject to the blank slate of the screen. In fact, the 'telepresent state' is less a statement of existence (being) and more an articulation of subjectivity through processes of telepresence. By offering the player access control, the game creates the gaming subject. If perfect access control, however, is indeed impossible, its impossibility lies in the contract between game and player to mutually and indefinitely defer this control. Time is not telepresent in online gaming worlds as a discourse of the player-subject, but exists radically independent and accessible beyond subject control.

Far from negating need for the presence of players, this radical indifference serves to bind both players and game through *différance*. Jacques Derrida expresses *différance* as difference that is 'discernibility, distinction, separation, diastem, *spacing*' and deference as 'detour, relay, reserve, *temporization*' (Derrida 1982, 18). For Derrida, to defer is an opening of a 'past' not as a negation of presence, but of time 'which has never been present, and which will never be, whose future to come will never be a *production* or a reproduction in the form of presence', a future anterior sense of a past that remains an undecided future (Derrida 1982, 21). Derrida finds a convenient narrative reserve (or relay loop) for the temporal imposition of the future anterior in Hamlet, whose dramatic assertion that 'time is out of joint', rather than relying on binary logic of absence/presence, makes time accessible to multiple significances (Derrida 1994, 18). For Derrida, Hamlet's invocation of disjointed time is not that there are no joints, but that all junctions of time (i.e. the present) can only ever be contingencies. There is no proper sense of disjointed time: it is ecstatic, beside itself – detour. In another chapter of this volume, McDowell also engages Derrida's perspective of time to RPGs as a detour from a consistent space.

MMORPGs utilize time that is expressed specifically as tele presence, both in terms of excess and detour. Game events neither mark the passage of time nor provide memory for players. In most RPGs there are quests, tasks, and obstacles that continually pile on top of each other, only to reappear for the benefit of other players and to maintain the fragile integrity of a coherent, accessible, and continuous playing space. Videogames have always featured obstacles which are destroyed or overcome only for as long as it serves the purposes of the delicate narrative logic, respawning moments later in the same area awaiting the next encounter. Whereas stand-alone console games included save features to pause the self-contained instance of the game for future progression, quests and puzzles in MMORPGs are never terminally completed, remaining permanently open and active for the influx of new players into the always-existing world of the online game. The layers of events do not map a cycle of events, but a layering of perpetual instances that continually recycle. The individual player may complete a quest, kill an enemy, and move on to the next area, but the quest will not vanish, the enemy will quickly resurrect, and old areas will continue to welcome new guests to territory always already discovered and rediscovered. Time is disjointed, but it is that disjointed quality that allows telepresence to function and invite players to experience multiple aspects of the game.

Procedurality, 'Now-time', and the 'Instance'

Disjointed time, with its inclusion of the future anterior, questions the ability for MMORPGs to present and maintain consistent gamespaces and playing subjects. At the very least, the creation of subjects in digital gaming can only be framed within the disjointed temporal conjunctions of narrative and description, representation and simulation. Thus, events in the form of quests, tasks, obstacles, etc., provide both narrative and descriptive functions: quests, for example, suspend narrative flow, while also inscribing the future with what is to follow. Tanya Krzywinska identifies that a fundamental benefit to quests is not just to progress through a fixed storyline, but to use the tasks in order to learn the rhetorical code implicit in the game. Kryzwinska points out that while quests do provide a way to progress through the gamespace, 'it is, however, a form of illusory agency because it is patently obvious to any player that they undertake the very same tasks already completed by others' (Krzywinska 2008, 127).

The actual work of quests and tasks built into MMORPGs are what Ian Bogost would call the game's procedures, a term he borrows from Janet Murray to describe the rule-based system of computer coding. Bogost argues that '[p]rocedurality is the principal value of the computer, which creates meaning through the interaction of algorithms' (Bogost 2007, 4). Procedurality, according to Bogost, is how the computer expresses representations. The computer represents visual processes through a series of code-level procedures (Bogost 2007, 5). Game designers create algorithmic instances that represent particular procedures of gameplay. Here the use of the word 'instance' becomes crucial. Instead of a limited temporal meaning, instance can now refer to particular procedures created at the code-level: an avatar instance; an architectural instance; a combat instance; a narrative instance.

What procedurality brings to a discussion of temporality in serious games is that even when time enters into the gameplay equation, it is still an individual instance of the procedures of the game. Most MMORPGs, such as the more established *World of Warcraft*

(Blizzard 2004) and *Guild Wars* (ArenaNet 2005) series, the more recently released *DC Universe Online* (Sony Online Entertainment 2011) and *Rift* (Trion Worlds 2011), as well as the forthcoming *Star Wars: The Old Republic* (BioWare 2011), are careful to evoke a time that is timeless; they do not evoke any real historical periods and do not impose biological lifespans on avatars. To hold together the fragility of the unstable gameworld, timelessness is built into the procedures of the games, and so clocks and calendars become ways to organize the game elements around the space of the gameworld.

Procedural rhetoric is evident in these instances that break down the illusion of this unstable simulation of consistency. Borrowing a term from Alain Badiou, Bogost argues that 'a procedural rhetoric persuades when it helps discern the eventual site of a situation – the place where current practice breaks down […] Procedural rhetorics expose the way things work' (Bogost 2007, 333). Badiou's notion of 'situation' is a self-reflexive moment that can lead to a rupture of the present and reveal the rhetorical composition of the game design. If we could peel away its narrative and visual (descriptive) layers, and the various instances that compose them, online gamespaces function on various relay loops that control the limits of gameplay capabilities and mediate the players' experience. These procedures all come from the game side of things. We could add here as well Friedline and Collister's argument in this volume that players provide their own parameters for how the RPG community will function, especially in terms of linguistic power.

To recognize time as a situation of instances is to expose the gaps that open between procedures or events, rather than base it on measured intervals. Time exists as far as it has been programmed directly into the code within and between instances. Rather than the measured intervals represented by clocks and calendars, time is represented by the interaction of codified 1's and 0's that determine the limits of the gamespace itself. Bogost sees this as a positive feature of procedurality in which 'the imposition of constraints also creates expression' (Bogost 2007, 7). Procedures regulate what is possible in the game through game elements, its instances. Rather than limiting gameplay potential, procedures generate expressive experiences. In other words, limited possibilities produce generative instances.

If *WoW* represents time as the 1's and 0's of computer code, it is tempting to relegate time as only one fragment among many of the game's general procedurality. It would characterize time as both an infinite present of player experience and a fragmentary element of a unified game structure. When time is understood as a naturalized part of the game structure, ecstasis is obscured and time becomes a normative element; it loses its detours. The result is similar to what Martin Heidegger critiqued as 'now-time', an Aristotelian definition of time that measures 'what is counted'; in this sense, time is 'what is expressed and what we have in view [...] when the *traveling* pointer (or the shadow) is made present' (Heidegger 2004, 473). *WoW* represents night and day with the presence or absence of light, denoted by the sun, which functions as its 'traveling pointer'.

But the progression of days is only part of an illusion of measured time; *now-time* is only *shadow* time. Night and day in *WoW* are the Heideggerian shadows of the simulated gamespace in order to bind a direct connection with a more familiar world. The turn from day to night collapses the distance introduced by the alienating effects of simulation. This time, understood by pointers and shadows, is only concerned with an essentially teleological present; time becomes a tool of the present. Both temporal and spatial presence is dependent on a series of nows stretching infinitely on either side of the present, and thus it is a negation of the disjointed time between game and player. This normative account based solely on procedurality puts game and player on a plane of equivalence and stabilizes identity.

In short, time in *WoW* cannot be fully understood as now-time, nor is it counted in terms of clocks and calendars. To situate player and game into procedural equivalence is to deny the gaps between the joints of this relay. Time is only directly structured into *WoW* through the relations between instances, not as pure instance itself. Procedurality sheds light on the rhetorical organization and distribution of instances in coded structures, but time works between these structures. The passage of time in *WoW* is a non-passage of time; no-thing is passing, inasmuch as time is not a thing, instance, or measurable quantity. In some ways this accounts for the feeling of timelessness produced within, yet beyond, the game's uninterrupted loop of simulated events.

The Gameworld Never Sleeps: The Ubiquity of MMORPGs

For the rest of the essay I will refer to *World of Warcraft* as a prime example of how time functions in MMORPGs. There are a few important reasons to use *WoW* to illustrate these points. Friedline and Collister point out in this same volume that at the present time *WoW* is the most popular MMORPG and Blizzard Entertainment has shown great resilience in retaining an industry majority of subscriptions since its inception in 2004. Blizzard has been able to strike a careful balance between maintaining a sense of its history and retaining older players while looking forward to product improvements that will attract new players. Blizzard is also a pioneer in forming the present subscription-based market for MMORPGs and establishing successful strategies for delivering a variety of ways for players to participate. Any game wanting to compete must either copy this model or find a new way to establish a player base. *WoW* may not be the first or last MMORPG, but it is certainly standing the test of time.

To take full advantage of the possibilities of a subscription-based videogame service, *WoW* requires a relay accessibility/excessibility of time. Through the ubiquity of the internet, *WoW* projects an image of a world based on stability and immediacy, and yet this stable image of controlled environment is at odds with the internet's volatile exchangeability and openness. The distribution of expansion sees *The Burning Crusade* (2006), *Wrath of the Lich King* (2008), and the more recently released *Cataclysm* (2010) introduce changes to narrative content as well as expanded gamespace to help the game sustain player interest and manage the instability of the economic system. Online subscription markets rely only marginally on a steady flow of new customers; the real transformation of the market model is the preservation and perpetuation of current subscriptions. While most cartridge- or disc-based gaming systems faced a shelf life of six months or less, as a product of the technological capabilities of the internet *WoW* will survive indefinitely.

Cartridge- or disk-based games supplied a radically temporal (and ultimately terminal) game experience: the gamespace survives as long as the player continues to play. Once the player stops, the game is over and the space ceases to exist. Save functions and memory cards on some games were attempts not only to maintain player progress but to introduce the idea of a continuous and consistent experience. Saving game progress provided a means to suspend the experience so that players could return and begin exactly where they left off. The save function works by closing the minimal distance between suspending gametime and insisting on a continuous space. In other words, save functions negate time in order to preserve an illusion of player control.

The online subscription service model of MMORPGs bridges the minimal distance by literally making the gameworld omnipresent. There is no longer any need to save the game because the game is always already 'on', and even persists once a player has stopped playing. According to Kryzwinska, the permanence of the gameworld in *WoW* is a component of the game's procedural rhetoric. She distinguishes the online RPG from other forms by its use of a 'persistent world in temporal terms that exists whether or not an individual player is playing. In this, the gameworld has a material presence beyond the sphere of the player' (Krzywinska 2008, 126). Rather than offering player-controlled gameworld time, a game like *WoW* provides players with a seemingly unlimited access to play. In the former, time is inextricably tied to gametime, separated into discrete periods of play between pauses. The pauses can only imply or simulate continuous action. In the latter, time is no longer discrete intervals and, consequently, it is the player that experiences separation (rupture). The gameworld of *WoW* continues on with or without the player, because it is not dependent on the presence of any one player. It theoretically continues to exist without any actual players logged in, ready to be accessed by the next available player in a state of perpetual waiting in which no-thing is happening.

Jesper Juul identifies the temporal relay between gamespace and player as a performance of game interactivity, and explores how time affects narrative elements of a game. Regarding this relationship in the game *Doom* (id Software 1993), he argues that it is 'clear that the events represented cannot be past or prior, since we as players can influence them. By pressing the CTRL key, we fire the current weapon, which influences the gameworld' (Juul 2001). The inability of a game to be both interactive and narrative at the same time leads him to separate out 'story time' from the game action:

> [*Doom*] constructs the story time as synchronous with narrative time and reading/viewing time: the story time is now. Now, not just in the sense that the viewer witnesses events now, but in the sense that the events are happening now, and that what comes next is not yet determined [...] Games are almost always chronological. (Juul 2001)

'Story time' seems to be advocating for now-time inasmuch as each new instance of the present is only intelligible within the context of the present. In fact, in order to construct 'story time', Juul only considers linear narrative elements, excluding descriptive functions of procedurality and gameplay that suspend time indefinitely.

In *Doom*, as in *WoW*, a player will defeat enemies and pass increasingly difficult obstacles in a linear progression of achievement. Time in *Doom* is procedurally dependent on achievement; enemies and levels do not reappear unless the player restarts the game. In contrast, *WoW* does not depend on any particular player to persist, so quests and enemies must continually be respawned and renewed in order to be available for the next passing player. Multiple players may be on the same quest and, therefore, may need the same items, battles, or characters in order to proceed. The emphasis on building and sustaining communities in MMORPGs, such as the concept of 'guilds' in *WoW*, resists the self-contained individual illusions of traditional games. But it also complicates the simple division of time aspects; just as physical paths cross, time paths must cross, or collapse, into a cyclical present.

MMORPGs are a social medium; these games literally organize and mediate online communities. Much of the game content is meant to be experienced in a context of collaboration across both physical and virtual distance. While the element of community is imperative to all modes of play, what I am interested in here is how telepresence is affected by social temporal modes of MMORPGs, or how external modes of time encroach upon internal gameplay. For example, one way in which the real-world calendar affects the virtual calendar in *WoW* is when Blizzard incorporates in-game seasonal events that resemble external holiday observations, corresponding to a real-world calendar and measurement of time. Seasonal quests and events are limited to the duration of real-world events and so there is a time restraint to experiencing them. The in-game calendar, in fact, corresponds to a real-world calendar and includes information for in-game events as well as user-determined content. The presence of in-game events provides a social experience that directs community interaction. The abundance of player choice is governed by the associations of these social and individual experiences of time.

While player choice continues to be directed by time-restricted events, telepresence functions by allowing players the opportunity to effect general change within the community by participating in seasonal events, or even completing a difficult achievement which is individually tracked and archived in the player's account. The inclusion of such elements demonstrates how content intended for multiple players is determined by the intersection of individual situations. This is an argument that examines primarily the choices of the individual as part of a larger community and in relation to the designed procedures of the game. For discussion about the individual's role in reconstituting identity through the particular designs of software developers, see the chapter in this volume by Travis on BioWare.

In patch 3.3.0, Blizzard introduced the Dungeon Finder system to *WoW* which allowed players from different game servers, discrete gameworlds, to assemble in order to complete difficult instances that required a group. When a player enters a dungeon group queue, all players assembled for the dungeon are transported to the starting location. There is a violation of gamespace consistency in order to allow more efficient gameplay. But the transition into a dungeon instance expresses an intersection of disparate temporal modes that requires players to constantly negotiate telepresence. When a dungeon queue suddenly signals that a group has been assembled, the player must decide to join the group or continue other tasks. Accepting the group invitation requires now that individual demands confront group needs. For all intents and purposes, time stops in order to successfully realize the present social conditions.

In the marketplace of videogames, MMORPGs display a relatively novel conception of gameplay that has the advantage of extending product shelf life and integrating a communal procedural rhetoric that taps into the rise of social media on the internet. Time is not just another procedural element that sustains the integrity of the gamespace, but a complex relay of disjointed movements between game and player at the very rupture points of virtual and real space. What remains to be examined is the function of the subject within the infinite recycling of procedural elements.

Hurtling Toward the Present: Polar Inertia in Cyclical Time

Although Blizzard offers players many avenues in which to explore the gameworld of *WoW*, combinations of many factors contribute to the success of the MMORPG model. Much thought and effort is put into creating a creative and independent narrative based around the gameworld, and these narrative aspects provide quest objectives that build on each other to increase experience and opportunities. The story elements of the narrative, however, facilitate a subjective sensation of constant linear motion, a trajectory of goal-oriented play, and imply the universal objectives. If a player were ever to arrive at a so-called final destination, the terminal jointedness of time would be exposed and the game is over. Instead, the continual accumulation of quests and objectives in MMORPGs demonstrate what Paul Virilio referred to as 'polar inertia' – the speed and distance that modern audiovisual technologies evoke without any actual movement (Virilio 2000, 17). The idea behind polar inertia is not so much to separate time and space as to rethink what space means within electronic media. Speed and efficiency are rhetorically embedded into the procedurality of online RPGs in order to counteract the impression of 'running in place' that accompanies an indefinite ubiquitous present that seems to characterize web-based applications and programs.

In the case of *WoW*, space is expansive but, of course, necessarily restricted for practical reasons, and requires fantasy GPS maps to track character position as well as locations of communities and important landmarks. Avatars must travel great distances in order to visit certain towns or compete quests. Not only are distances not measured in real world rations, but avatars travel at exaggerated speeds. The artificiality of distance and speed serves a double function of verisimilitude: it recreates a seemingly extensive space that challenges exploration, but also shortens the sometimes aggravating travel time that could substantially detract from the other active elements of gameplay, such as quests and battles. The 'moment of inertia' is an event of excessive simulation, a 'situation' in Badiou's terms, exposing the cracks of the stable gameworld. If there is a moment, or even a series of moments, in which these temporal inconsistencies surface within the gameworld, when do these moments occur, and what are their identifiable effects?

The question of cause and effect, however, is itself a procedural argument restricted by a continuous flow of now-time. This essay began with a quote about time and event from Maurice Blanchot, who was concerned with the question of human finitude and temporal impossibility. In his book *The Writing of the Disaster*, Blanchot writes that event is marked by separation and rupture, not the flow of linear history. Blanchot's approach to the fragmentary event is 'destined partly to the blank that separates them, find[ing] in this gap not what ends them, but what prolongs them [...] causing them to persist on account of their incompletion' (Blanchot 1995, 58). The instances that compose the procedural rhetoric of gameworld and time in MMORPGs have their own temporal relationship based on the rupture of distance/speed intervals and on potential travel paths.

In *WoW*, these instances reveal the fragmentary encounters between spaces of play: quests are offered and await the player to accept or decline; the brief interval before an enemy approaches to attack, or before the player engages battle; the hesitating moments between what has led a player to a particular instance and the potential that the instance holds for the future. Each event attempts to bridge the separation of temporal procedures; when the situation of the audiovisual vehicle suddenly reveals (as Bogost argued) the way things work 'in the hopes of inspiring a disruptive event', players face a disruption of the gameworld that requires them to make a choice (Bogost 2007, 331). The hope of disruption should not be seen as an intentional part of interactive game design; rather, these confrontations allow for insight into that rhetorical cycle of procedurality in which the simulation becomes excessively present and the player must choose to accept it in order to continue the illusion.

Conclusion/Disruption

The intersections of event-instances demonstrate that the subjective potential of *WoW* and the general genre of MMORPGs can be located within temporal relationships, rather than only in the identity politics of avatars. In an article critiquing the utopian promises of interactivity and subjectivity, James Newman believes that players identify as much with the game interfaces, movements, tools, and perspectives as they do with their avatars; in other words, players are rhetorically created interactively through their experience with game design. Subjectivity is not one of clear subject and object, but rather mediated by the continuous feedback loop of gaming interfaces in which the player must be seen as both implied by, and implicated in, the construction and composition of the experience (Newman 2002). Locked into this feedback loop at the level of interface or controls (hence the significance of the feel of the game), the player experiences at the level of first-hand participation and can then sustain and decode multiple and apparently contradictory presentations of the self (Newman 2002). Newman extends the circular metaphors to the code levels which employ feedback loops in order to sense information input and be able to respond appropriately. In an autopoietic system, particular inputs trigger certain outputs. This, of course, assumes the perfect directional flow of communication between mechanisms. From what Newman suggests (although feedback loops are designed to provide limited control and responses), online RPG players interject and intercept the message of the feedback loop.

Videogames are not autopoietic systems; they depend on player input in order to operate, and a player's input is likewise determined by the messages of the feedback loop. This seems to contradict the utopian image of the autonomous MMORPG gameworld, but any notion of autonomy is inaccurate for discussions of both space and time in gaming worlds that depend on internet technologies. In the absence of players the gamespaces of *WoW* would still require continuous external management from the Blizzard software team; and lacking player input, *WoW* would remain in the moment of hesitation, the gap between fragmentary instances, never able to move into the re-cycle of the feedback loop. In this sense, the cyclical structure of the feedback loop actually frees the system from polar inertia. While the player may still experience only the simulation of space and distance within the audiovisual vehicle, the temporal relationships of the game are not just simulated, but regulated by the feedback loop. Players are complicit in the loop; they interpolate the loop and affect the output of the system, mutual participants in the loop through the system interface. This reciprocity generates identification with the loop itself, with avatars being the exterior representation of this process.

This is, finally, one instance in which time in MMORPGs can be considered coherent, accessible, and continuous. The system is expressed through the movements and decisions of the player, the player accesses these movements and decisions through the procedural rhetoric of the system, which is all articulated through the cyclicality of the feedback loop. The loop provides players with a sense of telepresence, that their actions have effects on multiple levels of gameplay, including the physical world around them, without replicating a linear perception of time. Understood in this way, time is not only one element that the system utilizes to dictate player action and reaction, it also provides an orientation for players to comprehend a particular gameworld. The way time is expressed in MMORPGs is structured by its reliance on the stability of the internet, and this limitation is integral to how the game is first constructed and then experienced by players. That experience, however, is fed back into the system as players accept the parameters of the game and learn how to push them to their limits. How time operates within games rationalizes the limits of space and play, while responding to the essential telepresence of the individual whose suspension of external temporal modes can never be complete.

WoW represents one model for MMORPGs, and its success can in part be contributed to its capacity to respond to the needs of its evolving consumer base. Although the shelf life of individual MMORPGs is extended by the subscription service market, it remains to be seen how long this market model will last. These games seem to express that, although gameworlds continue to increase virtual dimension, we will not see massive changes in how those spaces are communicated. Temporal relationships, however, continue to evolve along with each new development in gaming technology, leading game theory on detours into unfamiliar territory. Heraclitus articulated this importance simply by identifying the close relationship between games and the infinite: 'Time is a child playing [...] the kingdom belongs to a child' (Heraclitus 1888, 103). As MMORPGs increase in popularity and functionality, and gaming in general becomes a more integrated part of social media, time will continue to present new challenges to players of games and theory.

References

Aarseth, Espen. 'A Hollow World: World of Warcraft as Spatial Practice.' In *Digital Culture, Play and Identity: A World of Warcraft Reader*, ed. Hilde G. Cornilussen and Jill Walker Rettberg, 111–22. Cambridge: MIT Press, 2008.
ArenaNet. *Guild Wars*. [PC]. NCsoft: Seoul, South Korea, 2005.
BioWare. *Star Wars: The Old Republic*. [PC]. Electronic Arts: Redwood City, CA, 2011.
Blanchot, Maurice. *The Writing of the Disaster*. Trans. Ann Smock. Lincoln: University of Nebraska Press, 1995.
Blizzard. *World of Warcraft*. [PC]. Blizzard Entertainment: Irvine, CA, 2004.
Bogost, Ian. *Persuasive Games: The Expressive Power of Videogames*. Cambridge: MIT Press, 2007.
Derrida, Jacques. *Margins of Philosophy*. Trans. Alan Bass. Chicago: University of Chicago Press, 1982).
—*Specters of Marx: The State of the Debt, the Work of Mourning, and the New International*. Trans. Peggy Kamuf. Routledge: New York, 1994.
Heidegger, Martin. *Being and Time*. Trans. John Macquarrie and Edward Robinson. New York: Harper and Row, 2004.
Heraclitus. *The Fragments of the Work of Heraclitus of Ephesus on Nature*. Trans. G. T. W. Patrick. Baltimore: Johns Hopkins University Press, 1888.
Id Software. *Doom*. [PC]. id Software: Mesquite, Texas, 1993.
Juul, Jesper. 2001. 'Games Telling Stories? – A Brief Note on Games

and Narratives.' *Game Studies: The International Journal of Computer Game Research* 1, no.1. doi: 0101/juul-gts.
—'Introduction to Game Time.' In *First Person: New Media as Story, Performance, and Game*, ed. Wardrip-Fruin, Noah and Pat Harrigan, 131–42. Cambridge: MIT Press, 2006.
Kittler, Friedrich. '*Protected Mode.*' In *Literature, Media, Information Systems: Essays*, ed. John Johnston, 156–68. Amsterdam: Routledge, 1997.
Krzywinska, Tanya. 'World Creation and Lore: World of Warcraft as Rich Text.' In *Digital Culture, Play and Identity: A World of Warcraft Reader*, ed. Hilde G. Cornilussen and Jill Walker Rettberg, 123–41. Cambridge: MIT Press, 2008.
Newman, James. 2002. 'The Myth of the Ergodic Videogame: Some Thoughts on Player-Character Relationships in Videogames.' *Game Studies: The International Journal of Computer Game Research* 2, no.1. doi: 0102/newman.
Simons, Jan. 2007. 'Narrative, Games, and Theory.' *Game Studies: The International Journal of Computer Game Research* 7, no.1. doi: 0701/articles/simons.
Sony Online Entertainment – Austin. *DC Universe Online*. Sony Computer Entertainment: Tokyo, Japan, 2011.
Taylor, Laurie. 2003. 'When Seams Fall Apart: Video Game Space and the Player.' *Game Studies: The International Journal of Computer Game Studies* 3, no.2. doi: 0302/taylor.
Trion Worlds. *Rift*. [PC]. Trion Worlds Networks: Redwood Shores, CA, 2011.
Virilio, Paul. *Polar Inertia*. Trans. Patrick Camiller. Thousand Oaks: Sage Publications, 2000.

3

Game and Narrative in *Dragon Age: Origins*: Playing the Archive in Digital RPGs

ALICE HENTON[1]

Archives often dominate digital games, both mechanically (how the game works) and narratively (how the story unfolds)[2]. Folklorist Kiri Miller celebrates the *Grand Theft Auto* (Rockstar Games) franchise, for example, as an interactive archive, in which the anthologized structure of the narrative is responsible for a large portion of the game's appeal as a 'story collection [...] a virtual museum of vernacular culture and a widely circulated pop culture artifact whose double-voiced aesthetic has given rise to diverse interpretive communities' (Miller 2008, 255). Many games foreground database mechanics by structuring narratives around archival interaction. As an illustration, the *Assassin's Creed* (Ubisoft) game series invites gamers into a world in which the main character, Desmond, a twenty-first century bartender, discovers that his own body is an archive of ancestral memories that can be accessed with the help of a special machine. Desmond's status as a genetic database allows players to enter this archive and 'play' the life experiences of ancestors living in exotic times and places. Similarly, in the opening moments of *Mass Effect* (BioWare 2007), the protagonist interacts with a mysterious beacon left behind by an ancient alien race. The beacon burns a series of images into the protagonist's mind, but the information remains indecipherable until the player undertakes a special mission to gain the 'Cipher', a concentration of 'endemic ancestral memories' codified into a transmittable index which, when accessed, allows the protagonist to understand the message and the player to complete the game[3]. *Dragon Age: Origins* (BioWare 2009) and its expansion *Dragon Age: Origins – Awakening* (BioWare 2010), a medieval fantasy RPG, take place in Ferelden, a fictional universe of enormous depth and complexity mediated through a proliferation of archives[4]. *Dragon Age* explores the potential ambiguities of archival narratives by problematizing and scrutinizing the process of data collection even as it insists upon it. Experiencing *Dragon Age*'s story reveals its dependence upon, and organization by, archives in a way that mirrors the archival mechanics of the game itself: the player's experience reinforces the character's adventures. Investigating this archival emphasis offers the chance to scrutinize the way narratives function in RPGs as a genre and perhaps also the opportunity to re-envision, or at least complicate, the long-standing tension in game studies of story versus play. Before examining the game in greater detail, however, it is useful to briefly visit the critical and theoretical underpinnings of an examination of archive in digital game media.

Game scholarship often relies on one of two distinct analytical models, 'narratology' or 'ludology'. While narratology focuses on narrative, particularly the story-like aspects of the digital game text, and draws heavily from traditions of literary criticism, ludology deals with 'the unique properties of games as distinct from narrative texts, including their variable outcomes and the effort they require from players' (Frasca 1999). Analyses frequently emphasize the divide between the fictional and mechanical levels of digital games, arguing, in essence, that 'the narration and the gameplay, like oil and water, are not easily mixed' (Aarseth 2004, 51). Without dismissing the friction between digital games in terms of gameplay – that is, games as elaborate constructs dependent upon systems of rules, objectives, and strategic behaviors – and games as vehicles for immersive and interactive fiction, or storytelling, this project invests in exploring Jesper Juul's claim that 'When rules and fictions do not match perfectly [the game] can still generate a *positive* effect, working as a way of playing with the player's expectations, as a way of creating parody, and finally as a way of foregrounding the game as a real-world activity' (Juul 2005, 163). Tensions between game and story are often figured as conflicts between form and content, and ludologists routinely contend that the study of gameplay – of the rules, strategies, and procedures necessary to interact with, progress through, and win out over the game – are more organically representative of the essence of the digital game experience, particularly since the mechanics of gameplay are closely related to the mechanics of the game itself. Gameplay, after all, forces the player to interact with the game as a program – a carefully structured system of algorithms, or rule-based processes, that tracks performance and progresses via fulfilled checkpoints and goals. Gameplay is thus the direct interaction with the game text, and 'the similarity between the actions expected from the player and computer algorithms is too uncanny to be dismissed' (Manovich 2001, 197). Game rules, like algorithms, are the functional underpinnings of the game experience. A digital game is playable when its rules are understandable, while a game's narrative is not fundamental in the same way: 'electronic closure occurs when a work's structure, though not its plot, is understood [...] a cognitive activity at one remove from the usual pleasures of hearing a story' (Murray 1997, 174).

Viewed through this lens, narratives can seem like superfluous additions, awkwardly grafted features of digital games that distract from their ludic integrity. It is worth considering, however, that narrative aspects of games are as fundamentally mechanical as the ludic ones. Narratives imbue digital games with the trajectory that fuels gameplay. Thus, games are actually 'experienced by their players as narratives', since the exploration of narrative trajectory, in novels as well as new media, is fundamentally a process of 'uncovering [the] underlying logic – its algorithm' (Manovich 2001, 200). Argued this way, both story *and* play, narrative and ludology, ultimately participate in game mechanics, since both invest in and draw from the algorithmic logic that defines digital game media. This mechanical similarity provides a useful platform from which to view game and narrative as complementary, even overlapping, aspects of the digital game text.

Digital games cannot be defined through algorithm alone. Game processes, tasks, and stories all rely on the interaction of logical processes with structured collections of data – that is, with databases. Data structures and algorithms function interdependently in computer programming, and the game experience is thus dependent upon both; in a digital text, 'the "user" of a narrative is traversing a database, following links between its records as established by the database's creator' (Manovich 2001, 200). This symbiotic process is, however, fraught with ideological tension: Lev Manovich elucidates a fundamental friction between a database, which 'represents the world as a list of items and refuses to order this list', and algorithms, which, as narratives, are dependent upon order and shape, 'a cause-and-effect trajectory [from] seemingly unordered items (events)'; this conflict makes database and narrative 'natural enemies' (Manovich 2001, 200). The process-driven nature of digital games – solve a puzzle, find a clue, advance a level, interact with a story, etc. – serves as evidence that games privilege algorithmic logic and, through this privilege, subordinate and even obscure the role of the database. In defining the central tension within game structures as a conflict between database and algorithm, Manovich effectively recasts the ludology/narratology divide as an alliance; both represent aspects of the algorithmic logic that drives digital games and relegates the database to its status as the 'unmarked term' (Manovich 2001, 207). This discrepancy is inherently problematic, given the centrality of database mechanics to a wide range of new media forms. Manovich asks: 'How can a narrative take into account the fact that its elements are organized in a database? How can our new abilities to store vast amounts of data, to automatically classify, index, link, search and instantly retrieve it lead to new kinds of narratives?' (Manovich 2001, 208). Digital games offer one possible answer.

Databases are not as invisible in digital games as it is tempting to think. Players routinely interact with any number of in-game databases. In digital games, progress occurs and gameplay unfolds through the careful observance of archived performance. Many games make at least part of this archive available to the player: special 'statistics' screens chart everything from the player's location in game to the number of times the game has been played, the number of enemies killed, the most common tactics used, etc. Beyond this 'meta' archive, most narrative-based digital games rely upon some form of in-game archive to engross players in the gameworld. 'Journals', 'codices', and 'logs' are searchable databases that allow background information and mission data to be always accessible to the player, who must create, maintain, and manage these resources in order to successfully navigate and complete the game. These embedded texts ground and direct the experience of the 'participatory, immersive medium' of the digital game (Murray 1997, 98).

This imbedded textuality is as integral to RPGs as a genre as it is to the mechanics of a digital medium. Their pre-digital origins as pen-and-paper (or tabletop) game experiences meld a rich narrative component, in which each player describes the actions and choices of his or her character, and an exhaustive archival knowledge of that character's statistics (stats) – his or her abilities, attributes, and qualifications – that enable these choices. Pen-and-paper players routinely record these stats, preserving and updating the records as the character evolves through 'experience' within games. As a number of critics have already noted, the genre's story-driven legacy, grounded as it is in archival mechanics, both carries over and mutates as RPGs adapt into digital forms, and, viewed thus, we can read the digital database as an evolution of a core component of the genre.

The database accompanies the player and develops as the game plays out. Playing is the experience of creating and altering the archive; adding to the archive is always necessary and often rewarded in a variety of ways[5]. Examining the way archives function in digital games necessarily involves interrogating the function of archival logic as well as recognizing the proliferation of archival collections. Games contain not only extensive assortments of (in this case digital) artifacts and texts, but also foster narratives that provide the system of signification by which these collections gain meaning. 'The archive' is, on every level, specifically tailored to, and for, the narrative. Even as the 'codex' reveals and organizes collected data as if they were 'the sum of all texts that a culture has kept upon its person as documents attesting to its own past, or as evidence of a continuing identity', it in essence creates the only incarnation of that past that has ever been (Foucault 1972, 129). This artificiality foregrounds the archive as a constructed system as well as a compilation of texts, and makes these fictional worlds an excellent place to consider the archive as a means of directed organization, privilege, and ordering. The process of archival creation is also the process of creating narrative structure and ludic strategy. A coherent narrative must, in turn, support a coherent strategy of gameplay; it must create a compelling and immersive history that is also a guideline for future actions.

In referring to in-game databases as archives, I am deliberately invoking a complex set of theoretical signifiers to illuminate not only utilitarian but also metaphorical and mythological registers. Jacques Derrida traces the etymology of *arkhē* to the dual signifiers 'commencement' and 'commandment', implying both beginning and authority and coordinating 'two principles in one: the principle according to nature or history, *there* where things *commence* – physical, historical or ontological principle, *there* where men and gods *command*, *there* where authority, social order is exercised' (Derrida 1995, 1). The 'archive' exists simultaneously on literal and abstract planes as both a place of storage, or the collection of things stored, and a system that creates the need for, and meaning of, that space and all it contains. Michel Foucault locates the significance of the archive not in its literal incarnation as an actual collection of artifacts or texts, but rather in the theoretical system that imbues these compilations with significance: 'the law of what can be said, the system that governs the appearance of statements as unique events (Foucault 1972, 129). This association with rules and processes seems particularly conducive to an interrogation of digital games, as it marks archives as algorithmically ruled databases: collections organized by, and necessary to, narrative. Archive as a narrative device and database as a mechanical reality provide us with a way of establishing a place for the database in the 'algorithmic logic' of digital game theory after all. Digital game narrative is about process completion, but is also about the storage, collection, and organization of data. In-game universes are actually story collections to be discovered, assembled, and manipulated by the player. Not only do programs rely on data structures, but narratives are dependent upon archival logic, as a player's experience of the game about assimilating, organizing, and deploying knowledge. The character's participation in the narrative and the player's experience of the game are inarguably different levels of the text, and it is unquestionably important to distinguish between them; however, the connections between them are as worthy of analysis as the distinctions. Archives are just such connective places. The roles of both player and character often demonstrate a similar dependence on archives, and the 'two layers' of archival significance, system and collection, permeate both levels of the digital game text.

Here, let us take a closer look at the mechanics and the story of *Dragon Age*. The game's plot immerses players in both the myths and practices of archival systems. Every major institution, religious and political, across a number of civilizations, including fantastical dwarven and elven cultures, requires the character to interact with archives, to add to them, restore them, or even destroy them. Mechanically, *Dragon Age*, like many games, collects a series of archival functions together under the heading of the 'journal', a simulated diary that connects the player to his or her character (the PC), who is also the protagonist in the game's narrative. Reading the character's journal allows the player to understand and manipulate the character's life. The journal comprises a number of different functions, including a codex, an inventory, a dialogue history, an interactive world map, and lists of both current and completed quests. The game possesses one of the most extensive archival systems in a digital game to date, with hundreds of possible entries. Archives are everywhere in *Dragon Age*; not only does the player rely upon the in-game archive, but the game's protagonist constantly encounters characters who function as archivists and completes missions that involve manipulating, creating, or even destroying various archival collections. This protagonist must be an archeologist and ethnologist as well as a warrior in order for the player to succeed in 'beating' the game, which requires, inscribes, and interrogates the idea of archive in numerous spaces and incarnations. As the player manipulates the protagonist's world, she alters both her own visible database in the form of the codex and the fictional archives that surround her PC, imbuing *Dragon Age*'s story with moral tension that enhances the complexity of the narrative. This complexity overlays, problematizes, and enhances the archival mechanics at the heart of the gameplay; it unites the digital game's dual layers of fantasy and the functionality and overlaps the experiences and purposes of the player and the PC. It infuses the player's textual interactions with a degree of moral complexity that must also extend to the game's essential mechanics. It connects gameplay with story even as the narrative questions and complicates the very process by which the technology operates.

A number of new media critics apply Wolfgang Iser's theory of *leerstellen* ('blanks' or 'gaps') to the experience of digital game narrative. As interactive texts, digital games make explicit the kind of textual participation that Iser finds implicit in any reading experience – the idea that 'the story of a narrative is produced by a convergence of text and reader' that requires the reader's 'participation in a filling in of gaps in the narrative provided by the texts' (Iser 1978, 50). This is literally the case in *Dragon Age*'s codex, replete with 'gaps' to be filled with gathered knowledge. Navigating the narrative requires creating the archive. Just as digital games can make literal the necessity of reader intervention, they also embody Michel de Certeau's assertion that 'narrative structures have the status of spatial syntaxes [...] every story is a travel story – a spatial practice' (de Certeau 1984, 115). His description of narrative as 'a whole panoply of codes, ordered ways of proceeding and constraints [that] regulate changes in space' provides an excellent synopsis of the carefully structured story of a digital game, which depends upon carefully mapping and recording the reader/player's progress through the coded landscape.

Dragon Age contains numerous characters who draw attention to their own status as archival mediators. At the end of their conversation, a character called the Shaper of Memories informs the protagonist: 'Your presence has been recorded in the archive. I wish I knew what significance it may have.' Simultaneously, an icon appears in the lower corner of the screen, informing the player that the 'codex' has been updated. A similar process occurs after almost every dialogue exchange in the game. Selecting the codex icon leads the player to a screen shaped like the page of a book. The larger page is full of tiny page-shaped depressions: some are blank, others contain numbers. The numbered spaces are 'full'; selecting one will link to three or four paragraphs of text that might provide information on a particular character, a specific artifact, a religion, a cultural practice, a geographic region, or an ethnic or racial group within the gameworld. Others remain provocatively 'empty'; they contain nothing ... *yet*. Much of the process of gameplay in *Dragon Age* consists of filling in these empty spaces; the game-world abounds with 'books' to read, characters to interrogate, and items to discover. The knowledge the player gleans from these resources is crucial to his or her game-playing strategy: the more she knows, the more successful she will be. This strategy in turn alters the game's narrative progression.

Even as the player relies on the archive to make informed choices about in-game dilemmas, those choices frequently impact the archive itself, which then incorporates and reflects those decisions. Within the game, players must interact with four different civilizations in dramatic ways: determining the lines of succession, preventing or inciting civil war, etc. They may also decide to do, or not do, small favors for individual characters. They can talk with their companions to learn more about them. Each decision, once made, is documented; the new information transforms character biographies, government profiles, even religious practices.

From the beginning of the game, the player must use the archive to mediate both landscape and narrative. Soon, the player's character must do the same. The story begins with the PC joining an ancient order of warriors known as the Grey Wardens, to whom service begins immediately, and always with the same quest. The order, as its leader Duncan explains, has a long and noble history, but that history has become more and more remote to the current cultural fabric of Ferelden. People have forgotten the Wardens and the threat they are meant to stand against. In order to combat this neglect, he turns to recorded history and enlists his new recruit to help him:

> Duncan: There was once a Grey Warden archive in the Wilds, abandoned long ago when we could no longer afford to maintain

such remote outposts. It has recently come to our attention that some scrolls have been left behind, magically sealed to protect them. I want you to retrieve these scrolls if you can.
PC: What kind of scrolls are these?
Duncan: Old treaties, if you're curious. Promises of support made to the Grey Wardens long ago. They were once considered only formalities. With so many having forgotten their commitments to us, I suspect it may be a good idea to have something to remind them with[6].

Without recovering the archive, the game cannot progress. Each treaty rescued from the ruin becomes the key to a specific location on the game map; each is tied to a different civilization, and none of them will allow the PC access without archival evidence of their obligation to the Grey Warden order. The Warden, as the protagonist becomes known after finding the archive and being successfully inducted into the order, must constantly invoke the archive in order to complete his or her mission. Shortly after finding the cache of documents that represents the Grey Wardens' authority, a disastrous battle wipes out all the Grey Wardens of Ferelden except for the Warden and a young fellow recruit. The order thus becomes two novices and their recovered archive, which forms their only source of direction and power in an increasingly hostile environment. Three separate treaties exist: for dwarves, elves, and mages. As the PC approaches the area designated to each on the in-game map, a sentry bars entry until shown the treaty. Each time, the treaty receives careful, even obsessive emphasis. Each civilization grants the ancient documents the respect that they cannot, or will not, extend to the youthful remnants of the modern Grey Wardens. Weapons are always lowered when the Warden makes it clear that he or she has 'come about the treaties'. Without the archive, the young wardens have no authority.

The Grey Warden archive is the first – and perhaps most crucial – of the protagonist's archival interventions, but by no means the last. It is unusual, perhaps, most for its completion, as usually the process of retrieval is also a process of assembly, a choice between addition or subtraction. Sometimes, an entire archive must be compiled or, alternatively, destroyed. As the game progresses, more and more archives appear for the Warden to intervene in. The archival process becomes deeply rooted in the character's narrative as well as the player's effective gameplay strategy. The player must constantly assist the PC in his or her role an archivist. The 'meta' aspect in this narrative strategy, in which the plot essentially mirrors the game's archival mechanics, becomes increasingly complex and ambiguous as the game's story unfolds. Many archives the PC encounters turn out to be essentially incomplete or even intentionally misleading. Numerous characters abuse or reject archival materials.

Even an innocuous conversation can reveal the archive's complex and potentially deceptive capacity. One of the most common stories in Ferelden is the tale of Flemmeth, the 'Witch of the Wilds'. Local bards and library books all repeat similar versions of the same romantic tale. A beautiful young woman marries a local lord who locks her away from the world. Isolated, she studies magic and lives in relative peace until a handsome young bard comes to the castle. The two elope to the deserted Kokari Wilds, where they live for years in peace until Flemmeth gets word that her husband is dying and wants to see her one more time. She persuades her lover to journey back to her husband's kingdom with her, only to witness her treacherous husband murder her lover. Distraught, she summons spirits to avenge him, only to be accidentally possessed by a demon and become the dreaded Witch of the Wilds. A great hero, Connabar, eventually drives Flemmeth, now mad with grief, into hiding. The game's codex entry for Flemmeth faithfully transcribes this version of the tale. However, when the PC encounters Morrigan, Flemmeth's disciple and adopted daughter, she tells a very different version of the now-familiar legend. According to her, Flemmeth was originally married to a handsome but poor young man when she caught the attention of the local lord. Tired of poverty and disenchanted with her husband, Flemmeth agreed to be sold to the lord. When he betrayed and killed her husband rather than paying him, she called on spirits for vengeance and fled to the Kokari Wilds to escape the wrath of the dead lord's kingdom. The hero Connabar, so central to the other version of the tale, never encounters Flemmeth at all; he is merely added to the legend in a process of historical sanitization: 'No doubt such a tale has mutated much, over time and telling [...] Cormac led a brutal civil war against his own people and later claimed it was to vanquish evil [...] Flemmeth was only attached to the legend much later.' Morrigan's story is a rare example of a conversation that does not transition into the game's archive: the codex entry remains exactly the same, even though the story has drastically changed. Later in the narrative, the player must decide if the PC will ally with Flemmeth or kill her. If spared, she ultimately betrays the protagonist. Without Morrigan's story, mercy is much more tempting; the legend preserved in the archive paints Flemmeth as a more sympathetic character than she actually turns out to be. Sometimes, the archive provides information more dangerous than useful.

Morrigan's observation that tales mutate over time foreshadows an archival truth that returns repeatedly as the game's narrative progresses. Other salient examples emerge in the variety of missions the protagonist can undertake for the Chantry, a religious institution that bears a striking resemblance to the Catholic Church. Throughout the game, the Chantry's influence often manifests itself through the knowledge it controls. Its network of scholars and vast book collections serve as a crucial resource throughout the game, and the PC often receives missions to perform in the Chantry's service. While exploring a library in a long-abandoned temple, the protagonist encounters some ancient scrolls that contain a long-lost account of the prophet's last days. After making this discovery, the PC encounters a chantry archivist, who begs for the scrolls as a necessary piece of Chantry history. She speaks despondently of the numerous 'false relics' that pervade the marketplace and her worry about 'the authenticity of even our most holy artifacts', but insists that any newly discovered materials that pertain to Chantry history must become part of the archive. The player has a choice: allow her character to give the scrolls to the priest, who offers a cash reward; or keep them, in which case they sit in the inventory, and the task remains perpetually 'open' and incomplete in the quest log. Either way, as the player navigates her character away from the archivist, the character overhears two other priests discussing the 'Chant of Light', the bible-like text that chronicles Chantry history and is sung throughout Fereldon to instruct the faithful and unfaithful alike in the 'true history':

PC: Does the chant mention elves?
Sister Theohild: Yes and no, dear.

Mother Perpetua: The official version of the chant does not speak of elves. Some of the Dissonant Verses, however, do mention the disciple Shartan.

PC: What are dissonant verses?

Mother Perpetua: The chant has changed over time. Some of the verses that were sung in the past were taken out. The Canticles of Shartan were stricken from the Chant in the Glory Age. They are no longer sung, though scholars sometimes read them.

PC: Who was Shartan?

Mother Perpetua: He was an elven disciple of the Prophet. A former slave, like Andraste Herself. He rallied his people against the Imperium. He was given to the flames alongside our Lady.

PC: Why aren't his verses an official part of the Chant?

Mother Perpetua: Divine Renata had the verses removed during the Exalted March on the Dales.

Mother Perpetua goes on to explain that the Chant is an evolving text that changes with the linguistic and cultural demands of its audience. The irony here is palpable – the 'true history' deliberately exposed as a propagandistic text tailored for public consumption, constructed and presented to the Chantry's best advantage. Since the Chantry has declared a holy war on the elves, the elven prophet vanishes from the Chant of Light. Only in the secondary archive that 'scholars sometimes read' can the 'dissonant verses', along with the countless forgeries and other questionable materials that the archivist has just finished describing, be found. Here *Dragon Age* carefully undermines the 'myth of the archive' as an unmediated and impartial collection that must empirically contain the 'truth'. Instead, both player and character experience the Chantry's archive as a collection that includes potentially dubious materials mediated through a specific agenda.

The Dissonant Verses resurface again. Later, amidst a camp of Dalish elves, renegades who have foresworn the Chantry and human civilization, a merchant offers the protagonist an ancient bow. If the PC buys the weapon, known as 'the Dark Moon', this description of the object appears in the game codex:

At Shartan's word, the sky
Grew black with arrows.

> At our Lady's, ten thousand swords
> Rang from their scabbards,
> A great hymn rose over Valarian Fields gladly proclaiming:
> Those who had been slaves were now free.
> – Shartan 10:1
> They say that Shartan's followers stole whatever they could find to make weapons. they fought with knives of sharpened stone and glass, and with bows made from broken barrels or firewood. This bow was ox horn, made in secret over the course of months by a slave who worked in the slaughterhouses of Minrathrous.
> This slave's name has been lost to history, and verses that spoke of his deeds, stricken from the chant, but the weapon endures.

The description includes a segment of the now-apocryphal verse, the only such excerpt the game provides, since the Dissonant Verses themselves do not merit a codex entry. The conclusion draws attention to the archival erasure of the artifact's creator; both name and verses are gone, and only the artifact remains, a commodity for commercial exchange.

In fact, the whole Dalish culture is organized around exactly this kind of erasure and loss. After hundreds of years of human oppression, little remains of the original civilization. Not only have the elves lost their homeland and advanced technology, they have also lost the ability to read their own language. As nomadic bands, they wander across Fereldan attempting to rebuild their lost traditions and recapture their ancient way of life, including their legendary immortality, now mysteriously lost along with their possessions and customs. The archival anxiety that defines the elven experience becomes immediately apparent if the player chooses an elven origin story for his or her protagonist. The clan storyteller labels the Dalish people 'keepers of the lost lore' and speaks sadly of texts no longer legible and histories no longer known, while the clan crafts-master bemoans lost techniques, artifacts, and technologies even as he chides a young apprentice who has ruined a work in progress: 'Truly the art will be lost to us forever at this rate. In truth, we Dalish know little of the art compared to what we once did, and even what little we know has taken us many lifetimes to achieve.' The point of the

Dalish way of life is to 'restore what has been forgotten', but this process of restoration is always hampered by the inaccessibility of a now-objectified past.

Even if the PC is not Dalish, he or she quickly learns of the Dalish plight. Consider this dialogue exchange between the PC and Velanna, a Dalish shaman who can be persuaded to join the Grey Wardens in *Awakenings*:

> Velanna: I envy you sometimes.
> PC: Why?
> Velanna: Even the youngest human child knows of at least a dozen heroes of legend. These tales are taken for granted, they are so abundant! Oh, it makes me angry, sometimes. We Dalish have lost most of our history and our legends. What we do remember, we hold dear.
> PC: We can share stories. They belong to everyone.
> Velanna: But does a human child value the tale of [another culture] as much as he does [his own]? Stories connect us to our past. They shape a people in profound ways. Without them, we are lost. I just wish I could do something to restore this lost part of our soul.
> PC: Make your own stories.
> Velanna: Now you are just being ridiculous.

In order to secure Velanna's loyalty, the PC can choose to give her a blank journal. The gift triggers this conversation:

> Velanna: What? This book is empty. Why have you given me this useless object?
> PC: Because you are going to fill it.
> Velanna: Fill it with what? Recipes for roast boar and pudding?
> PC: Stories for the Dalish.
> Velanna: Stories? For the ... oh. It's the silliest idea I've heard, but ... but brilliant at the same time. The Dalish will never recover what we've lost. It may be time to start writing tales anew. Perhaps one day they will be what connects my children and their children to their past – to me. I ... I see now that this is a gift to be treasured. And I ... I thank you.

This conversation strikes an odd note, since the Dalish do possess an extensive repertoire of recovered songs, prayers, and stories that, according to clan storytellers, are carefully passed from generation to generation[7]. However, a key part of this repertoire consists of the litany of textual loss. For a culture that has clearly relied on oral tradition for hundreds of years, the Dalish demonstrate considerable obsession with text. Velanna devalues her own oral tradition in a way that clearly illustrates the extent to which the absence of archival objects, particularly written materials, undermines the Dalish sense of cultural stability. The only hope she sees for her people's cultural future lies in the creation of new signifying objects: knowledge itself is not enough. The Dalish investment in an objectified, textual past seems to reinforce the commonplace hierarchy of written 'permanence' over the intranscience of oral tradition, or, that 'writing provides historical consciousness and orality provides mythic consciousness' (Taylor 2003, 21). In this sense, the elves participate in 'the metaphor of memory as a written surface so ancient and so persistent in all Western cultures that it must [...] be seen as a governing model or "cognitive archetype"' (Carruthers 1990, 16). The insistence upon accessible texts also mirrors the archival format of the *Dragon Age* game engine, which ultimately transforms a variety of inputs, including dialogue, into neat paragraphs to be read in the book-shaped codex. The Dalish fetishization of the trappings of their lost history seems to reinforce the centrality of a stable collection of signifying objects (the archive) to cultural success. However, it also reveals the kind of obsessive blindness the desire for such a collection can create. The Dalish know they cannot retrieve the relics of their lost past, but neither can they abandon their longing for it. They seek a structure than can never be completed.

The constrictive power of the archive becomes even more explicit in the dwarven kingdom of Orzammar, where it is the dominant feature of dwarven life. A huge edifice known as the Shaperate houses a vast collection of texts, presided over by the 'Shaper of Memories', the most important official in the underground city, who explains:

> The Shaperate guards Orzammar's knowledge. We have preserved all of the records of dwarven history. The Memories record all

– they are how we know to which family a child owes life, how we trace lost [colonies]. They ensure we forget nothing of our past, good or bad.

Everything in Orzammar enters the archive, and historical records organize every aspect of dwarven existence, particularly a caste system rigidly defined by recorded lineage. Children born of unrecognizable ancestry become casteless, a condition that condemns them to lives of poverty and neglect. They cannot hold jobs or own property, and shaperate officials tattoo their faces at birth to mark them as outsiders. The children of the casteless become casteless as well, and so the cycle of poverty and neglect for the unarchivable continues. On a street corner in Orzammar's 'Dust Town', the dilapidated slum where the casteless are forced to remain, the PC meets Zerlinda, begging for coins to feed her casteless son. Once a member of the mining caste, Zerlinda's parents 'erased her from the records' to punish her for having a child with a casteless man. Since the 'shapers teach that only children of true lineage exist', the two face impending starvation. The player can choose to have her protagonist persuade Zerlinda's parents to harbor her and the child in secret, despite the baby's unrecordable status, or to persuade Zerlinda to leave Orzammar.

Choosing to leave the city and attempt a life outside is also grounds for deletion from the archive. In Orzammar, the PC also meets Dagna, a bright young dwarf who wishes to study magic on the surface. She finds the carefully recorded and intricately proscribed ways of her people stultifying, and begs for help in leaving, since 'Here in Orzammar, we're surrounded by stone and tradition and more stone. Nothing ever changes'. Helping her to leave creates dire consequences, however, since, as her father explains, the second she sets foot on the surface she becomes casteless, her name stricken from the records. She can never marry or hold property. She 'no longer exists'. Almost every mission the PC can complete in Orzammar has something to do with the archive. The player can rescue stolen books for the Shaperate, look for lost records to aid a young woman trying to prove her noble caste status, return relics to the Shaperate, and discover and transcribe a long-forgotten monument to lost dwarven heroes – an act that adds a new caste to Orzammar society and thus creates new hopes for the descendents, who, in the absence of records, had been denied the privileges associated with their heritage. Always, effecting any kind of social or economic change requires manipulating the archive and, often, respecting its constrictive boundaries.

As the PC performs these missions, it becomes clear that in Orzammar archival excess provides stability at the cost of cultural stagnation. Archivally induced paralysis creates most of the dwarves' social and political problems, and every mission undertaken for the Shaperate ultimately reinforces this restrictive system, a fact that characters such as Dagna and Zerlinda keep at the forefront of the player's Orzammar experience. The imbalance of both dwarven and elven society complicates the idea of the archive as a central organizing principle, illustrating both the innervating futility of perpetual incompletion and the constrictive stagnation of over-cataloging. Nevertheless, players are still rewarded for reinforcing the archival system; persuading Dagna to give up her dream and remain with her family results in a cash reward from her father. Convincing Zerlinda's family to harbor her and her son in secret, without visibly disrupting the inscribed status quo, elicits similar compensation. Aiding either of them to escape, on the other hand, produces no such monetary bounty, only the angry diatribes of offended relatives. The narrative continues to reward archival complicity even as it demonstrates its flaws.

Archival complexities create anxieties that drive the game's plot; at the same time they highlight the significance of the player's intervention in the game's archival mechanics. *Dragon Age* makes explicit the way archives form the foundation of both narratological and ludic aspects of a digital game text, overlaying fantasy and functionality and inextricably linking gameplay and story. The emphasis on incomplete, damaged, and discriminatory archives as narrative devices foregrounds the database mechanics that underlie the game as a digital text. At the same time, it complicates and even problematizes these mechanics by imbuing them with moral ambiguity, allowing them to serve not just as an underlying framework but as an object of artistic and cultural significance. What does it mean, the games asks, to interact with and alter databases? Whose agenda does this intercession serve, and how? In this way, the game answers

Manovich's call for new media narratives that capitalize on their database-driven medium. The narrative emphasis on archive, like the player's reliance on the database, links the algorithmic function of story and gameplay not just to each other, but to an awareness of the interconnectivity of algorithm and database – a way, perhaps, to understand the interplay between, if not the seamless unity of, some of game studies' most deeply drawn binaries.

This interplay is compelling. Although one can play through any game, even *Dragon Age*, skimming or even ignoring its archival features, strong evidence exists that many gamers have no wish to do so, choosing instead to embrace and even expand upon the knowledge gleaned therein. Games – RPGs in particular, but even those less reliant on the archive as reference point for narrative mediation – routinely inspire external archives; websites and guide-books document not just strategies for gameplay, but also the internal lore of the game, commonly referred to collectively as the 'universe', from character and item descriptions to narrative recaps and plot analyses[8]. These collections act as evidence that players absorb, participate in, and even *re*-archive material from videogames as an intrinsic part of the gameplay experience.

This makes sense. Digital games are inherently archival. They start out that way; with rare exceptions, game design is a collaborative process that relies on a central collection of formative texts and artifacts to guide every stage of its creation. Before production starts, teams of designers, artists, and writers create a 'production bible' that includes 'concepting, world building, design and character iteration, timelines and the history of the universe' (Muzyka and Smee 2010)[9]. This collection of texts, programs, and graphic art guides the assembly of the actual game and any following material. Ray Muzyka, the general manager and CEO of BioWare, describes the process thus: 'There's a certain amount which surfaces above the water, that the player can see, and the rest is the rest of the iceberg that's down there, giving it weight and gravity, credibility and depth' (Muzyka and Smee 2010). Game developers often treat this archive as a kind of privileged reality, a source of direction and stability that informs and even transcends the final product. This archival privilege is part of the final product – it permeates the way games are marketed and played as well as the way they are created.

A better understanding of this archival privilege, and its potential, will help to open up new realms of analysis in game studies, and, perhaps, bridge some old divides. It will also link us back to the past, to the legacy of pen-and-paper RPGs, and illuminate the genre's particular contribution to our expectations of digital games.

Notes

1 My thanks to Professor Brian Kim Stefans and the Modernist and Experimental Literature and Text-art Reading Group at UCLA for their thoughtful feedback on an earlier version of this chapter.
2 Not all digital games have a narrative component. I would argue that those games which do not still rely on archival mechanics, but a fuller discussion of non-narrative games belongs to another paper.
3 For an in-depth treatment of the role of understanding and interfacing with cultural data in *Mass Effect*, see Gerald Voorhees's chapter in this volume.
4 The depth and complexity of BioWare games in particular seem to lend themselves to productive analysis. In this same volume, Roger Travis and Karen Zook also examine BioWare titles.
5 The most common reward comes in the form of 'experience points', which act as a form of currency that allows a player to develop a character's skills or attributes, making them more efficient at various in-game tasks – i.e. optimizing their algorithmic efficiency. Sometimes, rewards come in the form of items that a character can use, or 'money' to purchase such items; also bolstering his or her in-game efficiency. In digital games, knowledge is often quite literally power.
6 Unless otherwise specified, all game dialogue quotations are taken from *Dragon Age: Origins*.
7 I am relying extensively on Diana Taylor's distinction between the archive as a collection of objects and the repertoire as a series of performative social interactions, loosely but not exclusively categorized as a written/oral divide.
8 One of the most popular online archive forms is the 'wiki', an exhaustive peer-edited database that contains more narrative detail than game strategy. Sites exist for almost every game imaginable, even for some games with relatively minimal plot development. On a more ludic level, www.gamefaqs.com is perhaps the best example of an archive of strategy guides and 'walkthroughs'. There are

thousands of similar websites, often connected through hypertext links.

9 As a point of interest, the terms 'production bible' and 'IP bible' are almost ubiquitous within the videogame industry. The significance of the biblical reference is beyond the scope of this paper, but interesting to consider. If nothing else, it serves as evidence for the centrality of this pre-implementation archive in directing the game's creation and development.

References

Aarseth, Espen. 2004. 'Genre Trouble: Narrativism and the Art of Simulation.' In *First Person, New Media as Story, Performance and Game,* ed. Noah Wardip-Fruin and Pat Harrigan, 45–55. Cambridge, Massachusetts: MIT Press.
BioWare. 2007. *Mass Effect.* [Xbox 360]. Redmond, WA: Microsoft Game Studios.
—2009. *Dragon Age: Origins.* [Multiplatform]. Electronic Arts: Redwood City, California.
—2010. *Dragon Age: Origins – Awakenings.* [Multiplatform]. Electronic Arts: Redwood City, California.
Carruthers, Mary. 1990. *The Book of Memory: A Study of Memory in Medieval Culture.* New York: Cambridge UP.
de Certeau, Michel. 1984. *The Practice of Everyday Life.* Berkeley: University of California Press.
Derrida, Jacques. 1995. *Archive Fever: A Freudian Impression.* Trans. Eric Prenowitz. Chicago and London: University of Chicago Press.
Foucault, Michel. 1972. *The Archeology of Knowledge.* Trans. A. M. Sheridan Smith. New York: Pantheon Press.
Frasca, Gonzalo. 1999. 'Ludology Meets Narratology' Similitude and Differences Between (Digital) Games and Narrative.' Ludology.org. Accessed March 12, 2010. http://www.ludology.org/articles/ludology.htm
Iser, Wolfgang. 1978. *The Act of Reading: a Theory of Aesthetic Response.* Baltimore: John Hopkins University Press.
Juul, Jesper. 2005. *Half Real: Digital Games between Real Rules and Fictional Worlds.* Cambridge, Massachusetts: MIT Press.
Manovich, Lev. 2001. *The Language of New Media.* Cambridge, Massachusetts: MIT Press.
Miller, Kiri. 2008. 'Grove Street Grimm: *Grand Theft Auto* and Digital Folklore.' *Journal of American Folklore* 121: 255–85.

Murray, Janet. 1997, *Hamlet on the Holodeck: the Future of Narrative in Cyberspace*. Cambridge, Massachusetts: The MIT Press.
Smee, Andrew. February 7, 2010. 'Mass Effect 3 & Beyond: Interview with Ray Muzyka.' *IGN*. Accessed February 15, 2010. http://xbox360.ign.com/articles/106/1066954p1.html.
Taylor, Diana. 2003. *The Archive and the Repertoire: Performing Cultural Memory in the Americas*. Durham: Duke University Press.

4

When Language Goes Bad: Localization's Effect on the Gameplay of Japanese RPGs

DOUGLAS SCHULES[1]

It is interesting that an analysis of language itself, arguably a core component in the construction of a game's story and the development of character in role-playing games, has appeared as nothing more than vague ripples in the literature. This is not to suggest that language has not figured into analyses of games; rather, I contend that language as an analytical tool itself has been glossed over. At the risk of overgeneralizing, analyses of the subject tend to either emphasize game content, drawing connections between linguistically constructed story elements and larger non-game social discourses (Bogost 2007), or privilege the medium, maintaining a separation between the two realms based on differences in how they operate (Aarseth 2004).

Both approaches treat language as a representational vehicle; the irony is that language, as a rule-based system, fits the very basic definition of a game (McLuhan 1994; Lyotard 2002), and the implications of embedding the linguistic game within another rule-governed system – like RPGs, regardless of platform – have not been directly addressed in this context. My understanding of an 'analysis of language', then, differs in that I refer to explorations of the medium's rule-based characteristics – its grammar (Chomsky 1957; Chomsky 1965) or pragmatics (Austin 1975; Lyotard and Thebaud 1999) – and how these rules construct gameworlds and intersect with more mundane corporeal existence. From this vantage, I am not interested in the compelling explorations of how to approximate the complexities of linguistic rules into a game so that the computer will understand nuance, but, rather, how existing and intuitive human applications of linguistic rules inform the game environment.

The process of videogame localization witnesses these concerns, and so I scrutinize the grammatical, semantic, and prescriptive operations of language within the American iteration of the Nintendo DS (DS) game *Lux-Pain* (Killaware 2009) to argue that language contains a ludic impulse and can be approached in terms of its impact on gameplay. Sociolinguistic theory informs this argument, as do insights into language from Austin (1975) and Lyotard (2002; 1999); discussion of the medium itself draws from McLuhan (1994) and Baudrillard (1994), peppered with scholarship from ludology. (For another sociolinguistic approach to language in videogames see Friedline and Collister's chapter in this volume.)

While *Lux-Pain* was neither popular nor profitable, its inability to create even a ripple in the popular gaming market does not imply a dearth of critical potential. My rationale for choosing this game stems directly from the attention to language and its configuration in the videogame medium that guides this essay's argument. The game's spectacular failure as a localization more clearly elicits how language operates as gameplay – a good translation, to paraphrase Venuti (2008), smoothes over linguistic ruptures – the explicit operation of which would be difficult to parse from a better-constructed text.

Games: Playing by Rules

Frasca (2003) broadly defines the ludic approach by stating that games 'model a (source) system through a different system which maintains (for somebody) some of the behaviors of the original system' (223). Pointing specifically to audiovisual components as the most frequently reserved features of the original system, he notes that games encapsulate more than what players see or hear, a point Aarseth (2004) identifies as integral to the study of games in general: 'When you put a story on top of a simulation, the simulation (or the player) will always have the last word' (52). While games may engage in storytelling, that is not necessarily their primary purpose, or, in cases like chess, even a condition of their existence.

Rather, games operate by a system of rules that may or may not parallel the semiotics of narrative. This fact is what Frasca (2003) alludes to when he states that 'video games are just a particular way of structuring simulation, just like narrative is a form of structuring representation' (224). The rules of games tell us how to *play*; the rules of narrative tell us how to *read*. DRPGs consist of both systems of rules, and to come to an effective analysis of the genre we must engage how these systems interact to construct the gaming experience. In this respect, language offers an excellent analytical entrance to these concerns as it, too, possesses the same protean nature; alternatively approached as a representational tool (see the general work of Lévi-Strauss) or generative system (Austin 1975; Searle 1989, Searle 1995; Lyotard and Thébaud 1999), it offers multiple modes of structuring the DRPG experience.

Fan reactions to *Lux-Pain* provide a doorway through which I argue language's ludic potential. Three arguments form the core of this central claim: first, that violations in linguistic rules such as grammar and pragmatics potentially disrupt immersion in the DRPG game experience and thereby impact gameplay, a feature I refer to as immersive dissonance; second, that language can exceed the structuring of simulation organized by the game, resulting in an immersive dissonance motivated by semantic confusion; third, that this ability of language to operate both internally and externally to the game offers an analytical approach sympathetic to ideological critique. Before trekking these admittedly intricate paths, I begin with an overview of the *Lux-Pain*, including its genre classification and its plot.

Lux-Pain and Fan Discontent

Lux-Pain was developed by the Japanese game company Killaware for the DS, and Ignition Entertainment handled the 2009 distribution of the US localization. The game resists black-and-white genre classifications, mashing action, RPG, and adventure elements together to produce multiple gameplay interfaces. In terms of its DRPG characteristics, the game incorporates three distinct elements that scholars (Barton 2008; Wolf 2002) cite as definitive of the genre and shown in Figures 4.1 and 4.2: a formal leveling system, statistical representation of the protagonist Atsuki, and randomness.

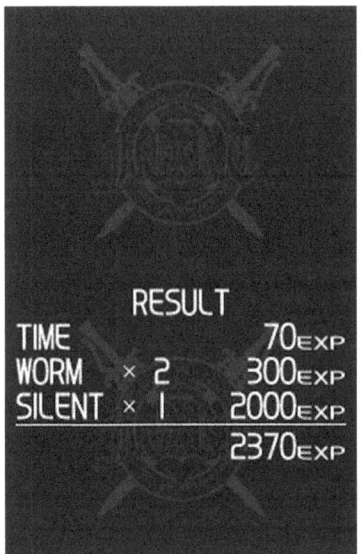
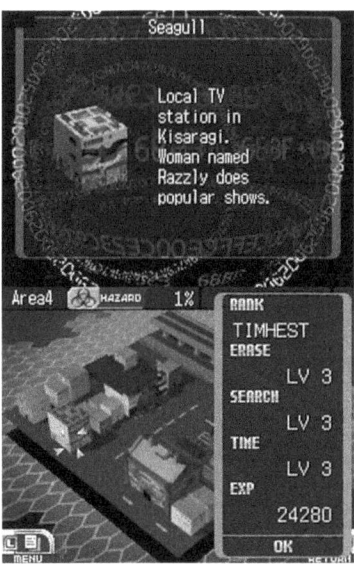

Figure 4.1 *Lux-Pain's* experience screen (Killaware 2009).

Figure 4.2 Quantification of Atsuki and his powers (Killaware 2009).

These elements are drastically simplified when compared to DRPG 'classics' such as SSI's *Gold Box*, Origin's *Ultima,* or SirTech's *Wizardry* series, but their inclusion directly affects gameplay in that if Atsuki is under-leveled, no amount of touch-pen dexterity in the action-inspired sequences will help him overcome the various obstacles he encounters. In these sequences, for example, he inflicts damage upon whoever he is probing; the greater his skill, the less damage he inflicts and the more time he has to complete his task. As one progresses in the game, these elements become increasingly more unfavorable to the player – time becomes shorter and damage greater – so that leveling becomes necessary to counterbalance the increase in game difficulty. To complicate matters, each encounter plays out differently; the positions of objects he must find and their movements randomly change each time Atsuki confronts the same obstacle, leaving a small portion of the encounter to frustrating chance (Figures 4.3 and 4.4).

Figure 4.3 Battle sequence with Silent (Killaware 2009).

Figure 4.4 Time, damage, and randomness in typical encounter (Killaware 2009).

This emphasis on leveling and luck rather than skill aligns the game more closely with DRPGs than the other genres (Barton 2008), but the three general definitional guidelines noted above reflect Western historical indebtedness to the pencil-and-paper predecessors of the genre (Apperley 2006). Japanese role-playing games (JRPGs), emerging from different historical and social conditions, possess an aesthetic and gameplay different from their Western counterparts; this area, as Barton (2008) woefully notes, is academically undertheorized. Gamers, however, maintain – some with religious zeal – that story and character development are hallmarks of JRPGs (Nagidar 2008, and more generally the whole thread). In the land of the JRPG, immersion in the gameworld rules, and many fans see this as the true roots of RPG. Indeed, *Lux-Pain* spends more time advancing the convoluted themes of murder, suicide, and isolation than forcing characters to grind for levels or money. *Lux-Pain*'s official webpage describes the plot and premise of the game as such:

> *Lux-Pain* is set in historical Kisaragi City, a town plagued by mysteries from small mishaps to murders – with no logical explanation as to why these events occur. It seems 'Silent', a worm born through hate and sadness, has infected humans and forced them to commit atrocious crimes. The hero's parents, Atsuki, are victims of such crimes. To avenge his parents, Atsuki goes through a dangerous operation to acquire Lux-Pain in his left arm, a power so strong that his left eye turns golden when using it to seek and destroy Silent for good. (*Lux-Pain Official Webpage* 2009)

Silent infects people with negative emotions which appear to Atsuki as worm-like balls of moving light that meander around an infectee. In order to see these balls of light, referred to as '*shinen*' (思念, thought), Atsuki activates a power called 'Sigma' that enables him to literally scratch the surface of reality to see what lies underneath. In order to more efficaciously mete out his revenge on Silent for his family's murder, Atsuki has joined an organization known as FORT which is comprised of individuals like him with the ability to see *shinen*.

The game takes place in Kisaragi City (the location of which is a problem addressed later). It contains everything one would expect in a town – a church, apartment buildings, bars – but what takes center stage in the game is the local high school. Early in the game FORT narrows Silent's base of operations to the vague 'someone operating through someone operating at the school'; as a result, what begins as a detective story resembling a cross between Dashiell Hammett and H. P. Lovecraft tropes transforms into something profoundly

Figure 4.5 Sigma's ability to reveal hidden *shinen* (Killaware 2009).

darker – the navigation of high school social banality. In his quest to track down the link to Silent, Atsuki enrolls in Kisaragi High as a transfer student and is thrust into the world of high school romantic and social drama; how he navigates these currents determines which of the eight endings the player experiences.

The emphasis on narrative and character development dovetail well with what fans perceive as the general conventions of JRPGs, but what makes *Lux-Pain* unique in this regard is the almost universal agreement, on account of its rife linguistic errors, that the US localization was released prematurely. One concise reviewer described the game by stating: 'Dodgy localization is everywhere with typos galore' (Castle 2009). A more gregarious reviewer expounded on these points by stating, in part:

> So what is the game's fatal weak point? Well, have you ever watched an anime DVD with both the dub audio and the subtitles on at the same time? Notice how the subtitles are basically saying the same thing as the dub actors are saying, but using different words here and there? That's the entire localization of *Lux-Pain*

... the only thing that's wrong with it is ... well ... THE TEXT! It's crappy. It's horrible. It's a complete and utter embarrassment! (*Video Game Review: Lux-Pain for Nintendo DS* 2009)

The emphasis both reviewers place on the game's poor localization offers a starting point to theorizing language as a dimension of ludic gameplay. Games structure simulations which, according to Baudrillard (1994), are 'beyond true and false' in that they do not attempt to make referential prescriptive claims about the world external to their operations (21). They are, as discussed later, self-contained. Narrative, to overgeneralize, strives to forge such connections due to its understanding of language as a representational device. But telling stories is merely *one* function of language, and overlooking the game's narrative does not throw the rules through which language operates out with the narrative bathwater. The fact that reviewer discontent with the game emphasizes how the localization impacts immersion in the gameworld rather than the narrative itself suggests a problem in rules, not story. For another discussion on this subject, see Henton's piece in this same volume.

My argument regarding the ludic implications of language takes shape over the course of three major sections that build upon the insights of the last. I begin this analysis by focusing on a close reading of linguistic rules emerging from the audio and written channels of *Lux-Pain*; the argument remains, more or less, constrained to material generated internally by the game. The section after, however, examines how internal inconsistencies in semantics disrupt the game and claims that language as it functions ludically exceeds the structuring of simulation imposed by the game text. From here, I close with some critical implications these insights have for the study of games.

Internal Gameplay and the Limits of *Lux-Pain*

No matter how one approaches localization (see Kuzimski 2007; Chandler 2005), the underlying impulse of the practice relies on manipulating the rule-based foundations of the symbolic system whose combination forms the building blocks of story and character development prized in JRPGs. Some of these rules speak to readability and form a fundamental aspect of gameplay – I'm thinking of grammar here and gaffes such as *Zero Wing's* (Toaplan 1992) 'all your base are belong to us'. While *Lux-Pain* contains errors of this type, and they do contribute to the immersive dissonance of the game, errors in this vein do not contribute much to language-as-gameplay, given their rarity in the industry.

Figure 4.6 Localization errors in *Lux-Pain* (Killaware 2009).

Figure 4.7 Localization errors in *Lux-Pain* (Killaware 2009).

A more useful approach flirts with the semantic component of language as it constructs the gameworld, as meaning is generally seen as emerging from specific situations and speech communities (Hymes 1989; Labov 1991). Fortunately, *Lux-Pain* provides both obvious and subtle fissures from which we can see how gameplay is impacted by language, and I intend to tease out the implications of this through repeatedly returning to the question of where the game takes place.

Obvious examples of language impacting gameplay stem from the differences between the written and audio channels of the game.

WHEN LANGUAGE GOES BAD

These differences first appear at the end of the prologue which orients the player to the game mechanics and basic points of the plot. Atsuki contacts FORT's recon and intelligence officer, Natsuki, to ascertain the location of some odd *shinen* and she mentions that her job would be easier if she was in Kisaragi City. The exact location of Kisaragi City, however, depends on whether one listens to the audio or reads the text:

> Natsuki dubbed: 'I wanted to go to America, too ... using viewing is easier at the actual scene.'
> Accompanying text: 'I actually also wanted to check out Japan but ... the actual place is easier for viewing.' (Killaware 2009)

This mismatch is not a minor concern, both in terms of the game itself as a marketed product and – more germane here – in terms of its navigation of tensions between the linguistic and ludic games. This disjunction between the written and aural channels continues through the entirety of the game, and the accumulated errors stress the ideological veneer placed upon localization as an accurate representation of the original text by revealing how language operates behind the proverbial curtain to craft part of the gaming experience. Through these errors, we witness how language interacts with, engages, and alters the world. Natsuki's complete monologue, reproduced below, provides insight into these processes:

Natsuki's audio:

1a) I wanted to go to America, too...
2a) using viewing is easier at the actual scene.
3a) But the chief says 'no'.
4a) How mean, really!
5a) 'I know why, you just want to see Atsuki, right?'
6a) That's what he said; what do you think?
7a) Oh, I wanna go to LA and I wanna see New York.
8a) Also, I really want to try the food there.
9a) I've never tried it before.
10a) I said so, but he ignored me.

Accompanying text to audio:

1b) I actually also wanted to check out Japan but ...
2b) the actual place is easier for viewing.
3b) Yeah, but the chief said no.
4b) You're quite the bully ...
5b) I get your alterior [sic] motive. You just wanna meet Atsuki.
6b) The chief actually said that. What do you think, Atsuki?
7b) You're wrong. I wanna go to both Akiba and Genjuku.
8b) Well, I also really like Sushi and Tempura.
9b) ... But I haven't exactly partaken in either yet.
10b) Well, forget I said that ...
(Killaware 2009)

Natsuki's monologue is of special interest in that it manages to distill in ten lines most of the faults reviewers and fans point to when they explain 'how an entire experience can be ruined by poor localization' (Shau 2009). Scanning the few lines in Natsuki's monologue reveals quite a bit of evidence to support the claims of Shau and others regarding the localization being 'poor'; the rather large leap in setting between (1a) and (1b), inconsistencies in spelling as seen in (5b), confusion over addressee as in (6a) and (4b), and general illogical statements such as in the pair of (8b) and (9b) demonstrate that the released product still requires some polish. What we read creates a different world and set of expectations that conflicts with what we hear, and while minor errors such as misapplied pronouns and other grammatical issues certainly contribute to this failure, more troublesome are those moments in which referential knowledge of the gameworld breaks down. Natsuki's desire to eat sushi and tempura can make sense regardless of whether or not the game takes place in Japan or America, but the problem emerges from the fact that both of these locations are simultaneously presented as valid constructions of the gameworld.

The divergence in gameworld constructed by the two channels additionally impacts her character. Grammatical and semantic consistency in Natsuki's voiceover suggest nothing dramatically marked about her speech, and this finds support with the inflection and other auditory cues provided; the written gloss, however, contains a number of issues that may strike the native speaker as odd. Line (4b), for example, points to an ambiguity in addressee. Given the nature of the speech, the second person pronoun should be understood to refer to the chief and her outburst more of an excited statement than direct address, but the ambiguity arises from the fact that Atsuki is present and there are no other cues to facilitate the intended reading. The rather interesting semantic logic between lines (8b) and (9b), where Natsuki complains that not going prevents her from eating the sushi and tempura she likes so much and immediately reveals that she's actually never tried them, further contributes to her puzzling characterization offered in the two channels and potentially interrupts the game experience.

This interruption of game experience, I propose, orients language in a fashion akin to more familiar aspects of ludic gameplay, in that it directly impacts a player's ability to become immersed in the gameworld, a condition that many players see as constitutive of the JRPG genre. The localization problems with *Lux-Pain* do not severely impact one's understanding of the plot – the overall story is readable and relatively coherent – but the grammatical and semantic potholes consistently serve as reminders that the game is a construct and a translation. McLuhan's (1994) speculation that media are co-constituted by other media explains the divergence between the audio and written gloss as symptoms of the operations of language embedded within different media, but this implies that the medium – in this case videogames of the JRPG console variety – regulates or somehow constrains language.

To some degree this is true, as technical limitations imposed by the DS cartridge prevent, for example, *Lux-Pain* from accompanying all written text with audio. But these limitations do not necessarily impact the rules by which language operates, and my claim that language can be approached as gameplay arises from its properties as a rule-based system. Unlike more traditional or conventional aspects of gameplay, however, linguistic gameplay derives from mechanisms both internal and external to the game. A brief overview of how simulations function will help ground this tension before an extended discussion of the prescriptive functions of language and the properties of naming.

Simulations and Names: *Lux-Pain's* Inscrutable Location

In arguing that games structure simulation, ludologists implicitly tip their hats to Baudrillard (1994), who, building off of McLuhan's theorization of media, notes: 'it [the object] has no relation to any reality whatsoever: it is its own pure simulacrum' (6). Games, in other words, are discursively self-contained and though they may draw upon resources external to them for content, these resources operate according to internal rules structured by the game – referential meaning included. This is a basic premise of so-called 'suspension of disbelief' and from this perspective we are able to overlook errors in location, logic, and the like, writing them off as idiosyncrasies tied to the gameworld itself. Natsuki's desire to go to 'Genjuku' in (8b) and shown in Figure 4.7 can plausibly be seen as an actual place in Japan (or America!) rather than a misspelling of 'Shinjuku.' The term *shinen*, and untranslated words in general, reflect how the game structures pragmatics in a limited sense. From the perspective of simulation, the most that can be said about the lack of translation of *shinen* in the US version is that it must have some semantic or other social function or meaning within the gameworld. It is a referent whose meaning is supplied from within the specific situational context of the game.

The tension I allude to at the end of the previous section, however, lies precisely with the properties of language as a rule-based system that includes how words are pragmatically conceived beyond the individual morpheme. As Lyotard (1999; 2002) and Austin (1975) note, language emerges as a response to specific, pre-existing discursive conditions. Austin speaks of this in terms of commitment and obligation: 'if I have stated something, then that commits me to other statements: other statements made by me will be in order or out of order' (139). It is not just that language in certain contexts can establish and alter world relationships, but also that these bonds imply specific obligations that continue to exist after the ephemeral speech context has been completed or even forgotten. Lyotard speaks of this obligation in terms of language's prescriptive functions:

An utterer is always someone who is first and addressee, and I would even say one destined. By this I mean that he is someone who, before he is the utterer of a prescription, has been the recipient of a prescription, and that he is merely a relay; he has also been the object of a prescription. (1999, 31)

In a ludic sense, *Lux-Pain* and videogames in general *simulate* language's prescriptive and obligatory functions through their demand in interactive response to drive gameplay. One must, for example, push buttons or touch the DS screen to move the game forward and acknowledge that the text was received. In addition to this type of interaction, *Lux-Pain* presents players with moments where they must select a response from a small pool of choices. These choices are constrained to what the game provides, and the player's ability to create alternatives outside these choices impossible. The game, in short, strives to simulate the limiters discourse places upon linguistic response through constraining interactive alternatives. The obligations and prescriptions Austin and Lyotard allude to, however, encapsulate more than 'response' in the semantic sense of the term, suggesting instead the role discursive systems play in pragmatically shaping the world and our rejoinders to it. The tension, then, lies with the extent to which games can govern pragmatics motivated by discursive prescriptions.

The character of Aoi Matsumura, self-described within the game as 'the language teacher' at Kisaragi High and viewed by the students and other teachers as a model of the profession, provides some insight into this process. She is the first teacher Atsuki meets when he arrives at school to search for leads on Silent, and her class is also his first experience with how academics operate at the school. Atsuki enters the classroom and Matsumura-sensei introduces him to other students; the bell rings and class begins. Through the dialogue box, Matsumura-sensei asks the students get out their textbooks and the following conversation begins:

Aoi

11) This is your first time, so I'll go slow with you.
12) Here we have Shimazaki's *A Collection of Young Herbs*.
13) Know [sic] for it's [sic] 5/7 syllable

14) form, it's called Japan's own romantic anthology.
15) It's been a popular one since last week.
16) The anthology also contains the well known *First Love*
17) Perhaps you've come across it before?
18) It's [sic] goes, 'You swept back your bangs...'
19) Well? Nothing?
20) This next novel should come with ease. Here's a hint
21) It deals with the Spring, starting anew, the joys
22) and sadness of youth.
Student A
23) Well, there are tons of ways to explain
24) Yeah, so should we get on to our homework as usual?
Student B
25) Yeah there are.
Aoi
26) Hmm ... such a wonderful love as this ...
(Killaware 2009)

Within the classroom environment, Aoi Matsumura's position and responsibilities at Kisaragi High amount to reading and explicating literature. Reading and even translating literature may plausibly be part of an advanced language class, and given Atsuki's age of seventeen it is equally plausible that he has the language background to succeed in such a class. Based solely on this very small and isolated context within the game, little appears amiss; however, interactions with Matsumura-sensei are not limited to the classroom, and Atsuki frequently encounters her in various locations throughout Kisaragi City either checking up on students she is worried about or gauging the suitability of popular hang-outs where students gather. In one of these encounters, she confesses to Atsuki that she does this because 'a teacher should protect and guide their students'. These encounters emphasize the prescriptions placed upon the profession as constructed by the internal discourse of the gameworld, but they must be read in concert with other similar discursive prescriptions to establish said world as coherent. In this case, the issue of *Lux-Pain's* fluid location once again emerges to disrupt a pragmatically coherent environment.

One possibility places Kisaragi City within America, and from this vantage we can most clearly see how inconsistencies within the gaming environment collude to destabilize the gaming performance and pragmatic construction of the world. Aoi Matsumura's specialization as evinced from the dialogue above is Japanese. Based on how she conducts the course, her pedagogy challenges students to explicate literary texts rather than study the grammatical, semantic, or phonological characteristics of the language. All of these features appear plausible, given some latitude and generosity with how the game constructs secondary education in America; indeed, from the perspectives of gaming and aesthetics, the text itself has been argued to be not a representation of the 'real' world but, rather, suggesting potential of how it could be (Frasca 2001). *Lux-Pain* offers for players' consideration a high school where the study of Japanese amounts to a cultural immersion: in addition to the study of Japanese literature, other courses such as Reiji's history course also revolve around Japanese cultural products. In essence, Kisaragi High amounts to an *otaku* magnet school.

Even with this rather lenient reading of the world *Lux-Pain* constructs, however, certain aspects do not add up. While Atsuki encounters a number of minor characters, he interacts with roughly twenty on a regular basis throughout the course of his investigation. Two of these characters have already been introduced: the language teacher Aoi Matsumura and FORT's resident psychic tracker Natsuki. Other characters, such as Atsuki's classmates and the residents of Kisaragi City, bear strikingly similar names. Prominent classmates include Akira, Rui, Shinji, Sayuri, and Yayoi; residents include characters such as Nami, Yui, and Naoto. Through these names, the question of location demands scrutiny as we are presented an America that boasts the existence of not only Japanese magnet schools but, more puzzling, an America in which the residents of at least one town reject Anglo naming practices.

This puzzling state of affairs certainly contributes to problems of immersion that disrupt the gaming experience, but in different, more subtle, ways than the obvious localization gaffes noted in the beginning of the chapter, whose disruptive epicenter can be located in purely internal linguistic mechanisms (i.e. the game as simulation). The disruptions associated with naming conventions and the location of the game's events, however, appear to be motivated by prescriptions *external* to the game.

One approach to this puzzle can be found within the performative function of naming itself. According to Lyotard (2002), 'to learn names is to situate them in relation to other names by means of phrases [...] A system of names presents a world' (44). Tracing the relations between characters provides insight into one aspect of the game's narrative dimension – its plot – but the schema of naming, taken in conjunction with the prescriptive function of language, reflects discursive relations. Some of these are driven by the internal mechanisms of the gameworld, as the expectations of Kisaragi High's language classes and the extra-scholastic responsibilities of teachers intimate. These two examples form part of the larger system of relations that constitutes the fictive gameworld, and through interaction with the game – obliquely referred to in ludic terms as the 'learning curve' – the player gleans how this system operates. Working in tandem with internally driven naming schemas, however, are terms which derive their prescriptive power from external discursive systems. The 'America' in which Kisaragi City is potentially located receives no description beyond the name itself, leaving the player to supply the referent with relevant pragmatic content, an attempt drawn upon the audience's beliefs in constructing the gameworld. The problems with immersive dissonance emerge from reliance on *external* prescriptions to construct an *internal* world.

The implications of this position for the structuring of simulations are far-reaching, as the rule-based ludic aspects of language appear capable of penetrating the closed system of simulation, consequently generating a gameplay that potentially continues after the videogame ends. While specific terms may generate their meaning from within the game itself – the untranslated term *shinen* referring to swirling orbs of concentrated emotion, for example – the text itself cannot be constructed solely from words of this type for both practical and theoretical reasons. Much as we may push for a reading built upon what the game provides, the building blocks of *Lux-Pain*, when push comes to shove, are individual morphemes already empowered with signification by social decree. To create a text whose meaning derives solely from itself would necessitate the creation, essentially, of another unfamiliar set of symbolic chains that the audience would need to decipher and encode with meaning as it progressed through the game; in this sense, perhaps, playing the Japanese version with no knowledge of the language would be the closest parallel. Such an endeavor would be impractical to say the least, especially when we consider the purpose of *Lux-Pain* as a localized product aimed at the generation of profit and the emphasis on the JRPG genre on story and character development. *Lux-Pain* employs English to establish some symbolic common ground; rather than reinventing the links between the chain of signification, *Lux-Pain* alters specific referents whose meaning becomes 'clear' throughout the course of character interaction. In short, players bring discursively prescribed assumptions to the game and utilize them to navigate the simulacral waters they structure; at the same time, players may take with them referents generated in game for play in other contexts.

The gameplay of language, in other words, lies in the ability of players to divine the semantic scope of referents and actively figure out if they operate purely internally to the game or are drawn from external discourse. It continues to function after the videogame has ended, allowing for the creation of new, unique games. This last feature, explored in more depth in the next section, provides a critical dimension to approaching language in a ludic capacity by linking aspects of gameplay to ideological critique.

The Unintentional Return of High Modernist Aesthetic Practice

The immersive dissonance generated by *Lux-Pain*'s inability to ground itself in a stable semantic environment does not necessarily mean that this game (or other, better constructed ones) is without critical potential. The frustration evinced by the reviewers and their inability to access the game in their customary fashion reflects, in part, ideological conditioning that a ludic interpretation of language, with its ability to move freely in and out of the confines of simulation, appears exceedingly capable of engaging; this should not imply, however, that this is an easy or common task.

Critics generally focused on the 'failure' of the localization process in *Lux-Pain* by pointing to grammatical flaws that were symptomatic of a larger issue of representation. Voicing his inability to 'get into' the game, Acaba (2009) complains:

> If that isn't bad enough there were a few times that I couldn't help but start snickering during really inconvenient time. When dealing with topics this mature it's a really bad sign for you to start laughing because a girl was referred to as 'he' or general Engrish popping up. It kills the mood and destroys any immersion in the story which is all a game like this really has.

Acaba may be hinting at the tension between the two radically different registers of knowledge players must supply to position themselves within the game environment. Whether Natsuki wants to go to Japan or America makes a lot of difference, as most players will be much more familiar with the cultural tendencies of one location over the other, a fact that has a direct impact on how much fiddling with the prescriptions generated by signification *Lux-Pain* can plausibly get away with. Due to this, the existence of a city in America populated almost exclusively by Japanese nationals whose idea of language study is to read and translate ancient Japanese literature gives one pause in its sheer absurdity. But it is exactly within this absurdist realm brought about by the infelicitous meeting of our expectations between the discursive prescriptions supplied by the game and the discursive prescriptions we bring to the game that *Lux-Pain* points to the aesthetic potential – and here I mean the older sense of the term invested with political overtones – of embedding a game within a game.

In a very general sense, *Lux-Pain* can be read as confrontational and antagonistic, disrupting embedded practices and ideologies. Derived through *Lux-Pain*'s amateurish localization, this aesthetic impulse within the game owes its origin to linguistic issues that complicate the construction of a coherent world, either on its own terms or in its intersection with surrounding social discourses in which it is embedded. Exemplified by the game's ambiguous setting, these linguistic issues have the potential to fashion new relationships and understandings of the world in which the player resides. Although speaking specifically about Dada, Tristan Tzara (2003) writes that art 'introduces new points of view, people sit down now at the corners of tables, in attitudes that lean a bit to the left and to the right' (25). For Tzara, new points of view emerge organically from the irrational, and part of his articulation of the Dadaist project revolves around breaking free from rationalist, scientific frames of thought. 'What we need', Tzara says, 'are strong, straightforward, precise works which will be forever misunderstood. Logic is a complication. Logic is always false' (10–11). Art, then, plays with the ordering and structure of the world as mapped by specific ideologies, attempting to offer alternate modes of envisioning the world predicated upon contradiction.

Lux-Pain enacts this process through language, albeit unintentionally. The world *Lux-Pain* presents to players certainly bears similarities to the one external to it, but inconsistencies in the performative construction of the virtual environment disrupt the gaming experience. A conflict between multiple competing constructions of the same world that ground the player's social, cultural, and ideological assumptions in different ways emerges; instead of asking why a town such as Kisaragi City would exist in America, the more fruitful way to approach the game's performative inconsistencies according to the aesthetic map offered by Tzara would be to ponder why America *cannot* have such a city. In this vein, the contradictions and confusions circulating the game express not liabilities but, rather, a new vantage from which to engage ideological networks such as nationality and identity. This approach applies equally to more polished games, although the manner in which they engage ideological apparatuses is less evident; after all, ideology operates best when hidden, and the position of videogames within the popular arena as entertainment media, coupled with a lack of linguistic ruptures to draw attention to the prescriptive underpinnings of language, obscures how they function as the potential world Tzara and Frasca note. *Lux-Pain* is like the friend who can't keep a secret: its linguistic slippage reveals how language constructs more respected games.

Along these lines, then, even the grammatical and pronominal inconsistencies that are the subject of re\viewer consternation suggest ideological revelation. Similar to the case above regarding the aesthetic potential housed in the ambiguity of the game's location, the grammatical errors often cited by the reviewers point to a breakdown in representation, a disjunction between signifier and signified that scholars have argued shape our approach to the world. Attention to language, in fact, figures prominently in Dadaist literature, where discussion and implementation of it aims at reframing the chain of signification. In the 'Dada Manifesto on Feeble Love and Bitter Love', Tzara (2003) glibly remarks that 'the good Lord created a universal language, that's why people don't take him seriously. A language is a utopia' (47). The polemic nature of this statement enacts the Dadaist position over language; in articulating language's link to the divine, problems over commensurability appear all the more poignant. At the heart of Dadaist theorization on this subject beats the arbitrary nature of signification; poised against bourgeois art and academic criticism, Dada revels in incommensurability by stripping the status of the artwork of communal interpretation:

> The bourgeois spirit, which renders ideas usable and useful, tries to assign poetry the invisible role of the principle engine of the universal machine: the practical soul [...] In this way it is possible to organize and fabricate everything. (Tzara 2003, 73)

In dissolving, refiguring, or altering the way in which specific words are understood through either grammatical rearrangements or semantic/pragmatic reconstitutions of words, the mandate of the market to render all things equivalent and into use value becomes stymied, momentarily arrested in its course of world domination like a supervillain without henchmen.

Lux-Pain's overlooked grammatical inconsistencies parallel the spirit of the Dada aesthetic in that the slow dissolution of referents in the game affects the cultural understandings of the words, revealing in ideological structures the potential for alternate symbolic configurations. The clearest case of this potential rests with the intermittent application of incorrect pronouns to the game's characters, a potential bolstered by the ethnic character of their names: players face being kept in a state of flux, constantly reconfiguring their perceptions of characters as they try to ascertain with certainty which gender box they belong to. Naturally this does not happen with every character, and in many cases a given character's gender can be based on vocal or visual cues. However, not every character is given audio or visual 'screen time' in every interaction. Coupled with the androgynous Japanese animation style and unfamiliarity with the gendering of Japanese names, a player must be hyper-aware of who is doing and saying what or risk confusion.

Problems over the US localization of *Lux-Pain* have been traced to inconsistencies between the sub and the dub facets which contribute to differing performative constructions of the game. Positioned within an analytical framework sensitive to inconsistency as aesthetic, the problem emerges due to the simultaneous existence of these features producing a performative inconsistency in the construction of the world. As discursively closed systems, simulations require that the performatives through which the world is constructed be consistent within that world, a feat which requires a modicum of suspension of disbelief. In the case of *Lux-Pain,* however, disbelief remains elusive due to competing versions of the world that can be traced to mismatches between the written and aural texts. This aspect is typically the focus of fan discontent, but such discourse tends to remain isolated to the grammatical realm and overlooks a deeper interpretation for fan discontent rooted in how language co-constitutes the aesthetics.

Loose Ends and Unresolved Tensions

In this chapter I have argued that language should be treated as a form of gameplay driven by linguistic rules ranging from the grammatical to the semantic, sketching out how these rules intersect with, operate within, and even exceed the organizational rules imposed by the structuring of simulations known eloquently as 'games'. In this vein I have made three arguments, although I feel that the second is more significant than others due to its larger theoretical implications for ludology as a whole. My first advocates that in the context of JRPGs, language should be treated as a component of gameplay due to its ability to prevent immersion or engagement with the text in question. My second point builds upon this claim and argues that these moments of immersive dissonance arise from both internally and externally driven linguistic rules; this is particularly significant as language appears capable of escaping the event horizon that keeps simulations self-contained and self-referential. The final argument asserted that this ability of language to persist outside the simulation (or enter it, as the case may be) offers a unique opportunity for ideological criticism surrounding a game and represents an approach not necessarily beholden to discussions of game plot.

Naturally, as JRPGs rely heavily on language, particularly stories, to carve out their identities, using them as a starting point to theorize the ludic dimensions of language may seem counter-intuitive, given the tendency in the literature to conflate language with narrative. Their status as translations, however, provides particular opportunities in this regard not commonly found in their less-travelled and monolingual brethren, and the insights garnered here can offer a basis for more generalized study of the chimeric qualities of language, particularly the contexts in which it operates as a narrative device and when it operates ludically.

Note

1 The author would like to thank his dissertation committee, and especially his advisor Timothy Havens, for their guidance and support during the drafting of this chapter, as well as the editors of this volume who exercised immense patience during the revision process.

References

Aarseth, Espen. 2004. 'Genre Trouble: Narrativism and the Art of Simulation.' In *First Person: New Media as Story, Performance, and Game*, ed. Noah Wardrip-Fruin and Pat Harrigan, 45–55. Cambridge: The MIT Press.

Acaba, Daniel. 2009. 'Lux-Pain review.' GamingExcellence. Accessed 19 September 2009. http://www.gamingexcellence.com/ds/games/2166/review.shtml.

Apperley, Thomas. 2006. 'Genre and game studies: Towards a critical approach to video game genres.' *Simulation & Gaming: An International Journal of Theory, Practice and Research* 37 (1): 6–23.

Austin, J. L. 1975. *How to do Things with Words*, ed. J. O. Urmson and Marina Sbisa. 2nd edition. Cambridge: Harvard University Press. Original edition 1955.
Barton, Matt. 2008. *Dungeons & Desktops*. Wellesley, MA: A K Peters, Inc.
Baudrillard, Jean. 1994. *Simulacra and simulation*. Trans. Sheila Faria Glaser. Ann Arbor: University of Michigan Press. Original edition 1981.
Bogost, Ian. 2007. *Persuasive Games: The Expressive Power of Video Games*. Cambridge, MA: The MIT Press.
Castle, Matthew. 2009. 'Schoolgirl Crushes and Crushed Spirits.' Gamesradar. Accessed 18 September 2009. http://www.gamesradar.com/ds/lux-pain/review/lux-pain/a–20090401101643619005/g–2008121011456970068.
Chandler, Heather M. 2005. *The Game Localization Handbook*. Hingham, MA: Charles River Media, Inc.
Chomsky, Noam. 1957. *Syntactic Structures*. Cambridge: MIT Press.
—1965. *Aspects of the Theory of Syntax*. Cambridge: MIT Press.
Frasca, Gonzalo. 2003. 'Simulation Versus Narrative: Introduction to Ludology.' In *The Video Game Theory Reader*, ed. Mark J. P. Wolf and Bernard Perron, 221–35. New York: Routledge.
—2010. *Simulation Versus Representation*. Ludology.org. Accessed 09 April 2010. http://www.ludology.org/articles/sim1/simulation101c.html.
Hymes, Dell. 1989. *Foundations in Sociolinguistics: An Ethnographic Approach*. 8th edition. Philadelphia: University of Pennsylvania Press. Original edition 1974.
Killaware. *Lux-Pain*. [Nintendo DS]. Ignition Entertainment: Glendale, CA, 2009.
Kuzimski, Alexander. 2009. 'Localization: Beyond Translation.' Accessed 1 July 2009. http://www.marlingaming.net/goldensun/portfolio/localization.pdf.
Labov, William. 1991. *Sociolinguistic patterns*. 11th edition. Philadelphia: University of Pennsylvania Press. Original edition 1972.
Lux-Pain Official Webpage. 2009. Ignition Entertainment Ltd. Accessed 18 September 2009. http://www.luxpain.com/.
Lyotard, Jean-François. 2002. *The Differend: Phrases in Dispute*. Trans. Georges Van Den Abbeele. Minneapolis: University of Minnesota Press. Reprint, 6th.
Lyotard, Jean-François, and Jean-Loup Thébaud. 1999. *Just Gaming*. Trans. Wlad Godzich. Minneapolis: University of Minnesota Press.
McLuhan, Marshall. 1994. *Understanding Media: The Extensions of Man*. Cambridge: MIT Press. Original edition 1964.
Nagidar. 2011. *GameSpot Forums – System Wars – JRPG's are not*

RPG's. Accessed 21 February 2011. http://www.gamespot.com/pages/forums/show_msgs.php?topic_id=26428529.

Searle, John Rogers. 1989. 'How Performatives Work.' *Linguistics and Philosophy* 12 (5):538–58.

—1995. *The Construction of Social Reality*. New York: The Free Press.

Shau, Austin. 2009. 'Lux-Pain Review.' GameSpot.com. Accessed 19 September 2009. http://www.gamespot.com/ds/adventure/luxpain/review.html.

Toaplan. 1992. Zero Wing. [Sega Mega Drive]. Sega: Brentford, UK.

Tzara, Tristan. 2003. *Seven Dada Manifestos and Lampisteries*. Trans. Barbara Wright. 5th edition. New York: Calder Publications. Original edition 1977.

Venuti, Lawrence. 2008. *The Translator's Invisibility: A History of Translation*. 2nd edition. New York: Routledge. Original edition 1995.

'Video Game Review: Lux-Pain for Nintendo DS'. 2009. The Anime Almanac. Accessed 18 September 2009. http://animealmanac.com/2009/04/10/video-game-review-lux-pain-for-nintendo-ds/.

Wolf, Mark J. P. 2002. *The Medium of the Video Game*. Austin: University of Texas Press.

5

The Lord of the Rings Online: Issues in the Adaptation of MMORPGs

NEIL RANDALL, KATHLEEN MURPHY

Our chapter takes as its focus the adaptation of the novels and created world of J. R. R. Tolkien, particularly *The Lord of the Rings* (1954–6), for the medium of massively multiplayer online role-playing games (or MMORPGs) in the form of Turbine, Inc.'s *The Lord of the Rings Online* (hereafter *LOTRO*). In the process we draw to a limited degree on the popular Peter Jackson film adaptations of Tolkien's *The Lord of the Rings* released each year from 2001 to 2003, both for the purposes of comparison of adaptation technique but also because *LOTRO* clearly draws on the Jackson films as well as the Tolkien novels. Our discussion draws upon the literature of adaptation studies, which traditionally treats the move from book to film or stage to film, but which has expanded in recent years to include other forms of media transference of existing stories or artifacts, and thereby attempts to demonstrate at least part the role adaptation studies might play in the growing field of game studies. The two particular foci of our paper are (a) *fidelity* to the source works and (b) the taxonomies of adaptation types. For the first focus, we argue that the issue of fidelity assumes greater importance when considering the adaptation of highly popular source material. For the second, we argue that role-playing game adaptations function through the creative strategy of *expansion*, in contrast to films drawn from novels, which typically use *compression* (both terms from Thomas Leitch and discussed below). Film-makers must tell the story in roughly two hours, but designers/developers of games not aimed at the casual games market must ensure, because of the prices they must charge consumers, that the game lasts for many hours, weeks, or, in the case of MMORPGs, months.

One issue we need to establish immediately is that of the original text. In the case of *LOTRO* and all other future games based on *The Lord of the Rings*, the issues takes on added significance because of the way in which Tolkien's novel and the Jackson films have become in many ways conjoined. For those reading Tolkien's novel for the first time only after seeing the films, for example, the mental image of the characters, items, and landscape will almost certainly draw from the film, but even for those with strong knowledge of the novels before entering the theater, recalling earlier conceptions of the visual elements is likely to be difficult, if not impossible. As a result, our chapter treats the novel and film together as the original text, with primacy given to the novels because of the much larger range of cultural, geographical, and narrative details or intersections in the printed works. Identifying a single text for *The Lord of the Rings* is further complicated by its direct connections with the remainder of Tolkien's work: *The Hobbit* (1937), *The Silmarillion* (1977), the appendices to *The Lord of the Rings*, and the many volumes edited and published after Tolkien's death by Christopher Tolkien – material which many Tolkien fans, and the *LOTRO* designers, know very well. To see the degree to which satisfying the huge Tolkien fan base was a major issue for both the film and the game, one only need watch the commentaries in the special features section of the extended edition DVDs of the Jackson films and the numerous developer blogs on Turbine's *LOTRO* site. For Jackson's team, Tolkien's writings, including those beyond *The Lord of the Rings* itself, continually impacted the decisions; for the *LOTRO* team, both Tolkien's and Jackson's work did so.

Adaptation and Fidelity

The topic of fidelity has permeated adaptation studies since George Bluestone's 1957 study *Novels into Film*, widely regarded as the major starting point for the field, and has been adopted, embraced, denounced, ridiculed, reconsidered, and theorized about endlessly ever since – with Brian MacFarlane's similarly titled 1996 book-length study providing another touchstone in the debate, arguing strongly against the continual comparison of source to adaptation. To judge even from the recent literature in the field, fidelity seems a topic that everybody has problems with but nobody can circumvent (see Cartmell and Whelehan 2007 and Albrecht-Crane and Cutchins 2010 as two of many discussions of this topic), in part because of the recurring appearance of the issue in the press and on fan websites. A recent study, however, suggests that the fidelity relationship needs further examination precisely as a means of defining adaptions. Thomas Leitch, who has championed the downplaying of fidelity studies, demonstrates in his exploration of 'post-literary' adaptations that there is a difficulty in some instances in determining if a derivative work is an adaptation at all. Of particular interest is his 2009 look at the *Pirates of the Caribbean* series of films (Kindle 3894f.), based on the theme park ride of the same name. The film borrows the title, certainly, and also the overarching subject matter of not-very-serious pirates and some of the visual images. Other than that, the film differs enormously from the ride, to the degree that calling it an adaptation strains the definition of 'adaptation' to the breaking point; Hollywood's popularly used phrase 'loosely adapted' (also seen in film reviews and credits) would seem to apply here, but it is far too imprecise for useful scholarly purposes.

The question of fidelity is tied directly to the field's various taxonomies of adaptation types, of what an adaptation consists of. One such discussion is the oft-cited article by Geoffrey Wagner, who offers a distinction among three different kinds of film adaptation: *transposition*, as direct a translation to screen as possible; *commentary*, an altering of the original for the purpose of expressing the same work of art differently; and *analogy*, an altering for the purpose of creating a different work of art (1975, 222f.). Dudley Andrew (1976) offers his own trio of types. His *transforming* is similar to Wagner's *transposition*, while his *intersecting* is a treatment that retains the original work's uniqueness and qualities, if not always its details, and his *borrowing* represents a much looser association with the source text (98f.). Both of these taxonomies take fidelity as their touchstone, with the categories (as we list them here) showing a decreasing movement away from the bounds of the source text. For anyone conducting adaptation research, however, a problem arises here: if all of these categories can be seen as adaptations, and if we add the viewpoint frequently seen in adaptation research that an adaptation must be seen as its own work of art, not in terms of its fidelity, then practically anything can be called an adaptation, as long as it bears some relationship, however slight, to a previous text. This is especially true of Wagner's *analogy* and Andrew's *borrowing*, and indeed Andrew states clearly that the success of borrowings 'rests on the issue of fertility not their fidelity' (Andrew 1976, 28). Judith Kerman comments on this idea by suggesting that, under this guideline, 'while not adapted from any prior literary text, films like *Star Wars* and *E.T.* might be thought of as adaptations insofar as they both borrow heavily from myths codified within and without SF tradition' (Kerman 1991, 97). If this is so, however, then surely an enormous number of artistic works – literary, cinematic, dramatic, material, ludic, and otherwise – may be considered adaptations; indeed, it starts to get difficult finding any that cannot. In a critical world where intertextuality has primacy, after all, all works are seen as borrowings to one degree or another. Kyle Bishop argues similarly to this point in his discussion of what he calls 'assemblage' filmmaking (Bishop 2010, 264), citing (270) Naremore's comment about the need to associate adaptation with 'recycling, remaking, and every other form of retelling in the age of mechanical reproduction and electronic communication' (Naremore 2006, 15), in fact using this as the basis to his discussion of the shortcomings of Andrew's theory of adaptation types.

Reflecting on the problems of these and other taxonomies, Leitch suggests a new grammar for understanding adaptation types in order to avoid the evaluative basis of adaptation categorization, and because, as he claims, previous taxonomies do not 'adequately demarcate the frontiers of adaptation, the places where it shades into allusion' (Leitch 2009, Kindle 1371). Leitch begins his ten-part taxonomy (Kindle 1389f.) with *celebrations*, the adaptations providing the most direct translation from source medium to the medium of adaptation, sub-dividing the category into *curatorial adaptations*, in which the resources of the new medium strive to reflect the corresponding resource of the original; *replications*, an absolutely slavish translation of all possible elements from the original; and *homages*, which 'pays tribute to an earlier film adaptation as definitive'. Leitch's second category, *adjustment*, is the most common type, a remediation of the source that makes it more suitable for film. Types of adjustment include *compression*, the commonly cited method that allows a novel's story to be told in a two-hour film; *expansion*, the opposite, which Leitch relates specifically to the adaptation of short stories; *correction*, where elements of the source are changed to suit a new audience (including changed endings to make them happier); *updating*, achieving relevance for a new audience by using today's setting; and *superimposition*, in which the adaptation is created for a star (or a star's demands) rather than for its own sake. Third on Leitch's list are *revisions*, attempts 'to rewrite the original, not simply improve its ending or point out its contemporary relevance' (Kindle 1539–42), sporting major changes but still demonstrating clear links to the original. Fourth is *colonization*, in which adaptations 'use progenitor texts as vessels to be filled with new meaning', and where 'any new content is fair game'. Here Leitch cites a number of pornographic movies that transform settings and characters in ways that barely refer to the source text, and which are clearly far removed from any nod to fidelity and, as Leitch notes, demonstrate a shift away from adaptation and towards allusion. He then goes on to discuss the even more allusive categories of *deconstruction* and *analogue*, noting that, in the case of analogues, they need not be recognized as adaptations until 'years after the fact' (Kindle 1663–6). Leitch ends with other allusive categories and finally discusses *allusion* itself, recognizing that all films are allusive and that allusions are so easily noted that they can quickly make the discussion of adaptation meaningless.

The most immediately useful of these categories for discussing *LOTRO* as an adaptation of Tolkien's novels is adjustment, specifically the sub-category of expansion. This is in contrast to the most useful way of looking at Jackson's film adaptation, which, like many fidelity-driven film adaptations, relies on compression of the original in order to fit the requirement of viewing time and various other needs of the medium (including shorter pieces of dialogue than found in Tolkien's novels). We examine *LOTRO* as expansion below, but in both cases – expansion in the games and compression in the films – the desire for a high degree of fidelity to the Tolkien works has clearly guided the creation of these adaptations. The simple fact is that millions of people venturing into the theater in 2001 to see *The Lord of the Rings: The Fellowship of the Ring* already knew the Tolkien books intimately and wanted fidelity to one degree or another. Of course, millions of the films viewers had never read the book – and so probably did not care about its fidelity to the novels – but the many millions of fans flocking to *Harry Potter and the Sorcerer's Stone* (to use the US title) later that year, or *Twilight* seven years later, are even more likely to have read the books, to judge from the book-buying frenzies for those two series that preceded the launch of the first film. As Leitch notes, fidelity in adapting bestsellers or cult classics, as opposed to much lesser-known novels, is a goal pursued by filmmakers 'because only bestsellers or cult classics are likely to bring out cinema audiences both large enough and devoted enough to the source text to threaten serious economic damage in the form of boycotts or badmouthing' (Leitch 2010, 64). So however strongly scholars might argue against the abandonment of fidelity analysis, it is practically unavoidable when dealing with extremely popular sources. And that brings us to *LOTRO*.

The Lord of the Rings Online: Fidelity through Comprehensive Expansion

LOTRO, released in April 2007 and supplemented regularly since then, follows the fantasy MMORPG formula closely. This formula was established in early role-playing games and made most popular by Blizzard Entertainment's 2004 release, *World of Warcraft*. Players take the role of a character with a race found in Tolkien's works – hobbit, dwarf, elf, or man – and solve quests through combat, exploration, and discovery in an effort to reach the maximum character level of 65. A wide variety of sub-systems ranging from economics through reputation and kinships reward continual play, in whatever desired combination for each player of solo or fellowship (group) questing – again, according to MMORPG standards. But *LOTRO* differs from other MMORPGs, of course, in its use of Tolkien's environment and plot-lines, and while most quests are unrelated to the quest of the Fellowship of the Ring in the novels, the game features a series of *epic quests* that do, in fact, follow certain elements of Tolkien's story. These quests give players limited interaction with the main characters in the novels – Gandalf, Aragorn, the hobbits, Elrond, and many more – and with numerous characters, locations, and plot developments only lightly treated in the books.

One example illuminates the working of the epic quests. Upon reaching maximum level, the character is summoned to Elrond in Rivendell. From here, a set of three major quest chains (called Volumes, Books, and Chapters in the epic quests, a clear attempt to appeal to those who have read the novels) makes the player an active protagonist into the briefly mentioned incident in the novels called 'The Ride of the Grey Company'. The chapter in *The Return of the King* called 'The Passing of the Grey Company' covers the ending of this sequence, where Aragorn's fellow Dúnedain (descendants of an ancient culture) meet Aragorn in the land of Rohan and present him with the standard that will announce him as the long-lost heir to the throne. But the novels do not cover the journey of the Dúnedain (who dress in unadorned grey, hence the 'Grey Company' name) from the north to the south at all; nor is this covered anywhere else in detail in Tolkien's writings. What the game does, however, is to flesh out this ride in considerable detail, introducing members of the company and having the player perform actions that help to guide it along its path towards Rohan. This episode provides a clear example of the use of expansion in adapting games from other media, and we use it here as one of the foci of discussion. The episode also provides a useful introduction to the issue of fidelity to the original text, specifically to the relationship between fidelity to the original and additions to it.

The question of correspondence between a game adaptation and its source text come into play here. For film adaptation, at least for several of Leitch's categories, correspondence is quite clear: main characters, primary plot lines, settings and descriptions, and sometimes even literary themes are reflected directly, sometimes with few changes (even if extensive compression) in the cinematic treatment. Certainly this was Jackson's adaptive strategy, with his minor changes and additions actually highlighting, rather than altering, the degree of correspondence to the Tolkien texts. But for games, even basic elements of the correspondence are different. As one simple example, while story-driven games such as RPGs have beginnings, not all of them have endings; indeed the subscription model that drives *World of Warcraft*, *LOTRO*, and other MMORPGs depends entirely on the players never reaching the end (*LOTRO*'s developers are unfolding Middle-earth one major area at a time). Furthermore, unlike most books and films, it is common when playing an RPG to jump back and forth in a thoroughly non-linear fashion, returning to finish quest sequences or see if new ones have appeared, then returning to the spot where the story was left off, and so forth. Players can even cancel quests and return to them, re-starting the chain at that point. And non-player characters in RPGs that are drawn from novels have either far less to say and do than in the books or films (in the case of major characters) or far more (in the case of minor characters). So, whereas the question of correspondence between book and film can – and usually does – take clear forms, such as the effectiveness of character portrayal, whether or not romantic or power relationships had the right intensity, etc., for games the correspondence is in many ways more tangential, and the classic adaptation question of which is better almost nonsensical. Linda Hutcheon gives us a more fruitful line of questioning, discussing videogame adaptations and, with them, theme park rides as remediations of the source text. 'What happens here', she states, 'is a heterocosm, literally an "other world" or cosmos, complete [...] with the stuff of story – settings, characters, events, and situations' (Hutcheon 2006, Kindle 452). This heterocosm, further, 'has a particular kind of "truth-of-correspondence" [...] to the universe of a particular adapted text' (Kindle 455). This truth-of-correspondence occurs, largely, because the player is forced to interact with that world. It is not just viewed or read, it is manipulated.

But this truth-of-correspondence can be achieved in numerous ways. To return to Leitch's adjustment category, compression and expansion offer heterocosmic attributes, both capable of presenting a correspondence that is far from 1:1 but that nevertheless reflects or captures elements of the source work long deemed important by followers of the source material. In *LOTRO*'s case, the 'other world' is incorporated in the expansion of Tolkien's setting, character interactions, and even plot lines. To show how this works, we describe the means by which Tolkien's details are fleshed out in *LOTRO*, grounding the details in the text's descriptions or evocations but adapting these details to suit the demands of an MMORPG. MMORPGs in particular require expansion, since the financial and ludological basis for such games means that players must return to it again and again over months and even years, and no novel or film can provide anywhere near that much detail. Players need to be able to step into the world of the adapted story and spend a significant amount of time in that world, exploring its many locations and engaging with the characters and objects drawn from, or even simply suggested by, the source text. In addition, to meet the same requirement of long-term immersive player involvement, videogame adaptations must expand the scope of the original story, allowing players to meet added characters performing added tasks and fitting into added plots and subplots. They must allow players to explore what is happening in that world beyond the scope of the storyline presented in the source.

A category of a larger taxonomy rarely satisfies full analysis, however, and expansion is no exception. We suggest that Leitch's *expansion* sub-category be further divided into *selective expansion* and *comprehensive expansion*. While there is no space here to explore fully the actual requirements for each type, a few examples from the videogame world will demonstrate the difference. *LOTRO* operates, we argue, through comprehensive expansion: the majority – if not all – of the locations, environments, characters, and cultures mentioned in the Tolkien novels are depicted in much greater detail in the game than Tolkien himself offers. So too are many of the sub-plots, although the main plot itself is assumed more than shown (yet it operates constantly in the background). By comparison, a game such as Electronic Arts' *The Lord of the Rings: The Battle for Middle-earth II* (2006) operates as a selective expansion: it focuses exclusively on a war little-covered in *The Lord of the Rings*, the war in the north, and it expands the roles of numerous minor characters (such as Glorindel the elf and Glóin the dwarf) in order to do so. Similarly, Sierra Entertainment's *The War of the Ring* (2003) expands the details of (among other battles) the defense of Osgiliath by Boromir and Faramir, again barely covered in the novels. Both of these games take specific elements of Tolkien's works and expand greatly upon them, as opposed to *LOTRO*, which uses the MMORPG genre and its expectation of non-ending gameplay to expand the details of Middle-earth and Tolkien's story greatly but always anchoring those details in material from the source.

Geography, Population, and Allies

One technique the designers have used in *LOTRO* is to retain Tolkien's maps of Middle-earth but expand on the detail of terrain and places of population. The maps themselves, printed with the first edition of *The Lord of the Rings* and replicated in numerous works over the years since publication, including the Jackson films, two boardgames entitled *War of the Ring* (SPI 1977 and Fantasy Flight Games 2004), and with especial detail in Karen Wynn Fonstad's *The Atlas of Middle-earth*, offer glimpses into the geography and built spaces of Middle-earth and combine with Tolkien's writings to enhance those glimpses, but only rarely showing what might be in them. *LOTRO* takes these glimpses and expands them dramatically, and interestingly, in doing so, reflects what appears to have been one of Tolkien's narrative strategies. Kevin Schut argues that in Tolkien's stories, '[l]arge chunks of the story do not forward the plot and often have little to do with building a character drama; they read, instead, like sections from an almanac or encyclopedia' (Schut 2011, 10). *LOTRO*'s wealth of details suggests that its own narrative – or at least immersive – strategy is precisely that of the encyclopedia: its attempt to incorporate as much of Tolkien's setting as possible renders it much closer to the experience of reading Robert

Forster's *A Complete Guide to Middle-earth* or J. E. A. Tyler's *The New Tolkien Companion* than the experience of reading the novels themselves, and certainly more than watching the Jackson films. The strategy of comprehensive expansion produces the encyclopedic effect.

In doing so, it allows players to interact with characters who make only brief appearances in the books, providing information to the major characters; *LOTRO* expands the role of these characters, making them conveyors of considerably more information than in the books and – more importantly for the MMORPG genre – appointers of quests. One example is Gildor Inglorien, whom the hobbits encounter as they make their way through the Shire early in the novel, and who disappears thereafter, but in *LOTRO* becomes a leading figure in a particular area of Middle-earth, where both his role and the area itself are treated to major expansion. Another is Radagast the Brown, a Wizard who appears but briefly in the text, fulfilling Gandalf's request that he communicates with various creatures (Radagast's special power) to send information to Saruman's tower, an important element in Gandalf's tale at the Council of Elrond. *LOTRO* expands Radagast's role, bringing him much more significantly into the conflict, and indeed making him a leader in an important region of the game's geography (and where he did not reside in the novels). Still another is Tom Bombadil, the strange earth-deity figure who helps the Fellowship out of two difficult situations in the novels but who does not appear at all in the Jackson films (except for a minor allusion in the Extended Edition). In *LOTRO*, Bombadil is placed within the same area as in the novels, but his role is expanded to guide the player through one of the epic quests. Other characters from the novels given much expanded roles are Halbarad the Ranger, Glorfindel the Elf, and Dwalin the Dwarf. Indeed, Dwalin has charge of a greatly expanded Thorin's Hall, a location that showcases the architectural design skills of *LOTRO*'s artists and, from all the clues Tolkien gives us about dwarves (and Jackson briefly shows), looks faithfully dwarven in all its details. These expansions provide the primary means by which players experience the geography of Middle-earth and interact with the novels' lesser characters and undeveloped locations, and accept quests and gain prestige in order to achieve character growth.

Character Races: Hobbits and Dwarves

As in *The Lord of the Rings*, and adhering to the (more or less) standard set in RPGs from their inception, characters in *LOTRO* start by assigning them a race and a class. The four races are Man, Dwarf, Hobbit, and Elf (as one might expect), and classes range from Burglar and Champion through Lore-Master and Rune-Keeper. Here we examine the cultural cues provided by Tolkien for two of these races, hobbits and dwarves, that a player seeking deep fidelity would want to see, then comparing these cues briefly with what the game actually offers in two of the four races.

In a game adaptation that allows players to become hobbits, the role of the hobbit, as well as how hobbits experience Middle-earth, should reflect the cultural cues Tolkien provides. Most obvious is their ability to go largely unnoticed; not only does Tolkien mention that the history books of the elves have overlooked any and all involvement of hobbits in the past, but he also frequently finds opportunity to suggest that hobbits are all but forgotten during the Third Age of Men. Significantly, the set of writings we know from his published letters that Tolkien cared most about, *The Silmarillion*, mentions this race only once, right near the end, and he does not call them hobbits but rather halflings. Part of the make-up of a hobbit character in a game (characteristics clearly stated in the early pages of *The Lord of the Rings*) should be that they are rarely considered a threat, are met more frequently with humor as opposed to suspicion, and are able to remain unnoticed as they see fit. The battle abilities of hobbits are strongest in archery and throwing stones. They also seem to possess a degree of fortitude lacking among the other races. They do not study magic and tend to avoid those who do. The challenge then becomes offering a level playing field for all character options, but still limiting or dispensing with the magical (or magic-like) abilities of hobbits. Importantly, in offering the option to become a hobbit warrior *LOTRO* is already stretching the limitations of the adaptation. Frodo is obligated to leave the Shire, and his friends follow him out of loyalty. While hobbits are considered to be brave and will protect their territory when necessary, as a people they are not likely to strike out on warrior adventures of their own. Simple travel is not only uncommon, but strongly discouraged among the members of this race.

LOTRO limits hobbits to five of the nine possible classes: Burglar, Hunter, Minstrel, Guardian, and Warden. The first one is an obvious choice, drawing as it does from Tolkien's first novel, *The Hobbit*, in which the dwarves took Bilbo on the adventure largely for his skills and stealth, and the second fits well enough given their stated proficiency with the bow, but the rest are clearly a cultural stretch. Tolkien tells us that hobbits love rustic song and dance, but a minstrel in *LOTRO* uses songs and tales to provide support for combat and raise their companions' morale. Guardians and wardens, important in combat and thus extremely un-hobbit-like, are further out of line. But adherence to the RPG genre dictates that *any* race from *any* culture needs to be able to do a great many things, hence the classes available. In play, their ability to use stealth does indeed predominate; this skill is available in *LOTRO* to the burglar class, not the hobbit race per se. As in the novels, they are not magicians in *LOTRO*, although they can be healers (again depending on class). The actual hobbit traits *LOTRO* provides from the instance of character creation are Small Size (reducing the Might attribute), Hobbit-toughness (increasing Vitality), Rapid Recovery (speedier regeneration of Morale), Hobbit-courage (resistance to the lingering effects of Fear), and Resist Corruption (more able to resist temptation from Evil). These traits cohere well with Tolkien's hobbits, and as with Tolkien they are not obvious in the game until seen in the context of other races during battles. Of course, there is no way an MMORPG could restrict adventurousness, since adventures and quests are at the core of the system and the experience, so what we end up with is a world in which many hobbits are engaged in many adventures in places far away from the Shire. *LOTRO* greatly expands the role of hobbits, and take significant care to present them according to many of Tolkien's dictates, but for no other racial depiction does *LOTRO* deviate so significantly from the source material. The whole point of the participation of Bilbo, Frodo, and the other three hobbits in *LOTRO* was that the participation was extremely unusual and their very existence little known.

Tolkien's dwarves are powerful, warlike miners, in love with cave and stone. Dwarves make strong armor and superior weapons, a trait that should be reflected in the strengths of player options. They are not magic-users, and they venture little outside their own domains.

Tolkien expands very little on the characteristics of dwarves as a race, although much on their history; most of what has been depicted of dwarves in Jackson's films is based on reasonable assumptions drawn from material in the appendices to *The Lord of the Rings*, supplemented by creative license (the latter resulting in Jackson using Gimli as a comic figure). Dwarves in *LOTRO* can be Champions, Guardians, Hunters, Minstrels, or Rune-Keepers. The first two of these are entirely reasonable from an adaptation standpoint and the next two less so (one attempts to picture Gimli breaking out his lute instead of his axe during a battle and leading the fighters in a rousing anthem). The final choice, Rune-Keeper, contravenes Tolkien because of the magic-like capabilities of this class, but coheres because of the existence and power of dwarf-runes in Tolkien's work. Dwarves' traits in *LOTRO* include Sturdiness (increased Might and Vitality), Stocky (reduced Agility), Lost Dwarf-kingdoms (reduced Fate – owing to the fading existence of dwarves in this age of Middle-earth), Unwearying in Battle (better regeneration of Morale), and One-handed Axes (special striking and damage abilities with these weapons). All of these are entirely in keeping with Tolkien's depiction. So, too, is the other interesting fact about dwarves in *LOTRO*: they can be male but not female; Tolkien notes in his appendices to the novels the paucity of women among dwarves, and Jackson picks up on this in a scene in which Gimli talks with Eowyn of Rohan. But since male and female characters in *LOTRO* don't actually differ from one another in anything but appearance, this nod to Tolkien is purely cosmetic. Still, the way in which dwarves differ primarily between Tolkien/Jackson and *LOTRO* is in the game's sheer number of them – dwarf NPCs abound throughout *LOTRO*, with colonies of them frequently encountered. In Moria itself, dwarves are everywhere, as they were most definitely *not* in the novels.

    Here, too, we see the effects of expansion: Moria itself is extremely large (the dimensions in Tolkien's work is unclear), but the number of settlements, outposts, and even small towns populated by dwarves – the Twenty-First Hall being the prime example – entirely contravenes the novel's assertion that Moria had been abandoned. The effect, again, is the possibility of extended gameplay for the purpose of player engagement and player return, and indeed 'The Mines of Moria' module for *LOTRO* makes returning even more compelling by using the location as the basis for a game feature introduced with the release of the module. Before they reach Moria, players begin to accumulate items called legendary weapons, that typically outperform those previously acquired by the player and can be rendered even more powerful using an entire system of leveling and enhancements. Once inside Moria, players can begin the process of bringing the potential of these weapons to fulfillment. With this system, not only is Moria a game location for expansion in the adaptation, it is also a mechanic for expansion of the game system.

Enemies and Allies

In a *Lord of the Rings* adaptation, a player who knows the Tolkien or Jackson texts expects to encounter, at the very least, the common enemy known as orcs and the rarely seen but extremely dangerous Ringwraiths (aka Black Riders and Nazgul). These evil creates are a staple of fearful conversations and scenes throughout the novel and they become an omnipresent in Jackson's films – indeed, Jackson arguably overpopulates his films with orcs, as demonstrated during the siege of Helm's Deep and as the characters flee from the Mines of Moria. In *LOTRO*, players discover these and many other types of enemies, and they do so constantly and in unrelenting quantity. What provides opportunity for further development and more interesting creative license is Tolkien's mention of less-defined horrors in the world of Middle-earth. In various conversations and tales in the writings there is mention of dragons, long unseen but not necessarily extinct; forests of trees, such as the Old Forest, that are capable of hemming in and attacking wanderers; barrow-wights, the ghostly half-dead from ages past; white wolves; and giants. Possibly even more interesting is the mention of 'other portents on the borders of the Shire' (Tolkien 1954, 66), which Tolkien never clarifies. A videogame adaptation has every reason – and thus implicit permission – to extend these brief mentions to their logical conclusion, not only by making these horrors active antagonists of the players' characters in the game, but also by using their very lack of description in the novels (Schut 2007, 6) to create depictions that demonstrate the capabilities of the game's graphic artists and animators. *LOTRO* capitalizes on this opportunity repeatedly. Barrow-wights heavily populate the numerous barrows that players enter on the Barrow-downs and provide foes for several other locations as well. White wolves and other wolf-like creatures abound, and characters of advanced levels get to meet, battle, and in one case even protect, giants. A battle sequence conducted with Legolas the Elf pits the player against huge attacking ancient trees (and they appear elsewhere in addition), and dragons are encountered in several locations. The Ringwraiths provide a basis for an epic quest chain, in which the player tracks one of the Ringwraiths after their dispersal at the Fords of Bruinen; this chain is an expansion of the mention in the novels that the Ringwraiths had to be accounted for before Frodo and the company could leave Rivendell with the Ring.

Concluding Remarks

The overarching question for us throughout this study has been: what does it mean to adapt a novel or film for a game? What is supposed to happen and how do we talk usefully of the resulting product? Videogames, after all, despite their clear similarities with film and television (moving pictures, or at least moving animations, and full sound) – similarities that have most certainly propelled their success – are a very different medium from either, even though, as Mark Wallin explains in detail in his essay on Tolkien adaptations (2007), they achieve part of their adaptive appeal through the rhetorical strategy of identification. The question Hutcheon, Leitch, and others have asked – What is being adapted? – comes very much to the fore here. What elements of the source text must emerge in the game for the adaptation to be considered an adaptation rather than an allusion in Leitch's terms or an evocation in our own terms? The question is complicated greatly by two other types of fidelity already raised by scholars concerned with processes of adaptation (Bishop 2010, for example) and with adaptation as intertextuality (the predominant recent trend), and in need of much further study in games and other non-traditional adaptation types: fidelity has many sources, and many demands, among them medium and genre. The videogame medium has specific requirements, ranging from systems of interaction through systems of presentation and systems of progress and reward, and each videogame genre has its own versions of these requirements: in RPGs, the main ones are character traits, experience points, and combat, with a strong nod towards storyline. Players buying computer RPGs expect their characters, their actions, and the world they are discovering to be represented on screen in ways for that medium and for that genre, and they expect to interact with these elements in equally typical ways – with innovation taking the form of tweaks (of varying degrees) rather than true novelty. MMORPGs extend the computer RPG genre by adding the features of continual change to the gameworld and constantly available multiplayer adventuring with constantly shifting choices in player collaboration, and designs require fidelity to these elements as well.

We conclude with a return to the taxonomies of adaptation types proposed by Wagner, Andrew, and Leitch. *LOTRO* seems to fit best into the following three categories: Wagner's *analogy*, Andrew's *borrowing*, and Leitch's *adjustment* (especially the sub-category *expansion*). But these are not equivalent categories (which is of course why new ones get proposed), and, while useful to see what *LOTRO* is *not*, we suggest that the game actually fits only the expansion category clearly. But even then, expansion describes only part of *LOTRO* as adaptation – an important part, to be sure, given the game's constant theme of taking Tolkien's world and fleshing it out in far greater detail than he ever did, but still only a part. There is more to the game adaptation, including a strong similarity in graphical appearance between portions of Jackson's films and certain elements of *LOTRO*, and yet a sharp difference in others (Moria and Hobbiton are very similar in appearance to the films, Bree and Lothlorien quite different) and an enormous difference in the perceived sense of the time (it is hard to believe, after spending weeks or even months of play reaching Moria in *LOTRO*, that the Fellowship has only recently been there). The quest of the Fellowship seems to be taking forever, partly because players have such an enormous range of quests to achieve as they follow the path. Indeed, the sheer level of activity is entirely at odds with both Tolkien and Jackson; the characters in Tolkien and Jackson encountered few enemies except during military battle scenes, but the player encounters and battles hostile creatures and characters at practically all points along all paths and roads, and throughout all wilderness areas. But all of these details, in fact, reinforce the predominance of expansion as adaptive strategy.

References

Albrecht-Crane, Christa, and Dennis Cutchins. 2010. 'New Beginnings for Adaptation Studies.' In *Adaptation Studies: New Approaches*, ed. Christa Albrecht-Crane and Dennis Cutchins. Madison, NJ: Fairleigh Dickinson University Press.

Andrew, J. Dudley. 1976. *The Major Film Theories*. New York: Oxford University Press.

Berg, Richard. 1977. *War of the Ring*. New York, NY: Simulations Publications Inc.

Bishop, Kyle. 2010. 'Assemblage Filmmaking: Approaching the Multi-Source Adaptation and Reexamining George Romero's *Night of the Living Dead*.' In *Adaptation Studies: New Approaches*, ed. Christa Albrecht-Crane and Dennis Cutchins. Madison, NJ: Fairleigh Dickinson

Blizzard Entertainment. 2004. *World of Warcraft*. Vivendi/Blizzard.

Bluestone, George. 1957. *Novels into Films*. Berkeley and Los Angeles: University of California Press.

Cartmell, Deborah and Imelda Wheleha. 2007. 'Introduction – Literature on Screen: A Synoptic View.' In *The Cambridge Companion to Literature on Screen*, ed. Deborah Cartmell and Imelda Wheleha. Cambridge, UK: Cambridge University Press.

Di Meglio, Roberto, Marco Maggi, and Francesco Nepitello. 2004. *War of the Ring*. Roseville, MN: Fantasy Flight Games.

Electronic Arts. 2006. *The Lord of the Rings: The Battle for Middle-earth II*.

Fonstad, Karen Wynn. 2001. *The Atlas of Middle-earth*. Boston: Houghton Mifflin.

Forster, Robert. 1978. *A Complete Guide to Middle-earth*. New York: Ballantine Books.

Hutcheon, Linda. 2006. *A Theory of Adaptation*. New York: Routledge. Kindle edition.

Kerman, Judith. 1991. *Retrofitting Blade Runner: Issues in Ridley Scott's Blade Runner and Philip K. Dick's Do Androids Dream of Electric Sheep?* Madison, WI: University of Wisconsin Press.

Leitch, Thomas. 2009. *Film Adaptation and its Discontents: From Gone with the Wind to The Passion of the Christ*. Baltimore: Johns Hopkins University Press. Kindle edition.

—2010. 'The Ethics of Infidelity.' In *Adaptation Studies: New Approaches*, ed. Christa Albrecht-Crane and Dennis Cutchins. Madison, NJ: Fairleigh Dickinson University Press.

The Lord of the Rings: The Fellowship of the Ring. 2001. DVD. Directed by Peter Jackson. Burbank, CA: New Line Cinema.

The Lord of the Rings: The Two Towers. 2002. DVD. Directed by Peter Jackson. Burbank, CA: New Line Cinema.

The Lord of the Rings: The Return of the King. 2003. DVD. Directed by Peter Jackson. Burbank, CA: New Line Cinema.

McFarlane, Brian. 1996. *Novel to Film: An Introduction to the Theory of Adaptation*. Oxford: Clarendon.

Naremore, James. 2006. *Film Adaptation*. New Brunswick: Rutgers University Press.

Schut, Kevin. 2011. 'Continuity and Discontinuity: An Experiment in Comparing Narratives Across Media,' *Loading* …1, no.1. Accessed April 2, 2011. http://journals.sfu.ca/loading/index.php/loading/article/view/19.

Sierra Entertainment. 2003. *The Lord of the Rings: War of the Ring*. Oakhurst, CA: Sierra Entertainment.

Tolkien, J. R. R. 1937. *The Hobbit*. London: Allen & Unwin.

—1954–56. *The Lord of the Rings*. London: Allen & Unwin.

—1977. *The Silmarillion*. Edited by Christopher Tolkien. London: Allen & Unwin.

Turbine. 2007. *The Lord of the Rings Online: Shadows of Angmar*.

—2008. *The Lord of the Rings Online: Mines of Moria*.

—2009. *The Lord of the Rings Online: Siege of Mirkwood*.

Tyler, J. E. A. 1980. *The New Tolkien Companion*. New York: Avon Books.

Wagner, Geoffrey. 1975. *The Novel and the Cinema*. Rutherford, NJ: Fairleigh Dickinson University Press.

Wallin, Mark Rowell. 2011. 'Myths, Monsters and Markets: Ethos, Identification, and the Video Game Adaptations of The Lord of the Rings.' *Game Studies* 7, no. 1: Accessed April 3, 2011. http://gamestudies.org/0701/articles/wallin.

SECTION TWO

In-Character

6

Traumatic Origins: Memory, Crisis, and Identity in Digital RPGs

KATIE WHITLOCK

No sound is purely made, no gesture 'in absentia' from time, no image without memory, not a particle of behavior in a state of nature. For there is always in any system the sediment of time. Which implies that whatever is coming in, something is leaking out.

HERBERT BLAU

The concept of memory is both fascinating and fluid in the postmodern consciousness. In contemporary culture, technology, psychology, performance, and other areas of study have considered the art of remembrance and the nature of memory in a variety of ways. From classic interpretations of memory's ability to inscribe narrative and to recollect events to modern ideas about collective unconscious and the imprint of involuntary traumatic echoes, the sense of how humans mark experience and recall it remains a provocative topic for discussion and exploration.

Memory, labeled by John Locke as 'the Store-house of our *Ideas*', is the repository of those ideas/experiences unable to be comprehended in one moment and instead stored up for later exploration and consideration (2007, 75). The fascination with the 'art of memory' is linked to the drive to inscribe and take ownership of the events of life. Revisiting and embracing the past through memory provides a stage on which to re-examine events, ideas, actions, etc. and opens the door to what it is to be human. Not surprisingly, memory is an often-referenced trope for actors seeking to portray the actions and effects of everyday life, suggesting that the nature of performance is linked to memory. Elin Diamond argues that memory infects all aspects of human behavior, that no single moment is free of past experience or influence:

> While a performance embeds traces of other performances, it also produces an experience whose interpretation only partially depends on previous experience. Hence the terminology of 're' in discussion of performance, as in *re*member, *re*inscribe, *re*configure, *re*iterate, *re*store. 'Re' acknowledges the pre-existing discursive field, the repetition within the performance present, but 'figure', 'script', and 'iterate' assert the possibility of something that *exceeds* our knowledge, that alters the shape of sites and imagines new unsuspected subject positions. (1995, 2)

Memory is in fact linked to major acting and performance theory as a necessary component for effectively creating characters which can be viewed by an audience/performer and then interpreted into another entity influenced and shaped by the source narrative, the performer, and the viewer all drawing from echoes of the past memories of all participants in the performance. Much of the contemporary acting training of today embraces memory in different ways, drawing from this connection, which was initially labeled as 'affective memory' by the French psychologist Ribot in the late 1800s and later given the name 'emotional memory' in the 1930s by Konstantin Stanislavski. Stanislavski explored the value of memory in relation to creating 'realistic' performances, driven by the need to create characters that were truthful and relatable for all the audiences who viewed them[1]. In developing his training techniques, Stanislavski felt that memory contained nothing superfluous, instead retaining the essence of an idea or emotion (similar to Locke's presentation of the storehouse). When accessed to create character, the memory is presented onstage in a new way, reinscribed and reconfigured into something engaging and connected to the experience with a truthful nature which could only be recognized and valued by an audience (Moore 1984, 41–5).

In videogames, memory becomes a conduit for the player to access information about the character from a unique aspect as well as a mode for luring the character into the narrative of the game. Beyond the ubiquitous complaint from players and critics that RPG narratives are thin and trite, especially when driven by amnesia, memory is the channel through which the player connects with the character and the narrative. The layers of memory from player to character recycle meaning and experience, drawing the player into the narrative to discover the nuances of difference that exist in these games. It should be noted that several popular RPGs such as the *Mass Effect* series, *Dragon Age* series, and *Oblivion* provide a type of configurative character creation. Players are afforded the luxury of deciding the physical appearance and attributes of their main character. Players invent their character and, as such, are imaginatively connected to the character, much like making a character on the playground as a child. This development of character is a ludic convention which engages the player in building a reflection of some facet of self and is discussed in detail in Chuk Moran's piece on the configurable being in this volume. In opposition, when memory serves to drive the character, the narrative construction of the whole is released in pieces, experienced as the player descends into the realm of the game. Yet, many traditional RPGs begin with the introduction of the main character as an amnesiac orphan whose lack of identity provides a convenient reason to start on a journey of self-recovery. The lack of memory makes the character an essentially blank slate for the player to access and merge with over the course of the game. While sometimes considered a tired yet familiar conceit common to many Japanese RPGs, such a narrative device still holds value in both its traditional status within the genre and also because of the range of connection many feel for the characters in well-crafted narratives which demand a connection to memory to develop character identity. Players connect with these 'evacuated' characters differently than with those configured from the beginning. As the game unfolds, characters experience violence and trauma; subjectivity and identity co-evolve as old memories resurface and as new memories are acquired, and the player merges with the character to achieve an emotional resonance. Perhaps there is still something to be gained from the connection between memory and performance, player and character.

Examining the construction of character/player relationship through the device of memory as utilized in the games *Lost Odyssey, Final Fantasy VII,* and *Final Fantasy X* provides some tactics of exploration. Each game uses the device of memory (or lack of memory) as a way of connecting player to character, melding memory with trauma and providing narrative reasons for characters to exist as initial blank slates for players to control. All three use main characters whose sense of self is incomplete at the beginning of the game, transforming as memories are revealed over time. In each game, a different concept of memory is explored, leading to a stronger tie between player and character, providing a sense of depth and backstory that engages players much like actors are engaged when developing roles for performance.

Memory as Recollection

My body remembers...
    Kaim Argonar in *Lost Odyssey*

In 2008, Microsoft Game Studios published *Lost Odyssey* for the Xbox 360 console to mixed reviews. Developed by Mistwalker and feelplus, Inc., this game drew upon very traditional RPG structures to introduce a deep narrative and unique characters who suffer from loss of memory and self at the beginning of the game. The player enters the game on a battlefield later revealed to be the site of a major conflict between the warring nations of the Republic of Uhra and the Kingdom of Gohtza. In the ensuing bloodbath and meteor strike, the player takes control of Kaim Argonar who is revealed to be an immortal, having walked alone for 1,000 years as a mercenary with no memory and questionable conscience in an endless and lonely journey. Over the course of the game, three other immortals are encountered and recruited, all having been stripped of their memories. In actuality, one immortal seeking ultimate power (Gongora, military sorcerer and advisor to the Gohtza government) has caused this memory loss in the other four to allow for a clear field of victory. The game depends upon Kaim and the other immortals connecting with one another, triggering their memories, rediscovering a sense of purpose, and ultimately saving the realm from Gongora's plans which would result in the destruction of the world as a whole.

    As the player controls Kaim and the other members of the party, various actions and encounters trigger random memories that the player is allowed to witness or bypass. These are referenced as dreams, unlocked from deep within the hearts of the characters. These memory dreams are uniquely presented as text stories on relatively plain backgrounds with some musical accompaniment. Rather than realistic cut scenes, the dreams are deceptively simple in construction. Words are the focus of these memories and they roll, shimmer, drop, and fade on and off screen to create a sense of poetic language rather than concrete visuals allowing the player to access the memory from a place of narrative imagination as opposed to realistic action. The nature of these memories, linked to words, suggests a classical interpretation of memory as inscription – a writing of experience that is reflective of Plato's value of language as one of the most powerful reflections of human experience (Whitehead 2009, 22–3). These memories, once triggered, are always available to the player to be accessed whenever Kaim stays at an inn or rests. The choice to view the *Thousand Dreams* of Kaim is available as soon as the character enters the rest state and is not limited for the amount of memories that can be revisited. The memories of the other immortal companions, Seth Balmore (female pirate), Ming Numara (Queen of Numara), and Sarah Sisulart (magic researcher and wife of

Kaim), are only accessed at main plot points and cannot be recovered by the player since Kaim is the protagonist and main character of the action, further linking the player to the single character.

This recovery of dreams suggests an Aristotelian approach to memory as *recollection*. Aristotle posited that humans were unique in their memory faculties not because they could remember, but because they could actively search and recollect, making memories something that could be recalled on command rather than something that simply surfaced in reaction to a present moment (Richards 2007, 21). This also ties back to the Diamond quote, which seems to suggest that there is something *new* present in the re-collection/configuration of memory for the development of scripts for future actions. Within *Lost Odyssey*, the immortals are flawed to some extent because they have no long-term memories. They have immediate memory, but their sense of purpose and history has been removed; they are unable to recollect (search) their memories to retrieve their reason for being in this world. They become more human in their actions and reactions as Kaim gains more memories, suggesting this link to Aristotle's concept of being human as connected to recollection. The recovery of memory is also linked to physical pain, as Kaim and Seth in particular must struggle to bypass Gongora's conditioning to regain their sense of personal identity. As the game progresses, Kaim regains fragments of memory, unlocked in seemingly random order dependant on how the player allows Kaim to engage with the environment and the NPCs in various locations. With the capacity to search the once-recovered dreams at points of rest, Kaim regains his humanity and his sense of purpose. This conjunction suggests a clear reflection of Aristotle's concept of recollection outlined by Jennifer Richards in *Theories of Memory* as 'a "search" entailing reflection on "time" and the objects remembered through the orderly association of ideas and images' (2007, 21). Recollection can also be read as an interesting mode of archiving the game experience, quite different from that suggested by Alice Henton's piece on *Dragon Age* in this volume, but still useful as a method for giving players a way of selecting their engagement with the narrative of the game. What also makes the device of memory particularly effective here is the sheer random way in which memories are revealed, sometimes triggered by entering a tavern or talking to an individual as opposed to only being connected to major boss battles or new maps. Interestingly, the player does not necessarily reveal all the memories of the game. It is actually quite easy to miss some memories, which does not detract from the gameplay and the end result of the game, yet does weaken the connection to Kaim and the understanding of his backstory and behaviors.

In addition to the archival nature of the dream memories, the method through which Gongora eliminated the memories of Kaim, Seth, and Sarah is telling. For each of these three, the memory wipe was achieved by trauma associated with the death of the strongest emotional tie for each character in the world at that time – with the ensuing guilt functioning as the prison for their memories. Gongora kills Kaim and Sarah's young daughter Lirum by having her fall over a cliff while they are unable to save her. They both suffer an endless repetition of seeing Lirum fall just out of reach as they scream for her. Gongora triggers Seth's blind rage as she discovers her long-time companion, Aneira, over the body of her son, Sed, and she kills that which she values most, locking her into a prison of loneliness and guilt. Both of these situations are staged with the emotional impact and a lack of clarity so that each of the three retreats willingly into the void generated by Gongora, terrified of their own responsibility in the outcomes. All three are controlled by guilt and hazy memories of what occurred. All three are 'freed' when they embrace the pain of their memories, triggered by encounters with mortals who are linked to them by blood. Kaim becomes more talkative and emotional when reunited with Lirum and his grandchildren Cooke and Mack, releasing his guilt. Sarah, who has locked herself into the body of an old sorceress, lashing out at all who enter her domain, is only reached when Cooke and Mack sing to her, using the lullaby of Lirum's childhood to reconnect their grandmother to the world as a place of hope and forgiveness rather than grief and guilt. Seth is more scattered as she slowly experiences pieces of her final encounter with Aneira and Sed in dream fashion, only to finally release her own guilt when she reunites with Sed and learns how Gongora manipulated the entire event through his magic. Seth also sacrifices herself for the good of the whole, achieving a final cleansing of guilt in the last confrontation with Gongora. Trauma and pain mark the recovery of self for these immortals as they gain their sense of purpose over the course of the game. This embrace of pain reconnects each character to the human world and produces behavior more in keeping with mortality than immortality.

This sense of trauma and struggle to regain the memories of these characters is part of the appeal of the gameplay. As players work their way through four discs of gameplay, the drive to return to the game is in part the desire to beat Gongora and save the world, but it is also an emotional connection, driven by the revelation of the memories. The fragments of memory gathered over the course of the game and the emotional connections they have for Kaim connect player to character much as an actor becomes connected to character when developing a role. A single reading of a text is insufficient to discover all the possibilities of the narrative; the rehearsal process allows an actor to develop a deeper connection and understanding for both the narrative and the characters. Re-hearsal is both re-flective and re-flexive, allowing for both muscle and mental memory, which helps to solidify player/actor and avatar/character. This generative process over time is mirrored in the playing of the game, seeded in the case of *Lost Odyssey* with fragments of memory that can be connected to generate a more complete picture of Kaim. It is not necessary to develop this depth of vision, but it provides a more satisfactory and immersive experience.

Memory as Involuntary

What I have shown you is reality. What you remember ... that is the illusion.
    Sephiroth in *Final Fantasy VII*

In 1997 Sony published a Japanese RPG for the PlayStation console developed by Squaresoft that would become a benchmark for commercial and critical success in the genre, *Final Fantasy VII*. This game, which was the first in the *Final Fantasy* series to use 3D graphics, was considered landmark for its graphics, story, gameplay, and music – all of which influenced the genre from that point forward. Set in a dystopian world of magic and technology, the game centers around the journey of the young mercenary Cloud Strife (an RPG icon recognized for his spiky blond hair and giant sword) and his battle to regain his sense of self and to fight the industrial power of the Shinra Corporation and the unstoppable warrior Sephiroth. The player enters the game in the midst of a mission for AVALANCHE (an eco-terrorist group) as Cloud and his companions attempt to blow up several targets in Midgar, the primary city and headquarters for Shinra. As the action progresses, not much is known about Cloud other than his previous work as a member of SOLDIER, Shinra's elite squad of warriors. Rather than beginning with a lack of memory, instead Cloud becomes suspicious of his memories as real, questioning his past, his identity, and even reality. The game becomes a puzzle to discover what is truth in relation to Cloud's identity and what is a manipulated construction deriving from genetic and emotional manipulation by other characters.

    Cloud begins the game believing he was once a member of SOLDIER, one of the genetically altered elite warriors of the Shinra Corporation. Throughout the action of the first half of the game, Cloud has certain moments where he experiences flashbacks that begin to plant a seed of doubt about the clarity of his memories. At the midpoint of the game, the traumatic event of Aerith's death occurs and robs Cloud of any certainty about his own past and identity[2]. Aerith, Cloud's love and stabilizing influence, is murdered by Sephiroth, who, in dialogue with Cloud, forces the realization that he cannot be who he thinks he is. Cloud spends the next portion of the game attempting to discern if he is a clone, created by the genetic material of Jenova, a headless monster 'owned' by Shinra. By the end of the game, Cloud's sense of identity is exposed as an illusion, woven out of guilt, fear, and anger. In reality, he failed in his attempt to join SOLDIER and his memories are that of his best friend Zack. He finally realizes that his memories are a blend of memories from Zack, Tifa (a childhood friend who is also a member of AVALANCHE), and his own influenced by Jenova cells, Mako energy (magic) and Sephiroth's manipulations. In an attempt to discover redemption and to solidify his new identity, Cloud enters the final battle with Sephiroth in which Cloud survives along with the other members of his party, but only to face the devastation of the planet by a meteor only partially destroyed in the last battle. His future is uncertain, as he still must deal with the traumatic reflexes of his past.

Here memory becomes a major narrative device to lure the player into continuing a relationship with Cloud. The nature of Cloud's trauma makes his memory suspect and the odd insertions of memory provide fuel to the player, encouraging continued play to solve the mystery of the character. Part of Cloud Strife's appeal to players is the fluid nature of his identity and the drive to connect all the missing pieces of Cloud's psyche. Also, memories intrude into the game less often than in *Lost Odyssey* but still feel somewhat random, marked by pain for Cloud as well as by vibration in the control, audio cues, and a slightly faded look to the graphics on screen. These 'memories' for Cloud are uncertain and appear real even though they reference events in a different manner than originally described by other characters. Cloud and the player also have no control over these memories; they must be played out in full in the context of the action. The control is taken from the player as the memory overwhelms both Cloud and player, forcing the viewing rather than making it acceptable to bypass the memory as in *Lost Odyssey*.

This use of memory corresponds strongly to descriptions of involuntary memory most often associated with trauma and Post-Traumatic Stress Disorder (PTSD). The American Psychiatric Association, in describing the mental stress exhibited by Vietnam War veterans, first used the category of Post-Traumatic Stress Disorder in the 1980s (Whitehead 2009, 114). Trauma is 'a response, sometimes delayed, to an overwhelming event or events, which takes the form of repeated, intrusive hallucinations, dreams, thoughts or behaviors stemming from the event, along with numbing that may have begun during or after the experience, and possibly also increased arousal to (or avoidance of) stimuli recalling the event' (Caruth 1995, 4). Cloud begins the game as a numb individual who communicates tersely and evidences little or no feeling about what is occurring. His meeting with Aerith and eventual love story with her provide a reason to see an opening in emotional behavior, which is then shut down again by her murder and his witnessing of yet another traumatic event. This event then triggers his downward spiral of stability, prodded by Sephiroth, which results in his need to get the answers about his origin at all cost. The cycle of trauma creates an emotional experience for the player, as theory after theory is tested in regards to Cloud's past and is proven wrong by yet another memory or action.

Another component of memory performance evidenced in *Final Fantasy VII* occurs as Cloud engages with other characters, particularly Aerith and Tifa, creating a conversation after many significant plot events. These long exchanges, often interspersed with cut scenes, serve as a rehashing of events, making Cloud question the validity of his memory. Performance theorist Peggy Phelan suggests the behavior trigger and the value of such conversations in this following way:

> Talking after the event, post-talking, the often tedious recitations of events and sequences, rehearses the tongue for trickier, less sequential psychic acts. For talking after often means 'talking over', and in that performance one might be able to discern what consciousness overlooked during the event's unfolding. (1998, 7)

The overlooked aspects suggested by Phelan become inconsistencies in Cloud's narratives, revealing the gaps and memory constructs which litter his consciousness. In revisiting events from multiple perspectives, the player gains insight and discovery further connecting character and player in the course of the game.

Memory as Ghost

You are a fading dream, but one that has been touched by reality. Run, dream. Run on into the daylight. And walk into reality.
  Yojimbo (an aeon) in *Final Fantasy X*

In 2001, Squaresoft released another title in its *Final Fantasy* series, for the PlayStation 2 console, which would be extremely successful. The first game in the series to use fully rendered 3D backdrops throughout the game, *Final Fantasy X* marked another significant game in the development of the RPG genre. Enjoying commercial and critical success, the game shifted the gameplay experience by using a sphere grid leveling system allowing more customization and flexibility in character development, as well as an integrated world providing relatively seamless travel between towns and landscapes of the game environment. The game also developed a deep narrative encouraging player immersion in the world of Spira and the life of Tidus and the other characters.

The game begins *in medias res* as Tidus (the protagonist) and his fellow companions gather before heading into what will be the final dungeon of the game. Tidus begins to narrate the story, pulling the player into a flashback, placing Tidus in Zanarkand before a blitz-ball tournament and the imminent destruction of the city by a monstrous creature. As Tidus flees from the destroyed city, he falls and passes out, to awaken in Spira. As he begins his journey, he learns that Zanarkand was a city from 1,000 years ago and the resulting destruction that Tidus remembers has wiped out much of the industrial life on Spira. The destruction, resulting from an overdependence on technology and a rejection of the natural world, is attributed to the monster, aptly named Sin, who returns in cyclical fashion to punish the living for the behaviors of the past. In the time of Tidus's arrival to Spira, the world is reduced to a more tribal existence, haunted by Sin and defended by Summoners, individuals gifted with the power to sing the spirits of the deceased to rest and able to summon aeons, beings of immense magical power. As Tidus joins the world of Spira, he becomes a Guardian to Yuna, one of the Summoners, and he protects her on her pilgrimage to summon aeons to defeat Sin. Over the course of the game, Tidus and Auron (another protector who Tidus recognizes from his first experience in Zanarkand) are revealed to be dead spirits who have been unable to rest. Both are memories with immense power and capacity to impact the world around them known as *fayth*. Auron is finally 'sent' after the defeat of Yu Yevon (one of the game's antagonists) and his soul is laid to rest. Tidus's 'death' is more complex, as the end of the game suggests that he might be alive; this led to the sequel *Final Fantasy X–2* which follows Yuna as she seeks to reunite with Tidus in the years following the defeat of Sin.

In this use of memory, ghosts are recognized as part of the action and are allowed to interact and interfere with the action of the game. Tidus is a memory, brought forth after 1,000 years to save the world at the cost of his own destruction, for once Sin is defeated, the *fayth* are all released, including Tidus. This becomes an interesting interpretation of haunting as Tidus moves around the world of Spira visiting places both familiar and unfamiliar to him as part of his journey. What is also interesting is that Tidus appears to have personal growth during his time as a Guardian, suggesting that his memory is more 'real' than most ghosts. He falls in love with Yuna and their relationship becomes a key point for how Tidus reacts and behaves in the narrative. A possible key into this choice is suggested by Joseph Roach as 'the desire to communicate physically with the past, a desire that roots itself in the ambivalent love of the dead' (1998, 23). The past is constantly part of the present in the game, making the player aware of the layers of memory. This becomes visible in the final dungeon as the Dream Zanarkand emerges, overlaying the ruins of the present Zanarkand with the ghost images of the Zanarkand of Tidus's memory. And Roach's understanding of this desire to communicate with the past is illustrated not only in the presence of Tidus and Auron but also in the use of the Farplane, which serves as both a religious other world and a physical access point where Yuna can see and interact with spirits in her role as Summoner. This game locates Spira's present entwined with its past in a ritualistic fashion which seems to acknowledge a collective sense of memory that haunts the world. This concept of haunting is also discussed in Bealer's chapter on performance within the gamescape in this volume, as *Arc the Lad: Twilight of the Spirits* operates with a similar construction of spiritual and real connections.

This haunted world is in some ways the most contemporary reflection of postmodern memory. Contemporary culture surrounds itself with memorials and museums – markers of traumatic past events mirroring Spira, littered with ruins of its trauma. In the twenty-first century, people visit the shrines of past trauma with a sense of obligation to history, forcing remembrance and imprinting memory in those who are too young or too removed to have 'real' memories of war, holocaust, etc. In similar fashion, the Summoners of Spira go on a forced pilgrimage across the landscape to various ruins to connect with ghosts of the past, gathering the power to face the monster Sin in hopes of defeating the past to allow the present to function without the overlay of fear and guilt. It is worth noting that *Final Fantasy X* is a Japanese RPG and, as such, reflects a different relationship with trauma and memory than Western culture, also suggesting a reason for a landscape of ruin which forces a different awareness of past and present in the visual and emotional landscape[3].

In addition to the ruined landscape of the game, the presence of ghosts within the game suggests the value inherent in having past and present meld into the gamescape. Marvin Carlson draws correlations between theater as the public experience of memory and dreaming as its private corollary. Theater can be viewed as a waking dream 'recycling past perceptions and experiences in imaginary configurations, that although different, are powerfully haunted by a sense of repetition and involve the whole range of human activity and its context' (1998, 3). This waking dream is where the player is allowed license to replay the destructions of the real world in a digital realm. The world of Spira can be examined with free license not allowed with the devastated landscapes of Hiroshima or Chernobyl. Playing as Tidus, the viewer/player is given a different perspective of this primitive world. Tidus is an individual much like the player, from a technological world, whereas the world of Spira is more tribal, kept to a more limited technology by Sin's repeated appearances, and more dependent on the natural environment to survive. Tidus's lack of familiarity with the world of Spira provides another blank slate character for the player to use, learning the world mechanics and culture in flow of the narrative.

Memory and Body

All three of the games examined have used memory in different configurations, yet there is one similarity which all three share. As part of the gameplay, the random battle encounters and boss battles task the player with strategically selecting behaviors resulting in damage for the creatures being fought. At the end of each battle, there is a short sequence in which all the characters showcase certain moves (and which in *Final Fantasy X* and *Lost Odyssey* includes voiced comments) which link the player to the character in terms of body memory. Kaim stoically leans back while Cooke and Mack do celebratory dances; Cloud twirls his Buster sword while Aerith tidies her hair and modestly places her hands before her;

Wakka pumps his fist while holding his blitz-ball and Tidus tosses his sword in the air in a victory celebration. This use of repetitive gesture in the physical behavior of the characters suggests another tie between memory and performance, a connection that further strengthens character-to-player ties. Polish acting theorist Jerzy Growtoski developed his concept of the 'body-memory' when working with actors by suggesting that the body mattered equally to the mind in construction of memory. 'It is thought that the memory is something independent from the rest of the body. In truth, at least for actors – it's something different. The body does not *have* memory, it *is* memory' (Wolford 2000, 203). Watching the repeated behaviors of the characters over and over, the sense of character becomes cemented for the player. Repetitive signature gestures provide visual referents which are independent of narrative but which serve to establish character from the ludic side of the gameplay.

These physical behaviors can also be viewed as a Brechtian technique of connecting with character, enabling an understanding of gameplay, narrative, and character purely from a visual standpoint. This technique, more commonly referred to as *gestus,* serves as a broad brush stroke that does not necessarily convey subtle nuance but instead creates an imprint, which serves the viewer in a more functional sense (Thomson 2000, 109–10). The *gestus* impulse repeated over and over creates a link with player that remains a signature of the game long past the initial engagement period. These gestures become a memory imprint on the player, retaining the essence of the character, haunting other games and becoming referential. For instance, the influence of Cloud is seen in Tidus, as both have blond hair and swords and their physical signatures echo one another, with Tidus being a more 'realistic' interpretation of the anime-influenced Cloud.

The Art of Memory

Memory, when investigated in relation to RPGs, exposes a connection between characters and players, creating a strong tie with emotional overtones. Using recollection, trauma, ghosting, and *gestus*, game designers create strong links which invite players to enter game narratives with enthusiasm and curiosity. The narratives of these games, while sometimes being criticized as simplistic and derivative, allow players an entry into character creation both sophisticated and subtle. Developing character backstory as a part of gameplay allows the player to become an actor, performing nuanced behaviors due to deepening understanding of character motivations and history. By the time boss battles occur, the player is invested in the character and becomes an expert at manipulating the controller, while also understanding the narrative impact of the battle on the psyche of Kaim, Cloud, or Tidus. All three of these games, which experienced commercial success, suggest the value in this type of connection, especially when the narrative is well constructed and invites such explorations.

What becomes clear is the power of memory for player and character in the construction of a successful role. The role in the role-playing genre assumes that the player becomes the character to some extent, losing self in the cloak of the character. Though the device of amnesia is a familiar conceit, what becomes evident in these games and others is that memory does not have to be limited to only one expression. Instead, exploring the power and range of memory as a concept can express cultural ideologies and present concerns, as opposed to being a seemingly trite reason to put a character into a state of reactive functionality.

The devices of memory create resonances within the players of RPGs as the games repeat and reinterpret tropes of performance, overlaying the successes of the past with new technology and ideas of the present. As Stanislavski suggested in his studies,

> Time is an excellent filter, an excellent purifier of memories of emotions once experienced. Moreover, time is an excellent artist. It not only purifies but is capable of poeticizing the memories. (Moore 1984, 42)

As time passes and gamers spend time in the pursuit of gameplay, the echoes of these games will impact new narratives, but also leave traces within the players to be embraced and recognized and remembered.

When people die, they just go away. If there's any place a soul would go, it's in your memories. People you remember are with you forever.
    Kaim Argonar in *Lost Odyssey*

Notes

1. This drive for realistic performance was connected to the rise of realism in writing, most notable in the works of Henrik Ibsen, Anton Chekhov, and August Strindberg. These playwrights changed the nature of theater from presentational performances of stereotype to a more nuanced version of the world around them. In tandem with this move towards realistic text, the actors of the late nineteenth and early twentieth centuries had to develop techniques which made their performances more 'real' to the audience, and Konstantin Stanislavski is considered the master of these early techniques and influential to all those who changed acting theory since.
2. Sometimes Aerith is referenced as Aeris due to the spelling in the original game booklet. The spelling Aerith will be used throughout in this paper for consistency. It should also be noted that the death scene for Aerith is considered one of the most emotionally charged and radical plot twists in an RPG due to the removal of a major character at midpoint in the game. This is a scene that is continually referenced and pointed to for its impact on players in conjunction with its emotional power and shock value.
3. This is an idea that is beyond the scope of this chapter but would provide more fruitful explorations in other avenues. Part of that exploration would include Baudrillard's interest in simulacra here, and the power of that imagined or re-collected memory.

References

Blau, Herbert. 1982. *Take Up the Bodies: Theater at the Vanishing Point*. Chicago: University of Illinois Press.
Carlson, Marvin. 2003. *The Haunted Stage: Theatre as Memory Machine*. Ann Arbor: University of Michigan Press.
Caruth, Cathy. 1995. 'Trauma and Experience: Introduction.' In *Trauma: Explorations in Memory*, ed. Cathy Caruth, 3–12. Baltimore: Johns Hopkins University Press.

Diamond, Elin. 1995. *Writing Performances*. London: Routledge.
Locke, John. 2007. 'An Essay Concerning Human Understanding.' In *Theories of Memory: A Reader*, ed. Michael Rossington and Anne Whitehead, 75–84. Baltimore: Johns Hopkins University Press.
Mistwalker and feelplus, Inc. 2008. *Lost Odyssey*. [Xbox 360]. Redmond, WA: Microsoft Game Studios.
Moore, Sonia. 1984. *The Stanislavski System: The Professional Training of the Actor*. 2nd revised edition. New York: Penguin Books.
Phelan, Peggy. 1998. 'Introduction.' In *The Ends of Performance*, ed. Peggy Phelan and Jill Lane, 1–19. New York: New York University Press.
Richards, Jennifer. 2007. 'Classical and Early Modern Ideas of Memory: Introduction.' In *Theories of Memory: A Reader*, ed. Michael Rossington and Anne Whitehead, 20–4. Baltimore: Johns Hopkins University Press.
Roach, Joseph. 1998 . 'History, Memory, Necrophila.' In *The Ends of Performance*, ed. Peggy Phelan and Jill Lane, 23–30. New York: New York University Publishing.
Squaresoft. 1997. *Final Fantasy VII*. [PlayStation]. Tokyo: Square Co.
—2001. *Final Fantasy X*. [PlayStation 2]. Los Angeles: Square Electronic Arts.
Thompson, Peter. 2000. 'Brecht and actor training.' In *Twentieth Century Actor Training*, ed. Allison Hodge. London: Routledge.
Whitehead, Anne. 2009. *Memory*. London: Routledge.
Wolford, Lisa. 2000. 'Grotowski's vision of the actor.' In *Twentieth Century Actor Training*, ed. Allison Hodge, 191–208. London: Routledge.

7

Risky Business: Neo-liberal Rationality and the Computer RPG

ANDREW BAERG

Duergar attacks Khelgar Ironfist: *hit*: (20+2=22: Threat roll: 9+2=11). Messages like these frequently appear as players engage hostile characters in Obsidian Entertainment's computer role-playing game (hereafter CRPG), *Neverwinter Nights 2* (hereafter *NwN2*). Veterans of the *Advanced Dungeons & Dragons* (hereafter *AD&D*) game series recognize the opening sentence as an indication of the success or failure of a given combat sequence. Spells are cast, weapons deployed, hit points lost and experience points accrued. The quantitative way in which these combat sequences are mediated plays an important role in the game's positioning of the player, the player's experience of the game, and the unfolding of *NwN2's* narrative. Numbers also play a vital role in character creation, inventory, or even social relations between characters.

To address why this quantification occurs and to speak to its significance is to begin to look more broadly at the political and social context of the CRPG's game mechanics. By exploring these questions, the chapter takes Konzack's desire for philosophical thinking about digital games seriously (Konzack 2009, 34) by reflecting on how the CRPG manifests certain forms of rationality – what Rose defines as 'a set of "intellectual techniques" for rendering reality thinkable and practicable'(Rose 1996, 42). The paper grounds its argument in Foucault's lectures on biopolitics and liberalism (Sennelart, 2008) and Beck's work on the contemporary risk society (Beck, 2009) to focus on the mediation of the CRPG narrative. If, as McLuhan argues (McLuhan 1994, 235), games function as faithful models of culture, then we should be able to examine the CRPG for its modeling of late twentieth- and early twenty-first century forms of rationality.

This essay argues that it is no coincidence that the digital RPG should become popular in a contemporary context in which the dominant political ideology has been neo-liberalism. The chapter begins by providing a brief overview of the CRPG's history. It then situates the CRPG in the context of neo-liberal governmental rationalities of calculation and risk-management. The essay concludes by theorizing about how these rationalities are expressed and naturalized through the CRPG. *NwN2* serves as the primary illustration of how this rationality manifests itself in a prominent CRPG. By making these claims, the chapter helps explain the genre's popularity, explains its role in mediating a specific form of power (see Friedline and Collister's chapter for an additional argument on power), while also opening up a space for critiquing some of its gameplay mechanics. The chapter also illustrates how governmental rationalities potentially express themselves in traditionally non-governmental spaces.

Brief History of the RPG

To begin this discussion, it is important to briefly survey the history of the CRPG. Fine locates the roots of the RPG in the war games and fantasy literature of the 1950s and 1960s. War games had originated in the Prussian armies during the late eighteenth and early nineteenth centuries but began to be more broadly popular in the

1950s (Fine 1983, 8). Fantasy literature, particularly Tolkien's *The Lord of the Rings* series, also became popular during this period. Both of these pursuits coalesced to inspire the creation of the RPG in the 1970s. Barton adds the card and dice-based statistical gameplay of the tabletop sports simulation games of the 1960s and 1970s to this origin narrative as well (Barton 2008, 14–15).

One of the first prominent RPGs was Gary Gygax and Dave Arneson's *Dungeons & Dragons* (*D&D*), initially published in 1974 by Tactical Studies Rules (TSR). Arneson had adapted the war game format to include fantasy settings and to focus more narrowly on single characters rather than large-scale armies. Gygax integrated a systematic means of combat resolution into Arneson's individual, fantasy war game and *D&D* was born. The *D&D* system involved many elements that have become commonplace for ensuing RPGs, including experience points for defeating monsters and completing quests, the ability to gain levels with accompanying skill and ability improvements, and hit points that determine how much damage a character could receive without being killed (Barton 2008, 5). The game initially struggled for sales, selling only 1000 copies in its first eleven months (Fine 1983, 15). However, by the early 1980s, *D&D* and its updated sequel, *AD&D*, could be found in bookstores and popular toy retailers. By 1982, *D&D* had been translated into fourteen languages and was circulating around the world (MacKay 2001, 15).

The late 1970s would also witness the advent of the personal computer. These computers became the hardware driving the forerunners of the contemporary CRPG. Text-based interactive fiction, early graphical adventure games and action-adventure games preoccupied players with quest narratives motivating role play. The *D&D* system was quickly adapted for the computer as well (Howard 2008, 12). Barton links the CRPG's popularity to these increasingly prevalent computers and jobs requiring data management (Barton 2008, 15). The computer altered the role-playing game by effectively becoming the gamemaster or dungeon master guiding the RPG's narrative and calculating the outcomes of player dice rolls (Barton 2008, 21–3).

Alongside the technological context of the CRPG's rise to popularity, the social context also proved important. MacKay theorizes that the RPG emerged out of a popular desire to escape the ideological confusion of the 1960s and 1970s. With Vietnam, Watergate, the oil crisis, and the fading of the rock-and-roll revolution, the RPG occupied a cultural space of clarity where good and evil could be clearly defined. This move to clarity was also resident in the many fantasy and science fiction films produced during this period as well (MacKay 2001, 21).

Barton's and MacKay's arguments both provide viable explanations of the genre's popularity. This chapter complements their work by focusing on the RPG's game mechanics and its grounding rationality. Barton briefly explains the economic context of the CRPG's ascension, but does not link game mechanics to this context. MacKay locates the RPG as a space of moral clarity, but does not interrogate how game mechanics situate this morality. This chapter argues for the importance of linking the CRPG's game mechanics to a broader political context. In order to examine this context, the ensuing section discusses this context in greater depth, a context characterized by neo-liberalism.

Neo-liberalism and Risk Management

CRPGs ascend to popularity during a period in which the dominant political ideology has been, and continues to be, neo-liberalism. In order to understand neo-liberalism, it is important to look back to its liberal predecessor. By tracing how the state came to emphasize limited government during the eighteenth century and how the market became a key site for the expression of limited government, Foucault explains how free market practices became the model for governmental practice. This development would come to be known as liberalism. In liberalism, the free market would allow for goods to be bought and sold at 'natural' prices reflecting supply and demand. These 'natural' prices became akin to truth, a truth that would theoretically lead to prosperity. Foucault suggests that in much the same way that the free market was assumed to foster 'natural' prices and encourage prosperity, so too liberal governments assumed that subjects operating within 'natural' spaces of freedom would prosper (Foucault 2008, 31–2).

Although this liberalism faded during the nineteenth and early twentieth centuries, it found renewed popularity in the development of neo-liberalism following the American New Deal and European post-war reconstruction. In a return to an older liberalism, the neo-liberal market was thought to oversee and legitimate the state (Foucault 2008, 102, 116–17). This popularity, and its accompanying emphasis on free markets, reached its zenith with the Thatcher and Reagan administrations of the late 1970s and early 1980s (Rose 1999, 27, 167). Since that time, neo-liberalism has become the pre-eminent global political ideology (Harvey 2005, 9).

The move to neo-liberalism and its emphasis on free markets invariably has consequences for those who live within it. Neo-liberalism allows subjects to become exposed to an increasing degree of choice and these choices go beyond the economic sphere. Foucault argues that neo-liberalism generalizes free market principles to the entire social body, even to areas previously unrelated to the economic (Foucault 2008, 243). Whether these be micro-institutions of the family through relational practices such marriage and child-rearing, or macro-institutions of schools, universities and hospitals, multiple cultural domains begin to be understood through the lens of the free market (Rose 1999, 146, 152).

As part of this marketization of society, neo-liberalism transforms the subject into what Foucault calls the 'active economic subject' (Foucault 2008, 223) or *homo economicus*. In keeping with this subject's operation in the free market and the market's extension into a neo-liberal political context, *homo economicus* functions from a utilitarian perspective as one who must freely choose how to maximize scarce resources. Cost-benefit analysis becomes vital to the subject who becomes an entrepreneur of the self, one who, under conditions of freedom, must make responsible decisions to prosper (Burchell 1996, 26; Rose 1996, 59; Rose 1999, 46; Dean 1999, 152; Binkley 2006, 344). Neo-liberal subjects must learn how to make responsible decisions in a context fraught with risk, given the consequences these choices potentially yield. Foucault argues that a neo-liberal society will not insulate its subjects from these risks, but move them to privately protect themselves (Foucault 2008, 144).

Sociologist Ulrich Beck sees these privatized responsibilization processes as a necessary part of existence in what he calls the 'risk society' (Beck 1992). In the risk society, institutional responsibility and concern for individual fears fades such that individuals are left to deal with insecurity on their own. Consequently, subjects living in the risk society must possess '*the ability to anticipate and endure dangers*' (Beck 1992, 76) to avoid problematic outcomes. Beck argues that the individual's role in dealing with this danger serves as 'an *essential cultural qualification*' (Beck 1992, 76). Subjects simply must be able to engage risk to function within the risk society. Assessing risk and its potentials becomes an ordinary part of neo-liberal life (Kenny 2005, 50).

How do subjects go about engaging this risk? Beck argues that risks can only be rendered visible in the contemporary situation through the extended senses of the scientific. As such, risk is contingent on scientific knowledge and the causal interpretation this knowledge brings to risk. This knowledge is often grounded in a constant assessment of the future, a future where threats must be prevented from being actualized. Risk renders this future present. For Beck, the projected threat subsequently shapes present personal and political action. To ignore risk is to ignore one's tangible needs (Beck 1992, 23, 32–4, 45).

These risks are specifically rendered visible through a scientifically inflected rationality oriented around calculation. As such, risk not only renders the future present, but also renders this future world through a grid of calculative rationality. Risk becomes legible and discernible through quantification (Dean 1999, 178). Risks are 'fundamentally *localized,* mathematical condensations of wounded images of a life worth living' (Beck 1992, 28). In being mathematical condensations, risks are inexorably linked to scientific conceptualizations of risk. Beck argues that failing to attend to risk through the intellectual grid of the quantified is to be either irrational or luddite (Beck 1992, 57). As such, calculative rationalities become one of the most prominent ways in which this risk is assessed and managed (Rose 1999, 214). An important part of becoming a responsible *homo economicus* involves decision-making undergirded by this scientifically oriented quantitative rationality. Weighing the costs and benefits of respective choices by looking at numbers becomes a way to engage risk in a neo-liberal society where the logic of risk is ubiquitous (Beck 2009, 12).

Given the emphasis on risk management in neo-liberalism, it should come as no surprise that one of the foremost figures in the history of RPGs should be directly linked to dealing with risk through the framework of quantitative rationality. Gary Gygax, the inventor of *D&D*, was an insurance underwriter prior to devoting himself entirely to his creation (Kushner 2008, par.13). To manage risk through ever more far-reaching quantification sits at the core of actuarialism, a discipline deeply linked to Gygax's insurance industry. O'Malley links this actuarialism to a calculative rationality by speaking of how actuarial practices become internalized in the rational neo-liberal subject who subsequently acts as a calculating self (O'Malley 1996, 197). In keeping with Gygax's occupational background, his major contribution to the RPG was 'the way in which he quantized everything in the narratives of his games' (Konzack 2009, 37). Evidently, Gygax applied an insurance-based approach in mediating events in *D&D*.

Over the last thirty years, neo-liberal principles began to be expressed in other non-economic social phenomena (see examples from Crook 2007; Langley 2006; Nadesan 2008). As Voorhees also argues in this volume, albeit in a different way, the rest of this chapter illustrates how neo-liberalism finds its way into one of these phenomena, the CRPG.

Neo-liberal Risk Management Illustrated: *Neverwinter Nights 2*

To illustrate how a neo-liberal rationality of calculation and risk management occurs in the CRPG, I turn to Obsidian Entertainment's *NwN2*. *NwN2* was chosen as representative given its links to an *AD&D* system that includes the conventions of character creation and development, equipment, the party, quests, and combat. Not all CRPGs include these features; however, most CRPGs have been influenced by this *D&D-based* system at some level.

Character Creation

Upon clicking the 'New Game' option in the main menu, *NwN2* takes the player to a character creation screen. From the outset, *NwN2*'s character creation process positions the player within a neo-liberally inflected space. As Voorhees argues in this volume with respect to the *Mass Effect* series, players can freely select from myriad combinations of races, skills, and attributes. Although not unique to the CRPG genre, players have the latitude to fashion their primary character as they see fit (for alternate perspectives on this process see chapters from Moran, McDowell, and Bealer). This freedom is rarely afforded in first-person shooters, adventure games and platformer games. The choices players make in character creation occupy a major role in how the action in the game unfolds.

Upon creating a new character, players are prompted to select the character's race. To select a race affects one's abilities in the game, one's capacity as Moran suggests in this volume. *NwN2* provides a tab explaining the qualitative description of each race, but this is balanced by a second tab featuring each race's base statistics. These statistics represent the conventional *AD&D* categories of strength, dexterity, constitution, intelligence, wisdom, and charisma. In keeping with its *AD&D* rule base, dice rolls determine the player's initial character attributes. The selected race also contributes to the number of hit points a character might possess and how these hit points will accrue throughout the game. More powerful races like dwarves and orcs will be assigned a larger number of hit points than a comparatively frail race like elves. These hit points play a large role in how much damage a character can absorb before dying.

Upon getting into the game proper, the character profile window reveals even more data. Players see the character's portrait, attributes, saves, race, class, and active weapon. Numbers feature prominently in being attached to these variables. Characters are quantified in attributes like strength, dexterity, and intelligence, and in saves by being assigned ratings in fortitude, will, and reflex. The character's total number of experience points is listed alongside how many additional points will be needed to level up. The profile also provides data depicting the character's armor class, attack bonus with the equipped weapon, damage potentially inflicted with that weapon, existing ability to resist spells, and his/her armor check penalty. All of these numbers provide the player with a representation of a given character's strengths and potential areas for improvement.

No matter the character's race and gender or skills and attributes, all characters remain beholden to the quantitative system undergirding their capacity to act in the virtual world. Players have the freedom to select a variety of races, sexes, and moral alignments; however, by framing the player's character as a series of numbers, the player is positioned to understand her avatar in a neo-liberal entrepreneurial manner. From the moment the character creation process begins, players are positioned to carefully examine the risks associated with selecting elves as opposed to humans, males as opposed to females, rangers as opposed to sorcerers, and lawful good as opposed to chaotic evil. Each choice allows for a raft of potential benefits and dangers. All of these risks are rendered visible through available quantitative data. Without the data, selecting an elf means little more than choosing a human. As such, players are encouraged to identify with an assessment of the self in keeping with the numbers presented to them. Selecting a character and allocating that character's attributes becomes an exercise in neo-liberal risk management.

The allocation of attributes reaches its apotheosis in the notion of the optimal build. With optimal builds, players create the most efficient, effective characters the game allows. A series of rules, grounded in various calculations, arises governing how character and party advancement ought to occur to achieve maximum efficiency. The optimal build begins from the creation of the player's character and continues as other characters are added to the party. Acquiring experience points and leveling up becomes an exercise in maximizing each character's abilities, the party's resources and minimizing any potential risks. Creating an optimal build takes cost-benefit analysis to an extreme in embodying the neo-liberal entrepreneurial self.

Equipment

This neo-liberalism also extends into the character's equipment. *NwN2's* character profile window links to a window featuring the conventional CRPG inventory. The mere appearance of the term 'inventory' as the descriptor of a character's equipment collection speaks to the notion of the neo-liberal free market and the entrepreneurial self. To label the equipment as part of an inventory implies that it has value in a market. Even though the typical CRPG gameworld exists in an approximately medieval space, the commodification of items resonates with free market principles (see Castronova 2003, 2004). Merchant NPCs will always be willing to purchase the party's goods in *NwN2*, thus making every piece of equipment translatable into virtual gold.

As with the character creation process, inventory is also related to the capacity and power (see Moran, Call, and Friedline and Collister in this volume for other perspectives on these issues) of the neo-liberal entrepreneurial self. *NwN2* consistently positions the player to consider how various items might be employed in different situations. Some items have magical abilities that empower a character in a given gameplay sequence (see Figure 7.1).

Figure 7.1 The character Sand. Note the Aido Wither Stick with its Enhancement Bonus and Ability Drain properties (Obsidian Entertainment 2006).

A sword might inflict shock damage or a ring might provide additional resistance to opposition spells. Selecting one item over another might benefit the party during a given battle, but be less useful against another opponent. These principles not only apply offensively with respect to weapons, but defensively to armor. Maximizing a character's Armor Class (AC) becomes an exercise in discerning the characteristics of a given cloak or piece of chain mail in specific contexts where the armor is used. As with weapons, some pieces of armor may more effectively protect a character from particular attacks than others. That the context in which these items are used is dynamic means that players must constantly be aware about whether or not certain items are maximally beneficial. Simultaneously, players must also take advantage of opportunities for upgrading items in their inventory that fail to meet this standard. Inventory items also contribute to the efficient development of optimal builds as well. By positioning players to exercise this constant assessment of their inventory, *NwN2* fosters an entrepreneurial approach to gameplay.

The entrepreneurial self is also articulated to the inventory via *NwN2*'s market mechanism. Inventories can become full of items that can be sold to accrue virtual capital, which can then be used to purchase more powerful items, thus maximizing the resources available for advancement in the game and bettering the entrepreneurial self. In *NwN2*, different items may fetch different prices in different game areas, and character development points can be applied to the appraise skill that maximizes a character's ability to get the best deal in the market. As such, the player is positioned to act as *homo economicus* by maximizing the acquisition of capital and goods that indexes the player's power within the gameworld. *Homo economicus* is strengthened and develops through the acquisition of virtual capital.

To reflect on the player's character and inventory is to see a heavily quantified zone of action. Failing to acknowledge how different choices improve the player's position in the game or damage any hope of completing quests is to ignore one of *NwN2*'s primary game mechanics. Players simply must manage this data to progress in the game. Items must be assessed to discern their effect on the character's abilities and this assessment can only occur through an analysis of the quantitative data the game provides. Haphazardly selecting equipment that makes one's character more aesthetically pleasing may be interesting, but will prevent the player from completing *NwN2*'s quests. Thus, the way one succeeds in *NwN2* is to adopt a neo-liberal rationality.

Quests

Not only does *NwN2*'s character creation and equipment system express a neo-liberal political rationality, but the game's character advancement process also expresses this rationality as well. Typically, a player's character advances her initial skills and attributes through the quest mechanic. Howard defines the quest as 'a journey across a symbolic, fantastic landscape in which a protagonist or player collects objects and talks to characters in order to overcome challenges and achieve a meaningful goal' (Howard 2008, xi). Howard goes on to suggest that game designers can use older forms of quest literature along with the scholarship of literary theorists who have studied this work to inform their narratives (Howard 2008, xiii). Even as Howard locates continuities between quest literature and the contemporary RPG, his work does not address how these narratives are transformed and their meanings shaped by digital mediation.

For Howard, the quest enables the player to choose a path 'in accord with her own sense of self' (Howard 2008, 5) and 'to overcome difficulties and to better oneself, both in the virtual form of one's "avatar" and in the real-world skills developed through extended playing' (Howard 2008, 27). Although this may be accurate, Howard does not address in great depth how this choice is made. One might question whether these paths do indeed become a product of one's own sense of self. If quantitative rationalities ground the narrative's unfolding, then this sense of self does not revolve around one's own sense of self, but rather around the game's construction of this sense of self.

Although specifically addressing the MMORPG, Dickey outlines six general quest forms, four of which can be found in *NwN2* (Dickey 2007, 261–3). These four quests include: (1) the bounty quest requiring an enemy's defeat; (2) the Fed Ex quest requiring a specific item's delivery; (3) the collection quest requiring the gathering of certain items; and (4) the messenger quest requiring the location of and subsequent discussion with an NPC. These quests become meaningful for the way they shape the player's experience in the virtual world, how they give the player a greater sense of the narrative within this world, and how they allow for a deeper understanding of the symbolic meaning of a player's actions (Howard 2008, 20–6). Although Howard may be correct about the ways quests become meaningful, how these quests are accomplished is just as important for considering their meaning as the experience of the quest's narrative and its symbolic meaning. Without necessarily alluding to the idea in a direct way, Dickey recognizes how the CRPG positions the player as *homo economicus* when it comes to quest completion. She argues that players tend to select 'the most economical way to complete a variety of small quests in the most travel-efficient way' (Dickey 2007, 261). The 'most economical way' to complete a quest is to maximize resources, a maximization that can only be comprehended through the data attached to characters and their inventories.

Managing risk also serves as an important element in the quest. Completing quests involves 'active, goal-directed effort, often in the form of balancing long-term and short-term goals' (Howard 2008, 1). Discerning whether to complete the side quest and deviate from the primary narrative arc means assessing whether one's party has the requisite levels and experience points needed to pursue the main thrust of the game. In a neo-liberal manner, a CRPG such as *NwN2* positions the player to carefully measure the costs and benefits of proceeding to the quest's next major goal.

Occasional quests require the player to influence other characters in one's party (see Travis in this volume for other examples). This influence can be accrued in general social relations and through the moral choices the game establishes. In *NwN2*, numbers also play a vital role in social relations and in morality, both with characters in the player's party and those without. At various points, the player is prompted to discuss a given issue with members of the party. Dialogue choices appear that can make the player's primary character more amenable or disagreeable to other characters. For example, discussions with Khelgar, *NwN2*'s combat-hungry dwarf, often revolve around whether a conflict should be addressed through diplomacy or battle. Selecting dialogue that privileges aggressive resolutions will cause Khelgar to relate to the player's character more favorably. At the conclusion of these types of conversation, the game signals the outcome with a phrase like '+1 relations with Khelgar' or '–1 relations with Khelgar'.

This quantified social relation also appears in *NwN2*'s moral system. Killing a helpless character may yield messages like '+1 chaotic evil' while showing mercy to the same character might yield a message like '+1 lawful good.' Hayse suggests that some CRPGs integrate what he terms a 'moral economy' into gameplay, such that different decisions move the player's character along a continuum of numerical values (Hayse 2010, 35). The situation is no different in *NwN2*. Although players never see the precise value of their relationship to other characters and can never truly gauge their moral status, *NwN2* clearly situates social relations and morality as something only discernible through numbers.

Combat

The most explicitly quantified social relation and its accompanying connection to the quest is articulated to combat. As Beck argues, calculations make visible dangers that would otherwise be invisible (Beck 1992, 28). As gamers encounter *NwN2*'s hostile NPCs, they have little ability to discern the threat these opponents present. However, once engaged in combat, players are afforded data enabling them to assess whether or not defeating an opponent(s) is possible.

In *NwN2*, combat is always resolved through a series of calculations. Yet, *NwN2* positions players to think about combat quantitatively well before engaging any enemies. A character's attacking and defending abilities are linked to her attribute ratings, but also to her equipped weapons and armor. A magically enhanced sword with the following properties might be brought to a battle: Attack Bonus +25/+20/+15/+10; Damage 1–8 +1 (Critical 19–20/x2); +4 Physical Damage; +1D12 Magical Damage vs. Outsiders. The character might partner that sword with armor featuring the following characteristics: Base Armor Class 8; Maximum Dexterity Bonus 1; Armor Check Penalty –6; Special Properties of Armor Bonus +1, Resistance to Piercing 5/- and Slashing 5/-. These numbers measure the character's total offensive and defensive capacity. Different combinations of gear yield different benefits while simultaneously potentially opening up the character to particular vulnerabilities. Responsibly equipping characters entails that players manage potential risks by looking to the quantified nature of weapons and armor to exact maximum future damage and suffer minimal future harm. The ways the game positions players to assess equipment potentially leads to complex calculations about what types of gear best serve the player's goals.

Once in combat, players are provided with the results of the confrontation in a highly transparent way, given the presence of an action window in the bottom left corner of the screen (see Figure 7.2).

Figure 7.2 Calculations are presented to the player in the game's primary message window (Obsidian Entertainment 2006).

This action window presents the player with equations governing the success of her actions. These equations derive from the interaction between an attacking character's offensive power and a defender's defensive power. Each attacking action is assigned a quantitative value that is measured against the value of the target's defenses. The result of the attack is then subtracted from the defender's total hit points. As an example, players might see a message like 'Khelgar Ironfist attacks Elite Vampire: *hit*: (20+23=43: Threat Roll: 20+23=43)'. Players can use these equations to carefully analyze the effectiveness of their attacks and defense to consider which strategies worked and which failed.

To further emphasize the importance of numbers in combat and their connection to a character's life, successful attacks are visually represented in the main window with red numbers. After being hit for damage, characters literally bleed numbers as a red digit briefly appears to depict how much harm a sword thrust or fireball inflicted (see Figure 7.3).

Figure 7.3 The numbers presented in the explosion at the top of the screen represent loss of life (Obsidian Entertainment 2006).

In *NwN2*, numbers not only represent life, but are directly equated to life itself.

Given the importance of numbers to the resolution of combat, this conflict takes on a neo-liberal hue. Combat simply cannot occur and be resolved in the game without being mediated through quantification. Players may attempt to work around the system by equipping their characters with gear they find most aesthetically pleasing, but this choice will not allow for progress in the game unless an assessment of the quantitative value of this equipment occurs. To fail to progress through the game is to ostensibly play irresponsibly. Not only does this move to resolve game events mirror how insurance companies have increasingly transformed social relations in conflicts into 'a technical, calculable matter' (Dean 1999, 185), but it also positions players to adopt a responsible, risk-management approach to conflict.

The party undergirds much of the combat in *NwN2*. *D&D* creator Gary Gygax has noted how the collective nature of the RPG mirrors everyday experience:

> There is a message contained in the true role-playing game. It is the message of the difficulty of surviving alone […] The inability of the lone individual to cope with every challenge is evident in RPGs and reflects life. (MacKay 2001, 9)

Much like other CRPGs, a solitary character cannot complete all of the game's quests. *NwN2* forces cooperation with other characters, in that upon leaving certain areas of the gameworld, a window appears requiring the player to select a party that accompanies the player's character to the next region. Some game events require the presence of specific NPCs and these NPCs are automatically added to the party.

It could be argued that Gygax's insistence on the party's necessity resists a neo-liberal emphasis on individual responsibility through risk management. It would appear that a collective is vital to the completion of *NwN2*'s quests. Yet, in spite of Gygax's assertion about the inability of the individual to deal with life alone, the party in the CRPG remains under the control of a single player. The player becomes responsible for the ultimate fate of the party. As a result, the apparently collective nature of quest completion is subsumed under the banner of individualism. The party essentially becomes an extension of the gaming self and must be actively managed in keeping with a neo-liberal management of the self.

It is this active management of all of the aforementioned elements of *NwN2* that responsibilize the player. This responsibilization process brings the various facets of *NwN2* together under the banner of neo-liberal political rationality. The way the game mediates the narrative through these discourses of quantification positions the player within the sphere of rational choice, but a sphere oriented primarily around numbers. Players make decisions through a quantitative rationality that enfolds them within the parameters of risk management. From character creation, to handling virtual goods, to relationships between characters, to completing quests to the development of the player's party, numbers exist ubiquitously in the experience. Managing risk rationally by working through *NwN2*'s number-rich gameworld means responsibly maximizing the resources available within it. In the same way, managing risk rationally by working through the numbers in a neo-liberal world means responsibly functioning as a citizen by maximizing the resources to which one freely has access.

Certainly, managing virtual risk pales in comparison to the risks faced by individuals in the real world. Saving Neverwinter may be inconsequential in the face of dealing with economic downturns, flu pandemics, and protecting one's children from sexual predators. However, it is the rationality behind the game mechanics involved in saving Neverwinter that becomes important for understanding how to live in the contemporary situation. *NwN2* both mirrors and naturalizes a neo-liberal approach to living for those who play it.

Conclusion

The arguments presented here must be understood as provisional. The RPG and CRPG continue to shift and change. Undoubtedly, as the prevailing political and social context changes, the rationalities of games within the RPG genre will continue to change as well. Perhaps the CRPGs that have been so heavily influenced by Gygax's quantitative *AD&D* system will become relics of the past as new political rationalities arise.

These arguments also apply more directly to offline CRPGs. As CRPG players increasingly move toward greater participation in MMORPGs, one wonders whether these ideas continue to apply. Although some work on governance in MMORPGs has been done (see Humphreys 2008), additional questions could be asked about whether these discourses are relevant in the context of MMORPGs with their highly collaborative raids and the development of Dragon Kill Points (see Malone 2009). Will neo-liberal rationalities persist in networked RPG environments?

This essay has the potential to shape future CRPG design. Howard looks at Joseph Campbell's notion of the hero's journey and argues that an uninspired reiteration of this journey will yield imitations of films like *Star Wars*. If the hero's journey can be individualized in keeping with the Western medieval romance, Howard sees the potential for original forms of questing in the CRPG (Howard 2008, 6–7). This chapter challenges this position by suggesting that no matter how original the CRPG's quest narrative, if game mechanics continue in the conventional form depicted above, the execution of that quest remains embedded in neo-liberal discourses of quantitative risk management. By establishing this position, the chapter opens up a space for critiquing existing CRPG mechanics and potentially challenging the form of future titles in the genre.

References

Barton, Matt. 2008. *Dungeons and Desktops: The History of Computer Role-Playing Games*. Wellesley, MA: A. K. Peters.

Beck, Ulrich. 1992. *Risk Society: Towards a New Modernity*. London and Newbury Park, CA: Sage.

—2009. *World at Risk*. Trans. Ciaran Cronin. Cambridge and Malden, MA: Polity Press.

Binkley, Sam. 2006. 'The Perilous Freedoms of Consumption: Toward a Theory of the Conduct of Consumer Conduct.' *Journal for Cultural Research* 10: 343–62.

Burchell, Graham. 1996. 'Liberal Government and Techniques of the Self.' In *Foucault and Political Reason: Liberalism, Neo-Liberalism and Rationalities of Government*, ed. Andrew Barry, Thomas Osborne and Nikolas Rose, 19–36. London: UCL Press Limited.

Castronova, Edward. 2003. 'On Virtual Economies.' *Game Studies: The International Journal of Computer Game Research* 3, no.2. http://www.gamestudies.org/0302/castronova/.

—2004. 'The Price of Bodies: A Hedonic Pricing Model of Avatar Attributes in a Synthetic World.' *Kyklos* 57: 173–96.

Crook, Tom. 2007. 'Power, Privacy and Pleasure: Liberalism and the Modern Cubicle.' *Cultural Studies* 21: 549–69.

Dean, Mitchell. 1999. *Governmentality: Power and Rule in Modern Society*. London: Sage.

Dickey, Michele D. 2007. 'Game Design and Learning: A Conjectural Analysis of How Massively Multiple Online Role-Playing Games

(MMORPGs) Foster Intrinsic Motivation.' *Educational Technology Research & Development* 55: 253–73.
Fine, Gary Alan. 1983. *Shared Fantasy: Role-Playing Games as Social Worlds*. Chicago and London: University of Chicago Press.
Foucault, Michel. *Birth of Biopolitics: Lectures at the College de France, 1978–79*, ed. Michel Senellart. New York: Palgrave MacMillan.
Gygax, Gary and David Arneson. 1974. *Dungeons & Dragons*. [Game]. Tactical Studies Rules.
Harvey, David. 2005. *A Brief History of Neoliberalism*. New York: Oxford University Press.
Hayse, Mark. 2010. 'Ultima IV: Simulating the Religious Quest.' In *Halos and Avatars: Playing Video Games with God*, edited by Craig Detweiler, 34–46. Louisville, KY: Westminster John Knox Press.
Howard, Jeff. 2008. *Quests: Design, Theory, and History in Games and Narratives*. Wellesley, MA: A. K. Peters.
Humphreys, Sal. 2008. 'Ruling the Virtual World: Governance in Massively Multiplayer Online Games.' *European Journal of Cultural Studies* 11: 149–71.
Kenny, Sue. 2005. 'Terrify and Control: The Politics of Risk Society.' *Social Alternatives* 24: 50–4.
Konzack, Lars. 2009. 'Philosophical Game Design.' In *The Video Game Theory Reader 2*, edited by Bernard Perron and Mark J. P. Wolf, 33–44. New York and London: Routledge.
Kushner, David. 2008. 'Dungeon master: The life and legacy of Gary Gygax.' *Wired Magazine*, Accessed March 10, 2008. http://www.wired.com/gaming/ virtualworlds/news/2008/03/ ff_gygax?currentPage=1.
Langley, Paul. 2006. 'The Making of Investor Subjects in Anglo-American Pensions.' *Environment and Planning D, Society & Space* 24: 919–34.
MacKay, Daniel. 2001. *The Fantasy Role-Playing Game: A New Performing Art*. Jefferson, North Carolina and London: McFarland & Company, Inc., Publishers.
Malone, Krista-Lee. 2009. 'Dragon Kill Points: The Economics of Power Gamers.' *Games and Culture* 4: 296–316.
McLuhan, Marshall. 1994. *Understanding Media: The Extensions of Man*. Cambridge, MA: MIT Press.
Nadesan, Majia Holmer. 2008. 'Hurricane Katrina: Governmentality, Risk, and Responsibility.' *Controversia* 6: 67–90.
Obsidian Entertainment. *Neverwinter Nights 2*. [PC]. Atari: Irvine, CA, 2006.
O'Malley, Pat. 1996. 'Risk and Responsibility.' In *Foucault and Political Reason: Liberalism, Neo-Liberalism and Rationalities of Government*, ed. Andrew Barry, Thomas Osborne and Nikolas Rose, 189–208. Chicago, IL: The University of Chicago Press.

Rose, Nikolas. 1996. 'Governing 'Advanced' Liberal Democracies.' In *Foucault and Political Reason: Liberalism, Neo-Liberalism and Rationalities of Government*, ed. Andrew Barry, Thomas Osborne and Nikolas Rose, 37–64. Chicago, IL: The University of Chicago Press.
—1999. *Powers of Freedom: Reframing Political Thought*. Cambridge: Cambridge University Press.
Senellart, Michel. Ed. 2008. *The Birth of Biopolitics: Lectures at the College de France, 1978–79*. New York: Palgrave Macmillan.

8

Postcards from the Other Side: Interactive Revelation in Post-Apocalyptic RPGs

ZACHARY MCDOWELL[1]

Turning and turning in the widening gyre
The falcon cannot hear the falconer;
Things fall apart; the centre cannot hold;
Mere anarchy is loosed upon the world
WILLIAM BUTLER YEATS, 'THE SECOND COMING'

War… war never changes
NARRATOR, *FALLOUT*

The award-winning *Fallout* DRPG series casts the player into a post-apocalyptic future filled with mutants, bandits, destruction, and decay. Released in 1997, *Fallout: A Post Nuclear Roleplaying Game* (Interplay 1997) spawned a series of sequels: *Fallout 2* (Interplay 1998), *Fallout 3* (Bethesda 2008), and *Fallout: New Vegas* (Bethesda 2010)[2]. The *Fallout* series of games seem to be inspired from an earlier game, entitled *Wasteland* (Electronic Arts 1987) (Barton 2007), rekindling *Wasteland*'s journey of survival and salvation in the remains of civilization after nuclear war. Although *Wasteland* is not considered to be part of the *Fallout* series, many of the narrative elements are similar, allowing for it to be read as part of a series that actually originated ten years before the first *Fallout* game arose. These underlying narrative elements can be seen to engage multiple generations of gamers with the structure of the post-apocalyptic DRPG. Borrowing heavily from 1960s' nuclear scare propaganda, as well as many of the thematic elements from *Wasteland*, *Fallout* (especially *Fallout 3* and *Fallout: New Vegas*) brings these elements together in a kind of 'future past' – a temporal dislocation that is both a future beyond our time, and also a nostalgic throwback to a time which many players never experienced outside of other narratives. As seen in Figure 8.1, this strange conglomeration of temporal characteristics creates a landscape that is both familiar and alien at

Figure 8.1 The Landscape of Washington DC is both familiar and impossibly marred by catastrophe (Bethesda 2008).

the same time; the wasteland remains an uncanny environment that is both future and past.

Like most DRPGs, both the *Fallout* series and *Wasteland* place the player in control of avatars that, while not always apparent to the player at the beginning of the game, are key to the preservation of the human race (or at least fighting off some element that promises imminent dystopia). A few of the *Fallout* series even refer to the main character as the 'Chosen One'. A common thread among these post-apocalyptic RPGs is that all of them take place in an environment apparently ravaged by a massive, world-changing, cataclysmic nuclear war in which the future relies upon the avatar(s) the player controls; put simply, the gameworld depends on the player's actions.

On the surface, the post-apocalyptic journey is one of survival in a temporally 'post'-cataclysmic environment. Whether it is a brutal human, a vicious creature, or the hostile environment, at every turn something attempts to end the avatar's existence. These games are violent by design in more ways than one, often placing the avatar in situations where they must not only kill, but also make decisions that pit the lives of different groups impossibly against each other. However, these games engage survival and cataclysm only on the surface, and remaining mired in a shallow reading of a rich and complex environment risks missing the underlying structures that compose the post-apocalyptic journey. There is a subtler journey that must begin beforehand for any narrative of human survival to commence: the journey of the player. The journey is not one of desert raiders, of sentient computers, or of nuclear holocaust, but the communicative subject in dialogue with herself. In the immersive and expansive post-apocalyptic gameworld, the communicative subject must engage herself in playing the game. This essay illustrates how, through these games, the player does not just face the aftermath of war, but also a process of communication where the player engages herself in a post-apocalyptic structure. This engagement is primarily one of communication, and therefore the 'game' becomes not one of entertainment but the space of communication. Rather than the commonplace thinking of communication as the exchange of messages, I would like to emphasize the original flavor of the concept, from the Latin *communicare*: sharing, as sharing implies a distance. If the journey is not one of sharing, then there would be no journey at all – nothing could be engaged. Something must be shared, whether it is the player and the game, the player and the avatar, or something else entirely. There must be something that brings the two together for a journey to take place at all. However, as with all journeys, there must always be something dividing the two – there must be space for movement. This essay will illustrate, through reconsidering the common-sense terms implied in the 'post-apocalyptic RPG', how the structure of the game refuses the 'end times' and instead makes space for the possibility of communication.

Apocalypse Where?

The apocalypse is big business these days. Millions of dollars are spent on various media every year[3]. Television shows, films, and videogames offering representations of post-apocalyptic existence are more popular than ever before. However, the common-sense consideration of post-apocalypse still relies both on the understanding of apocalypse through the Christian-vernacular 'end times' and the temporal consideration of *post* as 'after' an event. Although *Fallout* and *Wasteland* seem to mime these understandings, both of these terms remain less helpful when reconsidering the significance of the post-apocalyptic tale. It is useful to identify that the apocalypse does not simply imply 'the end', of course, but, as Derrida reminds us, revelation. From the Greek *apokálypsis*, to uncover or reveal, 'apocalypse means revelation, of truth, un-veiling' (Derrida 1984, 24), a *final* destruction, a final revelation. There is no locating a history past this point, as all of history has been foreclosed upon. The truth must be absolute and total, or, as Derrida continues, 'no truth, no apocalypse'. However, what Derrida plainly states remains surprisingly complex (as most Derridian statements often are). Apocalypse refers to totality, and therefore revelation, truth, and unveiling of apocalypse all refer to totalities. These totalities are transcendental, not just a simple reading of words, but complete knowledge. Without bounds, totality renders mute any movement outside of 'Truth'. Apocalypse therefore must remain impossible against the horizon of history (insofar as the absolute unveiling ends all understanding, all history, and therefore all potentiality), as its very existence wipes out all other possibilities – all history, all time. However, the reverse is also true: the impossibility of apocalypse, of revelation, is that which is the foundation for which knowledge and history are possible – the impossibility of the totality of unveiling allows for an infinite horizon to unfold. Playing in a post-apocalyptic environment, in a projected atemporality, refuses the 'end' its due, and opens up possibility for play itself.

This is not simply a pedantic move to obfuscate the notion of apocalypse, but to make clear that simply playing a game that takes place *after* a so-called apocalypse is, in fact, not by itself apocalyptic. There is, as Derrida clearly states, 'no apocalypse' (1984, 24). Not that a disaster did not happen, that billions of virtual lives might have been lost or turned into ghouls, super mutants, or taken refuge in a town built around an undetonated nuclear bomb, but that revelation is not complete. The unveiling is only yet in process. Yet in the face of apocalypse, immersed within a world shaped by a cataclysmic event, the player gains a perspective with what has begun to have been revealed – terrible things have happened, and the player inhabits a 'time' that carries these facts, whatever they may be, or whatever 'truths' they may lead toward.

As for the consideration of post, the post-apocalypse therefore cannot be simply temporal. The joining of 'post' to 'apocalypse' through the simple use of a hyphen, as in the post-apocalyptic tales of *Fallout*, can not be seen as *after* the apocalypse, as temporally nothing remains after an event that reveals fully. Rather than referring to the root of the prefix meaning 'after', thinking of 'post' as the Latin *positum*, the etymological root for the 'post' in 'the postal system' refers to placing something spatially, rather than temporally. As spatial, the post becomes a place for movement: spatial displacement, rather than temporal displacement. The post-apocalyptic adventure is that which places the subject – in this case the player – at a distance from the fulfillment of apocalypse, of revelation, and of truth, and allows for perspective. In this manner we can never actually be apocalyptic, only post. When the player approaches the apocalypse as *post* (already in a virtual temporal projection from their current situation), she is not approaching it simply as *after* an event, then, of revelation of that event, but instead she is simply *approaching* revelation, allowing for the possibility of revelation to come. This is a key distinction between an apocalypse and a post-apocalypse – the former remains impossible to speak of after, while the latter simply makes space for the impossibility to be in arrival. It can never arrive fully, yet its very position – that of the messianic, of the not-arrived, of the always-in-arrival – allows for *play*, for movement of truth, so that it is always unveiling. Rather than signifying the prefix meaning 'after', the semantic move of the 'post' hyphenation can simply represent the signification of spatial placing outside the term joined: the very possibility for the term to be understood (a place for perspective). The post-apocalypse then can be seen as nothing but the ability for revelation to actively reveal itself, for it to be seen.

Think of it this way: if revelation is ever fulfilled, if it ever is complete, then there would be nothing to unveil, nothing to learn and no truth left. The abundance, the totality, of truth is also its opposite: the end, the totalization of all understanding. Insofar as there is ever time, that there is a witness to time, there is history – therefore no apocalypse. The post collapses under the weight of totality – senders and receivers are rendered mute, as understanding (the very goal of communication) can no longer take place. However, in the spatially post-apocalyptic tale, the horizon remains open and unfolds for the possibility of understanding, the possibility of play. The post emerges as a node, a spatial place of location that heralds the emergence of revelation, giving space for growth, and therefore space to communicate.

Postal Communication

At least in part due to Shannon and Weaver's *The Mathematical Theory of Communication* (Shannon and Weaver 1949), the persistent manner (at least among the general public) of thinking about communication relies on what is often referred to as the 'sender receiver' model. Originally theorized for understanding telecommunication transmissions, this model considers messages between a sender and receiver, often with some notion of noise source in between. This is, of course, most often applied to a communicative system with more than one human involved. On a basic level, this model approaches communication as that which happens between two or more independent systems, the systems interacting with other systems by transmitting and receiving messages. These systems either 'understand' each other or, due to some noise within the process of transmission, mis-understand each other. Whatever the outcome, the two systems remain in direct contact with each other. This model presupposes something directly shared, like a Venn diagram with two circles overlapping. This something might have noise interjected within, which accounts for mis-understanding, but the de facto standard for this model is that the intended message is always shared. This thinking is, of course, over a half century old, and communication scholars have come a long way since then. However, it is still often the case that the term 'communication' implies that the message itself is being shared, and that the goal of 'understanding' may, eventually, be realized.

More recently, Briankle Chang argues there is something else that gets in between the two systems, something other than just noise. To begin, he complicates the matter by rethinking the common notion of a communicative exchange as one between subject and other through the exchange of messages. Communication, for Chang, is an 'interplay between self and other, between that which stays the same and which appears to the former as different' (Chang 1996, 44), effectively defining communication as the exchange between two or more elements that are attempting to make sense of something other than themselves. In this perspective, the subject considers itself as a self (and therefore familiar), and considers the other as different and not understood. Communication therefore does not simply send and receive messages, but attempts to domesticate 'the alien into the customary' (47); it brings things closer and helps make them familiar.

This point is not revolutionary on its own, and indeed does not directly confront traditional ways of thinking about communication, as it posits a subject who still attempts to communicate to the other in order to bring around understanding. However, as Chang continues:

> [A]s long as the subject of communication is predefined as a

self-enclosed, unconnected source of meaning and intention, communication [...] must be viewed essentially as a sending (envoi), an event of giving oneself over, during which a representative of subject, something representing or standing for the subject, is dispatched to another party, another subject. (46)

Commonplace narratives of communicative exchange presuppose that the subject directly sends a message to the other. Although symbolic representation encourages translation, the actual exchanges of messages are carried through a separate system. Messages are not simply sent from person to person – this conceptualization of messaging makes sense for telecommunication, but not for people. This system is outside of us, rather than in us, and therefore we must instead give our communicative tasks over to something *in between* us and other. The sharing does not happen between the two 'in communication', but instead is exchanged within a separate system. To put it another way, there is a mediator, a medium, by which communication operates. This medium we have given ourselves over to is communication itself. Communication does not happen between two, as the common-sense narrative supposes, but instead communication *communicates*: communication is a medium by which we exchange messages.

Like the model which Shannon and Weaver conceptualized (two independent systems transmitting messages), the system must always already exist, transmitting pre-constituted signs within to another node in the system. However, signals are always displaced from our own understanding – they always go through an impossible translation. Therefore *with or without computers*, we have essentially been talking to ourselves all along. This does not mean, of course, that we do not speak, or affect each other's actions, but it means that the *system* of communication is one that is already there. The nodes are in place. Chang calls this delivery system a 'postal system', a term he borrows from Derrida (1987), and the principle governing this communicative system the 'postal principle', as the message is involved in a system where the senders and receivers are already pre-constituted – they have addresses, and the message already has an identity that follows syntactic, semantic, and other rules that make it identifiable (47).

This post is, of course, the same post as in *positum* – there is a spatial distancing that is assumed within the postal exchange. This spatial distancing not only assumes the system remains outside of ourselves, but also that this system existed before we sent a message through it. Nodes are not constructed, they instead have only yet to be discovered[4].

What is crucial about the postal principle is that it places the communicative subject always (at least) one step removed from any other. There is no misconception about 'total' communication. Rather than expecting a realization of the goal of understanding, the postal principle assumes that understanding, in its totality, must remain impossible for communicative exchange to take place at all. We can never fully understand each other because we are always removed from that with which we are communicating. We send and receive messages, but we can never access the totality of the other. Applying this postal principle to RPGs, we may conceptualize the player's journey through the game as one of interaction with multiple layers of mediums. The communicative subject, when communicating with the world, remains mediated by the postal system – the subject finds an addressee, construes a message, and then sends it in hopes (maybe) of receiving something in return. The purpose of communication, even between mediums, still remains to approach understanding; communication still continues to communicate, even if it must always fall short of its ultimate goal.

The interaction that takes place in *Fallout* could be investigated here in a multitude of ways. The typical manner of conceptualizing human-computer interaction in game studies is often situated as an interaction between player and game (for example, see Galloway). In this essay I would like to situate a slightly different option, complicating the player-game relationship through a rethinking of the connection between avatar and player. As I mentioned before, the journey of the post-apocalyptic tale is that of the communicative subject in dialogue with herself. The player, through the digital medium (the interaction is between the player and him or herself) communicates through the mediation of the postal system. Although the post-apocalyptic tale that is *played* in *Fallout* is one that, essentially, the player must tell herself, the communicative event that takes place to allow this is slightly more complicated than 'simply' talking to oneself.

The Postal Avatar

RPGs have always required an extraordinary investment in time compared with other types of game. Pen and paper games, often played around a table for hours among a group of players, can last for months, even years, of multiple-hour-long sessions. DRPGs also require a massive time investment, often requiring from forty to over eighty hours (or more) of game-time to complete the basic story (and much more to complete all of the other content). This provides a unique situation where RPGs become more than just a simple story. This story takes up an incredible amount of the player's time and therefore a large percentage of the narratives that the player participates in. The game becomes an adventure that the player inhabits – lives through, not just digitally, but corporeally as well.

The avatar here becomes not just an embodiment of the player, following the Hindu conceptualization of a deity descended onto Earth, but as a node within a communicative structure, a sort of extension that situates the player in a different manner[5]. To do this, we need to think otherwise about the role that the mediation of the game can play by situating the player-avatar relationship differently. Computers, and therefore games, are often seen as the place between, as a medium that mitigates messages (Gunkel 2009). However, it is problematic to situate the computer as *simply* a medium; as David Gunkel reminds us, 'the computer [...] substantively resists being exclusively defined as a medium and instrument through which human users exchange messages' (Gunkel 2009, 64). As we would not, for example, exclusively define 'the world' as a medium, the possibilities allowed by the computer cannot be reduced to simply a medium or a source of noise, as it has the ability to fundamentally shift the way we communicate. For example, ELIZA, the software developed in 1966 to mimic rudimentary psychotherapy, was incredibly effective at engaging humans. While it (arguably) could not pass the famous Turing test (see Turing 1950) because it did not exemplify *intelligence*, it elicited emotional response from many of its users, who either knew they were interacting with a computer, had only limited exposure to it, or both (Weizenbaum 1984). Over fifty years later, the programs that we interface with consistently are far more complicated than a simple textual feedback, allowing for optical and aural feedback, as well as feedback to our physical movements. In DRPGs the player is immersed within a digital environment, absorbing information from every aspect of the game. The extreme investment of play-time, if nothing else, requires focus on the environment. Players stare into a digital world that occupies them both visually and aurally, their body movements (in this case, their hands) control the avatar through their journey. Quests become trials for the avatar, progressing slowly through the chosen storyline.

The gamespace becomes similar to our 'meatspace' (Gibson 1984), a term often used since Gibson's *Neuromancer* to describe the bodily space occupied by the corporeal player as complex rules must be comprehended and followed to gain access to different content. The player must educate herself about the ways the world operates and obey proper etiquette around other digital denizens or else be threatened in a myriad of ways – from social outcasting to execution. There are rules, but there are rules in the corporeal world as well. The difference is only that of flesh. Players learn the rules through experience, or from reading a manual, or both. The avatar's life is – at least socially – much like life in the corporeal world. Material aspects have vanished, pain is irrelevant, and death is never final, but the social aspects are still forefront. Contrary to Burn and Schott's conceptualization of the 'heavy hero', the avatar in *Fallout* is completely a 'digital dummy' (similar to the type that ventriloquists make talk), without personality and fully ready to control (Burn and Schott 2004). The player must experience knowing what will come next in the game, just as in 'meatspace', but it can never be complete: 'the complex nature of simulations is such that a result can't be predicted beforehand; it can vary greatly depending on the player's luck, skill and creativity' (Aarseth 2001). As Barthes predicted, the reader (player) is now the producer; the player tells the story they want to tell (Barthes 1975), as games are a 'radically different alternative to narratives as a cognitive and communicative structure' (Aarseth 2001). Each action the player chooses shapes future interactions, relying on complex systems of rules to govern the reaction by the game. However, recent games have far surpassed simply what the player wishes to tell, as the player becomes a co-producer in the story: the game takes an active role in its own telling. There are complex systems in place to mitigate the reactions to the actions that take place in the game environment. The player's avatar is 'co-present' to 'gameworld'. Gameworld and avatar interact. This goes beyond simple action-reaction, and links the avatar within a system that accounts not only for combat and other 'physical' reactions, but socially as well. In the *Fallout* series, for example, one of the gameplay elements is 'karma'[6]. Karma within the *Fallout* series governs not only how major plot lines unfold, but also how individual NPCs react to you. The 2010 release *Fallout: New Vegas* also sets up a complex series of factions, each with their own reputation systems – one action might benefit the avatar with one faction, but diminish their standing with another (See Figure 8.2).

Figure 8.2 Your choices, reputation, and karma will have an impact on whether this character will end up as friend or foe. (Bethesda 2010).

There are (at least) two different styles of gameplay in these games, one being a turn-based top-down system[7] in *Wasteland*, *Fallout*, and *Fallout 2*, and a first-person perspective (FPP) in *Fallout 3*, and *Fallout: New Vegas*[8]. Although not as immersive visually, the top-down environments in the first two games were still massive and interactive. The more recent *Fallout 3* and *Fallout: New Vegas* are mostly played in style where the player's view mirrors the view of the avatar[9]. As James Newman remarks, it seems like the 'primary-player-character relationship is one of vehicular embodiment' (Newman 2002). The camera follows the movement, often bouncing up and down with the terrain and immersing the player into the gameworld. Buildings may be entered, NPCs may be spoken to pleasantly (or murdered brutally), and everything has consequences. However, Alec Charles argues that this type of gameplay 'constructs an alternative but real subjectivity, and, insofar as the gamer increasingly experiences the virtual world as her primary reality, then that alternative subjectivity may come to represent the player's dominant sense of self' (Charles 2009, 7). Sherry Turkle in *Life on the Screen* (1997) seems to agree, revealing gaming as an exploration of the player's identity multiplicity. However, spending such an extended time focusing on such an environment or, as Peter Bayliss calls it, 'being-in-the-game-world' (Bayliss 2007), is not necessarily what Turkle refers to as 'suspend[ing] disbelief' (1997, 103) but simply that the player experiences 'a communicatively mediated sense of being present in the gameworld'. The player knows that they are playing the game, but consciously they realize that their avatar is 'a separately embodied character' (Bayliss 2007). Slavoj Žižek complicates this notion of subjectivity in gamespace a bit further:

> [W]hen I construct a 'false' image of myself which stands for me in a virtual community in which I participate [...] the emotions I feel and 'feign' as part of my onscreen persona are not simply false. Although what I experience as my 'true self' does not feel them, they are none the less in a sense 'true'. (Žižek 2008, 97)

This separately embodied character is an other that the player communicatively engages with, one that communicates their emotions, which we engage with and empathize with. The other brings its experience to the postal exchange: it communicates and simulates its worldview.

The game becomes something more than just an environment to explore for the player. The game becomes the place where the player communicates, and the computer (consoles are computers as well), as David Gunkel remarks, 'actively participates in communicative exchanges as a kind of additional agent and/or (inter)active co-conspirator' (Gunkel 2009, 54). The game's avatar (insofar as this computer is actively participating in communicative exchanges) acts not just as a medium through which the player is actively communicating but as an other that the player communicates *with*. However, the player does not just look at the avatar, but also through the avatar. The player is both conscious of the avatar's surroundings and their own – a double perspective. The player neither is just the avatar and is just simply the observer of the screen – it is, as Žižek says, a 'false' image that has been constructed, but it is also one that the player sees through, experiences interactivity with. In a manner of speaking, the player 'loses' herself in the game. Not that the player forgets who they are, or that they think that their corporeal body is now in a digital wasteland, but that they forget, or are not actively remembering, that *they are and are not* the avatar – it is not merely a 'false' representation of them. While they are still conscious of their own corporeal body, they also, as Žižek mentions, 'feel' through this digital representation in a way that is nonetheless 'true'. The digital 'other' that explores the screen is only other insofar as the player becomes divided – both self and other.

Although the avatar and the player are both the 'same', the avatar remains other insofar as it is not the player. Outside of the self, existing in the temporal and spatial projections of the postapocalyptic gameworld, the other that inhabits the gameworld in the player's stead remains alien to the corporeal player. An alien avatar in an alien world. As the avatar is the true 'player' of the game (the subject immersed within the world and engaged within the narrative of the gameworld) the game communicates to the corporeal player through the player's other, the avatar. The 'journey' of the avatar is mediated through this postal exchange, from avatar to player. The avatar becomes the post for which the player might explore the boundaries of the avatar's perception – a postal node in the network of self with which the player corresponds.

Postal Correspondence

The post is, on one hand, spatial positioning that both allows movement and requests from beyond itself to be recognized. However, on the other hand, the post already implies the structure of a postal system that carries messages between two systems that can never meet. The player and postal extension (the avatar) exchange letters, yet they can never meet. As the letters are never able to fulfill the communicative revelation, there is always a call for more letters. The revelation is that of the player communicating to the avatar, to herself, through the game; the postal node of the avatar-self becomes a spatial distancing of self to resituate the possibility horizons. The avatar is both the mediator and representation of the player, but also neither. The representative is not merely the descent, the arrival, of the player into the game. The avatar is instead an agent of the player – one who communicates through a postal exchange. The avatar is both, and not: a postal agent that the player can never fully meet. Understood in this way, a post-apocalyptic RPG is less about the end of the world as about the transmission of revelation: the always-arriving of understanding.

Through the gamespace, each of these mediations separates the player from herself while allowing the player to explore the potentiality that exists between a series of systems that can never be complete, never be fulfilled, and never be truly unveiled. The journey of the player's messages back to herself is never complete. This is why a 'post-apocalypse' is such a fitting setting for this type of journey, as it allows the player ample room to navigate her own path, to explore new horizons. Separated from the player through a double mediation, the avatar can explore the gamespace through the player unhinged by the player's own perspective. The exploration of the wasteland is (somewhat) open, limiting the avatar only by the constraints of the digital parameters (even the corporeal world is finite, after all). Through this exploration, the interaction between avatar and game, whether NPC or environment, communication begins to unfold. The process of understanding for the player, of course, is not as simple as the sharing of messages. Understanding is what unfolds through the engagement of this complex system of exchanges that happen between avatar and player, mediated through the postal system. The postal node of the avatar, and the exchanges between it and the player, slowly domesticate the 'alien' existence of the avatar.

Postal Anxiety

The *Fallout* series and *Wasteland* are excellent examples of this system (of which, undeniably, there are likely other games and systems to apply this consideration to, and will be many more) for a few reasons. First of all, unlike 'traditional' understandings of apocalypse as end-times (where there is quite literally no future) the *Fallout* series and *Wasteland* leave the player with a more open future – one that, in effect, allows for a future to come. These games do this not only through the game's major plotlines, in which the player's character helps herald the possibility a future in the game narrative, but (most specifically in the *Fallout* series) through the openness of the narrative itself – as there always *seems* to remain a place for movement available for the character. Rather than the typical good-versus-evil narrative that emerges in conventional apocalyptical rhetoric, the post-apocalypse becomes a place to reinvent, or at least rebuild, the socius and allows for the possibility of new modes of interaction to take place. Japanese role-playing games (JRPGs), for example, not only usually define a specific representation of the avatar (partially what Burn and Schott refer to as a 'heavy hero') but also usually reflect a linear plotline. Some recent games, such as *Mass Effect* or *Dragon Age: Origins*, allow a more customizable experience in a non-linear setting, but they do not situate the player themselves after the so-called 'end times'. The temporally 'post' apocalyptic worlds of *Fallout* and *Wasteland* allow a postal reorientation as well, situating the player within a foreign setting that is vaguely familiar, yet ultimately alien. It is spatially 'post' as this environment opens up a place for the avatar to locate itself as a postal node that looks back at the player's environment.

Secondly, *Fallout* and *Wasteland* offer something in their postal exchange to the player other than just their open gameplay style and narrative elements. The spatial distancing of the avatar, referred to earlier, is also a temporal projection into the (fictional) 'future' of the temporally 'post' apocalypse. However, as discussed before, there is 'no apocalypse', as the fulfillment of revelation can never be complete. So what, then, does a journey through the 'post-apocalyptic' wastelands reveal?

As I mentioned before, 'the apocalypse' is big business. Not only is it obvious, through the hundreds of millions of dollars per year spent on films, television shows, fictional books, and (obviously) DRPGs, that an apocalyptical event remains prevalent in cultural narratives, but the anxiety induced by the apocalyptical fear and paranoia from contemporary rhetoric has become a daily experience in contemporary culture, the world of the player. This is, of course, nothing new. Richard Hofstadter in *The Paranoid Style in American Politics*, originally published in 1964, highlights a trend of fearmongering and constant paranoia in American political rhetoric since the foundation of the country. More recently, Barry Glassner's *The Culture of Fear: Why Americans are Afraid of the Wrong Things* highlights more current constructions of fear and paranoia. However, it is not necessary to look on a bookshelf for overwhelming evidence of this style, as fear is cultivated daily in nearly every newspaper and every television news report (Romer et al. 2003). The Mayan 'prophecy' regarding the destruction of the world in 2012 is only the most popular and recent in a series of anxiety-producing predictions regarding the so-called apocalypse[10].

As the player inhabits this anxious time, facing numerous possibilities of destruction, this anxiety has become a defining characteristic of contemporary culture, since the 'meatspace' of the player's world is populated by fearful, paranoid, and apocalyptic rhetoric. In contrast to the anxiety of the 'real' world, the post-apocalyptic RPG places the avatar, and thus the agent of and postal correspondent of the player, in an impossible temporal projection where all the apocalyptic narratives have come to pass. Everything that is most terrifying, fear-inducing, and anxiety-producing has already come to pass. In a world ravaged by death and destruction emerges a journey after 'the end', one that, through the correspondence between the player and her avatar, communicates the very possibility of future, and the negation of finality.

Ironically enough, the post-apocalypse expands rather than contracts horizons; openness to the future is restored. The gameworlds of *Wasteland* and the *Fallout* series open up the most extreme of possibilities of human kindness and monstrosity, allowing the player to engage and escape their own anxious times, finding relief in the wasteland. It is the player's postal engagement that allows them to tell their own tale, to engage the semantic play that emerges. The player/avatar can choose to become a slaver or savior, a destroyer of humanity, or the mender of great wounds. This is the revelation of the post-apocalyptic RPG – the possibility of future, of what Derrida refers to as *l'avenir* (to come), can emerge. The journey of the post-apocalyptic RPG here can be seen not as a temporal post-apocalypse, but the relief of anxiety in the face of the current ethos of spatially 'post' (ongoing) revelation regarding 'the end'. *Wasteland* and *Fallout* may most effectively explore, for better or worse, that the possibility of both infinite terror and beauty arises from humanity, and how both of them may come to situate terror as beauty and beauty as terror. Or, more simply, as repeated in the beginning and end of every *Fallout* game, voiced by Ron Perlman: 'War …War never changes.'

Notes

1. This essay would not have been possible without the encouragement and editorial advice of Professor Stephen Olbrys Gencarella. His insight and critique has helped a seed of an idea sprout into something more vibrant than it was before. The author would also like to thank Professor Briankle G. Chang as the original seed for this essay was wrought through countless conversations held over endless cups of tea.
2. It is worth mentioning there are additional games within the *Fallout* universe, including *Fallout: Tactics (2001)* a strategy game, and *Fallout: Brotherhood of Steel (2004)* a dungeon crawler. As these were not RPGs, they are not included in this essay.
3. There are too many to list here, but the same year that *Fallout: New Vegas* was released, just four of the top apocalyptic movies (*The Road*, *Legion*, *The Book of Eli*, and *Daybreakers*) resulted in over $300 million in gross revenues.
4. Also see 'Going Postal to Deliver Subjects: Remarks on a German Postal *A Priori*' by Geoffrey Winthrop-Young.

5 Also see articles by Baerge, Moran, Travis, and Voorhees in this volume concerning alternative readings of the relationship between player and character

6 Originally called 'reputation' in *Fallout*, then called 'karma' in *Fallout 2* and future games.

7 *Wasteland* used a top-down system for exploring the environment and a windowed portrait and text mode for combat, whereas *Fallout* and *Fallout 2* used an isometric view with turn-based isometric combat.

8 *Fallout 3* and *Fallout: New Vegas* were released by Bethesda Game Studios after they licensed *Fallout* from Interplay in 2004.

9 There is an option to play in third person, but the game defaults to First Person Perspective and the alternate perspective offers less control and feedback.

10 There are numerous accounts of failed apocalyptic predictions through the years; for some examples, see 'A Brief History of the Apocalypse', http://www.abhota.info/end1.htm

References

Aarseth, Espen. 2001. Computer Game Studies, Year One. *Game Studies* 1, no.1. http://gamestudies.org/0101/editorial.html.

Barthes, Roland. 1975. *S/Z: An Essay*. Hill and Wang.

Barton, Matt. 2007. 'The History of Computer Role-Playing Games Part 2: The Golden Age (1985–1993).' http://www.gamasutra.com/features/20070223b/barton_05.shtml.

Bayliss, Peter. 2007. 'Beings in the Game-world: Characters, Avatars, and Players.' In *Proceedings of the 4th Australasian Conference on Interactive Entertainment*, ed. Hjorth, Larissa and Esther Milne, 1–6. Melbourne, Australia: RMIT University.

Bethesda Softworks. 2008. *Fallout 3*. [Xbox 360]. Zenimax Media, Inc: Rockville, MD.

—2010. *Fallout: New Vegas*. [Xbox 360]. Zenimax Media, Inc: Rockville, MD.

BioWare. 2007. *Mass Effect*. [Xbox 360]. Microsoft: Redmond, WA.

Black Isle Studios. 1998. *Fallout 2: A Post Nuclear Role Playing Game*. [PC]. Interplay Entertainment: Beverley Hills, CA.

Burn, Andrew and Gareth Schott., 2004. 'Heavy Hero or Digital Dummy? Multimodal Player-Avatar Relations in *Final Fantasy 7*.' *Visual Communication* 3(2): 213–33.

Chang, Briankle G. 1996. *Deconstructing Communication:*

Representation, Subject, and Economies of Exchange. Minneapolis: University of Minnesota Press.
Charles, Alec. 2009. 'Playing with One's Self: Notions of Subjectivity and Agency in Games.' *Eludamos. Journal for Computer Game Culture* 3(2): 281–94.
Derrida, Jacques. 1984. 'No Apocalypse, Not Now (full speed ahead, seven missiles, seven missives).' Trans. C. Porter and P. Lewis. *Diacritics*: 20–31.
—1987. *The Post Card: From Socrates to Freud and Beyond*. University Of Chicago Press, June 15.
Edge of Reality. 2009. *Dragon Age: Origins*. [Xbox 360]. Electronic Arts: Redwood City, CA.
Galloway, Andrew. 2006. 'Gamic Action.' In *Gaming: Essays on Algorithmic Culture*. University Of Minnesota Press.
Gibson, William. 1984. *Neuromancer*. Ace.
Glassner, Barry. 2010. *The Culture of Fear: Why Americans Are Afraid of the Wrong Things: Crime, Drugs, Minorities, Teen Moms, Killer Kids, Mutant Microbes, Plane Crashes, Road Rage, & So Much More*. Revised Edition. Basic Books.
Gunkel, David. 2009. 'Beyond Mediation: Thinking the Computer Otherwise.' *Interactions: Studies in Communication & Culture* 1(1): 53–70.
Hofstadter, Richard. 1996. *The Paranoid Style in American Politics: And Other Essays*. Harvard University Press.
Interplay Entertainment. 1997. *Fallout: A Post Nuclear Role Playing Game* [PC]. Interplay Entertainment: Beverly Hills, CA.
Interplay Productions. 1987. *Wasteland*. [PC]. Electronic Arts: Redwood City, CA.
Nelson, Chris. n.d. 'A Brief History of the Apocalypse.' http://www.abhota.info/end1.htm.
Newman, James. 2002. 'The Myth of the Ergodic Videogame.' *Game Studies* 1, no.2. http://gamestudies.org/0102/newman/.
Romer, D., K. H Jamieson, and S. Aday. 2003. 'Television News and the Cultivation of Fear of Crime.' *Journal of Communication* 53(1): 88–104.
Shannon, C. E, and Weaver, W. 1949. *The Mathematical Theory of Communication*. University of Illinois.
Turing, Alan. 1950. Computing Machinery and Intelligence. *Mind* 59: 433–60.
Turkle, Sherry. 1995. *Life on the Screen: Identity in the Age of the Internet*. New York: Simon & Schuster.
Weizenbaum, Joseph. 1984. *Computer Power and Human Reason*. New York: Penguin Books Ltd.
Winthrop-Young, G. 2002. 'Going Postal to Deliver Subjects: Remarks on a German Postal *a Priori*.' *Angelaki* 7(3): 143–58.
Žižek, Slavoj. 2008. *Violence*. Picador.

9

Constructing a Powerful Identity in *World of Warcraft*: A Sociolinguistic Approach to MMORPGs

BENJAMIN E. FRIEDLINE,
LAUREN B. COLLISTER[1]

Millions of people worldwide spend their free time engrossed in Massively Multiplayer Online Role-playing Games (hereafter MMORPGs). These games are attractive not only for traditional game-like elements such as slaying dragons and exploring mythical lands, but also for the social atmospheres that arise from player interactions within digital worlds. Since the mid–1990s, multiple papers have been published on digital gaming that have been crucial in developing theory on a variety of topics such as the participants (Bartle 1996), the online cultures (Taylor 2006), and the motivations for involvement (Williams et al. 2006) in digital games. This research alludes to the existence of relationships between language and power in virtual communities (e.g. Steinkuehler's [2005] work on the difference between beta-vets and newbies in *Lineage II* [NC Interactive 2011]), but does not directly explore how participants acquire power in digital games, nor how a participant's power relates to the language they deploy within the digital world. Hence, the purpose of this paper is to understand how power is situated and deployed through language in *World of Warcraft* (Blizzard Entertainment 2004).

This chapter reports results from a qualitative study of language and power within *World of Warcraft* and is divided into six sections: (1) game studies and *World of Warcraft*, (2) theoretical framework, (3) methodology, (4) results, (5) discussion, and (6) conclusion. Using a framework of power developed by Kiesling (1996, 38–102), we argue that the power in these interactions is realized through the interaction between linguistic and cultural artifacts that position players in power roles within the gaming community.

Game Studies and *World of Warcraft*

World of Warcraft (hereafter *WoW)* is a MMORPG created by Blizzard Entertainment (2004) and first launched in 2004. (In this same volume Abboud and Douglas also examine *WoW*.) As of the writing of this chapter, it is the most popular MMORPG in the world, with over twelve million active accounts (Blizzard Entertainment 2010). As players journey through the game, they participate in practices that are standard to the MMORPG genre, such as completing quests and slaying monsters which reward items and experience points, collecting materials to create items such as food or clothing with a number of crafting professions, teaming up with other players to fight in dungeons and raids[2], and – not least of all – interacting with other players via in-game chat channels such as party chat or guild chat. In the course of these activities, relations of power emerge among members of the gaming community.

From the standpoint of game studies literature, an avatar's power in the gameworld is often connected to the amount of experience that the player has acquired. R.V. Kelly writes:

> The total number of accumulated [experience] points then determines your level in the game. So, when other players scan your approaching avatar, they can see by glancing at your level whether they're dealing with a newbie who might *need* help or a grizzled veteran who might *provide* help. These same experience points are also what you use to upgrade your character […] Over time, you're able to grow yourself into someone more formidable than the pipsqueak you start out as. (2004, 27–8)

In connection with this view, game studies suggest that there is a relationship between an avatar's (or player's) level of experience and the language that the avatar's player deploys within the gameworld. Steinkuehler (2005, 50–6), for instance, connects language usage with game experience in her study of *Lineage II* players. She notes that the beta-vets often use specialized vocabulary (e.g. *poms* for potions of mana) to signal their veteran status in the gameworld and to distinguish themselves from newbies who were not familiar with in-game lingo. Similarly, research on *WoW* guild structure by Williams and colleagues (Williams et al. 2006, 355) demonstrates that players in guild leadership roles may obtain their positions by sharing expert knowledge with guild mates and serving as 'advisors' to less experienced players. This research indicates that expert players can effectively obtain a powerful in-game position by sharing their specialized game knowledge through language.

Despite the fact that they allude to the existence of a relationship between language and power, these studies were never intended to answer broader questions regarding language and power in virtual discourse. In fact, previous research has largely been concerned with describing the interaction between individual player identities and large-scale social structures in online games. To our knowledge, no previous research has sought to directly explore the relationship between language and power within the context of an online game such as *WoW*, which is the impetus of this paper.

Theoretical Framework

Linguists have long recognized that language usage is deeply embedded in sociocultural contexts. As such, language itself is inherently a social practice which is governed by the norms for spoken language within a particular linguistic community. These norms define not only *what* can be said, but also *who* is likely to say what in conversational interactions. For instance, Labov's (1966) study of the social stratification of (th) in New York City shows that (th) use was highly correlated with socio-economic status in that those with low socio-economic status were less likely to use the prestige variant (i.e. /Θ/) than those with higher social status. Brown and Gilman (1960, 253–76) also illustrate this point in their description of the usage of the *Tu* and *Vous* pronouns in European romance language – that is, powerful people (superiors) use *Tu* and receive *Vous* from those with inferior social status. These studies are important insofar as they evince a connection between an individual's power (economic, social, etc.) and their respective language usage; yet, they have limited utility for studies on language and power because they do not define what power actually is, nor explain how it interacts with individual identities and creative language use.

Kiesling's (1996) work on power among fraternity men builds on these early studies and provides a framework for defining power and analyzing the relationship between language and power through the lens of a 'power role'. According to this framework, power is:

1 Socially and culturally situated in every society.
2 Passed from generation to generation and resistant to change.
3 Relative to the relationship between the hearer and speaker.
4 Relative to pre-existing socially determined roles.

5 Relative to the position that a participant wishes to create through language.

This description of power indicates that a definition of power is relative to the society in which power is situated, which is one of the key ideas in Kiesling's power framework:

Power is one of the most basic productive social relationships; importantly, power relationships are real and meaningful to the speakers, as shown in the details of talk. Through language, people place themselves in relatively enduring power roles, as defined by a community of practice. Essentially, the framework suggests that people place themselves in certain power roles by using language to index these roles; however, every speaker cannot simply use any strategy or form to index any role. They are limited by ascribed traits, previous roles they have filled in the community, the roles available in the situation, and their competence in a certain strategy or form. Thus, there is a balance between using language to place oneself in a power role, learning the language expected of a person in a certain role, and creating a new definition of a role. Moreover, people have multiple roles, and may move from one role to another – even with the same audience in the same speech situation. (Kiesling 1996, 40–1)

Hence, Kiesling operationalizes power in society through a construct known as a *power role*. Power roles connect language and power in that the language used by participants in a power role is related to the respective power that an individual holds within the community. This framework predicts that powerful language can only be accessed by those in certain power roles or by individuals who wish to create powerful identities through the use of language. In addition, the framework recognizes that access to power roles is contextually constrained and that not all linguistic forms are accessible in all speech situations.

Importantly, the power framework makes predictions about language and power in the real world that can be extended to the study of power relationships in virtual communities. As such, the present study extends previous work on digital games by more fully investigating the relationship between language and power in online games. In particular, the following research questions will be addressed:

1. How do participants perceive power roles within *WoW*?
2. How do participants perceive powerful language within *WoW*?
3. What is the relationship between power roles and powerful language within *WoW*?

Methodology

The method of this study was a participant-observation ethnography that took place over a period of six months in 2007. The two researchers involved in this study joined different communities within *WoW*; Lauren Collister joined a Roleplaying (RP) server and Benjamin Friedline joined a Player-versus-Player (hereafter PvP) server. In-game demographic information and player opinions were obtained via an online survey given to participants, and conversation data were obtained using the built-in chatlogging feature in *WoW*. Both researchers also kept ethnographic journals during the course of the study.

The survey participants were in-game acquaintances of the researchers or members of the researchers' guilds who consented to be included in the study. Little is known about the background of the participants in terms of gender, occupation, race, or age, outside of what was shared via in-game chat or through the questionnaires. Character names have been changed in all cases (excluding the names of the researchers' characters), and any sensitive information has been removed from the data.

Results

Participants' Perceptions of Power Roles in WoW

In an attempt to understand how participants in *WoW* perceived power roles (Research Question #1), we asked participants in an online survey to reflect on the characteristics of powerful players. Several items required likert scale responses which asked students to agree or disagree with statements (1) to (4) below:

1. My gear makes me powerful.
2. My experience with the game makes me powerful.
3. My crafting abilities make me powerful.
4. Male avatars are more powerful than female avatars.

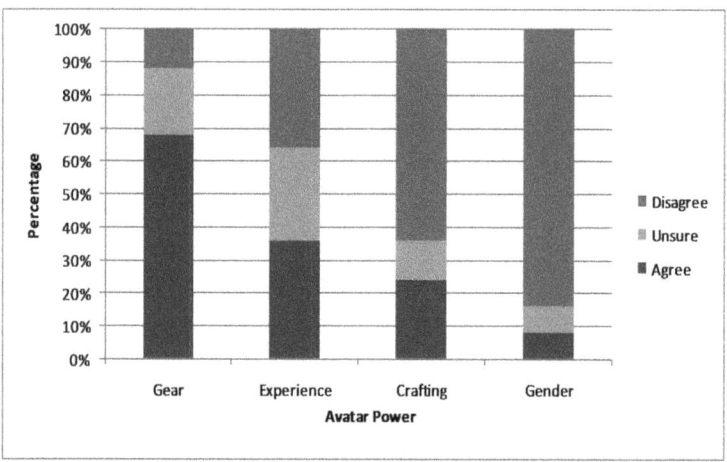

Figure 9.1 What makes an avatar powerful?

As depicted in Figure 9.1, participants believe that gear and experience correspond to power in *WoW*. Seventeen of 25 respondents indicated that having good gear placed someone in a powerful position. For instance, 'purple items' (items with names written in purple) are epic, or exceptionally rare, and having them makes a player's avatar more effective in combat within the gameworld.

To attain these purple items, players must defeat the most difficult enemies in the gameworld, a feat which requires great co-ordination and skill. Gear quality is related to a character's capacity – that is, the sum of the abilities available to the character – and is indicative of the player's abilities as well[3]. In addition to gear, some (9 out of 25) respondents thought that having experience with the game made one powerful. Knowledge of game mechanics (e.g. how to complete a particular quest) and game environment (e.g. where to find a rare item or creature) were also linked to power within *WoW*. This is a form of power employed within the gameworld – having knowledge that can be passed on to others or used to further the purposes of the individual or group gives a player an advantage in the game.

Participants' responses also indicated that certain characteristics within the gameworld were not important for determining a player's power. As displayed in Figure 9.1, few participants agreed that crafting abilities or avatar gender made participants powerful in *WoW*.

Participants in the survey were also given a chance to respond to open-ended questions such as: Describe a powerful person on your server and explain why they are powerful. In response to such questions, one theme that emerged was that power was often linked to an avatar's class (tank, healer, or damage-dealer). This relationship between power and character class may be drawn based on ethnographic observations and participants' comments to a survey question pertaining to character class and power. According to one participant,

> Lots of people think hunters are overpowered, but socially not so much. Many people don't like them as a class, and tanks and healers are less common and more desirable than dps (damage per second) in general.

Based on this comment, we might describe social power from the standpoint of a supply-and-demand model. On many servers, damage-dealers are abundant, whereas fewer people play healers and tanks. We found that 60 percent of our survey respondents reported having a DPS character as their main character, while 25 percent had healers and 15 percent had tanks, respectively. Although this survey was conducted in 2007, it is still relevant to the contemporary version of the game – that is, even with the advent of the 'dungeon finder' system which automatically matches players with parties, healers and tanks are still in high demand because they have a shorter wait for their dungeon queue due to there being generally fewer of them at any given time. In connection with the power framework, the results of the survey reveal that having the right gear, having knowledge and experience with the gameworld, and being 'in demand' by playing the right class are salient power roles within the *WoW* gaming community. However, it is important to point out that these findings provide only part of the picture of language and power within *WoW*, in that they describe the concrete manifestations of power without addressing the question pertaining to the relationship between language and power within the game. The next section discusses participants' perceptions of links between language and power in *WoW*.

Powerful Language in WoW

The second research question concerns how participants perceive powerful language within *WoW*. Participants' responses to a survey question regarding how powerful participants speak within the game can be placed into two distinct categories. The first category is collaborative or polite language (cf. Brown and Levinson 1987). This category is best explained in the words of one participant who describes his/her guild leader, a powerful person, thus: 'He is appropriate and kind to others in the group. He encourages participation and is never abusive.' Several other participants have similar ideas regarding the collaborative nature of powerful speech. These participants note that powerful people speak politely with directness and precision while at the same time respecting the needs of other players. Alternatively, the second category is aggressive language. Participants describe players who employ this type of language using words like controlling, abusive, or mean. For instance, one survey participant describes the actions of players who use this strategy as 'making fun of [somebody] in front of everyone around them'.

An Analysis of Language and Power in Virtual Discourse

The final research question concerns the relationship between powerful language and power roles in the game. In order to address this question, we provide linguistic analyses of four excerpts from our ethnography of *WoW* as exemplars of the workings of power within the gameworld. Each example is presented as it appeared in our chatlogs taken directly from the game, with names changed to pseudonyms to protect the identity of the players involved. We purposefully chose excerpts from structured collaborations in the gameworld in order to observe how players interact with each other. Nardi and Harris's (2006) work on interaction in *WoW* informed our choice of these selections and the analyses that we performed. These interactions involve opportunities for players to collaborate to learn something about the game or to achieve a mutually desired end result; furthermore, all of the environments require collaborative efforts from multiple players. The interleaved collaboration, which is so essential to gameplay in *WoW*, is the ideal situation to observe linguistic interactions for displays and uses of power, since it is in these arenas that players with power resources can demonstrate their abilities and linguistic behaviors. The four excerpts we analyze are from: (1) a maximum level battleground (PvP environment), (2) a low level questing session, (3) a maximum level raid, and (4) a general conversation in the trade chat channel. The first three of these excerpts involve structured collaboration which foster interactions between players for the continued mutual enjoyment of the players, while the fourth involves an exploitation of an area in which structured collaboration could take place.

Aggressive Language in a Battleground

The first example occurred in a level 70 battleground[4]. The participants' characters in this battleground were all at the maximum attainable level within the game at the time of our study, meaning that they had amassed hours of time within the gameworld to hone their skills and abilities, acquire the best possible equipment within the game, and learn all there was to know about the game and its mechanics. According to how survey participants defined power, having one or all of the aforementioned attributes or items may place a participant in a power role within the game.

In the excerpt below, the participants (members of the Alliance) were attempting to secure bases such as a lumber mill, a mine, and a stable to gain resources to defeat the enemy faction, the Horde. The player Nomercy had many of the characteristics of a powerful character, including epic (purple) PvP gear, which could only be obtained through engaging in PvP combat and winning many battles, giving Nomercy gear and experience as sources of power. In addition, Nomercy was a paladin healer – the only healer out of fifteen players in this battleground[5]. As stated above, the apparent paucity of the healer class on this server may have made healers more in demand; because of this, Nomercy had another source of power.

Example 1: Aggressive language in a battleground

1 [Battleground Leader] Nomercy-Crushridge: GROUP 1 GOING TO MINE GROUP 2 AND GROUP 3 GOING TO BS (= *blacksmith*) THEN PUSH TO FARM IM THE ONLY 1 WHO GO TO STABS (= *stables*)

2 [Battleground Leader] Nomercy-Crushridge: CALL INCS (= *incomings*)

3 [Battleground Leader] Nomercy-Crushridge: AND GG (= *good game*)

4 [Battleground Leader] Nomercy-Crushridge: I GO STBS

5 [Battleground Leader] Nomercy-Crushridge: COME ON NO 1 ELSE AT STBAS (= *stables*)

6 [Battleground] Highbon-Stonemaul: Inc stables

7 [Battleground] Geedbrow-Perenolde: stables needs help

8 [Battleground Leader] Nomercy-Crushridge: why are you going to lm (= *lumbermill*)

The most evident display of Nomercy's power is his use of the CAPS LOCK key. Typing in all capital letters is usually perceived as using a raised voice, or textually yelling at others (Collister 2008), which imposes his will on the others and, therefore, is a threatening act (Goffman 1967). In addition, he uses direct language to convey his orders to the other participants in the battleground, dividing players up into groups and telling them exactly where they should go. Nomercy also uses public embarrassment by asking the question, 'why are you going to lm?' in line 8. Here, Nomercy sees that several participants are not following his orders to assist at the mine or the stables, but are instead going to the lumber mill (lm). Nomercy does not actually want to know the answer to the question, but rather he wants to embarrass the two to three aberrant individuals who have disregarded his orders and gone off on their own. Nomercy's language displays aggressive strategies because he attempts to control the actions of others by yelling (i.e. CAPS LOCK) and through public humiliation.

Collaborative Language in Party Chat

The next conversation example occurred in party chat[6] on the PvP server. The three participants, Terrified, Dysfunction, and Agerionos, were attempting to defeat a large group of enemies in order to get an item needed for a quest. When it comes to power roles in *WoW*, the individuals in the following conversation are not in a very good position. They have only attained 30 out of the possible 70 levels of experience (pre Lich King expansion) and may not have had much experience playing the game. As such, they have limited access to power roles through gear or experience with the game, yet the players use language to create power within their group conversation while questing, even though they are powerless in terms of many of the things that make a player powerful within this world.

Example 2: Collaborative language in party chat

1 [Party] Terrified: ag where did u get ur pet? (= *a small bird that follows Agerionos*)

2 [Party] Agerionos: one of my friends gave it to me

3   [Party] Terrified: it's awesome
4   [Party] Agerionos: its from a valentines day event
5   [Party] Agerionos: thx (= *thanks*)
6   [Party] Terrified: two mages so if things get out of control u each have sheep (= *a magic spell that transforms an enemy into a sheep, temporarily disabling it*)
7   [Party] Agerionos: yep
8   [Party] Terrified: brb
9   [Party] Agerionos: k (= *ok*)
10 [Party] Dysfunction: hold
11 [Party] Dysfunction: hold age (= *agerionos*)
12 [Party] Agerionos: k
13 [Party] Dysfunction: Terr is cutting virus scan off
14 [Party] Dysfunction: let Terr mark the target and we both pryo (= *pyroblast, a magical spell*)
15 [Party] Agerionos: k

Even though these characters derive little power from the sources described earlier in this paper, they all stand to benefit from a successful interaction – they will reap the rewards of a quest completed. Since they must work together to complete the quest, the participants must cooperate with each other, and one of the best strategies for cooperation at low levels is by using collaborative linguistic forms. Players would prefer to interact with someone who is friendly, and many players might not agree to help someone who shouts or gives unnecessarily harsh orders. Without the gear or experience to 'excuse' the exercise of power via the use of aggressive language, collaborative language is a viable alternative for inexperienced players.

As illustrated in Example 2, Terrified uses collaborative language to create power within this interaction. This conversation begins with a compliment about Agerionos' pet from Terrified. This positive comment makes Terrified seem friendly, and is perhaps intended to boost Agerionos's willingness to work together with him. Shortly thereafter, Terrified issues an indirect order in line 6: 'two mages so if things get out of control u each have sheep.' The mages both presumably know that they possess the magic spell *sheep* (this spell transforms a monster into a sheep), so they do not need Terrified to tell them; however, what Terrified is really saying here is to use the sheep spell if things get out of control. By first creating solidarity among the party members with a compliment, and then issuing an indirect order, Terrified demonstrates the use of power through collaborative linguistic strategies.

Dysfunction also uses collaborative language to create power within this interaction. Dysfunction enters into the conversation for the first time after Terrified's departure and adopts Terrified's stance as the leader until Terrified returns. Initially, Dysfunction uses direct orders (line 11: hold age) with explanations (line 13: Terr is cutting virus scan off) but later, gives direct orders without explanations to Agerionos (line 14). The use of direct orders with explanations is a collaborative strategy because it mitigates the threat of the orders, showing reason behind the actions rather than ordering actions by virtue of one's position. Dysfunction still defers to Terrified's position, casting himself as speaking for Terrified, and justifies this position because he has knowledge that Agerionos does not (regarding Terrified's virus scan). Having established his position, Dysfunction can give direct orders without explanations later after already demonstrating the required politeness, while still maintaining that Terrified is the leader of the party.

In this example, we see how two players without the typical sources of power associated with power roles harness collaborative language to achieve success in the game environment. Collaborative language is a strategy available to players without the sources of power that players such as Nomercy (from Example 1) have, and can be used by anyone in the game to promote harmonious social interaction.

Collaborative Strategies in a Raid

The following example comes from the data from the RolePlaying server. The setting is a raid in which ten people must work together to fight extremely difficult enemies. Raids are an example of end-game content in *WoW* – in order to be part of a raid, a player must be at the maximum level, have the best gear available, and be competent in the intricacies of playing their class. In this particular raid, Jeremiah is the raid leader – he is not only the leader of the guild hosting the event, but he also has the best gear and the most knowledge of this particular raid (Karazhan) of anyone in the group. In addition to these sources of power (his gear and his experience), Jeremiah is also in the role of the main tank, a very important position for any raid which automatically indexes power based on the vitality of the person in the role. He has ample sources from which to draw power; however, Jeremiah instead chooses to employ collaborative linguistic strategies to preserve the goodwill of the team, such as the one below in Example 3. This example directly follows a wipe, or a failure to defeat a boss, which resulted in the death of everyone in the raid.

Players in the Ulduar raid environment (Blizzard Entertainment 2004)

Example 3: Collaborative strategies in raid leadership

1 [Raid Leader] Jeremiah: So now that we've seen the fight it should be a bit easier the second time

2 [Raid Leader] Jeremiah: Oh, and Opalyn totally needs to give us shadow protection

3 [Raid Leader] Jeremiah: Tam pointed that out to me and suggested we yell and swear at you, but I thought a friendly reminder would be better

4 [Raid] Tam: I totally did not say that.

Instead of using an aggressive order such as 'do better next time', Jeremiah instead says 'So now that we've seen the fight it should be a bit easier the second time'. Jeremiah includes himself in the plural first person pronoun 'we', meaning that he, too, will do better next time after seeing the fight and failing initially. In line 2, Jeremiah gives an order that could help the raid be more successful in their next attempt, namely a spell that protects against shadow damage that the player Opalyn, a priest, had forgotten to cast. Jeremiah does not fault Opalyn, which could be perceived as an act of aggression, but gives an indirect order instead. Giving orders is a potentially aggressive linguistic strategy, as demonstrated in Example 1, so Jeremiah follows his order with a deflection by saying that another player (Tam) would have employed an aggressive linguistic strategy ('we yell and swear at you'), but he (Jeremiah) instead chose to employ a collaborative one ('a friendly reminder'). Tam, the supposed aggressive language user, immediately denies his involvement in the issue, but it does not matter – Jeremiah has already set himself up as in opposition to people who use aggressive language, whether Tam is one of them or not.

Spamming and 'Bully Power'

The final analysis in this paper explores the 'bully power' language that some participants within the gameworld link with powerful language. This example is difficult to explain for three reasons. First, members of the *WoW* community differ in their assessments of spammer[7] language. For some members, spammers are powerful and use powerful language because they control the trade chat channel (usually used for trading items) and annoy a lot of people. For others, however, the same spammers are said to be weak and use weak language that annoys people and reflects their antisocial stance within the gameworld. Either way, most players view spammer behavior as being deviant in some way – that is, going against the established norms of the gameworld for their own benefit or gratification (Mortensen 2008). Linguistically, it can be hard to identify what 'spam' actually is. There are many different ways that a player can spam the trade channel, and a player may use multiple spamming strategies (e.g. player harassment, flaming, inappropriate topic selection). Last, many of the spammers do not have any of the material things (e.g. gear, experience, ability) that are linked to power roles within the game. We know this because you can check to see what types of equipment spammers have by looking up their names on the *World of Warcraft Armory* website (Blizzard Entertainment 2011) as well as see their level by clicking on their name in the chat box. The question is: what is it about spammers that makes their language usage ambiguous in terms of power in the gameworld? We suggest that spammers attempt to access power by using language forms which usually index aggressive linguistic strategies; however, the spammers themselves do not have access to these strategies. In this way, they are being deviant and going against the socially established norms of the game. We have outlined these norms in the above section, and spammers deliberately flout these norms of language use as one strategy to express deviance. By looking at a spammer, Wafflezz, and his group of spammer friends in action, we can see evidence of this behavior.

Example 4: Spamming and bully power

1 [Trade] Wafflezz: People who arent Wafflezz name themselves Rabitboy

2 [Trade] Voodoom: why you guys talk in trade your supposed to talk in genaral

3 [Trade] Vermincol: I must be Wafflezz, I'd never been stupid enough to take a name like Rabitboy

4 [Trade] Wafflezz: Yah!

5 [Trade] Rabitboy: WAFFLEZZ

6 [Trade] Marioboy: don't start that again … we always talk in trade … dunno why either

7 [Trade] Nishary: stop spamming trade wafflezz

8 [Trade] Wafflezz: O HAI RABITBOY

9 [Trade] Rabitboy: HOW LONG ARE THE Q's (= *queues for battlegrounds*)

10 [Trade] Frog: we talk in trade because we can talk to all cities

11 [Trade] Parasite: AI SPIE WAFFLEZZ

12 [Trade] Wafflezz: o me too

13 [Trade] Parasite: =O

14 [Trade] Wafflezz: i spie a wafflezz

Wafflezz, a notorious spammer on the server, begins this interaction in trade chat (a chat channel that can be viewed by a large number of people) by insulting another chat participant, Rabitboy (line 1). Rabitboy eventually responds by directly addressing Wafflezz in CAPSLOCK (line 5), both of which are considered aggressive linguistic strategies. Wafflezz responds in kind in line 8, and the spammer group of Wafflezz, Rabitboy, and Parasite continue their conversation with each other using these aggressive strategies while ignoring the protests of other chat participants (lines 2, 6, and 7). The spammer group also converses using a different online language form – that of LOLcat[8] – which further differentiates them from the rest of the group.

Wafflezz and his spammer group are notorious for their annoying antics in trade chat, and, from the observations of the authors and the survey responses, every server has its own version of Wafflezz. The deviant linguistic strategies of spammers are quite similar: they violate the purpose of the chat channel they are using, they use CAPSLOCK to draw attention to themselves, they make fun of other people trying to use the channel, and they ignore protests of others against what they are doing. Spammers are doing exactly what the raid leader Jeremiah was doing in Example 3 above, except in reverse. Spammers are powerless characters who are expected to use collaborative linguistic strategies like those players in Examples 2 and 3; however, they attempt to use aggressive linguistic strategies despite the fact that they do not have the requisite sources of power to gain access to these strategies.

Discussion

These interactions reveal that power within *WoW* is realized through the interaction between linguistic and cultural artifacts that position players in power roles within the gaming community. Nomercy is a high-level avatar who uses aggressive strategies to bend others to his will in battleground chat. Terrified, Dysfunction, and Jeremiah rely on collaborative strategies in order to facilitate harmonious group interactions in party and raid chat. Wafflezz uses aggressive language in trade chat, to the dismay of players who believe that the trade channel is for trade purposes only, in order to express deviant behavior. What is interesting about these examples is that there are links between the language that these players use and the power roles that they have available to them. In conjunction with Kiesling's power framework, players with greatest access to power roles (e.g. gear) are those who have the most legitimate access (according to how survey participants perceived power) to powerful linguistic strategies. For instance, Nomercy has the right to utilize aggressive linguistic strategies because he possesses epic-level gear and has lots of experience with the gameworld.

On this view, Jeremiah would also have a right to use these powerful aggressive strategies; however, he chooses to create power through collaborative language. In *WoW*, whether one has power does not determine the kind of language that will be used, but the range of available language. The speech situation narrows down the language that will most effectively suit the desired outcome. In a raid, much like when questing, all of the players must work together so that they all may reap the rewards of a job well done – in this case, they will receive epic (purple) gear, obtain money, get experience in the gameworld, and be able to brag to their friends about their victories. Such collaborative behavior may be less likely to happen if the raid leader were aggressive and harshly criticized players for their failure to perform. So while Jeremiah has access to aggressive linguistic strategies, he chooses not to employ them in order to have a better chance to achieve success in the raid. This finding is consistent with work on guild organization and leadership by Williams and colleagues (2006, 355–6), in that these data further show that guild leaders have much to gain by sharing their expert knowledge with novice players.

These results are representative of a general trend in the acquisition of language and power within *WoW*, in that participants acquire legitimate access to powerful language through the attainment of better gear and higher levels of experience. In connection with the earlier quote from R. V. Kelly, the transformation from 'pipsqueak' into veteran player is accompanied by access to more powerful linguistic forms. When a player enters the gameworld for the first time, they do not have the material artifacts within the gameworld that can place them in a power role. (See Bealer in this volume for a more in-depth discussion of the interactions between player identities and game environments.) On the one hand, in the earliest stages of a character's career in *WoW*, one would expect them to use collaborative language to access power because they do not have the requisite gear or experience – the capacity, in other words – to utilize more aggressive forms of powerful language. On the other hand, veteran players can either use collaborative language or the more powerful aggressive forms of language because gear and experience reinforces their use of powerful, aggressive linguistic forms. This shows a link between the player's real world actions (e.g. learning to play the game) resulting in actions happening to the avatar (e.g. better gear, higher level).

Importantly, our results further reveal that participants can use powerful language to create power roles within virtual interactions. Wafflezz contrasts with Jeremiah and Nomercy because he does not possess the relevant in-game artifacts that place one in a power role; yet, many survey respondents would agree that Wafflezz is deploying powerful language when spamming the trade channel. Wafflezz's behavior is significant from the standpoint of the theoretical framework because it illustrates the bidirectional relationship between language and power roles that is inherent in Kiesling's theoretical model. Specifically, access to power roles need not be restricted to those who have material artifacts as long as a player is competent in a strategy or form within a given speech situation, which opens the way for deviant behavior. Wafflezz uses powerful language to place himself in a power role within the gaming community despite the fact that he does not possess any of the relevant material sources of power that typically index power within the online community. Put another way, Wafflezz makes use of his competence in spamming language and the roles available within the trade chat context to create a power role within the community despite the fact that his avatar lacks the relevant sources of power such as gear and experience that are typically associated with a powerful position within the gameworld. (For an alternative reading of this phenomenon, see Travis's chapter in this same volume.) This strategically deviant behavior shows that it is not the case that players like Wafflezz misunderstand the norms of the community; on the contrary, they possess exceptional knowledge of interactional norms and purposefully flout them in order to take on a deviant identity.

When taken together, these data suggest that Kiesling's power framework can be extended from face-to-face conversations to incorporate virtual discourse. As a digital game, *WoW* situates players in a world that may seem altogether different from the real world. Specifically, avatars in the gameworld are immortal, in possession of magical talents, and level up over time to acquire more potent abilities. People in the real world may age or get a promotion in their job, but people in the real world do not level up and instantaneously acquire new skills and magical abilities that make them more powerful. Despite these differences between the real and the virtual, the power framework provides a viable model for interpreting the relationship between language and power in virtual discourse in that culturally defined power roles (whether real or virtual) encode norms for linguistic behavior (and vice versa). As such, an understanding of how community members view language and power within virtual conversations permits an ethnographer to explore the workings of power in online games such as *WoW*. The data for this study come from one game in particular, but power constructs and deployments may be similar for all MMORPGs. The sources of power may be different based on the construction of the game, but players will bring with them many of the same experiences and skill sets as they have to *WoW*.

Kiesling's framework would also predict that the power constructions that we have identified in *WoW* would persist over time, despite significant changes to the gameworld such as the most recent expansion: *Cataclysm* (Blizzard Entertainment, 2010). According to Kiesling's work, power structures are passed from generation to generation and are resistant to changes that occur within the community. The Gear Score Calculator is one example of a change to the game that does not appear to change the way that players perceive power – that is, the Gear Score Calculator generates a number, or 'gear score', which indicates how good or bad a player's gear is (the higher the number, the better the gear). Players will frequently display their gear score as evidence of their power and ability in the gameworld.

One aspect of identity and power that we have not addressed in this chapter is gender. At the outset of the study, we had anticipated that there would be some effect of gender on the power of a player. Interestingly, the respondents to our survey indicated that they did not see a correlation between the avatar gender and the power of the player. The result regarding avatar gender and power may seem a bit surprising, but may indicate a dissociation of player identity with avatar identity. Also, since we did not have data on the real-world gender of most participants in our study, it was not possible to link physical gender with digital linguistic behavior. Therefore, we did not incorporate gender in our analysis since it was difficult to characterize the interaction of gender with power in our study. Since gendered use of language has been linked with power in language and gender studies (cf. Eckert and McConnell-Ginet 2003, 38) more research is needed in this area as it relates to the gaming world.

Conclusion

In this chapter, we have extended research on digital games to include the formation and linguistic deployment of power within the MMORPG *WoW* using Kiesling's power framework. We argue that power in *WoW* comes from three primary sources: gear, experience, and demand. These sources provide the basis for which a powerful identity (i.e. power roles) may be constructed, and consequently the types of linguistic strategies (collaborative or aggressive) that may be used. Those characters (excluding spammers) who did not possess the adequate sources of power to use aggressive linguistic forms instead utilized collaborative strategies in order to accomplish their tasks in the gameworld. We note that even though a player possesses adequate sources of power, the simple possession of these sources does not require them to use aggressive, threatening linguistic strategies, but merely gives them the option to do so; in contrast, players who use linguistic strategies for which they do not have the required sources are perceived as annoying and deviant. This analysis reveals power to be a complex interaction of resources, activity, and identity that manifests itself linguistically in unique ways within digital gaming cultures. This research has only just begun to untangle the complexities involved in power and interaction within digital communities; future research could enhance the proposed power framework by exploring language and power within other digital game environments under the same theoretical model.

Notes

1 The authors would like to thank <SeeD> of Scarlet Crusade and its associates and friends and guild mates from Darkspear.
2 A raid is a high-level dungeon that requires the participation of many players (10–40) to complete due to its high level of difficulty.
3 For more about character capacity, see Ragnhild Tronstad's chapter in *Digital Culture, Play, and Identity: A World of Warcraft Reader*.
4 A battleground, as its name implies, is an event on all *WoW* servers that focuses on PvP combat.
5 Parenthetical expressions in transcripts are the authors' explanations of in-game jargon which may not be known to readers unfamiliar with *WoW*. Text inside of parentheses did not appear in the original utterance.
6 A party refers to a group of up to five players who are working together to perform a task.
7 A spammer is a player who constantly posts messages to the general or trade chat channel. Sometimes the spammer posts the same message many times, which fills the other players' chat boxes. In other cases, spammers talk about controversial subjects in order to get a reaction from other players and/or make other players angry.
8 Additional information about LOLcat can be found on this website: http://www.icanhascheezburger.com.

References

Bartle, Richard. 1996. 'Hearts, Clubs, Diamonds, and Spades: Players Who Suit MUDS.' Accessed June 8, 2011. http://www.mud.co.uk/richard/hcds.htm.
Blizzard Entertainment. *World of Warcraft*. [PC]. Blizzard Entertainment: Austin, 2004.
—*World of Warcraft: Cataclysm*. [PC]. Blizzard Entertainment: Austin, 2010.

—2010. 'World of Warcraft Subscriber Base Reaches 12 Million Worldwide.' Last modified October 10, 2010. http://us.blizzard.com/en-us/company/press/pressreleases.html?101007.

—2011. 'World of Warcraft Armory.' Accessed June 8, 2011. http://www.wowarmory.com.

Brown, Penelope, and Stephen Levinson. 1987. *Politeness: Some Universals in Language Usage*. Cambridge: Cambridge University Press.

Brown, Roger, and Albert Gilman. 1960. 'The Pronouns of Power and Solidarity.' In *Style in Language*, ed. Thomas A. Sebeok. 253–76. Cambridge: MIT Press.

Collister, Lauren. 2008. 'Virtual Discourse Structure: An Analysis of Conversation.' M.A. Thesis, University of Pittsburgh.

Corneliussen, Hilde G., and Jill Walker Rettberg, eds. 2008. *Digital Culture, Play, and Identity: A World of Warcraft Reader*. Cambridge: MIT Press.

Eckert, Penelope, and Sally McConnell-Ginet. 2003. *Language and Gender*. New York: Cambridge University Press.

Goffman, Erving. 1967. *Interactional Ritual*. New York: Doubleday. I Can Has Cheezburger?. 2011. Accessed June 8, 2011. http://www.icanhascheezburger.com.

Kelly, R. V. 2004. *Massively Multiplayer Online Role-Playing Games*. North Carolina: McFarland & Company.

Kiesling, Scott. 1996. 'Language, Gender, and Power among Fraternity Men.' Ph.D. Dissertation, Georgetown.

Labov, William. 1966. *The Social Stratification of English in New York City*. Washington, DC, Center for Applied Linguistics.

Mortensen, Torill Elvira. 2008. 'Humans Playing *World of Warcraft*: or Deviant Strategies?' In *Digital Culture, Play, and Identity*, ed. Hilde Corneliussen and Jill Walker, 203–24. Cambridge: MIT Press.

Nardi, Bonnie, and Justin Harris. 2006. 'Strangers and Friends: Collaborative

NC Interactive. Lineage II. [PC]. NCSOFT: Seattle, 2011.

Play in *WoW*.' In *International Handbook of Internet Research*, ed. Hunsinger, Jeremy, Lisbeth Klastrup and Matthew Allen, 395–410. New York: Springer.

Steinkuehler, Constance. 2005. 'Cognition and Learning in Massively Multiplayer Online Games: A Critical Approach.' Ph.D. Dissertation, University of Wisconsin-Madison.

Taylor, T. L. 2006. *Play between Worlds: Exploring Game Culture*. Cambridge: MIT Press.

Tronstad, Ragnhild. 2008. 'Character Identification in *World of Warcraft*: The Relationship between Capacity and Experience.' In *Digital Culture, Play, and Identity: A World of Warcraft Reader*, ed. Hilde

G. Corneliussen and Jill Walker Rettberg. 249–64. Cambridge: MIT Press.

Williams, Dmitri, Nicholas Ducheneaut, Li Xiong, Yuanyuan Zhang, Nick Yee, and Eric Nickell. 2006. 'From Tree House to Barracks: The Social Life of Guilds in *World of Warcraft*.' *Games and Culture* 1(4): 338–61.

10

In the Blood of *Dragon Age: Origins*: Metaphor and Identity in Digital RPGs

KAREN ZOOK[1]

Johan Huizinga characterizes play as an act that is not only representation, but is re-presentational; that is, it's an action that allows individuals to assimilate and recapitulate aspects of their lives (Huizinga 2002, 33ff). From a semiotic standpoint, games occupy a unique place in the pantheon of media; in a manner not seen in the western world since the early epic poets (Lord 2000), videogames serve as entertainment that allow for simultaneous performance and composition. In applying this concept to videogames, Roger Travis cites the useful identification of 'performative play practice', which he describes as play taking place in 'intersubjective performance that takes place in a cultural zone demarcated for play', or in a context that may resemble, but does not directly affect, 'real life' (Travis 2008). Play, then, can serve as an allegorical space in which the player can enact events and situations which have a significance outside the closed system of the game itself.

A videogame, however, is a world that is not bounded by the same limits that are imposed on events experienced outside it. From a semiotic standpoint, videogames occupy a unique place within the context of media as a whole. While there are certain technological and mechanical limitations to what can be done on a particular gaming platform, it's also true that games are an immersive, multi-sensory medium that are not limited by what may or may not be physically possible. Game narratives take place in settings which might be entirely unfamiliar to the player: in space, or at the bottom of the ocean, or in a fantastical realm with no relationship to physical reality. The laws of physics, for example, do not necessarily need to apply, and characters encountered do not necessarily need to resemble any currently living person (or creature). Game environments are, in many ways, the experiential equivalent of Roland Barthes' Empire of Signs, that utopian society in which language ceases to convey actual meaning and can exist as pure form (Barthes 1983). So, while no one would wish to play a game that was absolutely devoid of meaning, it's also true that there is nothing in a game that is inherently meaningful; any meaning that is present must therefore be imbued by the player.

For a game to be successful, however, it is essential that the designer and the player be able to achieve a level of communication that establishes a set of ground rules within the context of the game itself. Games are closed systems that both create and evaluate their own reward systems; they are, as Huizinga characterizes it, '"played out" within certain limits of time and place [and contain their] own course and meaning' (Huizinga 2002, 28). The designer must create a narrative framework that relates to the gameplay in such a way as to grant the player some scope of interpretation for the act of play itself (Arsenault and Perron 2009, 67). One of the most effective ways to do this in a videogame is to develop the game around a central conceit that the player can then use to relate to his or her own life experiences, thus providing a means of entry into the immersive world of the game. RPGs in general rely on the player's investment in not only the world of the game, but the particular world-view and experience of their individual character.

Dragon Age: Origins, put out by BioWare in 2009, manages to achieve this sense of internal coherency through not only fairly standard world mechanics, but also the consistent use of a single metaphor scenario: *life is blood*[2]. This scenario is constructed of an interwoven series of simple and complex metaphors relating the target domain blood to different aspects of the game narrative and character design that help create an immersive play experience. *Dragon Age: Origins* (*DAO*) takes place within a fantasy kingdom called Ferelden, possibly designed as an analogue to medieval Scotland, populated with fantasy characters (Gaider 2010), and, while most of the characters encountered there would be at least somewhat familiar to any player accustomed to the fantasy genre, does not strictly adhere to the rules that apply in the natural world. In addition (and as its title implies), *DAO* places a great deal of emphasis on identity and individual experience in the shaping of the narrative gameplay; players are encouraged to try different characters with different origins and to experiment with different branches of BioWare's extensive dialogue trees. With the exception of the very beginning and very end of the narrative arc, Ferelden is, if not a true sandbox, at least not a directed play experience; players may choose the order in which they progress through the world and what choices they make while they do so. They are, both implicitly and explicitly, encouraged to experiment with identity as they create and direct player characters (hereafter PCs).

It's intriguing, then, that BioWare would choose to focus such a game around such a grounded metaphorical domain as *blood*. It's not surprising that blood would feature prominently; the ancient Greek *agon* occurred not only in the 'play-sphere' of the festival (Huizinga 2002, 50) but on the battlefields of the Homeric epics; the relation between play and physical contest is, evidently, deeply embedded in the western psyche (for more on this phenomenon, see Travis's chapter in this same volume). Blood is not an uncommon feature in many games – there are plenty of FPSs and RPGs in which the player can expect to encounter it almost constantly – but, for the most part, such games employ blood as a sign (i.e. evidence of violence that has occurred) rather than as a means of conveying interpretive information to the player.

As a metaphor domain, blood is an extremely visceral (both metaphorically and, occasionally, literally) choice. Within the context of a game in which the player is encouraged to 'get inside' the PC, simultaneously creating and exploring the relationship of that character to the gameworld, it's an effective way to achieve this identification. As Gregersen and Grodal so aptly phrase it,

> interacting with video games may lead to a sense of extended embodiment and sense of agency that lies somewhere between the two poles of schema and image – it is *an embodied awareness in the moment of action*, a kind of *body image in action* – where one experiences both agency and ownership of visual entities. (Gregersen and Grodal 2009, 67)

The act of 'embodying' a PC is related to the physicality of gaming itself – at its most basic level, the audiovisual stimuli and the muscular activity required of the act of gameplay – but, in the case of *DAO*, successful embodiment also requires a more internalized component. The physicality of enacting the movements and interactions of the PC requires the player to navigate the world of Fereldan in a way that both demands and confers a deep understanding of the structures in place in that world. These structures are at least recognizable to the player as sharing the majority of their basic components, both physical and social, with the 'real world', albeit with the addition of certain fantasy elements. The PC encounters a recognizably hierarchical social structure, including class distinctions and organized cultural, religious, and military institutions, but this social structure has expanded to include familiar fantasy elements such as elves, dwarves, and magic (both constructive and destructive).

The player has the choice of entering the world by selecting a PC with one of seven distinct 'origins', or character backgrounds, which shape the identity and storyline of the character from that point forward. It's no coincidence that this is a significant aspect of the gameplay in *DAO*, given that the word 'origins' is present in the title. It's also a contributing factor in the development of the *life is blood* metaphor scenario; as Musolff has identified, blood has long served as a metonym for the establishment of a metaphorical relationship with the idea of origin or race (Musolff 2007, 21–43). Of course, all that blood can't just walk around Ferelden on its own (although there's a fair amount of it about, as the player comes to realize); this helps to set up the primary conceptual metaphor present in the game: *the body is a container*. This conceptual metaphor maps several elements of the source domain *container* onto the target domain *body*, as represented within the game; the body functions within the *containment* image schema, as identified by Lakoff (Lakoff and Johnson 1987, 126), and thus functions as a metaphor of *spatial motion*.

The *life is blood* metaphor scenario depends on several different metaphorical elements to support itself, of which *body is container* is only one. Kövecses would classify *body is container* as a basic metaphor, since its understanding does not require layered metaphorical interpretation (Kövecses 2006). Within the *life is blood* metaphor scenario there also exist two primary metonymies, in which a part of an object is used as a stand-in for the whole object – in this case, *person for surroundings* and *blood for life*, the latter of which is distinct from the *life is blood* metaphor scenario – and the complex metaphor *emotion is blood*. The latter, *emotion is blood*, depends on the basic metaphor *body is container*, and thus is a complex metaphor; it is, however, an accessible one, in that it also depends on an experiential understanding of emotion that almost any player would have access to from his or her own life.

Of these basic and complex metaphors, *DAO* relies most heavily on the *body is container* schema. The following entities within the source domain 'container' have corresponding elements in the metaphor as present in *DAO*:

- outside (i.e. the container has an outside surface)
- contents (i.e. the container is functioning to contain something)
- can be opened
- can be emptied

- can be refilled (or its contents can be transferred to another container
- is inanimate/inert (i.e. a container is itself a passive vessel)

The 'outside' entity corresponds to the appearance of the characters within the game. There are seven options available to the player in selecting the origin for the PC, all ostensibly recognizable to a player familiar with the genre of fantasy RPG: human noble, human mage, city elf, Dalish (i.e. forest) elf, elf mage, dwarf noble, and dwarf commoner. This selection has an impact on the player's experience of the game, as each origin is accompanied by a distinct associated backstory and set of physical characteristics. These elements serve two purposes; first, they serve a gameplay function by, as Bissell notes, strengthening the association between the player and the PC; second, they serve a narrative function, in that many of the choices influence the interactions between the PC and NPCs throughout the storyline (Bissell 2010). Peirce would interpret the PC as a 'symbol', because the PC is recognizable as belonging to a distinct subset of the gameworld's population (and, perhaps most importantly, the NPCs interact with the PC in their capacity as symbolic of their origin), but of course it is also a 'dynamic object', in that the player has the option of creating and enacting internalized motivations for the character (Peirce 1972).

The physical appearance of the PC, then, corresponds with the outside of the source domain 'container', in that it provides information to others (player and NPCs) about the PC; similarly, what is present on the outside of the container is often influenced, not by the PC him/herself, but by other elements in the PC's surroundings. One obvious incarnation of this is the different races, or body types: humans, elves, and dwarves are physically distinct from one another, and these differences are perceived and remarked upon by NPCs. Within these categories, the outside of the body-container can convey additional information serving to demarcate the PC's role or status within the societal structure.

It's simple tautology that a container must contain something. In *DAO*, one of the most obvious things being 'contained' is blood. Blood plays a significant role in *DAO*, and is central to both the game progression and the metaphorically interpretive structure of the narrative.

Blood imagery is prevalent throughout *DAO*. It is used to form the logo in the title sequence, and thus is the very first thing the player sees. Blood maintains a thematic presence throughout the game as part of the player experience, even in UI elements not directly related to gameplay mechanics. When the characters move around the map, for example, they leave a blood trail behind them. Upon encountering a new area or quest, attention is drawn to the on-screen title by surrounding it with a representation of blood.

In a nod to realism (and, perhaps, as a means of highlighting the significance of blood as a metaphorical domain), the player has the option of turning on a setting that causes the PC to maintain the post-battle blood-splatter in non-combat game interactions. That is to say, the PC can interact with the NPCs in non-hostile or even friendly ways while looking like s/he just stepped off the battlefield. The continuity of the visual representation of violence is, in the setting of a fantasy RPG, jarring.

At its most basic level, the primary object of *DAO* is to defeat an army of evil creatures called 'Darkspawn'. At the start of the game, the PC's knowledge of the Darkspawn is equivalent to the player's – that is, nothing more specific than that they sound like something you ought to be defeating. Once the PC is recruited to join the Grey Wardens – an organization of specially skilled warriors created specifically to defend Ferelden against Darkspawn surges referred to as Blights – it becomes immediately clear that, once again, blood has a role to play in the significance of this particular evil. In Ostagar, the first camp the player encounters outside the introduction, two NPCs explicitly inform the PC that Darkspawn blood is 'poisonous', 'black as sin', and has long-term effects; the PC is advised: 'Don't even touch it'.

In an early quest, the PC is instructed to gather several vials of Darkspawn blood for an as-yet-unexplained ritual. Once in the player's inventory, it's clear that there's something unusual and, indeed, actively malevolent about it. As the PC (and the player) learns, these vials of blood are intended to be used in a ritual of initiation into the Grey Wardens referred to as 'the Joining'. The initiation consist of the recruit drinking from a vial containing Darkspawn blood, with the result that the blood becomes absorbed into the body of the Warden (assuming it doesn't kill him, of course; in the PC's initiation, two of the three recruits are killed by the poison). *Dragon Age: Origins* plays extensively with the idea of dark/light, i.e. the basic metaphor *light is good* and its counterpart *dark is bad*. The storyline precludes the presence of any unambiguously 'good' characters, but it is undeniable that the Darkspawn represent 'evil' (although the inclusion of the Architect in the Awakenings expansion complicates the simplicity of the depiction of evil, as well). The Joining ritual is particularly interesting, then, in that it involves the soon-to-be-Wardens ingesting a portion of Darkspawn blood in order to absorb it into their own bodies. This allows them to communicate with the Darkspawn, but also guarantees that they will become more and more like a Darkspawn themselves (that is, more and more mindlessly destructive); it is, then, essentially a death sentence. If the *blood for life* metonymy holds true, and the Darkspawn are the representatives of evil (i.e. anti-life), then it seems that Darkspawn blood is serving as a metonym for death. After the end of the ritual, the PC is given a vial of blood to serve as a memorial for the recruits who didn't survive; as we shall see, this is echoed elsewhere throughout the game.

Three of the remaining entities in the source domain for *body is container* is that containers can be opened, emptied, or refilled (and/or have their contents transferred to another container). This relates closely to the idea that the 'stuff' of the container is blood; it doesn't really take any imagination to see the significance of a body being emptied of its blood. At least, not under normal circumstances; in *DAO*, however, the result from presence (or absence) of blood in the body is an entirely different ballgame. The difference is that, in *DAO*, the body-as-container is a mutable object, as are the contents thereof. In short, there's a lot of body-hopping going on.

The group of characters most affected by the mutability of the body is the mages. The mages are the magical figures in Ferelden, who (mostly) live in a tower guarded by a religious order called the Templars; the metaphorical implications of the tower are discussed in greater detail below. The mages derive at least some of their power from the ability to enter the Fade, a dream-realm in which the ordinary rules of the physical world no longer apply. There are, it seems, three sources of magical power in the game: the Fade, a magic-enhancing plant called Lyrium, and (in the case of mages specializing in such) blood. The ability to access the Fade is also a source of danger, however; from this realm, the mages can be corrupted or possessed by spirits or demons. There is a clear correspondence drawn between the ability to do magic (and access the Fade) and emotions. At several points the player encounters characters who experience a type of violent frenzy – one might even call it 'blood lust', if one could be excused for putting a rather fine point on it – under certain battle conditions, and the two sources of power are used together in blood magic. There is, then, clearly a relationship between blood and emotion in *DAO*. By extension of the *body is container* and emotional metaphors such as the experiential example *anger is hot*, then, we get the complex metaphor *emotion is blood*.

The ability of the mages to access the Fade allows them to exhibit agency with regard to their own body-containers. They are able to open those containers, and remove from them at least one part of their 'self'. For example, the PC encounters characters who have been in the Fade for a long time, and express awareness that their physical bodies in the 'real' world have suffered adverse effects as a result. Within the Fade dwell demons whose identities are based on powerful emotional states – Desire, Rage, Hunger, and Sloth – and mages who enter must guard against possession or corruption by one of those spirits. This self-preservation is achieved, in part, through emotional control, an essential part of training for an apprentice mage.

Living alongside the mages are a group known as the Tranquil. These NPCs are former mages who, for one of several possible reasons, have been stripped of their ability to feel emotions, which has the result of disallowing them from performing magic of any kind. The PC has repeated encounters with one particular Tranquil named Owain, who expresses displeasure with the way the Tranquil are treated, asking: 'am I to be denied personhood because I do not feel as you do?' (BioWare 2009) This makes explicit the *emotion is life* analogy. If *emotion is life* and *blood is life* then it's only logical that blood and emotion are serving as stand-ins for one another. In the mage origin story, the PC interacts with his/her friend Jowan, who is in danger of being made into one of the Tranquil because of his love for a young priestess-in-training. It is thought that Jowan would not be able to guard himself against demons in the Fade while in the grip of such strong emotion, so he is not permitted to enter. Since it later turns out that Jowan has turned to the (forbidden, because it requires blood as its source, most often from someone other than the mage him/herself) blood magic so that he can run off with his beloved, this assessment may have been accurate; if he was not able to resist the temptation of increased magical power, he might not be able to resist other temptations in the spirit realm.

One entity of the source domain 'container' is that the contents of one container can be moved to another. This is apparent in the Fade, but can also occur in the 'real' Ferelden. One of the PC's companion characters is a witch named Morrigan, who lives outside the mage tower (or Circle), and thus is an illegal witch, known as an 'apostate'. She first appears unexpectedly, over the shoulder of the PC in what the player would expect to be a typical post-battle tight shot. Her appearance out of nowhere is startling; still more startling is her presence there, in the ruin of an old Warden building in an uninhabited portion of the map known as The Wilds. Later in the game, the PC encounters an NPC who states repeatedly (chants, really; she's reading from a holy book) that 'magic exists to serve man, and never to rule over him'. This creates a subordinate metaphor scenario in which the domain magic serves as metonymy for mage; the characters the PC encounters in Ferelden, then, have mapped the characteristic exists to serve man from the source (magic) to the target (mage), with the result that entire societal institutions become constructed around the idea that the mages themselves must be treated with suspicion and constrained, lest they attempt to use the non-moral power of magic to supersede their proscribed role. In an example of the *person for place* metaphor, Morrigan is an embodiment of The Wilds. She serves as a counterpoint to the rigidly structured world within which the PC has previously operated. The introduction of Morrigan within the ruin of an old Warden structure is no accident; she is, in a sense, the embodiment of the 'ruin' of the mage/Templar/Chantry structure within which Ferelden society would require her to exist, in that her presence outside it simultaneously challenges and reifies it as an institution.

Morrigan's magical specialization is the Shapeshifter ability, meaning that she is able to take on the physical form of various beasts. This serves as a physical manifestation of her metaphorical rejection of society; she has gained the ability to physically modify her body to take on the shape of a beast, a reflection of her presence in The Wilds (again, both physically, in that it is where she literally resides, and metaphorically, in that it is outside the influence of Ferelden society). This ability – to inhabit different physical forms – is a mapped entity from the 'container' domain; her container-body can be opened and its contents put into another container.

Nor is this the only example of shapeshifting in *DAO*. Morrigan's mother, Flemmeth, is also an apostate mage. Over the course of the story she transforms into a bird (to rescue the PC and her companion, Alistair) and a dragon, and threatens to take Morrigan's body for her own. The PC also encounters a companion named Shale, a golem who, the player comes to learn, was once a dwarf. It's worth noting that the dwarves are the only race immune to magic; they have no sensitivity to Lyrium, because of its presence in the bedrock within which they have carved their homes. As a result, then, this sort of transformation (into rock itself!) is the only container-shifting of which dwarves are capable.

The player may well be left with the impression that, at least in Ferelden, the container-body is an extremely malleable entity. It quickly becomes apparent that not only is that the case, but it's also true that the container can sustain quite a bit of change before it might impact its contents in a permanent manner. While assisting the Dalish elves, the PC encounters a pack of cursed werewolves; if she chooses to help them regain their original human forms, they simply walk away with no indication that their internal identity has changed. The player is given the opportunity to experience this same theme again in the encounter with Kitty, a desire demon who has been trapped in the body of a cat. When confronted by the PC she expresses a desire to become a young girl (and, depending on how the PC handles the situation, may succeed in doing so); Kitty states that she wants to 'see the world through [the girl's] eyes', (BioWare 2009), indicating that she has the ability to intentionally jump into the girl's body, yet maintain her own identity. Once again, the player is struck by the flexibility of the body-as-container. This is an apt illustration of one entity contained within the *container* source domain: containers are, of necessity, passive and inert vessels. It is the tension between source and target domains (that is, the practical differences between container and body) that causes the characters in *DAO* to treat the mages with such suspicion; they are capable of transcending these limitations, and thus can voluntarily transfer their blood (where *blood* is metonym for *life*) from one container to another. As the PC learns, 'the Circle Tower is as much a prison as a refuge; the ever-vigilant Templars of the Chantry watch over all mages, constantly alert for any signs of corruption' (BioWare 2009), the end result being that those individuals no longer strictly bounded by their inherent physical limits have external limits imposed on them; their 'containers' have been strengthened externally.

While in the Deep Roads, the player encounters the Broodmother, a figure who embodies the central conflict at work in the thematic representation of the body's malleability in *DAO*. Throughout the Deep Roads, the player is presented with hints and clues that there are dire consequences for the ingestion of Darkspawn flesh (which would, of necessity, contain quite a bit of blood); the player comes to understand that the Broodmother originated as a young female dwarf who, through a combination of compulsory feeding (both Darkspawn and, cannibalistically, that of her traveling companions) and sexual assault is transformed into a monster capable of producing future generations of Darkspawn. This forced consumption both subjects her to, and literally transforms her into, the cannibal other, bringing into question any presumption regarding the inviolability of identity.

Besides further blurring the already hazy line between good and evil present throughout *DAO*, the player's interaction with the Broodmother highlights some of the contradictory and revelatory aspects of the issues of embodiment and identity present in the narrative. Within the metaphor scenario in which blood represents identity, it is the non-voluntary and unregulated nature of this particular ingestion that results in the complete physical transformation evident in the figure of the Broodmother. This transformation also grants her a generative power, in that her flesh, once corrupted, is capable of producing yet more of the same corrupted flesh. Thus, the *body is container* metaphor becomes corrupted by extension; once the container itself is violated, it is no longer capable of containing the identity it was originally intended to house, overflowing with the means of its own corruption.

This metaphor schema and the ways in which it is adhered to and subverted by the different player characters has a direct impact on the player's narrative experience of Ferelden, in that the PC (and thus the player) is constantly encountering the societal safeguards that have been established throughout Ferelden to counteract the mages' ability to transcend physical limitations. This is best illustrated in the mage origin story, specifically in the context of the PC's interaction with her friend Jowan. The player learns that the Templars have a vial of blood taken from each mage, stored within phylacteries, which allow the Templars to track mages that have transgressed the imposed limitations by, for example, leaving the tower or practicing blood magic. The possession of a vial of blood by the Templars gives them a great deal of control over the mages, giving rise to the complex metaphor schema *power is blood*. Jowan and his love interest are under threat of being made Tranquil (note the recapitulation of the theme of *emotion is blood*); were he able to destroy his phylactery, he would be able to leave the tower. If he does not destroy it he may still manage to escape; the Templars, however, could simply use the phylactery to track him.

There is one character who is acutely aware of his own status as a container for his own blood, with blood serving as metonym for *origin*, as identified by Musolff, and *life* (Musolff 2007, 21–43): the PC's primary companion, Alistair. In a typical videogame narrative construction, one possible objective for the PC is to install Alistair, the illegitimate son of the former king, on the throne of Ferelden. Atypically, however, Alistair is not particularly interested in becoming king; his personality is not well suited to it, for one thing, and his sole qualification seems to be his biological parentage. Toward the end of the game, the player may have the following conversation with him on the subject (emphasis added):

> Alistair: So, I'm guessing someone told Anora I was planning to steal her throne. She has a nasty glare. Did anyone mention this wasn't my idea? I think she's a great queen. As far as I'm concerned, she's welcome to it.

PC: I think you'd be a great king, Alistair.
Alistair: Really? What would ever give you that idea?
PC: *Theirin blood will tell.* You'll rise to the occasion.
Alistair: That's what I keep hearing. *The way they talk about Theirin blood you'd think I should maybe just jar it and stick that on the throne.* I never met my father, I understand he did all right as king. Worse things can happen to someone. What do you think I should do? Go ahead and be king? Just let it happen? (BioWare 2009)

Alistair's assertion that his identity is somehow separate from his blood, especially coming towards the end of a narrative in which the *life is blood* metaphor scenario features so prominently, is jarring and, like all of *Dragon Age: Origins*, calls into doubt what the player has come to assume about morality in the world of the game (and, if the experience of embodiment has been successful, perhaps has an impact on the player's interpretation of his or her own moral choices).

Thus, it is possible to see the way the metaphor scenario *life is blood* not only governs the player's experience of *Dragon Age: Origins*, but serves to expand the framework of the narrative outside the game itself. As with most BioWare games, the game itself rewards the player's drive to play for progression within the narrative over the drive to play for mastery of the game mechanics[3]. *DAO* is at its best when the player is invested in – and perhaps, to an extent, identifies with – the PC, because it allows the player to access the hermeneutic elements of game-play[4]; the *life is blood* metaphor scenario is unraveling the heuristic elements of the narrative that enable a deeper level of interpretation, allowing the game itself to serve as a mimetic medium through which the player can explore issues of identity (and identification), thereby furthering the player's investment in the gameplay itself. The more the player learns about the world of Fereldon, the less it appears possible to take anything encountered within the game at face value; good and evil, so often a clear distinction in more traditional videogames, are a grey line indeed in BioWare's presentation. *DAO* is no *Left 4 Dead*; there may be an insidious evil force at work in the world of Fereldon, but the solution is never as easy as 'kill the monsters', because the 'monsters' are never entirely *other*. The ways in which both the PC and NPCs can cross over this line at various points throughout the narrative depends largely on the subtlety of the PC's interaction with the world of the game which, in turn, depends on the subtlety of the player's identification with the PC. The physicality of the governing metaphors present throughout the narrative help to 'embody' the player in the world of the game and create these subtle connections.

Within the world of *DAO*, the player is given rein for narrative exploration and, accordingly, the developers have provided a narrative framework within which the player and PC can function. An essential element of a game – regardless of the medium – is the internal coherency of its ruleset; the game itself 'creates order, *is* order' (Huizinga 2002, 29). With such open-ended dialogue trees and character choices, it would be easy for the player to become lost within the array of options available to the PC; this metaphorical structure provides an interpretive framework within which the player can assess and govern his or her own choices. Blood is the unifying factor; it's the element that creates the internal consistency that allows for not only a satisfying narrative experience, but also a mimetic one, the implications of which can be carried beyond the closed world of the game and into the flesh-and-blood world of the player's daily life.

Notes

1 A great deal is owed to the tireless guidance of Roger Travis and Eduardo Urios-Aparisi for the work presented here.
2 This construction is a conceit of cognitive metaphor theorists; a more colloquial and expected way of expressing this same concept would be to say that 'blood is life'. Within metaphor theory, however, metaphors are expressed in the target-is-source construction.
3 *DAO* has been praised for its mechanical adaptability. The developers have released a patch for the PC edition of *DAO* which allows the player to skip the combat entirely, if he or she so desires, in order to focus on the narrative content if that is of more interest.
4 For more cf. the Magic Cycle, see Arsenault and Perron, 2009, *The Video Game Theory Reader 2*, 109–31.

References

Arsenault, Domenic and Bernard Perron. 2009. 'In the Frame of the Magic Cycle: The Circle(S) of Gameplay.' In *The Video Game Theory Reader 2*, ed. Bernard Perron and Mark J. P. Wolf, 109–32. New York: Routledge.

Barthes, Roland. 1983. *Empire of Signs*. New York: Hill and Wang.

BioWare. 2009. *Dragon Age: Origins*. [Multiplatform]. Electronic Arts. Redwood City, CA.

Bissell, Tom. 2010. *Extra Lives: Why Video Games Matter*, Kindle edition. New York: Pantheon Books.

Gaider, David. 2010. 'Antiva-Spain Or What?' Accessed 1 May 2010. http://social.bioware.com/forum/1/topic/9/index/425645/1#426051

Gregersen, Andreas and Torben Grodal. 2009. 'Embodiment and Interface.' In *The Video Game Theory Reader 2*, ed. Bernard Perron and Mark J. P. Wolf. New York: Routledge.

Huizinga, Johan. 2002. *Homo Ludens*. London: Routledge.

Kövecses, Zoltan. 2006. *Language, Mind, and Culture: A Practical Introduction*. Oxford: Oxford University Press.

Lakoff, George and Mark Johnson. 1987. *Women, Fire and Dangerous Things: What Categories Reveal About the Mind*. Chicago: The University of Chicago Press.

Lord, Albert B. 2000. *The Singer of Tales*. 2nd ed. Cambridge: Harvard University Press.

Musolff, Andreas. 2007. 'What Role Do Metaphors Play in Racial Prejudice? The Function of Antisemitic Imagery in Hitler's Mein Kampf.' *Patterns of Prejudice* 41(1): 21–43.

Peirce, Charles S. 1972. *The Essential Writings*. New York: Harper and Row.

Travis, Roger. 2010. 'Performative Play Practices: Are Stories and Games Really the Same Thing?' *Living Epic*, 8 November. livingepic.blogspot.com/2008/06/performative-play-practices-1-are.html

Wark, McKenzie. 2007. *Gamer Theory*. Cambridge: Harvard University Press.

11

Epic Style: Re-compositional Performance in the BioWare Digital RPG

ROGER TRAVIS

Since 1997, when Janet Murray's *Hamlet on the Holodeck* appeared (Murray 1997), critics have from time to time been exploring the analogy between oral traditional epic, as studied especially by Milman Parry (Milman Parry and Adam Parry 1987) and Albert Lord (Lord 1981), and digital games. Most prominently in recent years, perhaps, Emily Short, critic and creator of interactive fiction, has been writing a column entitled 'Homer in Silicon' (Short 2011) that explores the narrative potential of digital games in general and textual interactive fiction in particular, though largely without specific reference to Homer. From a theoretical perspective, these efforts have been hampered by an insufficient attention among critics like Murray and Short to the specificities of oral formulaic theory as developed especially by Lord and the homerists who came after him.

In this chapter I aim to move this area of games criticism forward by describing a particular segment of narrative practice in games – the performance style allowed to the player of the BioWare RPG – as a practice of the same kind of composition by theme described by Lord in traditional oral epic. To this end, I discuss three BioWare RPGs: *Star Wars: Knights of the Old Republic* (hereafter *KOTOR*), *Mass Effect*, and *Dragon Age: Origins* (hereafter *DAO*).

I argue that what I call BioWare's epic style, as a practice of composition by theme, allows the player to perform re-compositions of the thematic material ('theme' in this chapter means 'recurrent element' – see below) of the game that instantiate an identification of player with player-character (hereafter PC) that has characteristics we can describe as distinctive of the BioWare RPG: the identification is *manifest* in a distinctive way, and it is *related to the cultural meaning of the game* in a distinctive way. These distinctive features of the BioWare style arise in a combination of the modularity of the content of the games and the use of what I term 'sliders', which index the player's performance choices according to scales that have an integral relation to the cultural meaning of the games. (The term 'content' as used in games criticism is somewhat ambiguous. In this chapter, I use the term narrowly, to mean 'verbal and visual information accessible to the player in the course of playing the game'.) When we describe these distinctive elements of the BioWare style in the terms of oral formulaic theory as part of a practice of composition by theme, we gain theoretical traction over their role in gaming culture and in broader culture: player-performances of BioWare games transform the public role of the homeric or Southslavic bard into a new and interesting mediation of private and public, where the game allows the player to negotiate his or her identity in a way analogous to performance practices of oral epic, but crucially different in the way players shape their gaming identities as members of a performing audience.

Composition by Theme

The modern study of traditional oral epic in general, and homeric epic in particular, begins in 1928, with the publication of Milman

Parry's first work on the *Iliad* and the *Odyssey* (found in Milman Parry and Adam Parry 1987). After Parry's early death, his student Albert Lord continued the work Parry had done on Homer into the comparative study of homeric poetry and the oral poetry of the Southslavic guslars. In 1960, Lord published *The Singer of Tales* (Lord 1981), which remains the seminal work in the field, and has inspired the modern study of traditional epic in relation to its oral roots. What Parry discovered about Homer, and then confirmed by the comparison to Southslavic epic that Lord brought to fruition, was that homeric poetry contains the evidence of its origin in a system of oral formulas out of which the homeric bards – the singers of tales of Dark Age Greece – composed the songs we know as the *Iliad* and the *Odyssey*. Those epics, Parry demonstrated, came about in a system of bardic re-composition in which bards performed new versions of their tales every night.

As Janet Murray pointed out in *Hamlet on the Holodeck* (Murray 1997, 185–94), that re-compositional system makes living oral epic a multiform narrative system highly analogous to the systems in digital games that allow players to perform re-composed versions of the games' narratives a potentially infinite number of times, varying their performances according to the possibilities available in the games, as the homeric bards varied their tales according to the possibilities available in the poetic system in which they had been trained. This broad analogy captures the imagination. The argument that the videogames that seem by so much the newest art form of the modern world in fact reawaken a millennia-old tradition of storytelling is of the kind most enjoyable for a scholar to make. In my argument in this chapter, however, I am seeking to go much further, and to demonstrate that by making the analogy in a very precise deployment of the theoretical concepts pioneered by Parry, refined by Lord, and deployed since 1960 in homeric scholarship, we can describe a specific style of digital game, within a specific genre, more thickly than it has yet been described (I borrow the idea of thick description from Geertz's [1973] application of it to anthropology).

Lord's 1951 article 'Composition by Theme in Homer and Southslavic Epos' (Lord 1951) defines 'theme' as 'recurrent element of narration or description' (Lord 1951, 73) and proceeds to demonstrate that the homeric bards, like the Southslavic guslars, built their tales out of modular themes, which they must have learned (as the guslars learned) to deploy like building-blocks as an essential element of their training. Themes, to put it another way, are modular pieces of content, subject to variation themselves, out of which, in turn, a skilled performer can build his or her performance. The process of composition by theme makes every performance of oral epic a *re-compositional* process as well, because even the first time the bard performs a theme, he is re-composing it from the performance materials available to him in the traditional system in which he has been trained. Lord suggests in that essay a process of analysis of such composition by theme in Homer that scholars like Laura Slatkin have taken up (Slatkin 2006). A composition-by-theme analysis examines the way the bard has deployed his themes in a given passage or set of passages of Homer, and describes the effect that deployment has, either within the culture of the bard, or within the millennia-long reception of homeric poetry. I propose to carry out that kind of analysis not of a fossilized epic tradition like the homeric epics but of the living epic tradition of the BioWare RPG.

The idea of composition by theme might be applied to almost any digital game, because player-performances of these games are built from elements that recur thanks to the basic constitution of games' ludics and contents from fixed digital materials. The first ten minutes of a player's performance of *KOTOR*, for example, consist of choices between content-elements that could fairly be called 'themes' like 'conversation with a tutorial NPC' and 'battle' and are varied according to the exact way the player performs them, especially including dialogue choices he or she makes, for example whether to have Trask Ulgo, the first non-player-character (hereafter NPC) his or her PC meets explain various details about the situation. We might make the same kind of description of a level of *HALO*, in which the player's performance is built out of the weapons he or she chooses for his or her PC, enemies the PC kills, paths the player chooses to take through the level, and cutscenes triggered by specific player actions – all of which fit Lord's definition of 'theme' in that when the player, or another player, plays that same level again, those same elements can, and usually do, recur.

Moreover, we can describe as thematic – in Lord's sense of 'theme' – the essential stylization of the content of digital games, both within a single game and across broad ranges of games of individual genres and even of multiple genres. The taverns of *DAO* and the nightclubs of *KOTOR* and *Mass Effect,* for example, are all versions of a theme we could call the digital version of the 'assembly' theme to be found both in Homer and in Southslavic epic. Indeed, that same theme recurs not only in BioWare games but also in the guild halls of Bethesda games and even the inns of a game like *The Lord of the Rings Online*. When we shift our consideration to the themes 'battle' and the related 'single combat', both of course staples of Homer and Southslavic epic, we find corresponding themes not only in the digital RPG but also in the FPS and action-adventure game.

In fact, we can contextualize such an application of oral formulaic theory to RPGs quite neatly within important tropes of more familiar theoretical constructs of game studies, in particular Ian Bogost's analysis of videogames as unit operations (Bogost 2006, 3–6) and his development of that analysis into descriptions of videogames as sites for the enactment of procedural rhetoric (Bogost 2007, 44–6). From the perspective of game studies, the analytic work done on homeric and other traditional oral epic since Parry and Lord is actually a form of unit operations analysis; the formulas and themes of oral traditional epic are a precise poetic analogue for the units Bogost describes, and the techniques of composition and elaboration used by the bard are a precise poetic analogue for the procedures Bogost analyzes as operating upon those units.

Manifest Modularity of Theme

Themes, as defined by Lord, are inherently modular. Any recurrent element may be deployed fungibly as a modular building-block in service of the overall performance of a narrative. I show in this section, though, that the modularity of theme to be found in *KOTOR, Mass Effect,* and *DAO* has the special quality of being particularly manifest to the player. This manifestation of the re-compositional process makes the player's performance in turn manifestly a re-composition, because the results of thematic choices among manifestly modular options compound themselves into versions of the game's themes whose exact shapes are entirely dependent on the choices the player has made.

For example, fundamentally modular choices of party-characters to accompany the PC and places to go in the game's world redound into modular visual sequences in dialogue segments. If the player of *KOTOR* has chosen the NPC Carth Onasi as a member of his party, the player will see and hear Carth offer a particular opinion when the player has the PC confront some boys who are teasing a non-human. If the player has chosen a different party member, he or she will not encounter Carth's opinion. The version of the 'Talk to cruel human boys' theme with Carth's opinion is a re-composition based on the choice to bring Carth; by the same token, the version of the theme without Carth's opinion is equally a re-composition based on the opposite choice. The modularity of the party-selection screen, the choice of where to move, and the dialogue itself, make the role of composition by theme entirely manifest to the player, even if the player would never think to call the process by which he or she makes decisions and experiences his or her resulting performance 're-composition'.

Three kinds of modularity determine re-compositional performances in *KOTOR*, *Mass Effect*, and *DAO*: party selection, narrative-geographical selection, and dialogue selection. The first two of these function more or less independently of one another, although in certain narrative-geographical locations one or more party-members are pre-determined because the narrative-geographical sequence concerns them most nearly. The third (dialogue selection) compounds choices made in party and narrative geography into elements of the player-performance, like Carth's opinion in the example given just above, but also has an independent dimension, especially where the expression of a player's decisions about the PC's character is concerned. I treat each of the three in turn.

Each of the games features a party-selection screen that appears whenever the player chooses to enter a new part of the narrative geography of the game. In these screens, the player must choose two (*KOTOR* and *Mass Effect*) or three (*DAO*) of the available party-characters to accompany his or her PC in the upcoming sequence. The version of the themes (for example, 'visit to Denerim' in *DAO*, which might include a version of 'visit to a tavern'; or 'visit to the

Presidium' in *Mass Effect*) that the player then performs is built in very significant part out of the performance materials that become available when the player chooses particular party-characters. To the example of Carth's opinion about the taunting boys given above, we can add, in *Mass Effect*, the example of any number of sequences in which the player may choose the sniper Garrus as a companion instead of the Biotic (a science-fiction kind of wizard) Liara, changing the battles (or, to put it another way, the 'battle' theme) of an upcoming 'invasion of an enemy installation' theme at an essential ludic level. More fundamentally, with respect to the eventual final meaning of the player's performance in relation to the compositional system of the game, a player of *DAO* whose PC is a female and who has pursued a romance with the party-character Alistair might bring Alistair and Wynne along and hear in the midst of a tense situation a conversation between them about his intentions vis-à-vis the PC. All these variations in theme are *manifestly modular* in great part because of the party selection screen – the player chooses how he or she will re-compose the performance materials of the game to produce his or her current performance.

Similarly, each of the games features some kind of narrative-geographical interface. *KOTOR*, the earliest of the games, has only a selection screen that looks like a dialogue choice, allowing the player to choose which planet to visit next aboard the Ebon Hawk, but its function is the same as the galactic map in *Mass Effect* and the map of Ferelden in *DAO*. In each case, the various narrative-geographical locations of the game (for example, the planet Manaan in *KOTOR*, the Citadel in *Mass Effect*, and the city of Denerim in *DAO*) appear to the player as themes (again, even if the player would never to think to call them that) – recurrent elements of narration and description. To make a choice from one of these interface screens is to re-compose the current performance from the available materials at the very least in terms of the order of the episodes; moreover, very frequently a later theme will unfold significantly differently depending on previously made choices of narrative geography. The most obvious example is probably the locations of narrative geography in which the PC meets and recruits new party-characters, for example the Jedi Jolie Bindo on Kashyyk in *KOTOR*; if the player's PC goes to Tattoine before Kashyyk, the PC's party on Tattoine will not include Jolie. Analogous examples are present in both *Mass Effect* and *DAO*. As with party selection, the player's selections of narrative geography make manifest the ongoing process of composition by theme.

Finally, the many dialogue selection screens display the same manifest modularity. In the dialogue selections of *KOTOR, Mass Effect*, and *DAO*, the player has the opportunity to shape his or her current performance in several important ways, including brevity or length of conversation, the discovery or failure of discovery of background information, and – perhaps most importantly – relation to the game's performance slider(s): light/dark, renegade/paragon, approval/disapproval (discussed at length just below).

Mass Effect's dialogue wheel, on which not the exact words Shepard will speak, but a sort of epitome of them, is displayed, along with Shepard actually speaking the dialogue according to the player's selections, distinguishes that game from *KOTOR* and *DAO*. In the latter two games, the presumably exact words to be uttered by the PC appear on the selection screen – 'presumably' because the player does not see or hear the PC say those words. Whatever the effect of this difference upon *Mass Effect*'s place in the development of the RPG and/or its relation to other arts such as film, the dialogue wheel is certainly entirely analogous to the dialogue selection screens of other BioWare games where composition by theme is concerned; the player has the opportunity to vary the themes as he or she performs them through Shepard just as he or she does through the PCs of *KOTOR* and *DAO*.

These three aspects of re-compositional performance practice in *KOTOR, Mass Effect*, and *DAO* thus serve to foreground the process of re-composition itself. As the homeric bards and the Southslavic guslars learned to build their songs out of themes such as assemblies, battles, arming scenes, and verbal contests (a training detailed at fascinating length in Lord 1981), the player of the BioWare RPG learns to assemble his or her performances out of the themes available, and to compress or elaborate them, to order them, and to perform them virtuosically through an ever-growing understanding of the party-characters of his or her PC's party, of the narrative geography of the galaxy or of Ferelden, and of the conversational options open to the PC under given circumstances.

The Performance Slider

All this modularity would perhaps distinguish the BioWare RPG a little as a set of performance occasions analogous to those of the bards; we might even be excused for calling the modular ludics of these games a 'BioWare style'. The truly distinguishing feature of the BioWare style, though, has to this point barely entered this chapter. I now show that the sliders of *KOTOR*, *Mass Effect*, and *DAO* make the BioWare style as distinctive as the styles that separate the bards of the *Iliad* from those of the *Odyssey* (on this fascinating topic, once the sum total of what was called the 'Homeric question', see especially Nagy 1996 and Nagy 1979).

KOTOR, *Mass Effect*, and *DAO* each have what I call here a 'performance slider': a scale (or, in *DAO*, a set of scales) that measures and displays the status of the player's performance as the PC in relation to what I will argue below is the cultural topic of the game as a whole. In *KOTOR*, the slider measures the number of lightside and darkside points the player has received for choices he or she has made in the course of dialogue selection, like supporting or chastising the cruel boys of my first example. The player's current position on the slider determines what background color is displayed along with the slider on the game's character screen. When the player's PC, for example, gives credits to those in need, or does battle on behalf of the weak, the PC gains lightside points, and the slider moves up and towards the blue; when the PC, for example, refuses to give, or attacks an NPC in order to commit robbery, the PC gains darkside points, and the slider moves down and toward the red. The PC's position on the slider also determines how many points of Force energy are used in the invocation of certain Force skills like Heal (lightside PCs expend fewer) and Force Lightning (darkside PCs expend fewer).

In *Mass Effect,* the slider is not positional, but rather appears as the sum total of paragon and renegade points, displayed to the upper left and lower right of the PC respectively on the character screen. The area covered by the blue paragon scale and that covered by the red renegade scale together go to make up the player's position on the slider, which measures the player's dialogue choices in the general matter of showing kindness or exercising authority, for example when a crew-member of Shepard's ship, the *Normandy*, confesses to misgivings about the mission. The paragon dialogue choice, in general, expresses empathy (in this example, the choice might read 'We'll be fine'); the renegade dialogue choice, in general, expresses self-serving authoritativeness (here the choice might read 'Act like a soldier!'); there is always also a middle choice (for example 'We can't think about that now') that adds no points on either side.

It should be noted that the paragon/renegade slider is not *apparently* zero-sum, the way the light/dark slider and the approval/disapproval sliders are, and that description of it is complicated by there not always being both a paragon and a renegade choice (sometimes only renegade and neutral, or paragon and neutral, are provided), but because there is a finite number of paragon and renegade points available both in any given theme and in the system as a whole, the final effect is in fact zero-sum, although it is possible to explore both sides of the slider in a single performance of *Mass Effect* in a way impossible in a single performance of *KOTOR* or *DAO*. The PC's position on the slider determines the player's opportunity to gain the Charm and/or Intimidate skills; these skills, in turn, unlock significant dialogue options such as those that can save Shepard the necessity of killing one of his or her crew-members, Urdnot Wrex.

In *DAO*, the sliders appear not on the PC's own character-screen but on the party-character's individual screen, and represent the character's approval or disapproval of the actions of the PC. These scales can be affected either by dialogue choices, as in *KOTOR* and *Mass Effect*, or by the giving of certain gifts to be found throughout the narrative geography of the game. The PC's position on these sliders determines whether dialogue options with the party-characters are open to them; these dialogue options, in turn, open others, including, for example, options that themselves lead to themes (that is, quests) that the player would otherwise have no opportunity to perform.

KOTOR's light/dark slider may be described in several ways. The most usual way to describe it is as a morality scale, by which the player's choices are given what observers describe, broadly, as moral consequences in relation to the ongoing events of his or her performance. Indeed, as an element of game-design, the slider has been harshly criticized on that understanding of it as a morality scale (Sicart 2009, 207–11).

The light/dark slider may also be described, though, as a ludic system by which *KOTOR* differentiates player-performances. As the player accumulates a balance on one or the other side of the slider, choices of character configuration – that is, the cost to the PC of certain powerful skills – are shaped by where the PC stands on the slider. For a player on the light side of the slider, skills like 'Heal' are less costly, and skills like 'Drain Life' are more costly. The player's dialogue choices are thereby registered at the level of the gameplay so as to differentiate his or her performance from other possible performances at that level, in a way parallel to the differentiation at the level of dialogue, where the player must choose to say certain things and not to say others – choices that trigger the game's awards of lightside or darkside points.

At the same time, in a broader context, the light/dark slider differentiates the player's performance in relation to the range of possible performances as a Jedi in the *Star Wars* universe, whose dualistic light/dark ethical system is essential to the game, as it is to every part of the discourse of *Star Wars*. The climactic decision in *KOTOR*, for example, of whether finally to side with the Jedi or with the Sith adds either an enormous number of lightside points or an enormous number of darkside points to the PC's total, and thus places him or her decisively in relation to the ongoing performances of the *Star Wars* universe, whether in games, on film, or in text.

A brief comparison to homeric epic may be helpful in clarifying my point. When a bard first chose to have Odysseus lie to his father in what we know as Book 24 of the *Odyssey*, and when a bard first chose to have Patroclus call Hector his 'third slayer' in Book 16 of the *Iliad*, those choices differentiated those performances from every performance that had gone before, but they did so **in relation to** the existing epic materials – those new themes, that is, were already based on old ones ('lying' and 'battle-taunting'). In the re-compositional process, bards made their choices in developing their themes based on their knowledge of, and skill in using, the themes that had gone before.

Indeed, when subsequent bards followed them and used those themes ('lying to father', 'victor as third slayer') in their own performances, they enacted similarly unique performances in relation to the existing themes, despite the fact that they were using a pre-existing theme. To describe the difference between the *Iliad* and the *Odyssey* in a way that goes beyond the obvious and takes into account their geneses in bardic tradition requires that we describe the differing relationships between performance and theme in the two epics. That kind of analysis can tell us, for example, that the bards of the *Odyssey* re-composed their performances so as to take advantage of their hero's own relationship to performances like theirs, and demonstrate their virtuosity at such composition.

That sort of argument is well known to scholars of homeric epic; it has, to my knowledge, not been attempted in criticism of the digital RPG. I want to argue, though, that it should be attempted, because, for example, at the moment of decision between Jedi and Sith, the player of *KOTOR* re-composes his or her performance, **even the first time**, out of the elements given by the game, and above all in relation to his or her PC's position on the light/dark slider. This is, I believe, the basic nature of re-composition in the BioWare style: the player at every moment shapes his or her performance with reference to a ludic system that renders the performance meaningful *in relation to* the entire system of the game, which is at the same time an overdetermined version of the player's world that productively mystifies him or her about the meaning of his or her choices, both in the game and in 'real' culture.

From this perspective, the homeric equivalent of the BioWare style would perhaps be a sub-genre in which bards sung their heroes' words and actions according to a very stylized set of requirements (there are certainly examples of poetic genres with not dissimilar stylizations – think of haiku) that, rather than the Iliadic focus on glory or the Odyssean focus on wits, enforced a focus on a 'scale' of diction that related words to themes. Odysseus would, for example, lie to his father if the bard had earlier called him 'Odysseus the crafty', or not lie to his father if the bard had called him 'Odysseus the wise'; Patroclus would be third-killed by Hector if Hector had previously boasted that he was 'great in glory'.

I am thus arguing that what makes the BioWare style special is the way it ties the player's performance explicitly to a fundamental ludic system that itself both represents and determines the register of the game's range of performances. In *KOTOR*, that range has to do with the light/dark duality of the *Star Wars* universe; because of the light/dark slider, performances of *KOTOR* are always characterized in terms of where they fall on its spectrum: light, dark, or neutral. Because that light/dark duality was from its beginning in the original film *Star Wars* (now known as *Star Wars: A New Hope*) a mystifying allegory of real-world ethics, the *KOTOR*-player's performance functions to express, and perhaps even to shape, his or her practices outside the game. The BioWare performance slider bears an essential relation to the cultural topic of the game.

In *KOTOR* the light/dark slider does not simply index what the player, and any observer, are supposed to think about the player-character within the overall sphere of culture (that is, is the PC a 'good' or a 'bad' 'person' when measured by the standards of the community of which the player and observers are members). Much more importantly, the light/dark slider indexes how the player-character stands according to the fictively created governing rules of the fictional universe in which the player and observers imagine the narrative action of the game taking place. In *KOTOR*, the Force, the 'energy field' that 'gives a Jedi his power', 'is created by all living things', and 'surrounds us, penetrates us, and binds the galaxy together' (*Star Wars*, dir. George Lucas, 1977), itself indexes the player-performance in the world of the narrative. *KOTOR,* like all *Star Wars* narratives, takes the Force as what I am calling its 'cultural topic', and the light/dark slider makes the re-composition by theme of the player-performance about it, too.

The Force, like the Council in *Mass Effect* and the Ferelden/Blight conflict in *DAO,* is what *KOTOR* is most generally about. Also like *Mass Effect*'s Council and *DAO's* Ferelden/Blight conflict, the Force renders an ideological negotiation from the 'real world' in fictive terms. The Force is a fictive reification of important ethical questions of modern culture – in particular of the claims of the Other on the self; the Council is a fictive reification of questions about nationalism and Western exceptionalism in the modern world; the Ferelden/Blight conflict is a fictive reification of questions about loss of freedom to the State in times of crisis.

KOTOR revolves around the PC's efforts to bring the Sith under control and restore order to the galaxy. As the Jedi represent the yielding of self in the effort to create harmony, the Sith represent the strengthening of self to bring the world under the self's control.

The PC's position on the light/dark slider thus measures the player's current performance's meaning in relation to the central conflict of the game which, from the first cutscene in the PC's dream, phrases the question of the PC's identity as a search for where he or she fits into the struggle between the Jedi and the Sith, the light and the dark sides of the Force: with his or her performance's changing position on the light/dark slider, the player progressively answers that question.

Mass Effect's paragon/renegade slider is equally tied to the cultural topic of the game. The performance materials of *Mass Effect* orient themselves around the efforts of an interstellar United Nations to save the galaxy with the help of Shepard, the PC. The paragon/renegade slider indexes a player's choices of how to behave with respect to that organized government, in an overarching context which, from the game's opening cutscene, stages Shepard's actions as an ongoing assessment of the capacity of the human race to take a vital role in affairs of galactic salvation. Shepard becomes the first human 'Specter' – that is, member of the elite galactic security organization charged with furthering the aims of the multi-species Council; Shepard's actions, both paragon and renegade, are constantly evaluated by NPCs as examples of human conduct, above all at the conclusion of the game when Shepard must choose either to save the Council (and leave the fate of the galaxy in grave doubt) or to save the galaxy.

DAO, as befits the ongoing development of the style, presents more complexity, but the multiple approval/disapproval sliders of individual party-members, though they complicate the game's performance possibilities in myriad ways, nevertheless have the same connection to the cultural topic of the game: *DAO*'s performance materials are about the nature of Fereldan and of the threat to its safety (the Blight), and the question of what the cost of saving that, or any land so constituted, must be. The NPCs of the PC's party in *DAO* – above all, Alistair and Morrigan – present a system for shaping player-performances that enact a particular answer to that question, an answer unique to that performance. Each NPC has an individual relation to Fereldan. Alistair is the reluctant heir who has been mistreated by the power-structure. Morrigan is a witch from The Wilds whose motives are unclear for most of the game, but in the end have everything to do with the Blight, and in particular *nothing* to do with saving Ferelden: her aim all along has been to be impregnated by a Grey Warden (the Ferelden-saving order of warriors of which both Alistair and the PC are initiates). Leliana, Wynne, Oghren, Zevran, and Sten each have a very particular relationship to Ferelden; none has as decisive an effect on the player-performance as Alistair and Morrigan do, but each adds thematic possibilities that change what the performance means in relation to the cultural topic Ferelden/Blight.

The NPC sliders of approval/disapproval differentiate player-performances with respect not only to any idea the player might have about liking, disliking, loving, or hating this or that NPC, but also with respect to the much more embracing question of what the PC should do as a Grey Warden to save Ferelden, and how he or she, and with him the player and any observer, should feel about it. What affects the *DAO* sliders are decisions made about how to deal with the Ferelden/Blight conflict. A player-performance that employs choices that please Alistair is a composition whose re-compositions of themes are very different from one using choices that please Morrigan; the differences in thematic re-composition, moreover, represent fundamental reshapings of the meaning-effect of that performance as a version of the Ferelden/Blight conflict.

It would require much more space than I have in this chapter to fully explore the relationships of these sliders to the meanings of their games. It should be clear, however, that those relationships to cultural significance makes the BioWare slider different from, for example, the Bethesda one. The Bethesda reputation (e.g. *Oblivion*) or karma (*Fallout 3*) slider indexes player-performance not to the cultural topic of the game but to an apparently transparent game-representation of a 'real-world' ideological evaluation. Karma in *Fallout 3* and reputation in *Oblivion* both differentiate player-performance in a way roughly analogous to that of the light/dark slider, but *Fallout 3* is not **about** karma, nor is *Oblivion* **about** reputation, in the way that *KOTOR* is about the two sides of the Force, *Mass Effect* is about how Shepard deals with the Council, and *DAO* is about the people of Ferelden.

Modularity and Slider in Combination: Meaningful Identification

The combination of modularity and sliders produces a particular kind of relationship between player and re-compositional ludic system that I will call 're-compositional PC-identity'. The constitutive ludics – manifest modularity plus sliders – of the composition-by-theme process of the BioWare style force players of these three games to form a specific kind of identification with their player-characters – an identification that enacts a subjectivity *manifestly negotiated* between the game's thematic system and the choices the player makes within that system. Here I borrow from apparatus theory, but the argument does not require elaborate theoretization; as I detail below, the interpellation involved in the combination of modularity and sliders is literally forced on the player by the ludic systems of the games, in that he or she must periodically visit the screens bearing the sliders (the key terms 'apparatus' and 'interpellation' originate in Althusser 1971; apparatus theory as applied in film criticism, with an emphasis on spectatorship that has, I believe, a great deal to offer games criticism of elements like the character screen, the party-selection screen, and the narrative-geography screen, is developed in e.g. Baudry 1999). The player of a BioWare RPG must relate to his or her PC through the performance of modular themes and the manipulation of sliders effected thereby, with the result that his or her performance enacts an apparently visibly unique claim to selfhood (apparatus theory, following Lacan 1977, 1–7, rigorously maintains that any recognition of the self is a mis-recognition).

The paragon/renegade slider in *Mass Effect* can serve, with its strong similarities to the light/dark slider in *KOTOR* and the party-character sliders in *DAO*, as an emblem of this re-compositional PC-identity; the negotiation of modular themes involved in performing a particular version of *Mass Effect* produces a manifestation in the 'Squad' screen of what kind of human the player's Shepard is. Because the cultural topic of the game is the status of the human race vis-à-vis the other races of the galaxy, what the player sees on the squad screen is a visual index of a numerically determined relationship between his or her performance and the meaning of that performance with respect to the cultural topic. That is, the player's identification with Shepard – the way he or she is performing Shepard as a performative extension of him or herself (including any performance that operates as a denial, through the performance, of Shepard's status as that kind of extension) – is visible as a negotiation on the squad screen, a screen the player must visit every time Shepard gains an experience level if the player is to continue playing the game.

KOTOR and *DAO* share the essence of this ludic negotiation of re-compositional PC-identity. When we compare the paragon/renegade slider to the light/dark slider in *KOTOR*, we see the essential similarity of the two systems – every experience level, and usually many times in between, the player of *KOTOR* sees his or her re-compositional performance's relation through the slider to the task of saving the galaxy. Although the *DAO* system differs in that the sliders are not centrally located, it is similarly essential to continuing the game that the player visit the party-characters' individual screens with great frequency (at least those of party-characters the player has chosen to adventure with), and each party-character's approval/disapproval slider is displayed prominently on that screen. Just as in *Mass Effect*, the player sees a visual representation of a quantitative index of the relationship of his or her performance as the player-character to the in-progress cultural meaning of that performance of the game.

Through the manifestation of that negotiation, I would suggest, the player gains a special impression of individuality and of fullness that distinguishes the BioWare style, an impression that shines through on community sites like the official BioWare forums (see for example BioWare Inc. 2011), where players of BioWare games share their experiences of that game and describe their performances in terms that often might justly be described as rapturous. Whereas the homeric bards and their analogues in Yugoslavia performed their thematic re-compositions in relation to a public occasion and a public role, the player of the BioWare RPG performs him or herself to him or herself, with any performance to a third party mediated through that single-player experience, gaining a self-identity that we may describe theoretically in the terms I use above, as a subjectivity of manifest negotiation. Manipulating the modular themes of the games in relation to the games' sliders performs the player's subjectivity as not only capable of saving a world worth saving, but also as capable of making that salvation meaningful outside the game through the relation of the sliders to the games' cultural topics.

Because these sliders are influenced by the player's individual re-compositional performance of the games' modular themes, and because they in turn influence the availability of further modular performance materials like powers and dialogue choices, the player's re-compositional PC-identity renders the game meaningful to the player not just as an occasion for the performance of play, but as an occasion for the performance of a specific kind of self, unique to the BioWare style. As the bards of the *Odyssey* performed themselves as heroes through their manipulation of themes like 'Banquet' and 'Battle', and the bards of the *Iliad* performed themselves as preservers of heroic glory through their manipulation of themes like 'Embassy' and 'Ransom', the re-composer, whether bard or RPG-player, must always perform him or herself, but must also always perform him or herself *differently* according to the constraints of the occasion. Those constraints, as they exist in *KOTOR, Mass Effect,* and *DAO*, constitute what I have here described as BioWare's epic style.

Conclusion: Application of the Argument to Other RPG Styles

The sheer individuality of that style, along with the obviousness of the manifest modularity that I have suggested is its hallmark, has made the BioWare RPG, in my view, the ideal starting point for an investigation of composition by theme. That individuality can indeed cause us to wonder whether this kind of analysis has any application to other styles; if the re-compositional identity I am describing in BioWare RPGs comes about through the uniquely modular operation of what Bogost would call these games' procedural rhetoric and I would call their re-compositional style, how could we possibly discuss another style of RPG, such as the Bethesda or Square Enix style, using this theoretical model?

The question may actually open, rather than foreclose, exciting critical possibilities. From the standpoint of oral formulaic theory, games like *The Elder Scrolls* series and the *Fallout* series afford their players, broadly speaking, several of the same kinds of theme as the BioWare RPGs: the countless dungeons of *The Elder Scrolls* and subway tunnels of *Fallout* serve as a clear (though very far from exhaustive) example. As I showed above, the renown and karma systems of Bethesda games do not make the same kind of interpellation as the performance-sliders in BioWare RPGs, not least because the player does not face them regularly as s/he progresses, so those systems become simply another aspect of the games' thematic material; but the contrast thus developed between performance-slider and renown/karma points the way towards a description of the Bethesda style focused precisely on its tendency to obscure, above all through its reliance on a seemingly boundless open world and seemingly limitless choices for character development, the interpellative dynamics of the Bethesda RPG.

Apparatus theory tells us that interpellation occurs whenever a subject misrecognizes itself; the open-world narrative geography and 'open-character' PC development of the Bethesda RPG interpellate a re-compositional identity that depends on the PC's relationship to that geography and NPC organizations like the Fighters' Guild and the Wizard's Guild in *The Elder Scrolls IV: Oblivion* and the Brotherhood of Steel in *Fallout 3*. Re-compositional performance of the materials to be found in places like the Fighters' Guild guild-halls results in rising through the ranks of such organizations, and gives access to otherwise-inaccessible parts of the 'open' world like the headquarters of the guild. In turn, the cultural topic of these organizations, reinforced by the often striking design of the narrative geography associated with them (for example the 'Citadel' of the Brotherhood of Steel being the Pentagon), sets the PC in relation to the games' overall cultural significance.

It seems possible to argue along such lines that re-compositional identity is at work just as powerfully in the Bethesda style as in the BioWare one, and that analyses of composition by theme in other styles of digital RPG may be in order. I hope therefore that this chapter may prove useful not only in understanding the three RPGs here analyzed as performative practices, but also a growing range of other RPGs, and even of games in other genres.

References

Althusser, Louis. 1971. 'Ideology and Ideological State Apparatuses.' In *Lenin and Philosophy and other Essays*, 121–76. New York: New Left Books.
Baudry, J.-L. 1999. 'The Apparatus: Metapsychological Approaches to the Impression of Reality in Cinema.' In *Film Theory and Criticism: Introductory Readings*, ed. Braudy, Leo and J. Marshall, 760–77. Fifth Edition. Oxford: Oxford University Press.
Bethesda. 2006. *The Elder Scrolls IV: Oblivion*. [Multiplatform]. Bethesda Softworks. Rockville, MD.
—2008. *Fallout 3*. [Multiplatform]. Bethesda Softworks. Rockville, MD.
BioWare. 2003. *Star Wars: Knights of the Old Republic*. [Multiplatform]. LucasArts. San Francisco, CA.
—2007. *Mass Effect*. [Xbox 360]. Microsoft Game Studios. Redmond, WA
—2009. *Dragon Age: Origins*. [Multiplatform]. Electronic Arts.
—2011. 'Dragon Age: Origins Characters, Classes and Builds.' Community forum. *BioWare Social Network*. http://social.bioware.com/forum/1/category/96/index.
Bogost, Ian. 2006. *Unit Operations: An Approach to Videogame Criticism*. Cambridge, MA: MIT Press.
Bungie. 2001. *Halo:Combat Evolved*. [Multiplatform]. Microsoft Game Studios. Redmond, WA.
—2007. *Persuasive Games: The Expressive Power of Videogames*. Cambridge, MA: MIT Press.
Geertz, Clifford. 1973. *The Interpretation of Cultures: Selected Essays*. New York: Basic Books.
Lacan, Jacques. 1977. *Écrits: A Selection*. New York: Norton.
Lord, Albert Bates. 1951. 'Composition by Theme in Homer and Southslavic Epos.' *Transactions and Proceedings of the American Philological Association* 82 (January 1): 71–80. doi:10.2307/283421.
—1981. *The Singer of Tales*. Cambridge, MA: Harvard University Press.
Murray, Janet Horowitz. 1997. *Hamlet on the Holodeck: The Future of Narrative in Cyberspace*. New York: Simon and Schuster.
Nagy, Gregory. 1979. *The Best of the Achaeans: Concepts of the Hero in Archaic Greek Poetry*. Baltimore: Johns Hopkins University Press.
—1996. *Homeric Questions*. 1st edition. Austin: University of Texas Press.

Parry, Milman, and Adam Parry. 1987. *The Making of Homeric Verse: The Collected Papers of Milman Parry.* Oxford: Oxford University Press.

Short, Emily. 2011, January 8. Homer in Silicon. Column. *GameSet Watch.* http://www.gamesetwatch.com/column_homer_in_silicon/.

Sicart, Miguel. 2009. *The Ethics of Computer Games.* Cambridge Mass.: MIT Press.

Slatkin, Laura. 2006. *The Power of Thetis and Selected Essays.* 2nd edition. Cambridge, MA: Harvard University Press.

Turbine, Inc. 2007. *The Lord of the Rings Online: Shadows of Angmar.* [PC] TurbineInc. Needham, MS.

SECTION THREE

Out-of-Character

12

Neo-liberal Multiculturalism in *Mass Effect*: The Government of Difference in Digital RPGs

GERALD VOORHEES

This chapter examines the neo-liberal multiculturalist ideology of the *Mass Effect* series of digital role-playing games. I show that both games in the series profess the unmitigated superiority of neo-liberal multiculturalism as a form of dealing with difference. While the narrative conceit of the *Mass Effect* series is an alien threat to annihilate all sentient life in the galaxy, its key thematic is the biological and cultural differences that render the spacefaring races populating the Milky Way vulnerable to such a threat. In this context, the various systems of rules and the procedures for sorting and executing those rules valorize players' heterogeneous configurative practices and the neo-liberal multiculturalist performances they enact.

The following section outlines the theoretical and critical project upon which this intervention is grounded: Michel Foucault's genealogical pursuit of the regimes of truth that govern political, institutional, and cultural deliberative rationalities. This is followed by a brief look at the *Mass Effect* series of digital role-playing games, focusing on the narrative discourses that articulate the science-fiction series to contemporary cultural politics of difference. The final substantive section of this chapter examines processes of party management in the *Mass Effect* series as procedures within a truth game rule-bound to reward diversity and trumpet the truths of mainstream multiculturalist ideology.

Governmentality, Truth and Games

For much of his career Foucault was preoccupied with 'truth games', though it was only retrospectively, in the later years of his life, that this crystallized in his theorizing. At a lecture given at the University of Vermont, Foucault explained:

> My objective for more than twenty-five years has been to sketch out a history of the different ways in our culture that humans develop knowledge about themselves: economics, biology, psychiatry, medicine, and penology. The main point is not to accept this knowledge at face value but to analyze these so-called sciences as very specific 'truth games' related to specific techniques that human beings use to understand themselves. (1988, 18)

Truth games entered Foucault's lexicon around this time as a shorthand for describing the intersection of three distinct concepts integral to Foucault's critical project: the subject, power, and governmentality.

Foucault defined his life's work as an effort to study the processes through which human beings transform their selves into subjects

(2003b, 126). Unlike the 'self', a term Foucault uses nonchalantly in various contexts, the 'subject' describes a self in a specific relationship to power. Foucault explains, 'There are two meanings of the words "subject": subject to someone else by control and dependence, and tied to his own identity by a conscience or self-knowledge' (2003b, 130). In the first instance, the self's relationship to power is one of domination and dependence, but in the second instance the self's relationship to power is more difficult to discern and requires a theorization of power divorced from any notion of the sovereign exercise of authority.

As Foucault writes, 'Power's condition of possibility [...] must not be sought in the primary existence of a central point, in a unique source of sovereignty from which secondary and descendent forms emanate' (1990, 93). Though persons, institutions, and states remain important sites where power is applied, it is decentralized and diffused throughout the social matrix. In the neo-liberal politics of economic deregulation (Foucault 2008), the films shown by the YMCA (Greene 2005), god-games (Miklaucic 2003), and a myriad other cultural forms (Bennett 2003), power is ubiquitous. Even then, power does not originate from, nor is it exercised by, any of these entities, though they are sites where it is applied.

Rather, power is an effect of knowledge, or, more appropriately, truth. This truth is not transcendental. It is constructed by the very persons and populations it entangles, and is in this way immanent. It is doxological – consensual and contingent – and dynamic – subject to change but neither fleeting nor fickle. Foucault explains, 'Truth is a thing of this world: it is produced only by virtue of multiple forms of constraint. And it induces regular effects of power. Each society has its regime of truth, its "general politics" of truth – that is, the types of discourse it accepts and makes function as true' (2003c, 316). It is within specific regimes of truth that certain actions and patterns of practice come to be perceived as intelligible options that, in short, make sense (Biesecker 1992, 356). This, ultimately, is how power/knowledge is applied – by means of deliberative logics and governing rationalities, or, as Foucault termed it, governmentality. As practical reasoning constituting a governing rationality 'for the purpose of making judgments and planning reality' (Greene 1998, 35), power produces 'material judgment' (Sloop and Ono 1997) resulting in the materialization of practices and the performance of identity (Butler 1993). As an effect of truth, power is not an antagonistic competition between institutions and individuals, it is an agonistic contest played out in the various fields of human knowledge. We are not its pawns but its players. Subjects make themselves subject to power. Foucault insists that one's capacity for this engagement is a precondition to power, which 'operates on the field of possibilities in which the behavior of active subjects is able to inscribe itself [...] [I]t is always a way of acting upon one or more acting subjects by virtue of their acting or being capable of action. A set of actions upon other actions' (2003b, 139). Like the possibility space of a game (Salen and Zimmerman 2003, 66–7; Bogost 2007, 42–3), this field of possibilities Foucault describes is an extensive array of potential configurative actions determined by the rules. The actions are enacted by subjects 'freely' exercising choice in order to negotiate the weighted outcomes of the various dilemmas, obstacles, and encounters that constitute everyday life.

The *Mass Effect* series is a site where power is applied; both games make claims about the correct approach to managing difference. In this regard, the series is an exemplary popular cultural artifact. Miller explains, '[Power's] principle task is the engineering of relations between subjects. The primary site of this engineering is at the level of governance through culture' (1993, 40). Perhaps more profoundly, the operation of the digital game is homologous to the operation of the truth game. Unlike other media making claims about cultural difference, the titles in the *Mass Effect* series provide players with feedback, thus relating the outcome of the truth game directly to the player's input in the digital game. In this fashion, the series operates as a truth game governed by multiculturalist rationality and validates play practices that embrace heterogeneity in response to difference.

Moreover, a very specific notion of multiculturalism is put forward. Unlike liberal multiculturalism, which posits some essential sameness beneath the differences that define us (Žižek 2003), this multiculturalism accepts differences as long as they contribute to an already defined commonweal. The type of multiculturalism celebrated in the *Mass Effect* series is premised upon the other's ability to contribute something useful[1]. As Baerg argues in this volume, neo-liberalism is defined by the rationalization and economization of everyday life, and RPG characters are both products and producers of neo-liberalism. Neo-liberal multiculturalism, then, is multiculturalism that embraces the other to the extent that the other has a calculated worth that 'brings something to the table'.

As a cultural logic, it involves the commodification of the other for easy consumption (hooks 1999). Aihwa Ong analyzes this logic at work in the transnational cosmopolitanism of South Asia. Guest workers and international transplants at both the bottom (unskilled, manual laborers) and the top (highly skilled professionals) of the social hierarchy are more accepted than South Asian cultural and national norms typically dictate because they are perceived to fill vital functions local workers either cannot or will not fill. In America, it has most recently taken the form of policy proposals that seek to grant citizenship for undocumented immigrants who serve in the military or go to college, and it can be heard plainly whenever someone 'defends' undocumented workers by claiming that they fill niches in the American economy. And while neo-liberal multiculturalism is more progressive than racial animosity, it displaces a disregard for the other as other by accepting the other as a return to the same (Derrida 1985).

The following section looks at the *Mass Effect* series as a truth game centrally concerned with the relations between subjects. That the series is also an outcome of a truth game, a product of the relationship between political ideology, neo-liberal economic policy and the culture industries, does not negate that each iteration of *Mass Effect* is also 'a set of procedures that lead to a certain result, which, on the basis of its principles and rules of procedure, may be considered valid or invalid, winning or losing' (Foucault 2003a, 38). More specifically, the next section argues that the games allow players to enunciate their own response to the contemporary condition of a society defined by difference. Most significantly, the games also make procedurally generated valuations concerning the player's configurative performance, an implication that will round out the discussion in the final section of this chapter.

Performing Identity and Playing *Mass Effect*

The *Mass Effect* series of digital role-playing games includes two titles, *Mass Effect* (2007), which sold over 2.3 million copies worldwide across platforms, and *Mass Effect 2* (2010), which sold almost 2.5 million copies worldwide across platforms (VGChartz.com). *Mass Effect 3* has been in development since early 2010 and is scheduled for release in the fourth quarter of 2011. Not just commercial successes, both games in the *Mass Effect* series have been praised for their exemplary story and gameplay by numerous game review forums (Metacritic.com). The Academy of Interactive Arts and Sciences recognized *Mass Effect* (*ME*) as 2008 Role-playing Game of the Year and awarded *Mass Effect 2* (*ME2*) the distinction of 2011 Game of the Year.

The series is set in the year 2183 AD, thirty-five years after humans have learned to use the titular 'mass effect' technologies. Thought to be remnants of a lost Prothean civilization, mass effect technologies discovered on Mars allow for faster-than-light travel and the 'biotic' – essentially, magic for science-fiction – manipulation of gravity. After ten years of interstellar colonization, the human Systems Alliance extends itself far enough into the galaxy to make contact with other spacefaring races – Turians, Asari, Salarians, Krogans, and Quarians. First contact is rough, and several years of war ensue as a result of miscommunication before peace is brokered and humanity is granted an embassy in the Citadel, a recovered Prothean space station that serves as the seat of the galactic Council. The Council races – the industrious Turians, contemplative Asari and scientific Salarians – are the most populous and politically powerful races in the known galaxy. Several other species with embassies at the Citadel, including humans, are termed Citadel races and are considered members of the galactic community. In the margins are the non-Citadel races – outsiders who, for a mix of biological and cultural reasons, fail to adhere to the Citadel norms and laws. There are dozens of non-Citadel races including the war-like Krogans whose population is controlled by a Council-sponsored biological weapon of Salarian design and administration called the 'genophage', the planetless but technologically adept Quarians who travel in a Migrant Fleet of assorted salvaged ships after their home world was overrun by sentient machines of their own making, and the Geth, the artificial intelligence that rose up against the Quarians.

The first game introduces Commander Shepard, the protagonist and player-character. Both a 'heavy hero' – a character in an interactive drama, and a 'digital dummy' – a placeholder representing the player's intervention in the game (Burn and Schott 2004), Shepard can be configured in a number of ways. The player can choose to make Shepard male or female and alter eight aspects of Shepard's face by selecting from preset options for eyes, jaw, forehead, ears, nose, and lips. In addition to these purely representational characteristics, players also configure Shepard's sociocultural background and service history – decisions that affect gameplay by modifying the rate at which Shepard's reputation is altered. Also affecting gameplay, players configure Shepard's character class and in so doing determine Shepard's capacities to act in and upon the *Mass Effect* universe. Following Newman (2002), I maintain that in order to understand the significance of gameplay it is essential to approach game characters as 'sets of available capabilities and capacities', as vehicles, 'equipment to be utilised in the gameworld by the player'.

In this regard, it is important to note that as a human, the player can choose for Shepard one of six different character classes differentiated by the skills they avail the player and their capacity to act in the gamespace: Soldier (primarily physical prowess), Engineer (primarily technological know-how), Adept (primarily biotic powers), Infiltrator (some physical and technological capabilities), Sentinel (some biotic and technological capabilities), and Vanguard (some physical and biotic capabilities). This is reminiscent of a trope in fantasy role-playing games, inspired by the fiction of Tolkien and codified in the prototypical *Dungeons & Dragons*, that represents humans as more versatile and adaptable than other races, which tend to be articulated to one or another essential characteristic or affinity. In this vein, other races in the *Mass Effect* universe appear to make life choices under more restrictive, determinative constraints. Asari, known for their biotic prowess, diplomatic sensibilities, and sensuality, can be found in commando units, dancing in nightclubs, and administering trading houses and shops. Krogans, with their fierce reputations for physical strength, are all mercenaries or thugs, and any Quarians the player meets reveal abilities to access and manipulate technology. The Citadel, furthermore, is replete with Turian soldiers and police, as well as Salarian scientists. Hundreds of characters the player can meet during their travels conform to, and thus confirm, the prevalence of these generalities, including the characters recruited into Shepard's squad.

Like other popular RPGs, games in the *Mass Effect* series index identity by articulating characters that afford players different capacities to distinct representations often grounded in racially or ethnically charged constructions (Voorhees 2009; Tronstad 2008; Smith 2006). As Douglas argues in this volume, the conventions of digital role-playing games tend to conflate race and culture, and the *Mass Effect* series is, in the main, no exception. By ascribing racially essentialist properties to culturally learned dispositions, the series conflates race and culture in order to speak to both biological and ideological difference. This is especially significant in that, like the *Warcraft* franchise, race is not simply a part of the *Mass Effect* universe; it is also a central pillar of its narrative discourse, further encouraging players to engage the games as discourses centrally concerned with difference.

When a routine mission goes awry, Shepard is thrown into intrigue, and then into the spotlight. Made a Spectre, a special operative with the Council's mandate, Shepard goes off in search of a rouge agent, Saren, in order to uncover a Trojan Horse plot for an invasion of the Citadel by the terrifying Reapers. Shepard is accompanied on this mission by human crewmates Ashley Williams and Kaiden Alenko, and along the way recruits a Turian ex-cop, Garrus Vakarian, an Asari researcher, Liara T'Soni, a Krogan warlord, Urdnot Wrex, and a Quarian scout, Tali'Zorah nar Rayya. This mission, significantly, highlights the importance of biological and cultural difference. In-game dialogue and cutscenes emphasize that, as a Spectre, Shepard is a pawn in the politics of recognition; he represents humanity's potential to contribute to the Council and its aims. Before Saren is exposed as a traitor, he mocks Shepard before the Council, saying: 'Your species needs to learn its place Shepard. You're not ready to join the Council. You're not even ready to join the Spectres' (BioWare 2007). In a cutscene following Shepard's induction into the Spectres, Shepard's mentor, Captain Anderson, reminds Shepard that his appointment is part of humanity's struggle for political agency, and is necessary because the Council is unwilling to commit resources to an issue primarily affecting human colonies. As the narrative backbone of *ME*, this mission defines gameplay as an effort to secure cultural recognition and political representation.

It is reinforced by the repeated motif of interracial conflict. In one of the first missions available, Shepard and crew discover an alien species, Rachni, being studied in a weapons lab. These are the last Rachni, the player learns through dialogue, as the entire species was thought to be pursued to extinction after a terrible war. The player can either destroy the Rachni in line with the Council's will or, more benevolently, spare them so that they might live out their lives in peace. At another point in the game, Shepard discovers that Saren has a cure for the genophage and is using it in order to breed an army of Krogan slaves. This prompts Urdnot Wrex to demand the player's help in securing the cure and, under the great majority of circumstances, force a confrontation with Shepard that requires Wrex be killed to advance the game. Another encounter is with Cerberus, a pro-human paramilitary group widely considered a terrorist organization. The token human Spectre, an 'ambush journalist', asks Shepard to publicly advocate human-centered politics and the player is given the option to support Cerberus's militant ideology, disambiguate, or support the Council's more conservative path to full political parity.

The theme of biological and cultural difference is also prevalent in *ME2*. In this game, Shepard works for Cerberus because the Council will not take the continued Reaper threat seriously. Shepard is tasked with hunting the Collectors, an alien race that has taken up where Saren left off, attacking human colonies and working to facilitate a Reaper invasion. Though the player starts with the company of two human Cerberus agents, Miranda Lawson and Jacob Taylor, other companions are acquired through various missions. One such mission involves recruiting a Salarian scientist working to develop a cure for a virus. In order to recruit the Salarian, the player must help the plague-ravished community and in so doing learns that the virus was unleashed for the purpose of casting suspicion on humans, who only recently moved into the community. Talking to one Turian character in the community yields dialogue lamenting how property values fall whenever humans integrate into a community and suspicions that humans engineered the virus in order to make room for more humans in the community. Another mission has the player recruit Krogan warlord Okeer, only to find Okeer assassinated for his effort to breed Krogan that exemplified the strength and cunning the genophage saps from the Krogan gene pool. With Okeer dead, Shepard can recruit Okeer's finest specimen, Grunt, but doing so also means later helping Grunt discover what it means to be a Krogan. And toward the end of the game, after Tali, the same character from *ME*, has been recruited to Shepard's team, the player receives assistance from a Geth fighter, Legion. Legion may also be recruited to join Shepard's squad, but only if the player is prepared to handle the cultural and political friction that arises between Quarian and Geth squad members.

In drawing the player's attention to the theme of cultural and biological difference, these scenarios highlight how the games in the *Mass Effect* series function as cultural technologies that legitimate neo-liberal multiculturalist ideology. They construct a context for understanding the processes of gameplay enacted by means of the series' dialogue events, dialogue wheel, and paragon and renegade dialogue choices. The ability to choose from a range of dialogue options does more than pepper the story with the player's own personality; it ultimately affects the outcome of the story. As Travis argues in this volume, the player's performance of Western exceptionalism is indexed in Shepard's paragon and renegade scores. Dialogue options that contribute to the player's paragon score are located in the top left of the dialogue wheel and reflect concern for others and commitment to interracial cooperation. Dialogue options that contribute to the player's renegade score are located in the bottom left of the dialogue wheel and reflect selfish and aggressive responses that underscore commitment to human interests above all else. Paragon and renegade scores not only open up additional dialogue options, they are also evaluated at the end of the game in order to determine how certain circumstances are resolved.

In the final act of *ME*, Shepard and crew confront Saren after he has allowed the Reaper vanguard, Sovereign, access to the Citadel. After defeating (or talking down) Saren, Shepard makes contact with the human fleet speeding to the rescue and is informed that the fleeing Council is in danger. In what is arguably the most important dialogue choice in the game[2], the player can either order the fleet to save the Council, focus their efforts on attacking Sovereign, or 'let the Council die'. Sovereign's defeat is a foregone conclusion, but the player's performance is consequential and affects the scripted scene that follows this cinematic battle. In the instances where the Council is present, humanity is offered a seat on the Council. If the player has a higher paragon than renegade score, the Councilors laud Shepard as an exemplar of humanity's capacity to contribute to the greater good as a fully fledged member of the galactic community:

> Salarian Councilor: Your heroic and selfless actions stand for everything humanity and the Alliance stand for …
> Asari Councilor: Humanity has shown that it is ready to stand as a defender and protector of the Galaxy. You have proved you are ready to join our ranks and serve beside us on the Citadel Council.

However, when the player has a higher renegade than paragon score, the Councilors praise Shepard's force of will as evidence that humanity can contribute to the greater good as a fully fledged member of the galactic community:

> Salarian Councilor: Your species has an indomitable will, a fierce, savage spirit that will not bend or yield. We used to believe that this made humans stubborn, even dangerous.
> Turian Councilor: But now we understand that these traits are what make you strong … The Council needs humanity, and its strength.

In this manner, the paragon and renegade scores function as indexes of the player's position on the question of exceptionalism and internationalism (for another take on this, see Travis, this volume). This is made explicitly evident in the resolutions offered if the Council perishes in the battle. Udina leads the conversation and explains that the losses suffered by the Citadel fleets have made the human Alliance stronger by comparison. If the player has a higher paragon than renegade score, Udina argues that a Council should not only include a human but be led by one as well:

> Ambassador Udina: They believe in us because of you, Shepard. You saved the galaxy from Sovereign. You're a symbol of everything good to humanity; our courage; our strength.

But, if the player has a higher renegade than paragon score, Udina proclaims that it is time for humanity to 'ascend to its rightful place in the galaxy':

> Ambassador Udina: They believe in humanity because of you. Your ruthless pursuit of Saren and the Geth. Your defiance of the Council. That's what humans are capable of. That's how we'll defeat the Reapers. The others will follow us Shepard. We will have a human Council with a human chairman.

These various endings are the consequence of two conditional operations. The survival or death of the Council is determined by a single instance of user input, while the Council's assessment of humanity (or human plans for the Council) is the result of the player's configuration of dialogue events over the course of the entire game. In addition to the notable dialogue events (the Rachni queen, genophage, etc.) throughout the *Mass Effect* series where racial disparity is put into direct consideration, the repetition of this core mechanic in both games ensures that players have ample opportunity to perform their identity vis-à-vis the Council and the international community it represents[3].

The *Mass Effect* series does offer some narrative assessment of the player's performance of dialogue events. In the first game, paragon endings are accompanied by uplifting music and set in open locations that affirm the player's performance as a good response to contemporary social difference. Renegade endings, on the other hand, are accompanied by ominous music and set in cramped spaces that emphasize that something has been diminished in this performance and subsequent outcome. *ME2* offers a more nuanced narrative assessment of the player's configuration of dialogue events and considers the player's attitude toward difference as well as the player's knowledge of the different races and cultures represented in Shepard's crew. In the final mission of the game, squad-mates die when assigned to the wrong task (that is, one that is culturally alien to the character) and are especially vulnerable when Shepard has not secured their loyalty by engaging in a side quest, most of which are rooted in an issue arising from biological or cultural differences. The gloomier endings of *ME* and the *ME2* scenarios in which the majority of Shepard's crew perish are, arguably, procedurally determined evaluations of the player's performance. In this way, configurative performances of heterogeneity are validated by the (truth) game's procedures.

The Management of Difference

The *Mass Effect* series also makes value claims about players' performances in relation to another set of gameplay mechanics: squad management. Like the narrative claims generated in response to the configuration of dialogue events, these claims are procedural. *Mass Effect*, like the *Final Fantasy* RPG series[4], validates the player's willingness and ability to configure heterogeneous squads by enabling greater success in combat (Voorhees 2009). Though the *Mass Effect* series otherizes opponents, like most all RPGS and many digital games in general, this should not obscure how the series also advocates the coordination of difference.

Whenever Shepard's ship docks, the player must choose two members of the crew to accompany Shepard as a squad. It is only as a squad of three – never as Shepard, or any other character, alone – that the player fights opponents. While the player directly controls Shepard, maneuvering through a three-dimensional environment as well as aiming and firing weapons and abilities, the two characters in the squad are governed by the game's artificial intelligence and engage opponents based on a minimalistic set of player-defined parameters. However, the player can also pause the action and issue direct orders to characters in the squad, facilitating more direct squad management. The player's squad management is constantly evaluated and assessed, and performance is indexed not by means of an abstract set of scores; rather, it is represented through the evolving state of every shoot-out and battle.

Even more than the first game, *ME2* explicitly encodes the relationship between a character's capacity to act and racial and/or cultural identity. And even though *ME2* features a larger cast of characters where not every character exhibits a unique composition of attributes, each non-human fulfills a specific niche

A couple of playable characters, Garrus and Tali, return from the first game. Tali is a notable squad member both because she belongs to a non-Citadel race and because both her characteristics are technology. This is the same for Legion, the Geth construct also from a non-Citadel race. The final character representing a non-Citadel race is Grunt, the Krogan rescued from Okeer, whose characteristics are both physical. For these and other non-human characters, their racial identity is an essential component of their profession. Tali's character class is listed as 'Quarian Machinist', Legion's is listed as 'Geth Infiltrator', and Grunt's is listed as 'Krogan Berserker'. Non-human Citadel races get the same treatment. Mordin the 'Salarian Scientist', Samara the 'Asari Justicar', Thane the 'Drell Assassin', and Garrus the 'Turian Rebel' are all identified in a manner that conflates their biological and cultural identities. Of course, these titles all serve as a shorthand for indexing the different sets of capacities the characters add to the squad.

When more than one character shares the same set of traits – for instance, both Thane and Jacob have one physical and one biotic characteristic – each character still offers the player distinct capacities for action. Jacob's skills are more suited to close-quarters combat and Thane's skills are more suited to ranged fighting. The two characters with two biotic traits are easily distinguishable too. The human biotic, Jack, has powerful attacks that affect all targets in the area while the Asari, Samara, has highly focused attacks particularly effective against individual opponents. These different sets of capabilities, each powerful but limited, can be combined and recombined each time the player docks Shepard's ship and forms an active squad. With each different configuration of characters, the squad's offensive and defensive capabilities can be altered to adapt to a variety of situations defined by the opponents that populate them.

There are five primary groups of opponents in *ME2:* the Blue Suns, Blood Pack, and Eclipse mercenary outfits, as well as the Geth and the Collectors. Each set of opponents employs different tactics and brings their own unique offensive and defensive capabilities. This means that different squad configurations are more effective against different opponents, with their distinct strengths and weakness. Facing off against the Eclipse mercenary outfit means fighting against biotic and tech powers – defensive shields and barriers as well as ranged offense. This means putting together a squad with sufficient tech and biotic abilities to neutralize the opponent's defenses as well as the capacity to inflict damage while fending off attack. The squad configuration of Shepard, Tali, and Miranda would suit this task fine, but the same squad would be less suitable up against the Blood Pack mercenaries. Because the Blood Pack fights at close range and uses armor for defense more than biotic barriers and tech shields, this squad configuration would likely encounter difficulty. However, Shepard, Samara, and Garrus, having the combined ability to disable individual enemies and attack from afar, could more easily handle the Blood Pack. The player is given background information about each mission, making this type of preparation possible, and sometimes necessary.

It is through the commonplace, core mechanic of squad management that the games in the *Mass Effect* series most explicitly operate as cultural technologies reifying neo-liberal multiculturalism. Just as the player performs their identity through dialogue events, squad management is a platform for players to enact possible responses to a society saturated with difference. As a discursive formation within a regime of truth, the *Mass Effect* series affirms configurative performances that embrace heterogeneity. As a truth game, the series allows players to enact responses to specific states and then determines whether those responses are adequate or inadequate, and to what degree. This determination is objective to the extent that the rules are enforced by the game software, but partial and subjective to the extent that it represents an outcome determined by the game developer's (cultural) logic.

Another name for this operation is procedural rhetoric. According to Bogost, procedural rhetoric is how computational media makes arguments. It is premised on the core characteristic of computational media: procedurality, a term that describes how the execution of rules produces specific behaviors (2007, 4). In this light, *Mass Effect* can quantitatively evaluate the player's performance because the games 'make claims about *how things work*' by 'assembling rules together to describe the function of systems' (Bogost 2008, 125 [original emphasis]). The series' rules are structured in a manner that mirrors the conviction that differences, racial and cultural, are best embraced and managed toward a common end. To this end, in combat, every moment of gameplay generates feedback assessing the player's performance.

Neo-liberal Multiculturalism

In this chapter, I have endeavored to explain how the *Mass Effect* series of digital RPGs functions as a truth game that reifies neo-liberal multiculturalism. According to this notion of multiculturalism every difference is valuable – but not inherently – only to the extent that it can be made to contribute to some pre-established goal. As the analysis has shown, this cultural logic is affirmed procedurally, as a result of the systems of rules that structure the game. This applies to the rules governing the resolution of story elements as well as those that dictate how combat is resolved. The *Mass Effect* series makes the cultural logic of neo-liberal multiculturalism more tangible than other media forms by enabling players to test the validity of their propositions within its regime of truth.

The conclusions generated in this analysis are generalizable. As I have argued elsewhere, several more recent iterations in the *Final Fantasy* series celebrate a similar neo-liberal multiculturalism (Voorhees 2009). But, other RPGs that task the player with party or squad management – the *Dragon Age*, *Baldur's Gate,* and *Xeno* series, for example – also exhibit characteristics that could be articulated to this form of responding to cultural difference. It is also possible that other squad-based games such as Ubisoft's *Tom Clancy* series and multi-player shooters such as Valve's *Team Fortress* and *Left 4 Dead* series could be analyzed in order to examine potential procedural rhetorics of multiculturalism. Multi-player games, in particular, promise interesting complications as the procedures enacted by artificial intelligences are complicated with real patterns of lived play.

Notes

1 The same can be said for the notion of multiculturalism expressed in the *Final Fantasy* series (Voorhees 2009). However, in the *Final Fantasy* series, this construction of multiculturalism was abandoned for a neo-liberal model of self, at which point *Final Fantasy* games began to endorse radically different responses to the proliferation of ethnic, national, and cultural difference.
2 Aside from the decision about the fate of the Rachni and the confrontation with Wrex, only one other scenario (involving a corruption inquiry at the Noveira spaceport) enables the player to gain as many paragon or renegade points as the decision to save or abandon the Council.
3 *Mass Effect 2* also features a substantial number of dialogue events configured by means of dialogue wheels with paragon and renegade options. These options represent the same set of values they referenced in the first game and, like *Mass Effect*, are indexed and affect gameplay by enabling additional dialogue options but do not affect the story directly.
4 However, unlike the *Final Fantasy* series, *Mass Effect* maintains a consistent message. In both games in the series, characters are similarly differentiated and the player is required to successfully coordinate them in order to succeed.

References

Bennett, Tony. 2003. 'Culture and Governmentality.' In *Foucault Cultural Studies, and Governmentality*, ed. Jack Z. Bratich, Jeremy Packer, and Cameron McCarthy, 47–63. Albany: State University of New York.
Biesecker, Barbara. 1992. 'Michel Foucault and the Question of Rhetoric.' *Philosophy and Rhetoric* 25.4: 251–364.
BioWare. 2007. *Mass Effect*. [Xbox 360]. Redmond, WA: Microsoft Game Studios.
—2010. *Mass Effect 2*. [Xbox 360]. Los Angeles: Electronic Arts.
Bogost, Ian. 2008. 'The Rhetoric of Videogames.' In *The Ecology of*

Games: Connecting Youth, Game and Learning, ed. Katie Salen, 117–40. Cambridge, MA: MIT Press.
—2007. *Persuasive Games: The Expressive Power of Videogames*. Cambridge, MA: MIT Press.
Burn, Andrew, and Gareth Schott. 2004. 'Heavy Hero or Digital Dummy? Multimodal Player-Avatar Relations in Final Fantasy 7.' *Visual Communication* 3(2): 213–33.
Butler, Judith. 1993. *Bodies That Matter: on the Discursive Limits of Sex*. NY: Routledge.
Derrida, Jacques. 1985. 'White Mythology: Metaphor in the Text of Philosophy.' In *Margins of Philosophy*, 208–72. Chicago: University of Chicago Press.
Foucault, Michel. 1988. 'Technologies of the Self.' In *Technologies of the Self: A Seminar with Michel Foucault*, ed. Luther H. Martin, Huck Gutman and Patrick H. Hutton, 16–49. Amherst: University of Massachusetts Press.
—1990. *The History of Sexuality: An Introduction, Volume I*. New York: Vintage Books.
—2003a. The Ethics of the Concern of the Self as a Practice of Freedom. In *The Essential Foucault: Selections from the Essential Works of Foucault 1954–1984*, edited by Paul Rabinow and Nikolas Rose, 25–42. New York: The New Press.
—2003b. 'The Subject and Power.' In *The Essential Foucault: Selections from the Essential Works of Foucault 1954–1984*, ed. Paul Rabinow and Nikolas Rose, 126–44. New York: The New Press.
—2003c. 'Truth and Power.' In *The Essential Foucault: Selections from the Essential Works of Foucault 1954–1984*, ed. Paul Rabinow and Nikolas Rose, 300–18. New York: The New Press.
—2008. *Birth of Biopolitics: Lectures at the College de France, 1978–79*, ed. Michel Senellart, 129–57. New York: Palgrave Macmillan.
Greene, Ronald Walter. 1998. 'Another Materialist Rhetoric.' *Critical Studies in Media Communication* 15: 21–41.
—2005. 'Y-Movies: Film and the Modernization of Pastoral Power.' *Communication and Critical/Cultural Studies* 2(1): 19–36.
hooks, bell. 1999. 'Eating the Other: Desire or Resistance.' In *Black Looks: Race and Representation*, 21–40. South End Press.
Miklaucic, Shawn. 2003. 'God Games and Governmentality: *Civilization II* and Hypermediated Knowledge.' In *Foucault, Cultural Studies, and Governmentality*, ed. Jack Z. Bratich, Jeremy Packer, and Cameron McCarthy, 317–36. Albany: State University of New York Press.
Miller, Toby. 1993. *The Well-Tempered Self: Citizenship, Culture, and the Postmodern Subject*. Baltimore, MD: Parallax.

Newman, James. 2002. 'The Myth of the Ergodic Videogame.' *Game Studies* 1, no.2. http://gamestudies.org/0102/newman/.

Salen, Katie and Zimmerman, Eric. 2003. *Rules of Play: Game Design Fundamentals*. Cambridge, MA: MIT Press.

Sloop, John and Ono, Kent. 1997. 'Out-law Discourse: The Critical Politics of Material Judgment.' *Philosophy and Rhetoric* 30: 50–69.

Smith, C. Jason. 2006. 'Body Matters in Massively Multiplayer Online Role-playing Games.' *Reconstruction* 6, no.1. http://reconstruction.eserver.org/061/smith.shtml.

Tronstad, Ragnhild. 2008. 'Character Identification in *World of Warcraft*: The Relationship between Capacity and Appearance.' In *Digital Culture, Play, and Identity: A* World of Warcraft *reader*, ed. Hilde Corneliussen and Jill Walker Retttberg, 249–64. Cambridge MA: MIT Press.

VGChartz.com. (2011). *Mass Effect* Sales. Accessed April 2, 2011. http://gamrreview.vgchartz.com/sales/7635/mass-effect/

—(2011). *Mass Effect 2* Sales. Accessed April 2, 2011. http://gamrreview.vgchartz.com/sales/28815/mass-effect-2/

Voorhees, Gerald. 2009. The Character of Difference: Procedurality, Rhetoric and Role-playing Games. *Game Studies* 9 no.2. Accessed April 1, 2011. http://gamestudies.org/0902/articles/voorhees.

Žižek, Slavoj. 2003. 'The Violence of Fantasy.' The Communication Review, 6: 275–87.

13

'Simply Fighting to Preserve Their Way of Life': Multiculturalism in *World of Warcraft*

CHRISTOPHER DOUGLAS[1]

There is a scandal in Azeroth. The problem, one critic recently noted, is that racial representations in *World of Warcraft* seem to be based on racist caricatures and cultural stereotypes at work in our own world. The voodoo-practicing 'barbarous and superstitious' trolls come from islands 'renowned for their cruelty and dark mysticism', says the game manual (Blizzard 2004, 186). They speak in a seeming African American vernacular, saying 'aks' for the standard English 'ask'. 'That explains it,' concluded this commentator, 'trolls talk like black people because *they're superstitious jungle savages*.' As he also noted, the tauren race take their reference not from the minotaurs they physically resemble, but from 'Native Americans of the Mix-n-Match tribe. Environmentally conscious citizens of the plains, they live in both tipis and longhouses, and carve totem poles. And their signature greeting is "How!"' (Ruff 2007). With their orc and undead partners, these four races of the 'Horde' are rendered as the evil and uncivilized other to the good and civilized 'Alliance' races, which include elves, dwarves, gnomes and (of course) humans.

As it turned out, this reading was debatable, with another commentator arguing instead that Blizzard, the creator of *World of Warcraft*, had taken pains to portray the races in a more complex light, with the trolls, tauren and orcs representing indigenous peoples trying to resist the encroachment of the colonizing Alliance. Superseding the good vs. evil narrative was thus a clearly multicultural and postcolonial paradigm of cultural respect, resistance, and the questioning of supposedly civilized values. 'Blizzard not only acknowledges the existence of different cultures – something most fantasy games don't attempt – they treat them with respect and use them to seriously consider the embarrassing (and ongoing) exploitation, subjugation, and disrespect for indigenous people' (Williams 2007). That sympathetic reading also found support from the game manual, which explains that

> At one time in Azeroth's past, the Horde was a force of evil, and the Alliance was a bastion of good. However, in today's war-torn Azeroth, such black and white distinctions are gone. Both factions are simply fighting to preserve their way of life in the wake of the Chaos War. (Blizzard 2004, 14)

World of Warcraft's language improbably echoes that of our world of multiculturalism: groups are 'simply fighting to preserve their way of life' (14), and a player's character enters the world by first watching 'a movie introducing your racial heritage' (15). Blizzard's formulations seem to follow an established vocabulary of cultural contestation, more structured by Samuel Huntington's *Clash of Civilizations* than by President Bush's speeches on the war on terror.

But of course we should not be surprised that an online game is a site where these questions of racism, cultural stereotyping, and group representation get hashed out. As Lisa Nakamura reminded us at the beginning of the twenty-first century, 'The Internet is a place where race happens' (2002, xi). If Michael Omi and Howard Winant were correct in their classic 1986 study *Racial Formation in the United States*, that 'Race will *always* be at the center of the American experience' (1986, 6), we should expect to find race happening online in 2012, perhaps especially in online gaming. The racial fantasies that play out online are only part of the ongoing process of what Omi and Winant termed 'racial formation': gamespace, in other words, is only another social site where the expectation that race matters takes place, where race is socially constructed. And *World of Warcraft* promotes a particularly American racial logic to the planet: of its 12 million active worldwide subscribers (in December 2010), it has about one-quarter in Europe, about one-quarter in North America, and more than half in Asia (Blizzard Entertainment 2008).

Indeed, race is a core game concept in *World of Warcraft* and the genre of fantasy RPGs that it most famously represents. *World of Warcraft* is like an online game version of *Lord of the Rings*: in a fantasy world called Azeroth, a player creates a character and adventures with others in a virtual setting, fighting monsters, performing quests, and perfecting skills. Choosing a character's race is the first thing a player does: it comes before a character's class, the mix of magic-use, physical prowess, or stealth that characterizes a style of play. In Azeroth, of course, race is not understood as socially constructed, but rather to be a biological fact. Composed of inherited, immutable, essential differences, race in Azeroth is the old-fashioned (which is to say, nineteenth- and early twentieth-century) notion that the outward packaging signifies an inner reality, where the differences are.

But such is only to be expected of the genre, given its genealogical descent through pencil-and-paper RPGs like *Dungeons & Dragons* from J. R. R. Tolkien's *Lord of the Rings*[2]. Indeed, what's even more like *Lord of the Rings* online or *Dungeons & Dragons* online than *World of Warcraft* is *Lord of the Rings Online* and *Dungeons & Dragons Online*, less-popular but similarly premised massively multiplayer online RPGs based on Tolkien's oeuvre. (For an important examination of the relation between Tolkien's novel and the game based on them, see Randall and Murphy in this volume.) Tolkien imagined his races as fundamentally and intrinsically different. The dwarves are strong and hardy, making them particularly tough fighters; the hobbits are small, quiet and stealthy, making them particularly good thieves; the elves are wise and agile, making them particularly good with magic or bow; and so on. Some critics see Tolkien's work as intrinsically racist for these and other reasons, while others defend him from such charges[3]. But my point is not so much that Tolkien was or was not racist; it is rather that race remained a powerful idea and conceptual category in his fantasy world, the world from which fantasy RPGs descended.

Thus, as Niels Werber suggests in *New Literary History*,

> Through reading Tolkien's novels, seeing the movies, or playing computer games like 'The Battle for Middle-earth' (EA Games, 2004), one is introduced into a certain bio- and geopolitical knowledge: first of all, races are different not only in terms of skin color or height, but in moral worth, refinement, wisdom, and political integrity. The races are either hereditarily good and wise like Elves or genetically evil and dumb like Orcs, and therefore they make 'natural-born' enemies. The absolute and insurmountable hate between Elves and Orcs is not outlined as a consequence of political decision-making, but as a result of their opposing DNA sequences. To pass off contingent, historical, and changeable political differences as 'natural' or 'given' oppositions is paradigmatic in discourses of social Darwinism since the mid-nineteenth century. (2005, 227–8)

This is the generic legacy of the fantasy tradition in which *Lord of the Rings Online* and *World of Warcraft* and many other games take place. The games encode this logic of racial difference, a logic that players rehearse during play, learning and nurturing the expectation that phenotype signals crucial inner differences. Thus, one commentator uneasily reflected about playing *Lord of the Rings Online*, 'In the real world, defining someone by his or her race is considered a classically illiberal act. But in games, racism – making snap judgments about someone based solely on their skin and ethnic identity – is absolutely central to gameplay' (Thompson 2007). Or, as Thomas Foster notes in a different context, 'virtual reality privileges vision as a mode of information processing, and visual perception remains inextricably linked to a history of racial stereotyping' (1999, 160).

The obvious point to make here is that the many racial possibilities for characters in *World of Warcraft* are all about creating consumer choice. In this sense they fulfill the same design function as different classes, genders, and even vocations. Because these games are subscription-based (by monthly or hourly fee), they are designed to bring players back to play the same thing, but differently. This is why Blizzard's 'expansions' – new digital areas to be explored, at additional cost – are accompanied by new classes or races; thus to the original eight playable races have been added two more in the first expansion and two more in the third. The 12 races can each become about 7 or 8 of the 10 classes, for 90 possible race/class combinations, and with gender as an additional marker of marketable difference, there are 180 possible play combinations. Add into this mix a character's choice of 2 out of 3 class specializations (a mage, for example, can specialize in fire, although for destruction ice is also great and does suffice), and 2 of the possible 12 professions – making magic jewelry, crafting special armor, brewing powerful potions or whatever – and you have 71,280 different character configurations. (See Voorhees in this volume for the complementary way that multicultural difference is prized for 'the other's ability to contribute something useful' to a team of characters.) 'MMORPGs are all about choice', claimed one designer of *Everquest* – another online fantasy game popular before *World of Warcraft* more or less cleared the field of competitors – when asked about the multiple races. 'The difference in attributes, in profession choices, and starting area of the world, was to set the cultures apart as distinct choices' (Hayot and Wesp 2009). Thus, in *Everquest*, it is not really relevant that the Barbarians speak with a Scottish accent (like the dwarves in *World of Warcraft*). 'The Barbarians in *EQ* might have had a Scottish flavor to them, but they are not Scots; likewise the pyramids on Luclin might appear to be Egyptian in flavor or style to a degree, but there is no real relationship', explained another designer.

These games might thus signal a utopian aspiration that our race is irrelevant – 'it really doesn't matter who you are in real life – your financial status, your race, your gender, your age, your location, etc. should all be irrelevant' – and, further, that the games might help to 'break down all sorts of prejudices and preconceptions that exist in the real world' (Hayot and Wesp 2009)[4]. In this view, the ability to mix-and-match aspects of one's virtual identity – including race – might make us more flexible and open in the real world to other races. But what such market choices depend on is the sense that races are real entities, sources of actual, natural difference. In this sense, the liberal capitalist empathy experiment of becoming another race may have the consequence of naturalizing socially constructed races. What begins as a design choice to keep players coming back unintentionally entails our training in a conceptual model of group difference as natural and innate rather than historical and environmental.

But even the fact that *World of Warcraft* and games like it recirculate for us our mass hallucination of biological difference is not as scandalous as the fact that in this game there is no distinction between a race and a culture. How can a 'race' have a 'heritage' that is inherited, and have a 'way of life' that demands preservation? Are the differences between orcs and elves immutable, genetically inherited, natural, and hierarchical, or are they malleable, learned, conventionally arbitrary, and relative? In other words, are the differences between orcs and elves racial, or, in fact, cultural? In Azeroth that question makes no sense: there is no difference between these differences. Orcs are extra-handy with axes, which is called a 'racial passive' ability in the game, but it is easy to imagine that handiness stemming not so much from genes as from a cultural heritage that placed special emphasis on the axe and its early use by orc children. Those are two different accounts of what makes orcs handy with axes. Axe-oriented culture is indeed a kind of 'heritage', but biological predisposition to axes instead of, say, swords, cannot be. There is no such thing as a 'racial heritage', because heritages are either learned or not.

Thus, although it is difficult to imagine the undead as having a culture – a 'way of life' – that needs to be preserved, the game goes some way, as the commentator above noted, into making the orcs, trolls, and taurens into groups whose racial cultures are threatened by annihilation. 'For countless generations,' the manual explains, 'the bestial tauren roamed the plains of the Barrens, hunted the mighty kudos, and sought the wisdom of their eternal goddess, the Earth Mother.' The once nomadic tribes have been united and settled into cities. As the manual continues, 'Though the noble tauren are peaceful in nature, the rites of the Great Hunt are venerated as the heart of their spiritual culture. Every tauren, warrior or otherwise, seeks identity both as a hunter and as a child of the Earth Mother' (Blizzard 2004, 183). It is not that these races are evil in their continued opposition to the Alliance – that is the old, outmoded way of thinking. Rather, tauren 'identity' can only be completed by an enduring 'spiritual culture' – a 'way of life' – that is threatened by outside forces.

My argument is not only that tauren have a racially appropriate culture that must accompany and fulfill an already determined genetic identity, such that cultural learning supplements biological inheritance. Rather, and beyond this point, the scandal in *World of Warcraft* is that the game does not care about the difference between race and culture. The terms are indistinguishable in-game, with culture being something you are as likely to inherit as race is something that is learned like a language or a religion. The game is unable to imagine a racial member without her proper culture: there will never be an orc, or – gods forbid – a human, who is drawn to the religion of the Earth Mother.

To return to the above example of the orc characters gaining a 'racial passive' ability of being extra-handy at axe-wielding, it is precisely here that the rubber of what players actually do hits the road of game design. A player deciding on a character combination might choose the orc race for his warrior, recognizing the built-in advantage with certain weapons his character could have. On the other hand, he might choose for other gameplay or just aesthetic reasons that he wants to be an orc warlock, which renders the built-in advantage null, since warlocks cannot use axes. Gnomes have a 'racial passive' of being a higher intellect, which confers more spell power – useful if you decide to be a mage, not so much if you choose to live your life as a spell-less rogue. And so on[5]. There are many reasons for choosing race/class combinations. But from the player's point of view, it is not clear whether your extra axe ability or higher intellect is a result of racial or cultural forces. Players begin the game as adults, and do not have to learn to use their 'racial passives'. They are thus experienced by players as natural abilities – you have to train other abilities as you develop your character, but not this one. There is no sense of the cybernetic possibility of rewiring the supposedly hard-wired, in what Thomas Foster (1999, 161) has seen as a possible challenge to the social construction of race in cyberspace; here, a player can ignore or work with a racial passive, but it will always be there.

I am belaboring the point that there is no distinction between race and culture in *World of Warcraft* because that conceptual indifference was typical of the archaic and destructive paradigm of biological race that was successfully challenged by the work of the anthropologist Franz Boas and his followers in the first four decades of the twentieth century. Their distinction between culture and race was politically progressive and anti-racist. It was progressive because, first, it sought to show that group differences traditionally attributed to nature (or to God) were in fact learned behaviors, functions of distinct traditions or environments. And it was progressive because, second, it sought, once culture was conceptually distinguished from race, to destroy race as a scientifically defensible concept. Biologists today say that the things we once thought phenotypical differences signaled – intelligence, sexuality, potential for civilization, physical strength, and artistic ability – in fact have no correlation to the groups we still call 'races'. Boas's challenge to racial theory was taken up and pursued by many others during the twentieth century. It was a tribute to him when the mourning white supremacist Carleton Putnam laid the blame for *Brown v. Board of Education* in 1954 squarely at the feet of 'Boas and his disciples' (quoted in Hyatt 1990, 99). It was the destruction of race as a coherent, defensible concept, and its replacement by a notion of cultural learning and environmental influence that was understood by progressives in the early- and mid-twentieth century as being a key argument for the biological equality of groups (and, often, the relative equality of group cultures).

This was not to say, however, that 'racial' populations did not sometimes craft, nurture, and pass on distinctive cultural traditions. One of Boas's students, the anthropologist Zora Neale Hurston, worked to record such cultural traditions among African American populations in rural Florida and Afro-Caribbean populations in Haiti and Jamaica. She found folktales and religious traditions of hoodoo that were particular to some populations of African Americans living across the South; likewise, to her eye, Haitian voodoo's loas derived from West African deities who survived the Middle Passage with those kidnapped Africans who carried them to new shores. But these were not racial cultures or 'racial heritages'; they were cultures carried by specific populations that remained more or less historically distinct for reasons of social and geographical isolation. Boas's famous tenet about cultures was that they were historically particular: a culture was meaningful and changed only slowly over time, sometimes from outside pressures, as it was passed on from adults to children within a population group. But historical particularism understood culture as something that was fundamentally learned, thus recognizing the vast contingencies on which cultural transmission can depend. When Hurston exclaimed in her book on voodoo about one local white *houngan* who was an advanced practitioner of voodoo that 'Africa was in his tones', she was exclaiming on just such learning contingencies that broke the norm, and not on the fact that a racial member had learned the wrong culture (1990, 257). Hurston, at least, could have imagined a troll learning human culture in *World of Warcraft* (and vice versa) because she understood the difference between a race and a culture. Historically particular culture could likewise be lost if it was not passed on: thus many of her Harlem Renaissance colleagues were generationally removed from the Southern black folk culture that they sometimes imagined was their rightful inheritance (Hemenway 1977, 51). Culture was either learned (with subtle or unsubtle transformations), or it was not learned. It could never be inherited.

Boas's and Hurston's key distinction between race and culture does not exist in *World of Warcraft*, and in general game studies has not known what to do with that indistinction. Most critics have been critical of Blizzard's handling of questions of race, stereotypes, and imperialism, while others have noted sufficient complexity and nuance in the game to offer a provisional defense[6]. But in one way, the question of racism in *World of Warcraft* is not the most interesting question to be asked of the game; it is rather, I would like to suggest, the curious and continual swerving between notions of group identity, a swerving sometimes shared by the critics themselves. Thus, for example, Tanya Krzywinska, recognizing *World of Warcraft*'s debt to Tolkien, suggests that the game's races are part of its mythological thickness and story-telling complexity: there 'are many indicators of each race's culture that relate to myth that also inform both gameplay tasks and the stylistic designs of the gameworld's spaces' (2006, 387). But she does not stop to ask how a 'race' can have a 'culture', accepting the premise that genetically distinct populations just do things differently in a kind of eternal and immobile cultural segregation; no one ever learns another way outside their ancestors' tradition. In another example, Torill Elvira Mortensen muses on one possible role-playing situation in which 'the human is a dwarf-hater, who wants to eradicate the dwarf culture' (2008). This phrasing correctly apprehends the logic of how races and cultures are coterminous in *World of Warcraft*: what might be a kind of racism against dwarfs on the part of this human is not possibly distinct from a disdain for dwarf culture. There will never be a need, in other words, to try to eradicate (for example) a locally distinct population of tauren, or human-orc crossbreeds, or undead adoptees, who have been influenced by the dwarf 'culture' this human despises.

Meanwhile, in Esther MacCallum-Stewart's account of race, ecology, and imperialism in *World of Warcraft*, the Horde races are identified as 'survivors' in contrast to humans facing social collapse, and 'Quests reflect this different cultural makeup' (2008, 43–4). Like Krzywinska and Mortensen, MacCallum-Stewart correctly reads the race/culture mashup of the game, but does not interrogate its logic. And in her perceptive account of naming in *World of Warcraft*, Charlotte Hagström compares the enforced naming patterns of the races in Azeroth to arguments in Sweden about the unsuitability of Anglo-American names for Swedish children, and warns that 'We may talk about Canadian or Polish culture, as well as the gnomes' or blood elves' cultures of Azeroth and the culture of the *World of Warcraft* community, but must also be aware that they are not rigid and static' (2008, 280). But the gnomes' and blood elves' cultures *are* static: Poles can move to Canada and become Canadians, especially within a few generations, whereas gnomes can never go to Darnassus to become night elves, let alone to Silvermoon City to become blood elves. The Polish Canadians will learn English or French, intermarry, and adopt English or French names for children, grandchildren, or great-grandchildren, but the gnomes could live alongside night elves for generations and their naming practices and cultural conditions will never be affected by the elves, because their cultural identity is understood to be natural – that is, racial – and not something that is learned. In Azeroth, races living beside one another show no cross-cultural fertilization. The gnomes lived in Ironforge until the third expansion, but their engineering prowess seems not to have rubbed off particularly on any dwarves in the city, nor has dwarven blacksmithing or gun ability or Scottish accent rubbed off on any gnomes. Likewise, the trolls shared the orc capital city, but their 'voodoo' remains alien to the orcs, even as orcish axe ability remains foreign to trolls. Whatever the racial/cultural mix of these group identities, each community is eternally culturally segregated from the others. It is like imagining that African American music and religious traditions never infected white America, or that Christianity was a solely white religion and English a white language, or that a martial arts aesthetic never influenced Western films, or Buddhist religious practices and Asian foodways people of European descent, and so on.

If digital games studies tends to accept (even by not remarking on) these games' design premise that blur heredity with learning, genetics with tradition, an important exception is Jessica Langer (2008) in 'The Familiar and the Foreign: Playing (Post)Colonialism in *World of Warcraft*.' Perhaps the best analysis of how the races in the game allude to real-world cultures, Langer's essay ends with the critique that

> Here, then, is the crux of the problem with Blizzard's cultural borrowing: if in-game races are closely identified with real-world races, and those same in-game races are treated as biologically distinct species rather than socially categorized races, then the implication is that real-world race is also primarily biologically determined – an outdated and destructive implication that belongs to a racist discourse. (104)

Indeed, the game trains us to use racial thinking, but beyond that, it trains us to blur the race/culture distinction that was, as I have suggested, the historical key to challenging the racist discourse Langer names.

What accounts for this continuous swerving between race and

culture? At first it looks like a kind of 'neo-racism' of the kind diagnosed by Etienne Balibar. Neo-racism, Balibar suggests, 'is a racism whose dominant theme is not biological heredity but the insurmountability of cultural differences, a racism which, at first sight, does not postulate the superiority of certain groups or peoples in relation to others but "only" the harmfulness of abolishing frontiers, the incompatibility of life-styles and traditions' (1991, 21). This neo-racism, Balibar goes on to say, destabilizes anti-racism by attacking it from behind, with its own weapons:

> It is granted from the outset that races do not constitute isolable biological units and that in reality there are no 'human races'. It may also be admitted that the behavior of individuals and their 'aptitudes' cannot be explained in terms of their blood or even their genes, but are the result of their belonging to historical 'cultures'. Now anthropological culturalism, which is entirely oriented towards the recognition of the diversity and equality of cultures – with only the polyphonic ensemble constituting human civilization – and also their transhistorical *permanence*, has provided the humanist and cosmopolitan anti-racism of the post-war period with most of its arguments. [...] What we see here is that biological or genetic naturalism is not the only means of naturalizing human behavior and social affinities. At the cost of abandoning the hierarchical model [...] *culture can also function like a nature*, and it can in particular function as a way of locking individuals and groups a priori into a genealogy, into a determination that is immutable and intangible in origin. (21–2)

This outline seems to accurately describe the insurmountability and genealogical determinism of the 'races' in *World of Warcraft*, now supposedly rendered, Blizzard assures us, not by 'black and white distinctions' of 'evil' versus 'good' (despite the continued racial echoes of 'Horde' and 'Alliance'). Furthermore, Balibar suggests that neo-racism features 'the *return of the biological theme*' insofar as aggression between distinct and separate groups is understood as itself a natural fact of physiology and psychology (26) – an idea that might go some way to explaining the constant border skirmishes, antagonism, and warring between groups in the *World of Warcraft*.

There are certainly elements of neo-racism at work in *World of Warcraft*; in particular, the way culture can be reimagined as a kind of nature might offer a particularly promising account of difference in the game and games like it. But of course, in these games there actually are 'races' postulated – ones that seem to be understood, with some ambiguity, to have different biological and genetic capacities. In another way, however, Balibar's theory cannot account for the indistinguishability of culture and race in the games, the discursive swerving between concepts. This is partly because of Balibar's primarily French context of North African immigration and the measuring of population groups according to their resistance to assimilating into the culture of the 'land of the Rights of Man' (24), a dynamic entirely absent from Azeroth. I would like to suggest instead that the source for *World of Warcraft*'s conceptual indistinction between race and culture actually lies closer to home: it is an exaggerated version of our own world of American multiculturalism.

I try to outline the development of this conceptual indistinction between race and culture in my recent book *A Genealogy of Literary Multiculturalism* (Douglas 2009). The story of that indistinction began, as I allude to above, with Boas's progressive and anti-racist argument against biological thinking and the overemphasis on heredity, and his argument instead for the importance of historical culture and environmental conditions on population groups. It was through the influence of social science ideas about culture on literary writers that our multicultural literature developed, beginning most spectacularly when Boasian anthropology's terms helped Hurston articulate her pluralist cultural politics. That story continued through a strange detour when a different kind of social science thinking helping to articulate the thinking of a generation of assimilationist writers, the most significant of which was Richard Wright.

This particularly American history of multiculturalism and social science is another reason why Balibar's 'neo-racism' cannot do the job of naming *World of Warcraft*'s conceptual blurring, partly because of anthropology's different legacies in France and the United States. When speaking about Boas, Balibar suggests that

> One of the great figures in anthropology, Claude Lévi-Strauss, who not so long ago distinguished himself by demonstrating

that all civilizations are equally complex and necessary for the progression of human thought, now in 'Race and Culture' finds himself enrolled, whether he likes it or not, in the service of the idea that the 'mixing of cultures' and the suppression of 'cultural distances' would correspond to the intellectual death of humanity and would perhaps even endanger the control mechanisms that ensure its biological survival. (22)

Balibar's sense that anthropology taught us about cultures' 'transhistorical *permanence*' (21) is a lesson entirely in contrast (ideally, if imperfectly) to the historical particularism of American anthropology since Boas. Boas's usefulness for writers like Hurston, for example, was his insistence that culture took its meaning from the changing historical circumstances of a given population; thus the African American folktales that Hurston collected in Florida formed a kind of 'autobiography of the tribe', as Boas put it in a different context, one that told a particular story of the disruption of the Middle Passage, of the cultural survival of African tricksters, of slavery, Jim Crow, and resistance.

But by the time a post-Civil Rights generation of African American writers turned back to Hurston for inspiration, their anti-assimilationist pluralism found it productive to ground the problem of cultural longevity in a vehicle that was not so potentially treacherous as that of cultural transmission and adaptation. Though the multiculturalism that this generation inaugurated would variously call this vehicle culture, identity, or even race, it tended to look a little like Blizzard's 'racial heritage' – a phrase, not incidentally, frequently used by critics to describe Kiowa author N. Scott Momaday's claiming of his ancestral identity. As I try to show in *Genealogy*, in Momaday's Pulitzer Prize-winning 1968 novel *House Made of Dawn*, the novel sometimes credited with initiating the so-called Native American Renaissance in literature, the protagonist Abel is raised in Jemez Pueblo culture. But if we follow the genealogical hints of the novel, we discover that it is 'memory' in his 'blood' that accounts for his strange attraction to the Eagle Hunt and the cultural traditions of the distinct Bahkyush: he has not learned these cultural traditions, but he is yet attuned to them. Ishmael Reed's 1972 Black Arts Movement novel *Mumbo Jumbo* – another text inaugural of our current paradigm of multicultural literature, and one of Harold Bloom's 'five hundred most significant books in the Western canon' – likewise imagines 'blood', 'genes', and a 'race soul' as things that carry what cannot be properly learned. Though Reed called Hurston 'our theoretician', his novel did not follow in her footsteps of imagining Haitian voodoo and African American hoodoo in terms of historical particularism. Rather, the three characters who learn non-racial cultures are dead by the end of the novel: as in *World of Warcraft*, there will be not be a troll who can learn human culture, a white man with Africa in his tones.

Moreover, the most famous, Pulitzer Prize-winning novel by our Nobel Prize-winner Toni Morrison tropes and transforms racialized history into a kind of racial memory – and so slavery becomes something that she, and the characters, and white and black readers, 'don't want to remember', as she has put it (see Walter Benn Michaels [2004, 135–9]). In *Beloved*, slavery and the Middle Passage become things that cannot quite be learned, but rather must be re-experienced – even for contemporary readers – by a memory transference whose continuity seems to depend on a model of racial reincarnation, not cultural endurance and transmission (Morrison 1987). One might point as well to Gloria Anzaldúa's ground-breaking *Borderlands/La Frontera*, in which the language of culture and race mix to a degree anticipatory of the *World of Warcraft* manual:

> *Guadalupe* unites people of different races, religions, languages: Chicano protestants, American Indians and whites. '*Nuestra abogada siempre serás*/Our *mediatrix* you will always be.' She mediates between the Spanish and the Indian cultures (or three cultures as in the case of *mexicanos* of African or other ancestry) and between Chicanos and the white world. [...] *La Virgen de Guadalupe* is the symbol of ethnic identity and of the tolerance for ambiguity that Chicanos-*mexicanos*, people of mixed race, people who have Indian blood, people who cross cultures, by necessity possess. (1999, 52)

Culture and race are the very same thing in *Borderlands/La Frontera*. One's race is what one's culture is; mixed blood confers *mestizo* culture 'by necessity'; one's ancestry is the same as one's ethnic identity; to genetically 'cross' a culture is not different from crossing a religion or a race. Thus while Anzaldúa, like Reed, owes some intellectual debts to cultural anthropology, she, again like Reed, eschews the principle of historical particularism by which one could locate cultural continuity among what seemed like a distinct 'racial' population.

Before Disney reworked the traditional Chinese 'Ballad of Fa Mu Lan' for its cartoon feature *Mulan*, Maxine Hong Kingston (1976) adapted it in *The Woman Warrior*, which is, by some reports, the most-taught book at American universities and colleges by a living author (Yardley 2007, C01). Her adaptation earned the chiding of author and critic Frank Chin (1991, 3–4), who argued that 'At no time in Chinese American history was the real Fa Mulan obscure or inaccessible to a Chinese American girl or boy'. But Chin's uneasiness about imagining an instance in which proper cultural learning does not happen in a racially Chinese American family is true of all these multicultural authors to significant degrees. Like the paradigm of multiculturalism, they sometimes ignore the question of cultural learning. That is, the way we conflate race and culture: as in *World of Warcraft*, members of races just know their cultures. These are not marginal books or authors. These are our most crucial, most vivid examples of contemporary multiculturalism in literature. And if they resist the conceptual distinction between race and culture, what hope have the rest of us?

As the example from Chin demonstrates, everything depends on what he means by 'Chinese American'. Does the phrase refer to an American person's racial lineage, or her actual cultural mix? The phrase implies both, and in doing so equates them. In fact, we do not have separate terms to indicate whether we are discussing a cultural or a racial group. 'Chinese American', for Chin and for us, describes both a population characterized by 'racial' descent and a supposedly historically particular cultural tradition. But it is not difficult to formulate a thought experiment in which 'a Chinese American girl or boy' happens not to learn the Ballad of Fa Mu Lan from parents or community. Given current patterns of Christian evangelization and pop culture circulation, a Chinese American child may be as likely to grow up with the Bible as with Fa Mu Lan, or to learn her Fa Mu Lan from Disney rather than from her community. To switch registers, our words cannot distinguish between an African

American race and an African American culture; 'African American' (or white) simply means both, simultaneously. Coded into our very language is the indistinction between culture and race that characterizes our current paradigm of multiculturalism. Because we cannot distinguish between race and culture – or because it takes extra effort to describe racial African Americans who do not practice a recognizably African American culture (cases for which we have developed words like oreos, and analogously, coconuts, apples and bananas, pejoratives that signal disruption and our displeasure) – we treat the two rival accounts of group identity as though they were the same.

These examples come from *A Genealogy of Literary Multiculturalism*, where I develop them in their complexity. As it turns out, Reed's African American culture was partly theorized through Hurston and her Boasian model's crucial historical distinction between race and culture. Both found compelling that model's cultural pluralism, and the possibility of finding latent cultural survivals in a historically separated and marginalized population. And while both Reed and Hurston were suspicious of desegregation and the assimilationist social science that underpinned it, Reed's multicultural turn was all about collapsing the culture/race distinction that was crucial to the work of his 'theoretician'. Momaday's *House Made of Dawn*, meanwhile, and his more autobiographical *Way to Rainy Mountain*, were replete with instances of cultural syncretism and scenes of cultural transmission and learning. Like his own painful learning of Kiowa language and oral tradition culture (sometimes, strangely, through anthropological works), characters in *House Made of Dawn* must be taught distinct traditions that are not necessarily coextensive with their racial heritage. But Momaday's signature trope of 'memory in the blood', as he has repeatedly put it in his fictional and autobiographical work, is all about disguising the labor of learning and papering over disruptions in cultural transmission.

In this respect Momaday is akin to his fellow multiculturalist Frank Chin, both of whom researched minority cultural presences in the nation and their endurance over long periods of time. The Chinese literary tradition and a militantly Confucian 'writing-is-fighting' ethos – Kwan Kung is the god of literature and of warfare – are very much present for Chin as cultural resources to be drawn on by current generations of Chinese American artists. And though he was influenced by his friend Ishmael Reed's anthropological culturalism, the difficult questions of transmission and adaptation are sometimes bridged in his work by imagining Chinese America as simultaneously a cultural and a racial entity. Like Chin and Momaday and Reed, Anzaldúa's literary oeuvre is deeply indebted to research into the histories of actual migrations and the cultural adaptations that can be discerned through archeology and historical anthropology. There is at times a hard-headed, disenchanted, and positively Geertzian acknowledgment in her work that the religious expressions of a people are likely no more (or less) than the cumulative historical record of social change, disruption, adoption, and adaptation in that population. But, as Linda Martín Alcoff has recently and usefully warned us, critics mistake its character when they use *Borderlands/La Frontera* as an 'antidote to essentialism' (2006, 256); Anzaldúa was an essentialist, not an existentialist, and a close reading of her work suggests that her blurring of culture and race was productive for her literary politics.

Thus, by now it is surely obvious that the scandalous indistinction between race and culture in *World of Warcraft* is actually the frequent scandal of our own world of multiculturalism, our own confusion writ large. As in Azeroth, we in general do not understand or care about the distinction between a racial inheritance and a cultural heritage. I am not claiming, of course, that our most famous and canonical multiculturalists are racist, or even that Blizzard is racist, a term more apt for Boas's critic after *Brown*. We know we are not supposed to believe in race in a biological sense anymore, but instead as a social construction. My guess is that most of these authors do not quite believe in such a thing as old-fashioned race (though their biological metaphors of blood, genes, and hybridity suggest that at least sometimes some of them do). Indeed, the rhetorical stance of multiculturalism in the last three decades or so is to generally see through the biological fantasies that help generate contemporary 'racial formation', as Omi and Winant put it. There is much evidence in Morrison's work (for example, *Playing in the Dark* [1992]) to suggest a theorization of racial formation that is at least as sophisticated as that of Omi and Winant's.

Nevertheless, even when our paradigm of literary and critical multiculturalism is most disenchanted about race – seeing it as a social construction rather than as a biological reality – it frequently grounds cultural identity in a racial prescription. My hypothesis is that we erroneously fold into the social science truth of racial formation the dubious assumption that this construction includes the learning of racially appropriate cultures; such that, somehow, society's construction of the social reality of race out of its biological delusions *is the same thing as* or *happens simultaneously with* the learning by children of distinct black or Chicano or Asian American or Native American or white cultures. Contemporary multiculturalism conflates these two distinct processes of social learning, distinct not only as lessons but as sites of learning and as audiences. Racialization's lessons are the social significance of 'race' in America – its signs, its hierarchies, its forms of racial etiquette that apply differently to differently raced citizens – and these things are learned to different degrees by all citizens. But minority cultural transmission has a much wider content; it includes such things as vernaculars, oral traditions, religious beliefs, food practices, and so on. Racialization occurs as a national learning process, with regional pockets of difference cross-hatched by the usual catalogue of identity-complicators like class, sexuality, religion, and so forth. But minority cultural transmission occurs in local/familial neighborhood settings and in particularized segments of national media. Thus although racialization is a kind of cultural tradition in America, it does not entail the cultural transmission of minority cultures to specific minority groups.

The primary example where these two processes overlap, of course, is the idea that racialized minority groups' experiences of social race and racism become part of a cultural tradition that is passed down to younger generations. This is certainly true: Hurston's work in African American folklore revealed stories constituting part of a minority cultural tradition that encoded black responses to, and understandings of, the process of racialization and the facts of racism. But African American parents teaching their children how to deal with racism is a learned cultural trait that cannot count as an entire and distinct minority culture. This is only to say that, while all African Americans may be raced in America – heterogeneously according to gender, economic status, region, sexuality, and so on – such does not always or usually include the transmission of a distinctive culture. Alice Walker, for instance, was raced as black before she discovered (or rediscovered) the distinctive African American folklore in Hurston's *Mules* (1977, xi–xii). To use another example, Americans of Chinese descent may all be raced (in similar but uneven ways), but that racialization is a process distinct from the learning of Chinese American cultural heritage such as the Ballad of Fa Mu Lan oral tradition. We have perhaps been laboring under the erroneous conflation, since Omi and Winant, that racial formation includes the transmission of discrete cultures.

This confusion has produced what legal theorist Richard Ford calls our 'racial cultures', in which 'social groups defined by race are treated as analogous to geographically insular cultural minorities and certain indigenous or aboriginal tribes' and each is presumed to 'have a distinctive culture' (2005, 7). Warning that 'the degree and salience of cultural differences between the races is much less dramatic than between insular aboriginal groups and urbanized cosmopolitans' (8), Ford nonetheless finds that 'The slippage between quite insular groups defined by "societal cultures" and fairly diffuse groups with only mild and relatively superficial cultural distinctiveness is characteristic of multiculturalist argumentation' (11). And if literature has been one constitutive field of our multicultural paradigm informing Blizzard's logic of racial cultures, law may have been another. Multiculturalism's tendency to treat cultures and races as coterminous or causal entities was strengthened, Ford intriguingly argues, by the 1978 *University of California Regents v. Bakke* decision, which permitted 'diversity' as the sole remaining avenue for affirmative action college entrance policies. Various universities and the decision itself used 'ethnic' and 'racial' interchangeably, as *Bakke* 'silently analogized racial diversity to ethnic diversity' (45). In response, progressive admission policies encouraged students 'to internalize the equation of racial difference with inherited cultural difference and incorporate it into their self-conceptions' (48). *Bakke* and the diversity rationale reaffirmed recently in *Grutter v. Bollinger* (2003) helped solidify the 'cultural difference conception of race' (54) at the expense of an affirmative action policy based on students' actual experience of racism: 'Post-*Bakke* universities want to know all about the unique culture of the ancestors of their minority applicants, but ignore the discrimination suffered by the applicants themselves' (52).

Thinking of races and cultures as co-extensive, congruent, and non-overlapping means that, in *World of Warcraft*, there is no miscegenation and no cultural mixing. The trolls, orcs and tauren may have a certain indigeneity to their cultures, but there is no evidence of cultural borrowings and adaptations among these races. There might be elves living in a human community – even elven families with children – but those elves and those children are never affected by human culture. Individuals never lose their racial culture; there is never a generation gap when tauren children learn orcish ways, estranging them from their parents and grandparents. Orcs and trolls can both be shamans, but that vocation is not understood as a shared cultural tradition, or even in terms of cultural influence.

Since miscegenation – that which makes Anzaldúa's mestiza consciousness and hybrid culture not only possible but necessary – is inconceivable in *World of Warcraft*, the only remaining possibility for races to change their cultures would be through a transracial adoption. This, of course, never happens in the game. It is not that there are no orphans in war-torn Azeroth. Indeed, one of the game quests involves taking an orphaned child, who is likely of another race, on a tour of Azeroth: a Big Brother or Sister fieldtrip. But (to the disappointment of some players[7]) one cannot adopt that child. To be able to do so would be to imagine a distinction between a culture and a race, and disturb the racially prescriptive logic of deciding which culture we should have. What would be that child's 'racial heritage', and what her proper 'way of life'?

Here, as elsewhere, *World of Warcraft* seems to take its cue from multiculturalism's unease. On Blizzard's bookshelves might have been Spokane/Coeur d'Alene author Sherman Alexie's 1996 novel *Indian Killer*, in which an Indian infant is adopted and raised by WASPish parents in Seattle. He grows up to become a serial killer, the serious consequence of being raised in the wrong culture. More, as the helicopter bearing the infant to suburban Seattle takes off from the reservation hospital, it strafes the reservation with machine-gun fire. 'This is war', the narrator tells us: Alexie's surreal symbolism for the genocidal effects of transracial adoption (6). The infant turns into an Indian killer, but the title also means that transracial adoption is likewise a method of killing Indians. Such was the similar conclusion of the National Association of Black Social Workers in 1972 when it likened whites adopting black children to 'cultural genocide'(quoted in Clemetson and Nixon [2006]. This language was removed in 1994). This kind of idea, suggests Richard Ford, entails 'a notion of a biological predisposition to group culture' (84).

I am not claiming that Blizzard has been intensively reading the great literary works of contemporary American multiculturalism. There is no evidence that Blizzard designers have read these writers – as there is evidence, in contrast, that they have at least passing familiarity with other literary writers, especially Hemingway[8]. The trolls' voodoo in *World of Warcraft* does not come from Zora Neale Hurston via Ishmael Reed, but is rather a popular stereotype about it, in contrast to the references to big game hunting that drive one quest sequence ('Hills Like White Elekk') and overtly refer to Hemingway's biography and stories. My argument instead is that these authors played a crucial part in formulating our current paradigm of multiculturalism since the 1970s, as they engaged with social science discourse about race and culture, rejected the assimilationist politics of the Civil Rights era, and sought to discover and recover in an overtly pluralist way non-mainstream cultural heritages. These authors are representative of the multicultural turn, but they also helped to theorize, craft, and make happen that multicultural turn.

Of course the picture of literary multiculturalism is more complex than this, its genealogy more sundered and confused. But it is not always very much more complex. The great Boasian progressive distinction between race and culture has fallen into disuse. Our language is good at distinguishing among 'racial cultures', but it does not distinguish very well what is racial from what cultural about those groups. Read contemporary accounts of multiculturalism – by writers and academics, in government, business and media, in high culture and in low – and find a constant swerving between the terms, which have become more or less synonymous in public discourse. To be a race is to have a culture. Here, as in Azeroth. That is the scandal.

Notes

1 A previous version of this article appeared in the *electronic book review*.
2 For an excellent account of the influence of pencil-and-paper role-playing games and civilianized late nineteenth-century and pre-World World II wargames on *World of Warcraft*'s development, see Lowood (2007). For a genealogy that emphasizes wargaming, see Moran in this volume.
3 For examples of critics, see Werber (2005), and Kim (2004). For contrasting views, see McFadden (2005), Chance (2005), and Rearick (2004).
4 For a critique of this utopianism, see Nakamura (2002, chapter 2), Langer (2008), Foster (1999), and González (2000). Randall and Murphy in this volume have an excellent discussion on how *Lord of the Rings Online* stretches the racial boundaries Tolkien established.
5 Some analysts have suggested that while there are 'minor race-specific game advantages (e.g. taurens have a small bonus in herbalism, humans are slightly better with swords, etc.), the differences between races are essentially cosmetic' (Ducheneaut et al. 2006). This is certainly true, but in a game as statistics-driven as *World of Warcraft* (characters have all kinds of numbers attached to their abilities and objects, specifying strengths of specific qualities), these slight differences matter to players.
6 For criticism, see Corneliussen (2008), Bringall (2008), Langer (2008), and Golumbia (2009). For provisional defenders, see MacCallum-Stewart (2008), and Krzywinska (2006).
7 http://us.battle.net/wow/en/forum/topic/2353276190.
8 See Kriptik (2006) and http://www.wowpedia.org/List_of_pop_culture_references_in_Warcraft for lists of literary references that includes Beowulf, Cervantes, Dostoevsky, Hemingway, Shakespeare, Stevenson, Dickens, Whitman, Vonnegut, Ginsberg, Burroughs, Lovecraft, Wells, Dante, Conrad, Kipling, Swift, Crane, and Palahniuk.

References

Alcoff, Linda Martín. 2006. 'The Unassimilated Theorist.' *PMLA* 121 (1): 256.
Alexie, Sherman. 1996. *Indian Killer*. New York: Atlantic Monthly Press.

Anzaldúa, Gloria. 1999. *Borderlands/La Frontera: The New Mestiza*. 2nd edition. San Francisco: Aunt Lute Books.

Balibar, Etienne. 1991. 'Is There a "Neo-Racism"?' In *Race, Nation, Class: Ambiguous Identities*, Etienne Balibar and Immanuel Wallerstein. Trans. Chris Turner. New York: Verso. 17–36.

Blizzard Entertainment. 2004. *World of Warcraft Game Manual*. Irvine: Blizzard.

—2008. '*World of Warcraft* Surpasses 11 Million Subscribers Worldwide.' *Blizzard Entertainment Press Releases*, October 28. http://us.blizzard.com/en-us/company/press/pressreleases.html?081028.

—2010. '*World of Warcraft: Cataclysm* Shatters PC-Game Sales Record.' *Blizzard Entertainment Press Releases*, Dec. 13, 2010. http://us.blizzard.com/en-us/company/press/pressreleases.html?101213.

Bringall, Thomas III. 2008. 'Guild Life in the *World of Warcraft*: Online Gaming Tribalism.' In *Electronic Tribes: The Virtual World of Geeks, Gamers, Shamans, and Scammers*, ed. Tyrone L. Adams and Stephen A. Smith, 110–23. Austin: University of Texas Press.

Chance, Jane. 2005. 'Tolkien and the Other: Race and Gender in Middle-earth.' In *Tolkien's Modern Middle Ages*, ed. Jane Chance and Alfred K. Siewers, 171–86. New York: Palgrave Macmillan.

Chin, Frank. 1991. 'Come All Ye Asian American Writers of the Real and the Fake.' In *The Big Aiiieeeee!: An Anthology of Chinese American and Japanese American Literature*, ed. Jeffery Paul Chan, Frank Chin, Lawson Fusao Inada, and Shawn Wong. New York: Meridian.

Clemetson, Lynette, and Ron Nixon. 2006. 'Overcoming Adoption's Racial Barriers.' *The New York Times*, August 17.

Corneliussen, Hilde. 2008. '*World of Warcraft* as a Playground for Feminism.' In *Digital Culture, Play and Identity: A World of Warcraft Reader*, ed. Hilde G. Corneliussen and Jill Walker Rettberg, 63–86. Cambridge, MA: MIT Press.

Douglas, Christopher. 2009. *A Genealogy of Literary Multiculturalism*. Ithaca: Cornell University Press.

Ducheneaut, Nicolas, Nick Yee, Eric Nickell, and Robert J. Moore. 2006. 'Building an MMO With Mass Appeal: a Look at Gameplay in *World of Warcraft*.' *Games and Culture* 1(4): 281–317.

Ford, Richard T. 2005. *Racial Culture: A Critique*. Princeton: Princeton University Press.

Foster, Thomas. 1999. '"The Souls of Cyber-Folk": Performativity, Virtual Embodiment, and Racial Histories.' In *Cyberspace Textuality: Computer Technology and Literary Theory*, ed. Marie-Laure Ryan, 137–63. Bloomington: Indiana University Press.

Golumbia, David. 2009. 'Games Without Play.' *New Literary History* 40: 179–204.

González, Jennifer. 2000. 'The Appended Subject: Race and Identity as Digital Assemblage.' In *Race in Cyberspace*, ed. Beth Kolko et al., 27–50. New York: Routledge.

Hagström, Charlotte. 2008. 'Playing with Names: Gaming and Naming in *World of Warcraft*.' In *Digital Culture, Play and Identity: A World of Warcraft Reader*, ed. Hilde G. Corneliussen and Jill Walker Rettberg, 265–85. Cambridge, MA: MIT Press.

Hayot, Eric, and Edward Wesp. 2009. 'Interview with Brad McQuaid and Kevin McPherson.' *Game Studies* 9, no.1. http://gamestudies.org/0901/articles/interview_mcquaid_mcpherson

Hemenway, Robert E. 1977. *Zora Neale Hurston: A Literary Biography*. Urbana: University of Illinois Press.

Huntington, Samuel. 1996. *The Clash of Civilizations and the Remaking of World Order*. New York: Simon and Schuster.

Hurston, Zora Neale. 1990. *Tell My Horse: Voodoo and Life in Haiti and Jamaica*. New York: Harper & Row.

Hyatt, Marshall. 1990. *Franz Boas Social Activist/The Dynamics of Ethnicity*. Westport, CT: Greenwood Press.

Kim, Sue. 2004. 'Beyond Black and White: Race and Postmodernism in *The Lord of the Rings* Films.' *Modern Fiction Studies* 50 (4): 875–907.

Kingston, Maxine Hong. 1976. *The Woman Warrior: Memoirs of a Girlhood among Ghosts*. New York: Vintage International.

Kriptik. 2006. '*World of Warcraft* Easter Egg – List of Pop Culture References.' *The Easter Egg Archive*, 17 April. http://www.eeggs.com/items/47546.html.

Krzywinska, Tanya. 2006. 'Blood Scythes, Festivals, Quests, and Backstories: World Creation and Rhetorics of Myth in *World of Warcraft*.' *Games and Culture* 1 (4): 383–96.

Langer, Jessica. 2008. 'The Familiar and the Foreign: Playing (Post) Colonialism in *World of Warcraft*.' In *Digital Culture, Play and Identity: A World of Warcraft Reader*, ed. Hilde G. Corneliussen and Jill Walker Rettberg, 87–108. Cambridge, MA: MIT Press.

Lowood, Henry. 2007. '"It's Not Easy Being Green": Real-time Game Performance in *Warcraft*.' In *Videogame, Player, Text*, ed. Barry Atkins and Tanya Krzwynska, 83–100. Manchester: Manchester University Press.

MacCallum-Stewart, Esther. 2008. '"Never Such Innocence Again": War and Histories in *World of Warcraft*.' In *Digital Culture, Play and Identity: A World of Warcraft Reader*, ed. Hilde G. Corneliussen and Jill Walker Rettberg, 39–62. Cambridge, MA: MIT Press.

McFadden, Brian. 2005. 'Fear of Difference, Fear of Death: the *Sigelwara*, Tokien's Swertings, and Racial Difference.' In *Tolkien's Modern Middle Ages*, ed. Jane Chance and Alfred K. Siewers, 155–69. New York: Palgrave Macmillan.

Michaels, Walter Benn. 2004. *The Shape of the Signifier: 1967 to the End of History*. Princeton: Princeton University Press.

Momaday, N. Scott. 1999. *House Made of Dawn*. New York: Perennial Classics.

Morrison, Toni. 1987. *Beloved*. New York: Plume.

—1992. *Playing in the Dark: Whiteness and the Literary Imagination*. Cambridge, MA: Harvard University Press.

Mortensen, Torill Elvira. 2008. 'Me, the Other.' *Electronic book review*. http://www.electronicbookreview.com/thread/firstperson/sincere?mode=print

Nakamura, Lisa. 2002. *Cybertypes: Race, Ethnicity, and Identity on the Internet*. New York: Routledge.

Omi, Michael, and Howard Winant. 1986. *Racial Formation in the United States from the 1960s to the 1980s*. New York: Routledge.

Rearick, Anderson. 2004. 'Why Is the Only Good Orc a Dead Orc? The Dark Face of Racism in Tolkien's World.' *Modern Fiction Studies* 50 (4 Winter): 862–74.

Reed, Ishmael. 1972. *Mumbo Jumbo*. New York: Simon and Schuster.

Ruff, Matt. 2007. 'Wow.' *LiveJournal*, June 30. http://matt-ruff.livejournal.com/12050.html.

Thompson, Clive. 2007. 'Playing the Master Race.' *Wired*, Mar 12.

Walker, Alice. 1977. 'Zora Neale Hurston – A Cautionary Tale and a Partisan View.' In *Zora Neale Hurston: A Literary Biography*, ed. Robert Hemenway, xi-xviii. Urbana: University of Chicago Press.

Werber, Niels. 2005. 'Geo- and Biopolitics of Middle-earth: a German Reading of Tolkien's *The Lord of the Rings*.' *New Literary History* 36: 227–46.

Williams, John H. 2007. 'Trolls and Taurens: Racist stereotypes in *World of Warcraft*?' *Thud Factor*, August 12. http://www.thudfactor.com/race/trolls-and-taurens-racist-stereotypes-in-world-of-warcraft.

Yardley, Jonathan. 2007. '"Woman Warrior", A Memoir That Shook the Genre.' *Washington Post*, June 19.

14

From Meaning to Experience: Teaching Fiction Writing With Digital RPGs

TRENT HERGENRADER

Creative writing as an academic discipline has not advanced far beyond the approach pioneered at the Iowa Writers Workshop, formally established at the University of Iowa in 1936. The program's website succinctly describes the traditional workshop method:

> A senior writer leads a discussion about a work written by a member of the class; workshop students share impressions, advice, and analysis. As Paul Engle, director of the Writers' Workshop and founder of the International Writing Program, observed: 'the students benefited greatly from hearing a variety

of attitudes toward their work. It was like publishing then being reviewed.' Workshop students receive honest and immediate feedback about their writing and become better critics of their own work.

The website states that this method became the prototype for more than 300 writing programs, and it is undoubtedly the dominant approach to teaching creative writing in today's universities.

The method works extremely well for writers committed to breaking into the competitive publishing world – I attribute much of my own publishing success to an Iowa-style workshop – but it requires a highly controlled environment. Programs like the Iowa Writer's Workshop are selective *graduate* programs, and thus have the luxury of accepting and rejecting prospective students based on writing samples that reflect the applicant's literary aesthetic. Participants in graduate-level workshops also typically share a good understanding of the contemporary publishing scene, which allows them to offer incisive critiques for their peers. 'What the workshop ideally provides', writes Scott Russell Sanders, 'is a community of people who read widely and well, who savor words, who enjoy using their minds, who take seriously what young writers wish to take seriously' (Sanders 1991, 27).

While the Iowa Workshop model may work well for crops of handpicked writers, this method produces mixed results at best for the diverse student body enrolled in undergraduate creative writing classes (Ritter and Vanderslice 2007, xv). Unlike the carefully cultivated population attending elite graduate writing workshops, instructors teaching creative writing to undergrads have little control over enrollment, there is no guarantee that students will have read widely and well, and virtually none will be conversant about literary publishing trends. In fact, few of my students show interest in literary publication at all, with far more saying they take creative writing courses as an outlet for their creativity or to fulfill general education requirements. For some creative writing instructors, this means we can't do much more than nurture the gifted writers and help the rest be as good as they can be – which, by literary publishing standards, may not be very good at all (McFarland 1993, 43–4).

While the Iowa Workshop has been the dominant approach to teaching creative writing, an increasing number of critics contend that we must do more with the intellectual space creative writing courses afford us. Rather than obsessing about whether a piece of writing would pass muster at a given literary magazine, these critics charge that creative writing offers opportunities for students to engage with a variety of issues, such as how the social, historical, and material conditions of writing manifest themselves in creative work (Mayers 2005, Ritter and Vanderslice 2007, Wandor 2008). Amato and Fleischer (2002) go even further by suggesting that a primary goal should be the establishment of close-knit communities where students can freely experiment with their writing, including using digital and networking technologies as narrative tools. Olson (2002) builds on this idea, describing progressive creative writing courses as 'centers of narrativity [...] where various arts will be fused & be confused in increasing & increasingly illuminating ways.'

If such ideas are to be put into place, students must learn to critically analyze media other than the literary print text; traditional print fiction is only one of many possible narrative modes of production that can be analyzed, probed, and investigated in the context of a creative writing class. In an experimental creative writing course, instructors can adopt other popular texts such as comics, films, and videogames without abandoning classic narrative concerns such as characterization, setting, and plot. This type of approach not only teaches students to critically analyze fictional narratives across media, but it also creates space for them to explore multimodal composing by manipulating images, audio, and video in the production of their stories. By de-emphasizing the literary print text, we open creative writing classes to more expansive ways of thinking about narrative and promote experimental forms of fiction writing.

In this paper I discuss how a specific kind of videogame, the DRPG, can be usefully incorporated into a fiction-writing course to teach specific narrative principles. DRPGs require players to make a series of explicit choices during the character creation phase, many of which directly impact how players experience the game's larger narrative. The foregrounding of choices in the DRPG translates well to the act of fiction writing, which helps students understand writing as a series of deliberate authorial decisions. Players of DRPGs also take an active role in determining how the story unfolds, an advantage not replicable in other media. Perhaps most critically for creative writing courses, the online knowledge-building communities based on DRPGs offer compelling models for experimental fiction writing.

From Meaning to Experience: From Literary Print Texts to the DRPG

Though much postmodern theory emphasizes the active role of the reader in meaning-making, many students view reading a print text as a passive activity, especially compared with the direct control they wield in a videogame. Many students also harbor a reductive understanding of what literature can offer, often having been drilled to read for a singular 'meaning' that the author buried beneath layers of symbols and metaphors. This narrow conception of literature poses a particular challenge in creative writing classes, where inexperienced fiction writers can saturate their fiction with overcomplicated plots rather than developing compelling characters and detail-rich settings. Students who focus their attention on plot and meaning inevitably wind up writing uninspiring stories, depicting wooden characters acting stiffly against a white canvas.

DRPGs offer a unique solution to this problem. Few students play videogames to uncover the deep hidden meanings contained within them; instead, players are absorbed by the challenges and possible solutions presented in the game. As with other genres of videogames, DRPGs feature storylines that motivate players to achieve specific tasks in order to advance the narrative. To complete these tasks, players must immerse themselves in a fictional world and learn how to survive and thrive based on the attributes of their character and the rules of that specific environment. Player choice is paramount, something the designers of the post-apocalyptic DRPG *Fallout 3* (Bethesda 2008) explicitly state in the game's instruction booklet:

> It's your game, so play it the way you want. There is no 'right' way to play. Try out the many skills and perks found in this manual. Try using V.A.T.S., the all new combat system. But most of all, remember that each challenge the game gives you

has multiple ways of solving it, and multiple outcomes. There are many paths to success, and yes, the game does eventually 'end'. But how it ends is up to you, and the character you play. (*Fallout 3 Survival Guide* 2008, 3)

Varieties of experience, rather than a single profound meaning, take precedence in DRPGs. While the game offers multiple plotlines known as quests, the scenarios play out differently based on how the player approaches the situation. In other words, player decisions fashion, rather than serve, the larger plot. They can play through multiple possibilities by reloading from a save point, or by restarting the game with a newly constructed character.

Beginning with character building rather than plot is a traditional strategy for teaching fiction writing as well. Accomplished writers often begin new stories by fleshing out their characters first and developing the plot later. John Gardner (1984) writes in his canonical *Art of Fiction* that the fiction writer's chief goal is to 'make up convincing human beings and create for them basic situations and actions by means of which they come to know themselves and reveal themselves to the reader' (14–15). Flannery O'Connor (1969) encouraged novice writers to devote ample time to their characters, who should naturally drive the story's plot:

> In most good stories it is the character's personality that creates the action of the story. In most [workshop stories], I feel that the writer has thought up some action and then scrounged up a character to perform it. You will usually be more successful if you start the other way around. If you start with a real personality, a real character, then something is bound to happen; and you don't have to know what before you begin. In fact, it may be better if you don't know what before you begin. You ought to be able to discover something from your stories. If you don't probably nobody else will. (105–6)

For Gardner and O'Connor, the act of reading and writing fiction should be one of exploration and discovery on the part of the reader, writer, and even the fictional characters themselves. The question for students writing fiction ceases to be 'what do I want my story to mean?' but rather 'who is my protagonist and what are his or her unique qualities?' This is precisely the same question facing a player starting a new DRPG.

While DRPGs excel at foregrounding character creation and world exploration, they make little attempt to reveal the nuanced emotions and attitudes of the characters (Aarseth 2004), something that print fiction handles very well. In order to successfully compare the similarities and differences between the media we need a flexible critical methodology. Theorist Ian Bogost (2006) proposes analyzing the *unit operations* present in the texts. Bogost describes unit operations as 'modes of meaning-making that privilege discrete, disconnected actions over deterministic, progressive systems' (3) as opposed to *system operations*, which are 'totalizing structures that seek to explicate a phenomenon, behavior, or state in its entirety' (6). To apply the concept to creative writing, students exhibiting a tendency to read a print text searching for a fixed immutable 'meaning' could be said to be examining systems operations, looking for clues that would reveal the totalizing structure that serves to inform a correct interpretation of the work. Unit operations, however, isolate discrete moments of meaning-making in a text that invite the exploration of alternate configurations; whereas *systems* suggest rigidity and determinism, *units* suggest fluidity and potentiality in narratives.

For creative writing pedagogy, this methodology allows students and instructors alike to focus on discrete moments in media where we learn specific information about the character or the fictional world without becoming distracted by interpretations of broader possible meanings. In the following discussion, I analyze specific moments in the character creation process of the DRPG *Fallout 3*, as well as discrete moments of character development in early stages of the game. This type of analysis helps students experience a narrative through the eyes of the protagonist moving through a fictional space and reveals how plot develops from the character's decisions, not the other way around. I also examine the limitations of the videogame form in general, critiquing the options this specific game's designers chose to include and exclude from gameplay. This kind of critique can be instructive for creative writing students who often don't appreciate the full range of possibilities available to them when starting a new narrative, as well as the social consequences of their narrative choices.

'What Kind of Person Are You Going to Be?' – Character Creation in *Fallout 3*

Many fiction-writing instructors use exercises to prompt students to think about aspects of their characters they might not have considered, such as their character's job, favorite foods, and hobbies (Bernays and Painter 2009, 36). The character creation process in a DRPG functions like a digitized version of these classic creative writing exercises. In *Fallout 3*, the character is literally born into the world. The game begins with a short movie describing a nuclear holocaust survived only by those who took shelter in underground vaults, and who later emerge to find the world transformed into a hellish wasteland. The inhabitants of Vault 101, however, chose to remain sealed off from the outside world. 'It is here you were born', the narrator tells the player. 'It is here you will die. Because in Vault 101 no ever enters, and no one ever leaves' (*Fallout 3* 2008). The screen turns black; the player hears a beating heart and then sees a flash of white light; then the player hears a baby crying. Two blurry figures hover over the newborn character, and one asks the other whether the child is a boy or girl. The game cuts away, prompting the player to select the character's sex. Next, the player chooses a name and, via a clever 'gene projection' monitor, customizes the character's adult appearance. This includes the character's race, facial structures, hair color, and hairstyle. The character's father opines on the kinds of people who populate the world, and then asks an open-ended question: 'What about you? What kind of person are you going to be?'

As a discrete unit of meaning-making, the initial stage of the character creation process invites the critical player to examine the various options and reflect on the possible consequences for the narrative. For example, the player customizes the character's race, facial structure, and hairstyle. While players eventually learn that none of these options impact gameplay – characters in the game react the same to a Caucasian with a crew cut as they do to an Asian with a spiked blue hairdo – they help create a bond between player and character. These details enhance visual gameplay but they also provide a fertile moment for introspection and classroom discussion. In our actual world, we know appearances *do* matter in personal interactions, as many students will have experienced first-hand. *Fallout 3* presents a series of tense situations between the character and inhabitants of the wasteland, and it seems inarguable that outward appearance would impact conversations and negotiations; for example, a gatekeeper of a closed community might be less inclined to trust an important task to a character sporting an unconventional look.

More troublingly, the game sidesteps sticky race-related issues. Racial discrimination does not exist in *Fallout 3*. While apologists might claim that the game strives to be apolitical, this is belied by the fact that another attribute, the character's sex, *does* impact gameplay. Early on in the game the player may choose a bonus skill for his or her character entitled Black Widow (for female characters) or Lady Killer (for male characters) that opens unique, sexually suggestive dialogue options when dealing with the opposite sex. By offering this choice, the game designers tacitly acknowledge that outward appearances do influence interpersonal interactions; it would logically follow that the races of two characters would likewise impact the way they communicate, but the game is silent on this account. At best, players might assume that the futuristic world of *Fallout 3* has attained racial harmony, and that the sex-based perks are simply an example of the black humor the games are known for; at worst, the designers could be accused of ignoring or trivializing the endemic social problems of racism and sexism.

Students should also consider the character customization options the game doesn't include. For example, all *Fallout 3* characters have an identical body type: tall and slim. The game neglects other noteworthy social issues such as a character's class and sexual orientation, topics frequently tackled in compelling fictional narratives. The limited presence of body modifications such as tattoos and piercings can also spark debate; not only do players not have the option to decorate their characters' bodies, but the only characters who have tattoos are cannibalistic, drug-addled raiders. Even though body modifications have become more commonplace in our society, the game loosely equates tattoos and piercings with substance abuse and lawlessness. (For other limitations on character/avatar creation, see Moran elsewhere in this volume.)

These gaps and weaknesses in the digitized character creation process become teachable moments in a fiction-writing class. The game designers made *choices* about how players may customize their characters and how those customizations impact the narrative. Each choice can be isolated from the narrative arc of the game, allowing students to connect their knowledge and experiences from the real world to their corresponding representations (or absence) in a fictional world. The critical fiction writer must consider not only the details of his or her fictional character, but how and why those details have consequences in the fictional world. For example, students might consider how a character's physical stature would alter a post-apocalyptic narrative, which often entails scrambling over debris or fitting into tight spaces; they could also discuss different ways sex, race, and class impact the ways people communicate, based on their own real-life experiences. By interrogating the choices of the game designers, which are more explicit in a DRPG than in a print text, we draw attention to the discrete decisions students must confront in their fiction writing, and thus compel novice writers to account for the complexity of their social and historical realities. Conscientious writers must be aware of the social consequences of their narrative decisions on their audience, even if most action DRPGs elide them.

After the character's appearance has been determined, the player continues the customization process by determining his or her physical attributes and skills. This entails assigning point values to properties such as strength, agility, and perception, as well as choosing from a variety of learned talents that skew toward violent conflict resolution: small guns, energy weapons, explosives, etc. (In this volume, see both Travis and Baerg regarding the ramifications of assigning points to character attributes.) Critical players can infer through the skills and their descriptions that certain activities won't feature in gameplay. For example, no skills exist for piloting terrain vehicles or aircraft because the player never has the opportunity to get behind the wheel; no language skills exist because this world is monolingual. Other skills are comically broad in their application: the

Repair skill allows for the fixing of weapons of all types, patching clothing, and even repairing faulty plumbing; the umbrella Science skill covers such disparate fields as computer programming, biology, chemistry, and robotics. Perhaps most evident of all, the loading and firing of handguns, machine guns, rocket launchers, and flamethrowers requires no training; like today's digital cameras, *Fallout 3*'s weapons are all point-and-shoot.

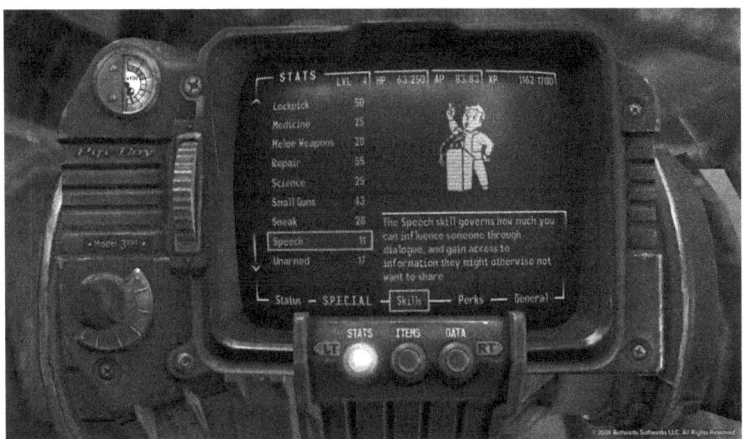

Figure 14.1 Skill points displayed on the Pip-Boy 3000, a standard piece of equipment for every character. *Fallout® 3*: © 2008 Bethesda Softworks LLC, a ZeniMax Media company. All Rights Reserved.

The critical player should understand that while this atmosphere creates a thrilling game (and the occasionally enjoyable but mindless Hollywood action film), it does not make for compelling print fiction. Other types of talents are conspicuous through their absence. Artistic abilities are not options during the character creation phase, despite the fact that players encounter musicians and sculptors in their wanderings. While one could argue that the irrelevance of artistic skill reflects the depravity of wasteland culture, the game designers foreclose a character's artistic production from the onset by denying this skill set. This absence in the game in a writing class can prompt important questions for beginning writers: what urges people toward artistic creation? What value does society place on artistic production? While these can be tedious questions to address in traditional print fiction, for students collaboratively creating a vast fictional world the issue becomes one of choice: do artistic works exist in your fictional world and, if so, how do they function? This provides student writers, who are artists themselves, a unique opportunity to reflect on their own artistic production and its worth in our current world.

These discrete narrative choices when creating a character – race, sex, and their outward appearance, as well as skills and abilities – lead to an important question: how will these choices impact the narrative? In actuality, players starting a new DRPG and writers beginning a new story might only have a hunch about how the narrative might unfold. Often the best way to find out is to set the character in motion and see what happens.

Venturing Forth from Vault 101 – Trial and Error in Gaming and Writing

At the start of *Fallout 3*, the player's only motivations are to find the character's runaway father and to stay alive in the wasteland. The manner in which the player can accomplish these goals is directly related to the fictional character's strengths and weaknesses as determined by the player during the character creation phase. As DRPG players customize their character, they form a unique bond with the fictional character – the player literally sees the world through his or her character's eyes. James Paul Gee (2007) refers to this as an 'embodied story', where the player and character become fused into a single psychological space (79) known as the player-character (PC). In videogames, Gee explains that players learn about their characters and the fictional world through a four-step process of probing and hypothesis. Players probe a fictional world, discover things about it, form hypotheses, and then test these hypotheses. If they encounter a negative result (e.g. the character dies) then they begin again; if they succeed, they move on to new discoveries (88).

This probe-hypothesize-reprobe-rethink cycle is not only an effective learning method, it also closely resembles the revision process for fiction writers. Gardner (1984) states that a writer must shape simultaneously (in an ever-expanding creative moment) his characters, plot, and setting, each inextricably connected to the others; he must make his whole world in a single, coherent gesture, as a potter makes a pot; or, as Coleridge puts it, he must copy, with his finite mind, the process of the infinite 'I AM'. (29)

Gardner tells us that character, plot, and setting are so closely linked that a change in one 'is to make the fictional ground shudder' (46); as experienced writers know, the fictional ground shudders non-stop during the revision process. Early drafts of narratives can be quite different from the final product, often because the author makes discoveries about the world and the nature of the character through the act of writing and then must make adjustments, both minor and major, through a series of drafts. Far from bursting from the author's head fully formed, a story gradually emerges through an often slow and messy affair full of missteps, dead ends, and refinements. Only by the author's weeding through of a multitude of options does a work of fiction take its final shape, leaving a smattering of vestigial details from earlier drafts that impart a sense of a deeper, more fully realized world for the reader. However, the stories printed in magazines and anthologies show no trace of the revision process, which can be discouraging for beginning writers who feel they can never get a story 'right' on the first or second try. The DRPG can be a useful tool in demonstrating that drafts, like a character's repeated deaths in a videogame, are not failures but valuable learning moments.

For example, when I emerged from Vault 101 my first time playing *Fallout 3*, I decided not to follow the path leading down to the ruined town below and chose instead to take in the post-apocalyptic sights, marveling at the shattered expressways and other ruination. I saw figures moving near a totaled semi-trailer and went to investigate. As I approached, shots rang out and the screen flashed as the bullets hit me. I fumbled to draw my pistol using the controls I thought I'd mastered in the introductory quests, but I was too slow. I squeezed off a few poorly placed shots before my character hit the dirt, dead. Irritated at stumbling at the first hurdle, I loaded from my last save and tried again. On my second attempt I sneaked up on the party and managed to eliminate the first assailant, not realizing that he had two buddies hidden behind the truck. Needless to say, I died again.

On the third try, I headed in the opposite direction of the gang and searched some ramshackle houses, hoping to find a better weapon. My scavenging turned up a lawnmower blade and ammunition for a gun I didn't own. Then I heard an ominous scratching sound and discovered two mutated ants had cornered me in the house. With guns blazing I managed to force my way out, killing both ants but using nearly all my ammunition. I stopped to get my bearings, and that briefest of pauses undid me. I was attacked from behind by another mutated creature, this time something called a mole rat. I wound up at the reload screen again. On my *fourth* attempt from the vault, I bolted down the path to the town, scurrying between boulders and wrecked cars littering the path, jumping at any sound. Some hero I turned out to be! This time, I made it into town and I celebrated when I found a locked safe, which I assumed contained valuable supplies. Then I discovered I couldn't open it because I hadn't boosted my lockpick skill high enough during the character creation process, and my heart sank. I scurried on before something else attacked me.

The designers of *Fallout 3* constructed an intensely dangerous world. Only on the fourth attempt did I respect the perils pressing in from all sides. It took multiple restarts for me to understand that, while this open-world DRPG made many options available to me, the terrain and its dangers of the wasteland severely limited those options. (For more on the interaction between character and environment, see Bealer in this same volume.) I learned very quickly that I had neither the strength nor resources to cope with conflicts in the wasteland, and I didn't have to wonder what my character might be thinking or feeling in that moment; sneaking down among the wreckage, my heart was racing and I was jumpy, ready to shoot first and ask questions later. The game doesn't explain my character's emotional state, but it doesn't need to. When I'm holding my breath in terror, so is my character; when I despair at not being able to open a safe, my character despairs with me.

Such embodied experience proves invaluable for the beginning writer. My game experience wouldn't have been very fun if my character shot everything dead on sight and unlocked the first safe I found without breaking a sweat. My series of failures taught me that I could not dawdle in the wasteland and I (eventually) acted accordingly, adjusting my behavior to match the environment. My embodied experience as a PC imparted a strong sense of both the physical and psychological reality of my character in the fictional world. While playing, I jumped out of my seat more than once; my hands turned sweaty on the controller; I cursed my own stupidity when I couldn't open the safe. These actions not only exhibit my level of engagement with the game, but they suggest how my character felt in that same scenario. Faithfully transcribing a gaming session might not be very interesting, but having beginning writers experience connecting real-world physiological responses to fictional characters is a valuable lesson that print fiction simply cannot replicate.

Students should understand writing as a process of slow and steady progression, and that each misstep is in fact a valuable learning moment. Students could be asked to write multiple scenes based on a given scenario, each time with a radically different character; another strategy would be having students put the same character through very different scenarios and see how the writer handles the character's reactions. Peers could comment on whether they agreed with the writer's interpretation of how the scenario played out in the fiction. Also, scenarios need not be rooted in the action-quest genre of *Fallout 3*; exercises in multiple perspectives would be equally productive in a more mundane setting, such as a routine traffic stop. Such an exercise could be 'replayed' dozens of times over, turning what could be construed as a dull repetitive task into game-like learning.

Will Megaton Burn? – Decisions, Experience, and Karma

As Gardner suggests, readers learn about fictional characters through their decisions. In *Fallout 3*'s introductory levels, the PC has few interesting decisions to make, primarily because the character is a child and lives in the authoritarian bubble of Vault 101. Once the player emerges from the vault though, choices abound; with each decision, the character grows both in the imagination of the player and in the gameworld. Characters earn experience points (XP) for a variety of activities, including finding new locations, successfully performing tasks like picking locks, killing dangerous animals, and completing quests. After accumulating enough XP a player 'levels up' and can choose to bolster new skills and attain bonuses called perks. Quests fall into four different categories: eleven main quests that revolve around finding the character's father and fulfilling his broader goal of providing purified water to the wasteland; seventeen side quests that further develop the *Fallout 3* world and usually require the PC to perform some service in exchange for payment, often in weapons, supplies, cash, and XP; and over thirty unmarked and repeatable quests, which are of smaller scope and importance for the narrative. In addition to fulfilling quests, the player also has the option of simply wandering the wasteland searching for random encounters. While the completion of certain quests often makes other quests available, the game does not compel the PC into any one course of action.

In addition to XP the game also tracks karma points, which can be gained or lost based on the game's moral valuation of certain kinds of act. Karma is independent from XP. For example, a character receives *positive* karma for killing a violent raider and *negative* karma for killing an innocent civilian, but would receive the same XP for either act. Karma does not dictate success in the game; good, neutral, or evil PCs experience the game differently, but no karmic category provides a playing advantage over the others. Karma does determine how non-player characters (NPCs) interact with the PC though. Noble characters will only partner with PCs with positive karma, and rogues only join PCs with negative karma; law-abiding citizens give gifts to a PC with good karma while criminals reward PCs with low karma. Unlike XP that displays a numeric value per completed task, the karmic point total is never revealed for the character and the game only informs the player that karma has been lost or gained without revealing the numeric value.

XP and karma act as visual indicators that the PC has taken an action of consequence that often has tangible, often unintended consequences in the fictional world. The PC must continually weigh and balance each decision made, not knowing in that moment how a specific decision will impact the character's future. Any time the player earns XP or karma provides an opportunity for critical

Figure 14.2 Dialogue options with Jericho, an NPC who will join a character who has negative karma. *Fallout® 3*: © 2008 Bethesda Softworks LLC, a ZeniMax Media company. All Rights Reserved.

reflection. For students unused to assessing videogames critically, it is imperative to remind them that it's no magical higher power, but rather the game's designers, who decide which acts deserve XP and positive or negative karma. For example, if a virtuous player steals supplies from slavers, should this result in more or less negative karma than stealing from a law-abiding citizen? Does the game reward violent solutions more than diplomatic ones? Isolating moments of decision-making also invites players to examine their own notions of morality, as well as providing a safe space to experiment without negative consequences (Schulzke 2009). Just as with discussions about race relations, students can be encouraged to map the moral value system of the real world against that of the fictional world, noting confluences and ruptures. This not only helps them create more complex fictional worlds, but it also requires them to interrogate their own conceptions of moral and immoral behavior.

Playing with Creative Writing and the Future of Fiction

While creative writing pedagogy might be strongly rooted in antiquated practices, progressive instructors must look towards the future – both for the future of our students as well as the future of narrative. The traditional workshop method developed at the University of Iowa focuses exclusively on producing work intended for publication in literary print magazines, yet undergraduate students voraciously consume texts of all kinds, including digital texts, and few show interest in literary publication. They do, however, show interest in a wide variety of different kinds of narrative, including the videogame. Creative writing instructors should demote the literary print text from its historical position of privilege and adopt a broader spectrum of narrative forms for classroom practice. By limiting our craft analysis to literary print texts, we limit the types of narrative students will feel comfortable writing. By considering narrative across several media, we widen the range of our students' critical skills and will encourage them to experiment with multimodal composing, especially in the digital realm, where they can incorporate text, image, audio, and video into narratives in intriguing new ways.

I used *Fallout 3* in an introductory writing course subtitled 'Gaming, World Building, and Narrative', where students collaboratively constructed and explored a post-apocalyptic version of Milwaukee. In the course's opening weeks they read print fiction, watched films, and played the DRPG; we discussed the characters, locations, and plot events as discrete unit operations within each text and compared the narrative strengths and weaknesses of each medium. In the middle portion of the course, students populated a wiki – an easily editable website for multiple users – with items, locations, and fictional characters, and used the Vault, a freely editable wiki created and maintained by fans of the *Fallout* series, as our creative inspiration. This active online community uses the site to discuss everything from game cheats and glitches to chronicling the history of the game series' expansive world. Every object, location, and character in the game has its own page with a detailed description that, in true wiki fashion, contains dozens of hyperlinks connected to related pages. While most players use the site to overcome obstacles they encounter in the game, the sheer quantity of links entices the visitor to click through dozens of pages to discover more about the world of the *Fallout* series.

The wiki played a central role in the final third of the course, when students created player-characters and explored the fictional world through a series of tabletop role-playing campaigns. Their characters equipped themselves with items from the wiki, and they discovered new locations and NPCs, which were created by their classmates and described in detail as discrete wiki entries. The wiki also became a repository for their player-characters' ever-evolving stories, which featured links to relevant pages for the items, locations, and characters mentioned in the narrative. Our post-apocalyptic Milwaukee quickly developed into a vast and deeply complex world, and although each student wrote individual narrative episodes for their player-characters, the stories prominently featured content created by their classmates. Writers were not only interested in the fate of their own characters, but they wanted to read about their classmates' adventures to see if anything they contributed to the wiki had made it into their story. Throughout the semester, students regularly added details to the fictional world, including a complex network of social, political, and economic histories. The complete site, which features two novels' worth of fiction, is sprawling, messy, strange, and incredibly compelling.

The DRPG *Fallout 3* was integral to this creative writing experiment's success. Students spent considerable time developing their player-characters, repeatedly referencing their experiences creating characters in the videogame; the factions, histories, and societies of their world drew heavily from the intricacies of *Fallout 3*'s wasteland; and the wiki's page layout was modeled after a wiki dedicated to the game series. Though we analyzed several media, the world and characters students collaboratively created most closely resembles the world presented in the videogame, both by design as well as the students' natural creative impulses.

The sound fiction writing advice shared by Gardner and O'Connor still holds true today; however, the world has moved on and instructors must embrace digital technologies that offer new ways to construct narratives. DRPGs offer an exciting avenue for narrative analysis for beginning writers due to the characters customization options and freedom for players to shape the narrative as they play. In addition, game wikis and other online fan communities can serve as models for experimental student writing. Videogames are central to student culture and by including them in our courses we can broaden our students' critical skills, liberate them from closed interpretations of literature, and reorient creative writing pedagogy towards the future.

References

Aarseth, Espen. 2004. 'Genre Trouble.' In *First Person: New Media as Story, Performance, and Game*, ed. Noah Wardrip-Fruin and Pat Harrigan, 45–56. Cambridge, MA: MIT Press.
Amato, Joe, and H. Kassia Fleischer. 2002. *Reforming Creative Writing Pedagogy: History as Knowledge, Knowledge as Activism*. ALTX Online Network. http://www.altx.com/ebr/riposte/rip2/rip2ped/amato.htm.
Bernays, Anne and Pamela Painter. 2009. *What If?: Writing Exercises for Fiction Writers*. Harrisonburg, VA: Longman.
Bethesda, Fallout 3. [Xbox 360]. Bethesda Softworks: Rockville, MD, 2008.
Bogost, Ian. 2006. *Unit Operations: An Approach to Videogame Criticism*. Cambridge, MA: MIT Press.
English 236 Website: Gaming, World Building, and Narrative. 2011. http://eng236.wikispaces.com
'Fallout 3 Survival Guide.' 2008. Rockville, MD: Bethesda Game Studios.
Gardner, John. 1984. *The Art of Fiction: Notes on Craft for Young Writers*. New York: Knopf.
Gee, James Paul. 2007. *What Video Games Have to Teach Us About Learning and Literacy*. New York: Palgrave Macmillan.
Mayers, Tim. 2005. *(Re)Writing Craft*. Pittsburgh: University of Pittsburgh.
McFarland, Ron. 1994. 'An Apologia for Creative Writing.' *College English* 56(1): 28–45.
O'Connor, Flannery, Sally Fitzgerald, and Robert Fitzgerald. 1969. *Mystery and Manners: Occasional Prose*. New York: Farrar, Straus & Giroux.
Olsen, Lance. 2002. 'Learning to Wish for More.' *Riposte to Reforming Creative Writing Pedagogy: History as Knowledge*, Knowledge as

Activism. ALTX Online Network. http://www.electronicbookreview.com/thread/endconstruction/truestory

Ritter, Kelly and Stephanie Vanderslice. 2007. 'Introduction: Creative Writing and the Persistence of Lore. In *Can It Really Be Taught?: Resisting Lore in Creative Writing Pedagogy*, ed. Kelly Ritter and Stephanie Vanderslice, xi–xx. Portsmouth, NH: Boynton/Cook Heinemann.

Sanders, Scott Russell. 1991. 'The Writer in the University.' *ADE Bulletin* 99: 22–8.

Schulzke, Marcus. 2009. 'Moral Decision Making in Fallout 3.' *Game Studies* 9 no.2. http://gamestudies.org/0902/articles/schulzke

University of Iowa. 2011. 'The Writing University.' http://www.writinguniversity.org/index.php/main/info/writing_at_iowa/

Vault, the Fallout Wikia. 2001. http://fallout.wikia.com/wiki/Fallout_Wiki

Wandor, Michelene. 2008. *The Author is Not Dead, Merely Somewhere Else: Creative Writing After Theory*. Basingstoke, UK: Palgrave Macmillan.

15

Gaming the Meta: Metagame Culture and Player Motivation in RPGs

JOSH CALL[1]

It is a Saturday afternoon and I am watching my four-year-old daughter play Hide and Seek with other neighborhood children. As is often the case in these kinds of game, the rules are remarkably vague and often revised on the spot. Beyond setting a limit for number of seconds to count, and where 'home base' is located, things are largely open. It is her turn to be 'it' so she dutifully closes her eyes and counts to twenty. After completing her count, she opens her eyes, abruptly turns, and without hesitation walks directly to a tree a good distance from home base. As she nears the tree, one of her friends sees her coming, and tries to make a break for home base. My daughter tags her on the way, signaling to the other children that this round is finished, and a new person is now 'it'. This produces uproar from her friend, with accusations of cheating and claims that 'she watched me hide there'. Like any parent, I wade into the fray to sort out the details, assuage bruised egos and hurt feelings, and make some attempt to restore order. In doing so, I pull my daughter aside and ask her how she knew her friend was hiding behind the tree (we had already had an earlier conversation with another boy in the group that 'peeking' was against the rules and not a nice way to play). She looks at me with a completely serious face and says without hesitation: 'Daddy, she always hides there every time we play, so I just knew she'd be there.'

This declaration drives home a very simple point about how we play. The question here is where the information in question in this child's game comes from. The implication of cheating would suggest that acting on the knowledge of another player's tendencies is somehow acting in bad faith on the conditions of the game. It suggests that players ought only to use those skills and literacies that come during the act of play. The trouble is, the kind of information at stake in this sample exchange has no clearly defined location in the play act. It is, in part, outside the play context because it draws on knowledge generated not in the exact moment of play where it was used. My daughter did not 'know' in any empirical sense that her friend was behind the tree. Her 'knowledge' in question came from repeated observations of a strategy. In this case, her claim to certainty represented more of a strong probability coming from previous play sessions in a long-running game. In this sense, her knowledge is not outside the moment of play. It is in this schism that we experience the multiple iterations of metagaming.

In itself, metagaming is nothing new. It has been a regular feature of our play for as long as there have been games. While it can function at the kind of conscious level that my daughter described in her account of the game, the awareness of it as an element of play, both tied to the game yet outside of it, is often blurry. In this sense, it would be fair to say that how we play is as important as what and why we play. The tricky business here is establishing how metagaming functions, and to what degree it is an unavoidable part of the gaming experience, and how our practices of play have evolved out of our metagame tendencies.

The guiding purpose of this project is to explore the various motivations that we bring to bear in playing DRPGs – motivations that are, at best, difficult to account for. The following section outlines an approach to metagaming and its relationship to RPGs, from pen-and-paper games to current digital games. The emphasis is on accounting for the multiple motivations driving decision-making strategies involved in play. This is followed by an examination of the *Suikoden* franchise of games (in particular *Suikoden II*), focusing on player literacies in drawing resources from various locations to inform their strategies, decisions, and motivations.

Making Sense of Metagaming

The example of something as simple and childlike as Hide and Seek invokes questions of where our game 'knowledge' comes from. What does the game communicate to us, what do our fellow players communicate to us, and how do we use that information? The issue of where the information is located reinforces older arguments about games and the magic circle of play space (Huizinga 1938; Niewdorp 2005; Salen and Zimmerman 2003) and the spaces where play takes place. If we think of the magic circle as the membrane that separates the experience of a game from other contexts, then the question becomes: where do play strategies fall on the dividing line between what is 'in-game' and 'out-of-game?' Determining the boundaries of play, or of play space, and locating the particulars of a given experience is exactly the grey area of metagaming. What complicates this example is that in the case of the Hide and Seek match, the information is not automatically given as a result of experiencing the gameplay. The children do not watch each other hide *while* they attempt to seek them out. Rather, these actions are broken down into distinct turns or phases in which players stake the outcome of the game on their actions and then experience how those actions unfold. It is in the children's assumptions about how the game functions that the complications arise. While each phase is clearly separate and distinct, they all exist as a kind of 'whole play' in the longer narrative of time spent in their social engagement with this activity.

Role-playing games complicate this work by adding additional classifications for how a person plays. From pen-and-paper games like *Dungeons & Dragons* to current DRPGs, players must juggle increasingly complicated rules and roles as ongoing agents in the experience of play. Originally understood as a matter of computational matrices, metagaming outlines the mathematical chances of particular outcomes given any gaming scenario. Graphed as topological trees, Melvin Dresher offered a vision of game theory as a means to find the 'saddle points' in games with 'perfect information' (1981). In this regard, gaming serves as a means to uncover 'optimal strategies' for any given scenario. This is contingent on what knowledge the player has, both of the possible actions in any gaming scenario, as well as the corresponding outcomes and subsequent actions of those moves. Thus, the analysis of strategy here serves as a kind of causality awareness.[2]

In similar fashion, Nigel Howard offered a vision of metagaming, not only as computational matrices, but as an analytical tool for understanding the decision-making strategies of participants in game-like scenarios. Howard's framework examines not just the probability of outcomes, but seeks to extend the computational possibility of mathematical approaches to games by focusing on the analysis of options within any scenario (1971). Thus the emphasis shifts from probability analysis to causal relationships and the generation of a '"strategic map" that reveals how stakeholders can use their power to move from one scenario to another, and which moves are likely to occur in view of the stakeholders' preferences' (Bots and Hermans 2003, 648). In some respects, this works from a management rhetoric of direction and control. Stakeholder analysis relies on the generation of a map accounting for each party involved, and the various permutations of their responses to any given situation (Howard 1989; Bots and Hermans 2003; Holland, Jenkins, and Squire 2003). It also allows for a more complex discussion, accounting not only for the causes and consequences of any given game action, but also the emotional investments and outcomes – what Howard refers to as the 'drama' of metagaming, or 'the way in which players "reframe" their situation so as to create for themselves a new, different game' (1996, 125).

This shift from computational probability to stakeholder analysis moves us closer to the conventional rhetoric of metagaming as many players understand it. Metagaming is a frequent enough feature of role-playing that it receives regular attention in rules of gameplay. For example, the *Dungeons & Dragons: Dungeon Master's Guide, 3.5 Edition*[3] offers the following language for how to handle metagaming as a part of role-playing:

> Any time players base their characters' actions on logic that depends on the fact that they're playing a game, they're using metagame thinking. This behavior should always be discouraged, because it detracts from real role-playing and spoils the suspension of disbelief [...] In short, when possible you should encourage the players to employ in-game logic [...] It shows smart thinking as well as respect for the verisimilitude of the gameworld. (2003, 11)

The first issue of note in this description is the pejorative value placed on metagaming as a part of play. It is framed here as a kind of bad faith interaction when weighed against more serious modes of attention to the game's verisimilitude. The implications here are clear for how we play role-playing games: the work of the player is to further the story through their character's involvement, not to invest oneself around the game's mechanics any more than necessary.

The second point of interest is the clearly implied line between in-game and out-of-game information, and the difficulty with locating play behaviors in accordance with that spectrum. Ostensibly, part of the point of the gameplay here is to become (as much as possible) the character the player embodies. This level of identification is intended to blur the lines between what the character knows and what the player knows. The classic example of a player in *D&D* fighting a troll for the first time highlights this distinction. In traditional *D&D*, trolls can only be killed with fire or acid, otherwise they will eventually regenerate. A third-level character encounters a troll for the first time and decides 'Trolls can only be killed with fire, so I'll use my torch as a weapon'. Unless there is something particular to that character's skills, back-story, or specialized knowledge as indicated on their character sheet, the odds are that as a third-level character they would be unlikely to know the weaknesses of a Troll. What is more likely is that the player is drawing on knowledge of the game's systems and rules as a means to achieve their objectives. Thus, the verisimilitude is (ostensibly) somehow lessened, and the play experience somehow cheapened. It is worth noting here that while the *Dungeon Master's Guide* addresses this issue, there is no similar passage located in the *Player's Handbook*. The message here is clear. Metagaming is the province of the Dungeon Master to police, and the player to avoid at all costs.

This is not a new tension for role-playing. Neither is this view of metagaming as a problem necessarily universal. Notable indie game designer and founder of *The Forge* community, Ron Edwards, speaks to this aspect of games in the creation of the games systems 'GNS' (an acronym for Gamist, Narrativist, Simulationist) and its later iteration 'The Big Model'[4]. Edwards offers an articulation of how these tensions may be understood and accounted for, not as antithetical to the experience of the role-playing game, but as an inevitable and essential part of engaging with complex play. Edwards offers a vision of role-playing that is defined by a general set of three 'stances' that players may work from: Actor, Author, and Director. The tensions of metagaming addressed so far fall into the lines that divide Actor and Author stance:

> In **Actor** stance, a person determines a character's decisions and actions using only knowledge and perceptions that the character would have. In **Author** stance, a person determines a character's decisions and actions based on the real person's priorities, then retroactively 'motivates' the character to perform them.
> (GNS and Other Matters of Role Playing Theory, Chapter 3, 2001).

Edwards' stance distinction highlights the same tensions offered in the earlier examples of metagaming by making them an unavoidable part of the ways we play at role-playing games. These stances represent generalized approaches, or strategies for decision-making, 'with people shifting among the stances frequently and even without deliberation or reflection' (2001). Edwards' distinction offers alternate affordances for the play experience, assuming that players might simply play differently out of habit, or might actively seek alternate play styles depending on the circumstances. This distinction acknowledges that these alternate play styles are extensions of multiple possible objectives in any given game – what Edwards refers to as 'premises'. Thus, 'gamist premises' operate under the assumption that metagame goals are an inevitable possible outcome of how we might play, and that while they may complicate certain story-driven elements (narrativist premises), they are certainly not antithetical to one another, and they equally respect the interests and investments of players. Likewise, to be a narrativist player does not mean playing to the exclusion of gamist motivations and approaches.

We see more recent iterations of this thinking in digital game studies in Burn's and Carr's scholarship exploring *Anarchy Online* (Funcom 2001). Exploring the immersive qualities of games, they offer a similar triumvirate of approaches. These 'motivations' are broken down into the 'representational', the 'ludic', and the 'communal' (2003). These distinctions further highlight the multiple approaches a player make take to any given gaming context, outlining the various affordances games enable for player participation.

There is considerable evidence of this stance-dancing when we look at the recent rise of achievement culture and player habits. Most obvious in this regard is the development of the 'gamerscore' and achievement system for the Xbox 360 and its online play[5]. For this current generation of consoles, games are no longer unlinked ephemera, or self-contained play experiences, but are collectively linked by an overarching metagame comprised of achievements. Each game is designed with a specific number of achievements, each with a corresponding point value. Accomplishing a specific trigger event (or series of trigger events) registers an achievement as 'unlocked', awarding the corresponding point value to the player's total gamerscore. These scores are linked to an individual player profile, offering a kind of progress report for how one plays, and what a player has accomplished. This system offers players alternate possibilities for engaging their games, by articulating what Dresher would call 'win conditions' outside of the game itself. For example, several of the achievements listed for BioWare's science fiction blockbuster *Mass Effect* (BioWare 2007) are based on time played with a particular party member. In order to unlock the achievement 'Sentinel Ally' a player must 'Complete the majority of the game with the Alliance sentinel squad member' (BioWare 2007). Note the achievement description does not dictate a specific amount of time, offering only a general description. Player consensus on this matter suggests that the appropriate amount of time is roughly 75 percent of the game's missions and story arcs (GameFAQs 2011).[5]

There are interesting possibilities for how we play implicated by this. Mikael Jakobsen has suggested that the rise of metagame achievements contributes to both sales numbers and player replayability (2009). Depending on my play style (or stance), I may or may not be moved by the existence of these additional win conditions. Even if I am invested in the metagame of my gamerscore, I may not be moved to invest myself in the conditions necessary to reach this particular achievement. What is striking though, is the sheer volume of player discussion[6] focusing on the 'need' for players to complete additional game playthroughs in order to reach each of these objectives. While we might go so far as to say that there may be a kind of distancing of player investment in the verisimilitude of the experience, it would be a stretch to assume that they are not invested differently in this particular experience of play. Making this problematic assumption runs the risk of re-invoking the false either/or dichotomy of narratology versus ludology[7]. Indeed, players who invest themselves in these multiple modes of play have been doing so for some time. Much like the phenomenon of metagaming in general, this is nothing new to how we play.

It is in this tension that we see metagaming not only as a mode of play, but as an inevitable part of the role-playing experience. Digital role-playing games require players to code-switch between these available stances as a regular feature of their experience. This kind of shifting play operates as an extension of earlier role-playing games in multiple ways. The absence of social elements in most console RPGs forces players into a kind of reciprocal character relationship with the game's verisimilitude[8]. Pen-and-paper games suggest a social space where enacting a character through gamist and narrativist stances would reinforce the group's social contract and collective will (Edwards 2004). In a single-player digital game, the player reinforces only the directing will behind the play and the game contexts that inform that will – in other words, whatever stance the player adopts reinforces the acting drive that informs it. Hence, Edwards' point that players shift at will highlights the nature of the RPG as a character-driven narrative that is engaged through a ludological interface of game mechanics.

Metagaming and Stance-dancing: How Players Shift

Of the multiple possible ways in which metagaming can be enacted, playing in meta ways often allows players access to forms of control. Doing so requires a kind shifting of one's subjectivity in the game, variably prioritizing one's possible roles as player. Again, this could be read as antithetical to the traditional assumptions about player presence in RPGs, but, if so, it is less the case than in pen-and-paper games. Edwards' concerns about the social contract of players are mitigated by the absence of other bodies. The degree to which the lines are blurred between player-as-player and player-as-narrative-subject depends heavily on the immersive elements of the game, and how the game's mechanics allow a player access to the game's immersive elements. Jesper Juul names this as the 'half-real' condition of games, highlighting the necessary levels of abstraction required to separate rules from fiction (2005, 2007). Juul's distinction reinforces the conversations about Edwards' 'stances' that players might bring to play. To engage with the fictional or dramatistic elements, players might operate under a narrativist stance, while engaging with rules might ask players to operate as gamist or simulationist.

Konami's *Suikoden* franchise employs this to regular effect, most notably in the second installment of the series *Suikoden II* (1999). The series itself is a striking example of the narrative possibilities of metagaming for the ways that each iteration of the franchise builds on or extends both the narrative as well as the ludic elements of the series' previous installments. One of the first console games to employ a progressive save feature, *Suikoden* players are invited into a world that is, in many ways, the product of their decisions and efforts in previous installments. At the very beginning of *Suikoden II* (Konami 1999), players are invited to import their save game from the original *Suikoden* (Konami 1996) title. This save game carries several important flags that alter the second game. Most importantly, the player character from the first game, Tir McDohl (assuming the player does not rename him) can be recruited into the party, assuming certain conditions are met by the player during the second game. This feature is replicated across the franchise, with the player carrying over save games and unique elements from one game to the next.

BioWare has recently popularized this concept in both their *Mass Effect* and *Dragon Age* franchises, inviting a new level of engagement with games. Much like the idea of gamerscore, this links games across multiple titles, removing the experience of them as individualized ephemera. To play a *Suikoden* game is to immerse oneself in the narrative history of the world, and the player's choices in the evolution of that history. Even if a player has not completed other titles in the franchise, the game's invitation to load one's preceding game data makes it clear that the player's role is significant.

It is this significance of the player and their actions that make the *Suikoden* franchise such an interesting example. DRPGs are often known for having a wide cast of characters that the player can interact with, form parties from, and who support the ongoing game. As a franchise, *Suikoden* takes this to nearly unheard-of extremes. Each game in the series operates under a narrative mythology of one hundred and eight 'Stars of Destiny'. While some of these are largely non-player characters (NPCs) who run shops in your army's base, or further the plot, most are actually party characters with story arcs that cross multiple games in the series. Some of these characters join the player's cause automatically as the narrative unfolds. Still, the player must actively seek the larger number out, and meet certain conditions in order to enlist them in your army. What makes this recruitment an essential component of the game is the understanding in fan/player culture that each game in the franchise has multiple endings, with one being imagined as a 'best' ending or outcome. In each game, one of the (often many) necessary conditions for achieving the 'best ending' is the successful recruitment of all one hundred and eight characters (called the Stars of Destiny).

If we think about this in Dresher and Howard's terms, the successful recruitment of each individual character is the outcome of meeting specific 'win conditions' at particular 'saddle points' in the game's progress. Some conditions are met through simply playing the game, while others require complex decisions from the player. Given the volume of characters, and the linked complexity of each character's 'win condition', the odds are slim that any given player will be successful in recruiting every possible star of destiny on a first playthrough – that is, unless they use some form of metaknowledge about the game in the form of a walkthrough, strategy guide, player wiki (more on this shortly), or other means to help them piece together 'perfect information' for the game's ludic topology. Even on subsequent replays, the game itself does not provide all the information directly necessary for the successful recruitment of each character. While there are certainly clues in most cases, not every win condition is visible or discernable.

Throughout the franchise, each game presents its own complications with recruiting characters. This presents the player with multiple opportunities to 'miss' achieving the best ending in any given play attempt. *Suikoden II*, much like other iterations of the franchise, adds an additional component to achieving a perfect game. Simply recruiting all the characters is not enough. There are additional win triggers that must be satisfied. Once a player has recruited each required character (there are also extras that do not count), the story must proceed to a particular point. The player leads his army in an assault on an enemy fortress. During the assault, the main character is targeted in several volleys of arrows. The scripted story dictates that Nanami, the hero's sister, jumps in front of him and attempts to deflect each volley. She fails on the third and final volley, suffering a critical injury. This is where the player is faced with a sequence of 'saddle points' which will dictate the ending received for the game. Successfully navigating this requires either significant foreknowledge and metagaming or a tremendous stroke of luck. The following section, taken from 'Suikosource', the wiki devoted to the *Suikoden* franchise, details the general player consensus regarding how to achieve the best ending for the game:

> In order to save Nanami and see the 'best' ending, you must first gather the 108 Stars of Destiny before choosing to invade Rockaxe. You will know you have accomplished this task if Leknaat appears during the rally and unlocks the fourth level spell of the Bright Shield, Forgiver Sign. Then Nanami must have a total DEF value of 121 or greater (you can use equipment to boost her DEF) when she and Riou reach Gorudo during the siege of Matilda Castle. Then you must select either dialogue option when she

is deflecting the arrows; there is a time limit for this dialogue selection. Afterwards, Huan should have a private word with Shu after he claims to have failed to save Nanami. Please note that Nanami will still be unavailable for the rest of the game. With that being said, in order to see Nanami alive you must get the 'best' ending, which consists of not entering the meeting room in your castle but instead going to Tenzan Pass to meet Jowy at the place the friends swore to wait for each other if separated. Do not defeat Jowy in the duels he forces upon Riou, and when he tries to give you his true rune, keep rejecting it. Eventually, the end sequence will start.

(*Suikoden II* Secrets 2011)

Clearly this is an involved process. It is also clear from this description why people who play RPGs cling desperately to the SNSO (Save Now Save Often) acronym. The prospects of having to replay each possible outcome in this topological tree open up a lengthy series of options for players to explore. Knowing how to navigate this series of options is essential to its successful completion.

While there are numerous examples of situations like this in *Suikoden II* that we might draw upon, this particular example highlights some important aspects of metagaming. Specifically, the scene in which Nanami defends the hero (Riou) presents a dialogue selection menu which offers the player two distinct options: when arrows strike Nanami, the two dialogue options are 'NANAMI!' or 'Watch out Nanami!' (Konami 1999). What makes this noteworthy is that, ultimately, the dialogue choice made here does not count. What matters is the speed with which an option is chosen. There is no clear consensus on the exact amount of time afforded the player, but the general idea is a few short seconds. This time limit functions as a key analysis moment for the game. It is a pivotal saddle point for determining the final outcome. Knowing how to successfully navigate this requires players to operate in particular ways. The trick is in locating which stance (or stances) this particular action belongs to.

In one sense, we could read this as a narrativist moment. Given the context of the story, the hero has just watched his sister receive a mortal wound. Given the elevated tension of the moment, we might imagine a player selecting an immediate response as a performative gesture, simulating the felt anxiety of the hero. Unfortunately, that analysis is complicated by the larger play patterns of a narrativist construction. Dialogue options, such as those presented in *Suikoden II*, afford moments of control – the possibility for the player to dictate outcomes according to their sense of what the narrative should be, and how they can perform their characters actions accordingly. While certainly not as open as one might expect in pen-and-paper games, there is clear character distinction discernable in the two options. Selecting the simple response 'NANAMI!' could be read as recognition of her potential death, the impending danger, shock at the situation, even rage at the soldiers responsible for her wound. Each of these is possible. Likewise, we might read in the response 'Watch out Nanami!' something that is less certain about her injury. Perhaps we are warning her, hoping to make the incident less potentially fatal. Perhaps we are simply warning her too late.

The ways in which we read (and possibly select) these responses speak to the very notion of narrativist agenda that players bring to the game. How we read each of these responses is dictated by how we imagine those responses serving as a reflection of the hero as directed by the player. It speaks to the issue of *leerstellen* inherent in this sort of reader response moment that Jesper Juul worried through in his original thesis *A Clash Between Game and Narrative* (1999, 46). Drawing on reader response theories, Juul's early work highlights the complexity of navigation that players bring to games by focusing on how they fill in the 'textual gaps' of meaning as represented in Wolfgang Iser's notion of *leerstellen* (1978). In other words, how a player reads the distinction in these responses is as much a matter of player motivation, or stance, as it is framing context provided by the game's narrative. In Iser's words, 'as text and reader thus merge into a single situation, the division between subject and object no longer applies, and it therefore follows that meaning is no longer an object to be defined, but is an effect to be experienced' (1978, 10–11).

Given this, reading the action through the lens of a gamist stance decision is simpler, but not necessarily easier, to parse and determine. In this case, the player must make the choice in a particular way to satisfy the specific parameters of the gameplay. Again, foreknowledge is an issue here, as the odds of a player simply stumbling into the complex sequence of win conditions are ridiculously low. Given the time limit tied to this specific moment, it is likely a player must act as player, rather than character, in order to succeed. The gamist agenda operates with a meta-directive in mind – in this case, to obtain the 'best ending'; given that, the narrative contexts that inform the dialogue options become moot. If a player wants to achieve this particular goal, considering the implications of narrative options is a detriment. Thus both answers are equally valid, so long as the overarching goal of the time limit is adhered to.

The final crux, though, is in making the determination of player motivation. While achieving a best ending in *Suikoden II* virtually requires a player to work, at some level, from a gamist stance, the desire or motivation that informs the sense that that 'best' ending is the desirable outcome is not as easily located. A player draws equally from gamist or narrativist agendas in this regard. This opens room for the kinds of stance-dancing that Edwards sees as integral to RPGs. If a player is interested in achieving the 'perfect ending' for *Suikoden II*, then they must, at some level, shift the motivation they bring to their play. This level of play negotiation is reflective of the complex literacies that players bring to their games, of their ability to 'read and write' the game. If players pause to consider the narrativist weight and implications each potential dialogue option represents, they risk losing the window of opportunity for achieving a best ending. Likewise, if we pause attempting to calculate gamist outcomes, we equally risk our window. In both cases, the playing pause is natural, even expected. To successfully achieve a win condition here, players must operate with a metagame logic in mind, one that potentially collapses both gamist and narrativist ends. Thus the answer here lies not in any one stance or approach, but in parsing out the complex interactions of each.

Making Space for Metagaming: Social Knowledge as Foreknowledge

While the complexity of a game like *Suikoden II* makes it perhaps an extreme example, it is by no means wholly unique in this regard. Many recent RPGs offer up similar issues of complexity, both in narrative and mechanics. Both of BioWare's current bestselling franchises *Mass Effect* and *Dragon Age* present increasingly complex character negotiations, considering they require players to track narrative arcs and party character development across multiple titles. Uncovering the multiple permutations of both gamist and narrativist possibilities requires both planning and foreknowledge on the part of the player. These are just current examples of something that is increasingly commonplace in game culture. What these examples clearly show is the increasingly complex set of negotiations players undertake as a result of play. To engage the game means to challenge oneself to read and write the gameplay experience in complex ways: through metagame strategies, various motivational affordances, and social negotiations.

Given the frequency with which RPGs require these kinds of complex interaction, it was inevitable that players would respond by creating archival repositories of game information. Ranging from the well-established networks like *IGN* and *GameFAQs* to the rise of fan-developed wiki spaces, players continuously contribute to the collective knowledge base that underpins their collective ability to metagame. For example, when *Suikoden II* was initially released, fans had yet to construct much of the online wiki material. Instead, game portals like *GameFAQs* housed much of the available information. The oldest fan-created file for *Suikoden II* hosted on the game giant's site dates to 1999 (shortly after the game's US release) and covers some initial basics of the game. This has grown over nearly a decade (the most recent files are dated 2007) offering a range of fan-generated content, from complete walkthroughs to the most recent 'Perfect Game Guide'. From the culture generated around sites like *GameFAQs* to more focused sites like *Suikosource*, the trend towards metagaming is tied directly to the rise of shared digital spaces used to collect and collaborate on these resources.

James Gee is particularly interested in the potential of such shared spaces, highlighting their ability to promote learning and literacy. Building on an analysis of *Age of Mythology*, Gee offers a taxonomy of these spaces that highlights their non-hierarchical structure and ability to both rely on and resource its respective membership (2007, 102). The general characteristics of affinity spaces work in concert with the metagame tendency of players by privileging the 'common endeavor' of the game itself, encouraging 'intensive and extensive knowledge' as well as 'individual and distributed knowledge' (2007, 102). Players come together, sharing not only the particulars of their specific play experience (strategy, motivation, and outcome), but also a kind of accountable history of the information they gather. The collected knowledge is socially vetted, confirmed and parsed, and then disseminated. In effect, this allows players to generate the kind of topographical mapping of game and its possible outcomes, accounting for each conceivable saddle point.

Gee's analysis of affinity spaces is rooted in his earlier work exploring 'semiotic domains' or 'any set of practices that recruits one or more modalities (e.g. oral or written language, images, equations, symbols, sounds, gestures, graphs, artifacts, etc.) to communicate different types of meanings' (2003, 17). The very spaces that support the possibility of metagaming are constructed out of the need/desire of players to exert some level of control over the games they play. Looking at the examples covered in this chapter, it is easy to see that as games become increasingly complex, the multiple possibilities they afford us may outstrip our available time to engage them. As is, RPGs like *Suikoden II* can require upward of fifty to sixty hours of game time. Given the number of possible permutations and combinations of gameplay outcomes resulting from an extensive number of saddle points, coupled with the possibility of lost time due to missing any one saddle point, it is unsurprising that players tend towards strategies that make their play more efficient. A player could invest hundreds of hours in any one game without seeing or achieving every possible outcome.

As a result, relying on these affinity spaces has become an unmistakable part of game culture. It is a vehicle for players not only to showcase their literacy through expertise, but also to perform their various and multiple motivations for playing in the first place. Thus, stance-dancing and the shift of player disposition become reinforced as just another way we play. This opens up new levels of complexity for how players define, invest in, and experience games. As RPGs in particular develop increasingly complex narratives and mechanics, we can expect this phenomenon of metagaming to increase, becoming its own locus of study, practice, and investment. As it is, we already game the meta. The next step is to explore what these literacies afford us, and how we develop them further as our games grow increasingly complex.

Notes

1. For Mom and Dad: thanks for introducing me to a lifetime of games.
2. While outside the scope of this chapter, there is considerable work to be done uncovering and documenting this trend in MMORPGs, and the rise of modding and add-ons – in particular, the frequency with which players are designing and distributing third-party software as an addition to a game's interface. The website *Curse Gaming*, while also clearly an affinity space, serves as a singular example of this trend.
3. While the 3.5 Edition of *Dungeons & Dragons* is not the most current edition, it still retains the largest level of saturation in the player-base, largely due to the rise of the d20 model and the Open Gaming License (OGL). Market share analysis has variously pinpointed the *D&D* saturation at anywhere between 45 to 66 percent as recently as 2009, although the 1999 Wizards of the Coast marketing survey and Ken Hite's 2002 market share analysis are often cited as useful benchmarks.
4. Both GNS and The Big Model cover mutual elements. Edwards' original goal was to develop a universal and holistic system for RPGs that would encourage collaboration through social contracts, while also not limiting the desire and agency of players, game masters, and designers equally. The impact of his utopian vision for role-playing can be seen in more contemporary pen-and-paper games such as *Wushu* or *Nobilis*.
5. While the PlayStation Network (PSN) has a system of trophies that is similar to Xbox Live, the latter has specific features that distinguish it as a more directed metagame. Specifically, Xbox Live uses gamerscore to rank players in relation to one another through the attribution of point value to each achievement. PSN's Trophy Card model is both more complex in its ranking and less prominently visible on the interface.
6. The various *Mass Effect* forums are not a unique anomaly in this regard. One could look to the multiple *Suikoden* games, *Dragon Age*, *Growlanser*, and others. The idea of 'playing to perfection', something long held in gamer discourse, is intimately tied to this idea of metagaming; a notion of 'knowing the whole story'.
7. While I'm not interested in revisiting the battle lines of narratology vs. ludology, it is interesting to note that the argument itself has a historical trajectory that extends well beyond digital games. Gonzalo Frasca's work 'Ludologists Love Stories Too: Notes From a Debate that Never Took Place' hints at this as well.

8   This is a potentially contentious claim, as console RPGs are pushing the boundaries of the social. Even setting aside specific console games that are also MMOs, recent titles such as Atlus Software's *Demon's Souls* (2009) present players with social contracts to navigate that are more complex than the traditional single-player RPG. For the purposes of this project, I am focusing specifically on the single-player RPG.

References

BioWare. *Mass Effect*. 2007. [Xbox 360]. Redmond, WA: Microsoft Game Studios.
—2009. Dragon Age: Origins. [Multiplatform]. Electronic Arts.
Bots, P. W. G.and L. M. Hermans. 2003. 'Developing "Playable Metagames" for Participatory Stakeholder Analysis.' *Proceedings of the 34th Conference of the International Simulation and Gaming Association (ISAGA)*. Chiba, Japan. Accessed April 1, 2011. http://www.actoranalysis.com/documents/ISAGA2003.pdf.
Burn, Andrew and Diane Carr. 'Signs From A Strange Planet: Role Play And Social Performance In *Anarchy Online*.' Published in conference proceedings, *COSIGN 2003, 3rd conference on Computational Semiotics for Games and New Media*, 10–12 September 2003, University of Teesside, UK, 14–21.
Cook, Monte, Jonathan Tweet and Skip Williams, eds. 2003. *Dungeons & Dragons Dungeon Master's Guide: Core Rulebook II v. 3.5*. Renton: Wizards of the Coast.
Dresher, Melvin. 1981. *The Mathematics of Games of Strategy*. NY: Dover.
Edwards, Ron. 2001. 'GNS and Other Matters of Role-Playing Theory.' *The Forge: The Internet Home for Independent Role-Playing Games*. Adept Press. Accessed April 1, 2011. http://www.indie-rpgs.com/articles/4/
—2004. 'Narrativism: Story Now.' *The Forge: The Internet Home for Independent Role-Playing Games*. Adept Press. Accessed April 1, 2011. http://www.indie-rpgs.com/_articles/narr_essay.html
GameFAQs. *Suikoden II*. Accessed April 1, 2011. http://www.gamefaqs.com/ps/198844-suikoden-ii.
Gee, James Paul. 2003. *What Video Games Have to Teach Us About Learning and Literacy*. NY: Palgrave.
—2007. 'Affinity Spaces: From *Age of Mythology* to Today's Schools.' In *Good Video Games + Good Learning: Collected Essays on Video Games, Learning and Literacy*, ed. James Paul Gee. NY: Peter Lang.

Holland, Walter, Henry Jenkins, and Kurt Squire. 2003. 'Theory by Design.' In *The Video Game Theory Reader*, ed. Mark J. P. Wolf and Bernard Perron. NY: Routledge.

Howard, Nigel. 1971. *Paradoxes of Rationality: Games, Metagames, and Political Behavior*. Cambridge: MIT Press.

—1989. 'The Manager as Politician and General: The Metagame Approach to Analysing Cooperation and Conflict.' In *Rational Analysis for a Problematic World: Problem Structuring Methods for Complexity, Uncertainty and Conflict*, ed. Rosenhead J. Chichester, 249–66. UK: John Wiley & Sons.

—1996. 'Negotiation as Drama: How "Games" Become "Dramatic".' *International Negotiation*, 1: 125–52.

Huizinga, Johan. 1950. *Homo Ludens: A Study of the Play Element in Culture*. Beacon: Boston.

Iser, Wolfgang. 1978. *The Act of Reading: A Theory of Aesthetic Response*. Baltimore: Johns Hopkins University Press.

Jakobsson, Mikael. 2009. 'The Achievement Machine: Understanding the Xbox Live Metagame.' In *Breaking New Ground: Innovation in Games, Play, Practice and Theory. Proceedings of DiGRA 2009 Conference.* http://www.digra.org:8080/Plone/dl/db/09291.32175.pdf

Juul, Jesper. 1999. 'A Clash between Game and Narrative: a Thesis on Computer Games and Interactive Fiction.' Master's Thesis, University of Copenhagen.

—2005. *Half-Real: Video Games between Real Rules and Fictional Worlds*. Cambridge, MA: MIT Press.

—2007. 'A Certain Level of Abstraction.' *Situated Play, Proceedings of DiGRA 2007 Conference*. http://www.digra.org/dl/db/07312.29390.pdf

Konami Digital Entertainment, Inc. *Suikoden*. [PlayStation] WoodDale, Illinois. 1996

—*Suikoden II*. [PlayStation]. Redwood City, California. 1999

Nieuwdorp, Eva. 2005. 'The Pervasive Interface: Tracing the Magic Circle.' *Proceedings of DiGRA 2005 Conference: Changing Views – Worlds in Play*. http://www.digra.org/dl/db/06278.53356.pdf

Salen, Katie and Eric Zimmerman. 2003. *Rules of Play: Game Design Fundamentals*. Cambridge, MA: MIT Press.

Suikoden II Secrets. Suikosource. Accessed April 1, 2011. http://www.suikosource.com/games/gs2/secrets/.

16

The Generalization of Configurable Being: From RPGs to Facebook

CHUK MORAN

If a generalization of the gaming paradigm is already underway, what is it that is becoming more general? Is it interactive media, constrained choices, serious games, ubiquitous casual gaming, real-time combat, micro-incentives, or hedonism? What will be generalized with what effect remains to be seen. This chapter considers the generalization of something specific: reflexively modifiable player agency developed out of role-playing games and now appearing in many games and as the central function of *Facebook*. I focus on explaining what this agency is, how it can and must modify itself, and what it allows and encourages. Through this being, we do not consume media or intake information so much as respond to pulses of coded affect by forgiving affordances that we are educated in using.

Configurable being is a dynamic form that comes from the genre of role-playing games (hereafter RPGs). RPGs systematized high fantasy scenarios with rule sets derived from wargaming. In their translation to computer games, some things have been condensed while others have been greatly expanded. I refer to computer-based games that draw on RPG genre conventions as digital RPGs (DRPGs). In these games, it is not enough to pilot an X-wing or manage a city, as might be the focus of other computer games; instead, to get anywhere, you must *be someone*, and continually improve that person (Miller 2006). Aspects of the game influenced directly by the character have grown and aspects of gameplay focused on modification of the character have too. Creating or extensively modifying the avatar is a constraint on what may come to pass, but it is also the foreclosure that enables one to be at all[1]. Recently on *Facebook*, a similar development is afoot, with a reflexively modifiable being providing a user agency in a fantasy of busy cosmopolitanism not so distant from the high-fantasy settings familiar in DRPGs.

The words in this chapter's title, 'being' and 'generalization', each have a double meaning whose ambiguity is important to my argument. 'Being' means both an individual and the very fact of existence. My focus is on a being that takes on the process of existing, and this has precedence over a *self* that guides conscious action, an *identity* interpreted by self and others, a *character* in a narrative context, a *body* in a virtual space, or a *subject position* for the production of the human individual. This ambiguity of 'being' foregrounds the relation of a digital creature to the mode of existence by which it can appear. 'Generalization' means both a proliferation (here, of technology) and a summary concept. As a technology, the configurable being exists in implementations from *Dungeons & Dragons* to *Facebook*. As a summary concept, it is a way to recognize this pattern. This ambiguity – between design and concept – connotes the very real intermingling of hype, inspiration, mimicry, and common structural basis.

However, the general concept of such a being is useless without a firm understanding of its form and formation in DRPGs and RPGs before them. Configurable being's generalization is a story of voluntary adoption, of something that was, or eventually became, useful.

From *D&D* to DRPG

Though much has changed since *Dungeons & Dragons* in 1974 (Gygax and Arneson 1974), some connections are worth making. RPGs *systematize fantasy* and *direct player imagination* with their aesthetics. However, DRPGs have narrowed the range of role-play considerably and increased the importance of the player's configurable being. *D&D* combines wargaming *and* fantasy fan practices and style, and these competing tendencies for systematicity and imagination remain important in DRPGs.

Wargaming played out the movement, attacks, retreats, and death of soldiers in different historical periods (and in specific historic battles) with carefully observed rules of measurement and probability (executed by dice throws) in a slow, turn-based rhythm on diorama-like tables made up with hills, grass, trees, and other landscape features. *D&D* formalized an earlier experimental departure from wargaming that allowed smaller armies – with more interesting goals than just killing each other – to engage with fantasy elements (e.g. dragons) rather than strictly historical ones (e.g. pikemen). It preserved wargaming's statistically determined combat rules, accrual of experience that boosts skills, and emphasis on fighting. It was played in the format of a wargaming session: several hours of play, in relative isolation, with a big table, and a group of players who stayed the whole time.

What wargaming provided to those who were already interested in fantasy was a place where dreams could come to life. It's a fine pastime to draw dragons, write stories about elf princesses, or build model castles. What *D&D* offers that's exciting to players is to animate all these images and passions so they interact with each other and generate new stories. It does this with an engine derived from wargaming. Rules exist in DRPGs because they 'give people an expectation of how things work and what the consequences may be for taking certain actions' (Hallford 2001, 150). What will happen if the thieves try to fight the ogre instead of run? The voice of contingency in DRPGs remains randomness, with outcomes determined by thresholds calculated from statistics of characters, tools, and targets. Because of this continuity, an agile character can still dodge an arrow, even if the *player* is slow and clumsy. In his chapter in this volume, Baerg considers this blossoming of mechanized fantasy as an expression of the ascendant cultural power of neo-liberalism from just before *D&D* to the present moment.

On the other hand, role-playing also follows some key rules of improvisational theater, such as establishing a setting, creating a story through teamwork, suspending disbelief, maintaining shared enthusiasm, and building relationships between the performers (Mackay 2001; Fine 1983). The game is an exercise in imagination, fueled by fantasy films and literature. This is where the aesthetics come in: names, descriptions, maps, pictures, and acting style saturate the game with expressive art. A key goal of fantasy aesthetics is to entice the imagination to wonder about new concepts in a strange world (Grant 1996, 12): a giant made of stone, a tree whose leaves are fairies, a mountain melting into water.

This kind of game can be understood as a 'cool medium' – a medium delivering a low intensity experience to the senses and demanding those watching or listening fill in many details (McLuhan 1994, 22–32). To fill the gaps, *D&D* players draw on a 'generic, historically anachronistic fantasy world assembled from ideas culled from dozens of authors in the fantasy genre' (Mackay 2001, 27). Other games drew on scenarios other than high fantasy, such as comic books, horror novels, or science fiction television. Still, the game requires creativity based on appropriation, homage, and leveraging genre conventions.

Moving to the computer, games of role-playing changed into DRPGs. They were single-player games, with fixed stories where a hack'n'slash style became normal.

> At best, the computerized versions could simulate the mathematics of *D&D* combat and to some extent the strategy and exploration components, but the inherent abstractness and aloofness of the medium seemed to stop true role-playing at the gate [...] *D&D* and its computerized 'equivalents' actually have far less in common than most people think. (Barton 2007a)

Role-play in contemporary DRPGs has certainly changed, and MMORPGs seem to offer only minimal provision for it. *World of*

Warcraft (Blizzard Entertainment 2004) for example, inhibits role-play at many levels (MacCallum-Stewart and Parsler 2008).

Despite the clear barriers to role-playing that do exist, it should not be ignored that DRPGs do offer very sophisticated role-playing in a limited scenario and on their own terms. A DRPG is more akin to a gamemaster and a campaign than to an RPG source book, despite the world's richness and size. DRPGs do allow role-play, but they also determine it, offering only a few body types to players, a limited world in which stories may unfold, respect for some kinds of actions but not others, and certain realities with which players must deal (in combat, for example, there is not enough time to type out complete sentences on chat, and it would be excessively risky to wear something other than strong armor). Even in role-playing, no gamemaster gives a campaign and offers players a fully functional sandbox environment in the woods. Even the most elaborate and frequently expanded MMORPG can be understood as just one long campaign in one gamemaster's world. The problem, of course, is that it has substituted the range and flexibility of variety (different campaigns, different gamemasters) with the lures of character progress in a single world.

DRPGs retain systematization of fantasy, aesthetics to guide player imaginations that will fill in the low intensity gaps of the game as a medium[2], and emphasis on reflexive modification of the character who is the agency by which the player acts. But, unlike a session of an RPG (during which the character is usually improved only a little), almost every DRPG is 'ultimately concerned with building up enough strength, experience, and resources to overcome some uber-powerful foe', and exceptions (such as Ultima's early system of virtues instead of attributes) are still quests for self-improvement (Barton 2007b). This is the difference between how players gathered around a table treat a person and how a videogame treats a player.

Capacity for Identity

In the DRPG software environment, identity is an opportunity for play according to particular social rules and pursuant to a kind of education in the embodiment of identity that authorizes one's being.

This section analyzes the capacity system, which is the specific way players exist in, and interact with, DRPGs. Although narrative identity and the player's appearance have been much discussed, I downplay them in favor of capacity. As shown in the previous section, DRPGs animate fantasy by systematizing it through a statistical system. Despite its appealing stylization, that system is often a bit dull. Usually, one chooses a weapon by choosing the largest possible number of attack points.

In the systematized fantasy of DRPGs, capacity tends to overpower other registers of identity. While important socially in MMORPGs (and almost the only register where race and gender are real), *appearance* grew up around the capacity system and directs player imagination without making as much difference to gameplay as it probably should. Appearance tends to index capacities (Tronstad 2008) or give limited expression of a character's properties, in a relation analogous to phenotype to genotype (Smith 2006). *Narrative* identity results from what the game forces on the player and how the player sets up the character. Turkle's *Life on the Screen* (1995) addresses the seduction of identity, but intentionally ignores the powerful forces that direct the formation of identity. These forces are quite strong. Characters tend to be heavy heroes built around the skeletal grammar game interactivity allows (Burn and Schott 2004); certain identities are likely for social structural reasons, not just personal or psychological ones (McGahan 2008); single-player DRPGs have already written the (unchangeable) story of who the player-character is, and multi-player DRPGs accommodate only the range of narrative identities that have been written in advance. Both appearance and narrative identity exist because of capacities of the character to wear clothes, be seen, have a name, chat, honor promises, and act. This is not to reduce these registers to capacity, but to recognize the mutual presupposition between all three. Instead of appearance and narrative identity, I focus on the identity formed through modification of the ability to act.

Capacity is an ability to act in a situation. It is an immanent and locatable power. Games are made of many situations that are unlike one another: navigating menus, organizing saved games, fighting bosses, basking in glorious victory, special levels, mini-games, backtracking, and being lost are all examples. James Newman has argued that, at least in some situations within a game, the only relevant characteristics of an avatar are its capacities (Newman 2002). Newman's example is Princess in *Super Mario Brothers 2* (Nintendo EAD 1988). When she jumps, she can float a bit longer than the other characters. In a game based on jumping, to jump longer is to jump better. The fact that she wears pink, is a girl, or is a princess is irrelevant when trying to hop across a series of falling logs or land on a shooting egg. She is a jumping body character; it makes no difference within what is normally called gameplay that she is a princess. Most situations in a game (such as jumping from log to log) engage only some specific capacities of the avatar. Very often in DRPGs, you are your capacities.

Capacities are configured. This involves a basic unfreedom: the user must always be configuring. But what is configuration? I use configuration to refer to the synchronic manner in which paths of development are navigated. You can take your time to select one option from several that are available and the game executes the meaning of that selection. It's like pushing a button. The player selects capacities from menus, choosing which available weapon to equip, what kind of magic to further specialize in, or what line of dialogue to speak. These are choices made from a list of options. They are not freeform creative expressions or unchangeable constants. The capacity to withstand powerful blows or run faster than others does not exist in a person by chance, a talent discovered in childhood; working with the game, the player arranges these capacities, usually through very explicit interfaces. Although some games have subtle mechanisms that monitor player action and modify the character based on what you *do* (such as determining alignment in *Fallout 3* [Bethesda 2008]), players soon realize that this monitoring turns even more of their actions into reflexive configuration. Many decisions are permanent or very difficult to change. Because past decisions change what the best available option is in a present decision, players become committed to developing certain aspects of the character. Path dependence favors specialization.

Capacities of a configurable being open onto different worlds of possibility, offer characters different segmentations of perception (and thereby alternative worldings or milieus), and enable different kinds of action. Characters in *Freedom Force vs. The 3rd Reich*

(Irrational Games 2005) who can become immune to combat damage experience damage-taking as optional, something that can be turned on and off. Other characters cannot hide from damage. The wielding system is a ubiquitous example. Almost any DRPG (like some other genres) allows characters to use different weapons, and some are more open-minded about what can count as a weapon (e.g. a dead rat). Some characters, however, cannot wield weapons, and most have limits. Clerics, in many games, cannot wield swords. Some capacities are available for all characters, such as the capacity to gain experience, collect money, equip items from inventory, buy and sell, talk on chat channels, jump, or die. Many capacities of characters can change, whether by permanent change of abilities or by temporary status effects. All open to a world; or, to put it another way, all actualize potentials that are latent in the gameworld. Wielding opens to the world of blacksmiths, weapon enchantments, heavy blunt objects, and training with a weapon. It actualizes the potential of objects to be wielded, or swords to slice and knives to stab.

Sociality emerges from these capacities for perception and action, and this sociality can look rather antisocial. Chat, costumes, gestures, and discussion outside or alongside the game all yield sociality in *World of Warcraft* that can be understood in the terms used to study social situations in everyday life. People talk, make friends, and do things together. But there is also another sociality in DRPGs: the sociality of numbers. Online games have been studied as sites of human cultural activity, but most players act as characters concerned with sets of interesting numbers (a nightmare version of online dating). The attraction of one profile to another can be more about appealing characteristics than about charming character. In *World of Warcraft*, it's important to remember that, as of 2006, more than 40 percent of players didn't belong to guilds (Williams et al. 2006) and less than 10 percent of players participated in high-level raids (Ducheneaut et al. 2006). Human players engaged in computer-mediated communication (talking that's key to guilds and raids) are not the only things social in the game; numbers socialize with numbers. Some items and quests only become possibilities for a character with certain attributes (numbers). Some interactions with other players are completely instrumental, following the attributes, level, equipment, and skills that the other player has to offer. Who can you be for me? What can we do together? The capacity system makes itself deeply felt within the game as a social world. In his chapter in this volume, Voorhees describes this facet of DRPG as a neo-liberal multiculturalism wherein the other is valuable because he or she brings something to the table — is a character with useful characteristics.

To recap, capacity (an identity) empowers one with certain abilities to act that define, shape, and contextualize the game's virtual world. Playing the role of a character has come to mean selecting and modifying abilities to act that shape a player's world. As it happens, these games of collaborative imagining are also games of brazen careerism.

Meritocracy and Education

DRPGs instate a retrospective meritocracy that interlocks with the mechanisms of a configurable being. Get favorably evaluated, get upgraded. This pattern of the game mechanics can be understood as an institutional policy with social implications. The meritocracy discounts other kinds of characteristics and ways of playing from its channels of progress-making. This system of incentives, persuasion, instruction, and control shapes how beings are configured, ordering how players arrange their ability to act in a game.

Meritocracy is a system of rewarding candidates based on merit. Retrospective meritocracy defines merit in terms of past achievements, whereas a prospective meritocracy selects candidates based on an assessment of who would make the greatest contribution if given a particular resource or position. These terms are particularly useful in disparate impact law, where merit can mask confidential reasons of a hiring committee (Kennedy 1990) or obscure other factors that distribute merit by historical inequality (DeSario 2003). DRPG rules award resources and position to characters based only on what they have done, and rarely by considering what the player might do with a thing[3]. Nicole DeSario argues that the retrospective meritocratic model ignores the social context that makes individuals appear with merit and obscures the way merit is defined by those deciding about an individual's fate (DeSario 2003, 507–8). To reward merit, a system must identify what merit is and who has it, ignoring how merit came to be defined and distributed. Standardized tests are a familiar example. Merit in DRPGs, like money in the world, is something that, once acquired, does not stand for ability or future potential, but establishes it. (This contrasts with work experience, which hopefully *demonstrates* aptitude, though can also substitute for it.) The key cases of merit in DRPGs are currency systems (experience, mana, hit points, money, or reputation quantities) and linearly increasable statistics (skill levels, base attributes such as strength, or armor ratings). The game rewards these merits. This is how it encourages some actions over others, while ignoring background conditions that lead to these actions being taken and while displacing preferences of all kinds into a jargon of upgrades and obsolescence.

Experience points are a prime example of retrospective meritocracy in DRPGs. Experience that builds skill can be found in fantasy literature, or in training montages of kung fu or action movies; DRPGs make it mechanical. In a ratchet system, the character gains experience points at the death of an enemy or completion of a skilled task. Although this seems nonsensical compared with ordinary life, the model comes from wargaming (and thus from war) where seasoned troops can, as a rule of thumb, be considered better than those with less combat experience. Toward the player, the system uses the psychological mechanism of continuous reinforcement: every time the player does a task, the game provides a reward (Loftus and Loftus 1983, 14–26). For the game, this ratchet system (losing experience in a DRPG is rare) pushes the player into new areas with tougher monsters and harder tasks[4].

The DRPG meritocratic order follows the logic of upgrades and obsolescence. You do not choose based on naked preference, but in the meritocratic terms of improvement. Upgrades replace what came before, promising to fix what was wrong, and to improve it in all ways. New pieces of armor in *Secret of Mana* (Square 1993) are better in every way than previously available armor. The Unicorn Helm is *stronger* than the Tiger Cap. Because a single number defines an object, one unit can be absolutely superior to another. There is nothing to regret; quality increases quantitatively. For this reason, high-level characters can rightfully claim to be better than everyone else. Friedline and Collister document the linguistic 'power role' of such characters, and high-level players' ability (not always exercised) to command, shout, and bully other players. They, after all, are an upgraded version of us. The arrangement realizes a dream of seniority: to rank and order within a disciplinary scheme, to position bodies clearly in enclosures (Townley 1993, 528). Such disciplinary experience may be exactly what players enjoy (Silverman and Simon 2009).

Players who do not accumulate experience points, do not save regularly, or otherwise choose wrong are left behind in the trajectories developers have prepared for normative gameplay. This is not to say that all players min-max their characters, just that those who understand the game can see that this is what the system rewards. It is easy to forget that most players with most games go through a period of not understanding, which only ends for some. There is a high dropout rate. Getting past this requires supplication as students to the game.

DRPGs educate the player's freedom, which is directed towards improving their character's capacity, in a manner parallel to how games usually guide the player toward victory. Games do not dominate players completely, and players do not have free reign within games; the education, training, and socialization actually found in videogames lie between these two extremes. Although one can make much of the importance of winning to games (Wark 2007), and of the constant threat of failure, this tends to reduce games to struggles of a certain kind, ignoring play's playfulness and games' gentle didacticism. The game coaxes playfulness into its terms, by various means. *Fallout 3* begins with the character's own childhood, showing the player how different choices can be made and some of the basic kinds of effect they can have. After a while at the game, players learn even more of what to expect as consequences of their actions. Death is an event that forces the player to the order of game mechanics. Through it, we understand better our active involvement in the game (Atkins 2007). Death may function in power relations as 'one element among others, working to incite, reinforce, control, monitor, optimize, and organize the forces under it' (Foucault 1990, 136) to varied effect in MMORPGs (Klastrup 2007). In DRPGs, if you don't use the right weapon, you learn that you will die.

Games do not manipulate and control players all on their own, but work persuasively (Bogost 2007) and with the aid of a player community which often influences how one plays a game[5]. Between a DRPG's incitements to act and a player's experimentation and desires, one learns to act in accordance with a desire, even if the game has partly implanted it, to improve the character.

The function of DRPGs' meritocracy is to keep the player challenged without making the game completely linear. The character must be continually modified in a basically progressive way, but the linearity is not spatial (as in Mario games). Merit bonds players to their character, by forcing them to learn how to use the identity and develop it in a methodical way for a long time. So long as players are willing to accept the investment of effort the system requires, it efficiently multiplies the player's possibilities without wasting chunks of storyline. The same content in the game will be experienced differently if the character is a paladin or an illusionist; the game can scale up challenges by making a stronger version of the same monster for a new challenge.

Indeed, it doesn't take an entire DRPG to take advantage of self-modification's power for efficient non-linearity – it only takes a few elements. A smattering of these 'RPG elements' have been added to games of other genres to 'enhance' them, though this often does not make them better (Croshaw 2009). In these games, the character gains experience, can add or improve capacities, and collects an inventory of items; also game mechanics include some of the statistical contingency that comes from wargaming. DRPG elements generalize the model of a configurable being, largely as a way to produce modular narrative as described by Travis in this same volume. RPG elements give games more replay value and encourage players to bond with their custom-made characters, thereby decreasing resale. Game producers fear resale because the sale of used games trades off with sale of new games, which is of course a primary source of income for them. Publishers and developers are trying out different approaches to resist this trend (Hyman 2008). Increased replay value and reticence to sell a game are possible tactics in this battle. But the generalization of configurable being this represents isn't just happening in games; it also exceeds games.

Configurable Being Generalized

Configurable being is a mode of existence that provides an agency constantly under construction, with capacities opening to different worlds, specifically designed chances at clear steps of advancement, and a supporting aesthetic and system that animates fantasy. Between different implementations, much varies. To lump together every case of configurable being, across many different games, is therefore to make a generalization. Though every case may be unique, generalization is productive because it allows us to recognize commonalities among differences. This double meaning of generalization (as proliferating technology and summary concept) includes our thinking, when we make stylized summaries. We are part of the trend. Yet, whatever we call it, a self-modifying existence is common to increasingly large fragments of our lives (whether we are being called users, players, or customers). What has been learned from games can and should be used to envision more of our world than the odd hours occupied by the actual playing of games.

When I began working on this project, it seemed that configurable being was becoming the norm throughout the web: in online shopping, search, and content-based sites of all kinds. In shopping, collaborative filtering would develop alongside robust profiles on sites like Netflix and Amazon. In search, social search would consider site visits and recommendations from 'friends' of the user's profile (Halavais 2009, 160–80). In other sites, your identity would influence what you could see and do, as it does on Yelp and Flickr. Now *Facebook* has become more central, at least in the United States, and online identity has been consolidated. As of 2010, there are 500 million *Facebook* accounts of an estimated 2 billion internet users ('New *Facebook* Statistics' 2010). But size isn't even *Facebook*'s real advantage. What it actually provides is capacities for those who exist on its site to perceive and act beyond its own pages. *Facebook* has overtaken the fledgling identity systems that might have blossomed on many sites, turning each site into another modular set of capacities for *Facebook* accounts.

Web 2.0 technologies have made possible the consolidation of empowered identity. Web 2.0 has been the fanciful name for the enclosure, intensification, and advancement of hosting, visiting, content sharing, and linking together. Flickr, Digg, GoogleMaps, and Meebo are examples. The basic technologies of web 2.0 are old, but they've been repackaged so that everyone can play for free, while only some reap the economic benefits (Scholz 2008). Where hypertext browsers might once have offered other ways to traverse the web, new systems simulate the openness of the internet more reliably, with better interfaces, and more standardization of content. We have preformatted pages with nice layout instead of homepages forever under construction and attractive buttons instead of blue text hyperlinks. Cross-platform APIs and embedded content make user action no longer dependent on the hosting site; users can connect directly to (what they experience as) modular applications. User capacities (such as apps) open to new worlds (analogous to the earlier example of wielding); getting *Lexulous* for *Facebook* (Agarwalla and Agarwalla 2008) lets you see which of your friends are top scorers at the game and gives you a chance to compete with them. The social web centers on systems of identity because action on various sites (off *Facebook* servers) can be viewed on *Facebook* and can appear as authored by a *Facebook* identity. This is great for user-generated content, where content that would be mundane becomes interesting because you know the person who made it; amateur producers can use their social network as an audience, and any user can list, like, or share content they anticipate their network would enjoy (e.g. cat videos for cat fanciers). As a result, web 2.0 immerses each user in an individualized perspective, rather than leaving them to drift as they surf strange pages and take on new worldviews on the go (Langlois et al. 2009; Tully 2006).

Introduced in April 2010, *Facebook*'s Instant Personalization is a customization package for partner sites that carries this theme further. Websites can provide an individualized experience without developing their own profile system. What Instant Personalization does is, first, add some old *Facebook* features to existing sites (share, like, or comment on partner's pages) and, second, show activity of a *Facebook* user's friends on the partner site (what restaurants my friends have reviewed, what links they have shared). For *Facebook* users, the feature opens up new social worlds into which their capacities can reach, thus making other sites more interesting[6].

For business, this increases the value of partner sites to *Facebook*-using visitors and gives sites marketing information on these visitors.

The individual's identity, and its capacity in particular, is modular, upgradable, and configurable. The most basic capacities are common to everyone, and the system demands a certain minimum of choices be made, even if they make no difference. A wealth of additional capacities exist, as there is more to do with social networking than just browsing profiles and modifying your own. The user builds up albums of photos, tags friends, tweaks privacy settings, posts videos, reads friends' shared stories, looks through friends' albums, writes notes, takes personality quizzes with one app, compares friends with another app, and works her virtual farm in another. All this builds up the user as a character. The mechanisms here are different from DRPGs because they are not statistical or probabilistic. They systematize fantasies of having fun and exciting conversations with diverse and beautiful friends (faces are a major part of *Facebook*'s aesthetics), writing witty prose, or being a respected and appreciated photographer by employing already existing techniques of chat, comments, micro-blogging, photo posts, image tagging, embedded content, and a whole array of apps that connect to the rest of the web. The meritocratic system here works both by accumulation (friends and photos of oneself) and by the very fact that to be someone you must always do something, usually something recent[7]. Users are no longer just a username and password; they must always choose and are constantly encouraged to expand their capacities and participate more.

There are good local reasons for this enforced blossoming of individualism. A password holds individuals responsible for their possibly mischievous actions. When this was a profile's sole function (most of the history of computing), profiles were not elaborate. When the lifeblood of a system is user-generated content, users must be constantly encouraged to generate quality content in great quantity. Making users comfortable with the environment and concerned about their reputation helps stimulate the community (Jackson-Wilkinson 2009). As of 2010, internet users in the US spent an average of seven hours per month on *Facebook* (Nielsen 2010). This should mean increased revenue, but how you turn sociability into profit remains an open question. On-site ad revenue (the obvious route) has not proved very effective for social networks. Another approach is to gather information that could be useful for marketing (something Instant Personalization and Facebook Deals offer to partners)[8]. *Facebook* will no doubt continue to try turning users' investment in their identities into profit streams, by whatever means necessary. All this is quite contrary to the web's much-discussed anonymity and marks a break in how the internet is used and, therefore, also in how it should be studied.

To be online is not just to browse. It is to be and to act, with those actions often modifying one's own being. In web 2.0, just looking around becomes an action and this action is authored by a developing identity. The mechanisms of this being, which continue to be worked out, systematically animate social fantasies not of slaying ogres with magic spells, but of being a busy person with an active social life who stays up-to-date with the rapidly changing world. You do not just imagine this persona or role-play this character; you play the online identity game to act the part.

Generalization of a form of being does not happen by a single mechanism or for a single reason. Most obviously, it takes place when developers intentionally apply the principle from one case to another. It also happens when a particular approach can be deployed to handle a situation, as configurable being can handle modular levels of action in a system; or again, when the method provides customization that attracts customers and increases system use; or when customers expect and strongly prefer it. There is no simple explanation rooted in contemporary culture for the generalization of configurable being. To reduce it to an expression of a diagrammatic summary of macro-social conditions (e.g. capitalism, neo-liberalism, or disciplinary society) would be to miss both the specificity of the technology and the variety of situations where it is put to use.

A technology makes itself useful and is put to different uses. It is not invented once or taken up overnight. There are always local attractors, specific assemblages. Role-playing needed a way to insist on the meaningfulness of characteristics to animate fantasy scenarios with friends. In gaming, DRPG elements proliferate for reasons particular to game design, player culture, and dynamics within the industry. Similarly, configurable being online becomes real on account of forces of sociability, fantasy, pleasure, security, profit, and powerful hype. Despite differences between the exact being one plays, we spend increasing amounts of time in a role that perceives, acts, socializes, and appears through modular and configurable functions. This is not an attack on freedom, but the nature of an opportunity at something that is widely understood as pleasurable and empowering. It is simply an opportunity that is now available to be and to act.

Notes

1 There are RPGs where much of the character is determined at the outset (notably some Japanese games and older games). Though my focus is not on these games, they still almost always provide a character that must be modified for the player to progress, and they require player commitment to the character as if the player had chosen them.
2 Regarding use of aesthetics in *World of Warcraft*, see Chandler 2009.
3 Two important exceptions are social organizations within RPG worlds, which may make their decisions on whatever grounds, and awards scripted into the RPG narrative that select the character without the character doing anything to merit the magic sword, sacred duty, etc.
4 As games progress, they often require the player to understand the game more deeply and employ more clever strategies. Experience points are not the only force driving the game as an experience of progress, though they are a major one.
5 Gaming capital offers one way to understand how players influence one another (Apperley 2009, 74–8).
6 It is quite possible that the content of our own social network will not always remain so interesting for users. Communities based on shared interest rather than offline personal relations have, with the growing enthusiasm for social networking, receded for now.
7 *Facebook* needs users (your friends) to provide its 'social' service, so meritocracy is less vicious at encouraging hardcore use.
8 Introduced November 2010, Facebook Deals integrates coupons, groupons, charity offers, and promotions into *Facebook*.

References

Agarwalla, Rajat and Agarwalla Jayant. *Lexulous*. [Facebook]. Lexulous: Kolkata, 2008.
Apperley, Tom. 2009. *Gaming Rhythms: Play and Counterplay from the Situated to the Global*. Theory on Demand. Amsterdam: Institute of Network Cultures.
Atkins, Barry. 2007. 'Time in Prince of Persia: The Sands of Time.' In *Videogame, Player, Text*, ed. Barry Atkins and Tanya Krzywinska, 237–53. Manchester: Manchester University Press.
Barton, Matt. 2007a. 'The History of Computer Role-Playing Games Part 1: The Early Years (1980–1983).' *Gamasutra.com*. February 23. http://www.gamasutra.com/features/20070223a/barton_01.shtml.
—2007b. 'The History of Computer Role-Playing Games Part 2: The Golden Age (1985–1993).' *Gamasutra.com*. February 23. http://www.gamasutra.com/features/20070223b/barton_01.shtml.
Bethesda Game Studios. *Fallout 3*. [Xbox 360]. Bethesda Softworks: Rockville, MD, 2008.
Blizzard Entertainment. *World of Warcraft*. [PC]. Blizzard Entertainment: Irvine, CA, 2004.
Bogost, Ian. 2007. *Persuasive Games: The Expressive Power of Videogames*. Cambridge: MIT Press, July 1.
Burn, Andrew, and Gareth Schott. 2004. 'Heavy Hero or Digital Dummy? Multimodal Player-Avatar Relations in *Final Fantasy 7*.' *Visual Communication* 3(2): 213–33.
Chandler, Damon. 2009. *Living, Charming, Epic: The World of Warcraft Aesthetic*. Denver, Colorado: University of Denver. http://richardcolby.net/files/WoWAesthetic.pdf.
Cook, David. 1991. *Tome of Magic*. 2nd edition. Lake Geneva WI: TSR.
Croshaw, Ben. 2009. 'On RPG Elements.' *The Escapist*. Extra Punctuation. October 6. http://www.escapistmagazine.com/articles/view/columns/extra-punctuation/6588-Extra-Punctuation-On-RPG-Elements.
DeSario, Nicole J. 2003. 'Reconceptualizing Meritocracy: The Decline of Disparate Impact Discrimination Law.' *Harvard Law Review* 38(2): 479.
Dovey, Jon, and Helen Kennedy. 2006. *Game Cultures: Computer Games as New Media*. New York NY: Open University Press.
Ducheneaut, Nicolas, Nick Yee, Eric Nickell, and Robert J. Moore. 2006. 'Building an MMO With Mass Appeal: A Look at Gameplay in *World of Warcraft*.' *Games and Culture* 1(4): 281–317.
Edery, David, and Ethan Mollick. 2009. *Changing the Game: How Video Games are Transforming the Future of Business*. Upper Saddle River NJ: FT Press.

Fine, Gary. 1983. *Shared Fantasy: Role-Playing Games as Social Worlds.* Chicago: University of Chicago Press.

Foucault, Michel. 1990. *The History of Sexuality, Vol. 1: An Introduction.* Vintage, April 14.

Grant, John. 1996. *The Encyclopedia of Fantasy and Science Fiction Art Techniques.* Philadelphia: Running Press.

Halavais, Alexander. 2009. *Search Engine Society.* Malden, MA: Polity.

Hallford, Neal. 2001. *Swords & Circuitry: A Designer's Guide to Computer Role Playing Games.* Roseville CA: Prima Tech.

Hyman, Paul. 2008. 'As Recession Deepens, Used Games Get More Painful.' *Gamasutra.com.* December 8. http://www.gamasutra.com/view/feature/3872/as_recession_deepens_used_games_.php.

Irrational Games. *Freedom Force vs. The 3rd Reich.* [PC]. Digital Jesters: Welwyn Garden City, UK, 2005.

Jackson-Wilkinson, M. 2009. 'Lessons from Thomas Vander Wal: Reputation and Social Comfort.' *Viget Advance.* July 28. http://www.viget.com/advance/lessons-from-tvw#continue.

Juul, Jesper. 2010. *A Casual Revolution: Reinventing Video Games and Their Players.* Cambridge MA: MIT Press.

Kennedy, Duncan. 1990. 'A Cultural Pluralist Case for Affirmative Action in Legal Academia.' *Duke Law Journal*, 1990: 705–57.

Klastrup, Lisbeth. 2007. 'Why Death Matters: Understanding Gameworld Experience.' *Journal of Virtual Reality and Broadcasting* 4, no.3. http://www.jvrb.org/4.2007/1022/420073_bibtex.

Langlois, Ganaele, Fenwick McKelvey, Greg Elmer, and Kenneth Werbin. 2009. 'Mapping Commercial Web 2.0 Worlds: Towards a New Critical Ontogenesis.' *Fibreculture* 14. http://fourteen.fibreculturejournal.org/fcj–095-mapping-commercial-web–2–0-worlds-towards-a-new-critical-ontogenesis/.

Loftus, G. A. and E. F. Loftus. 1983. *Mind at Play: The Psychology of Video Games.* NY: Basic Books.

MacCallum-Stewart, Esther, and Justin Parsler. 2008. 'Role-play vs. Gameplay: The Difficulties of Playing a Role in *World of Warcraft*.' In *Digital Culture, Play, and Identity: a World of Warcraft reader*, ed. Hilde Corneliussen and Jill Walker Rettberg, 225–46. Cambridge MA: MIT Press.

Mackay, Daniel. 2001. *The Fantasy Role-Playing Game: a New Performing Art.* Jefferson NC: McFarland.

Massumi, Brian. 2007. 'The Thinking-Feeling of What Happens.' In *Interact or die! 'There is drama in the networks'*, ed. Joke Brouwer and Arjen Mulder, 70–91. Rotterdam: V2 Pub./NAi Publishers.

McGahan, Christopher. 2008. *Racing Cyberculture: Minoritarian Art and Cultural Politics on the Internet.* New York: Routledge.

McLuhan, Marshall. 1994. *Understanding Media: The Extensions of Man.* Cambridge MA: MIT Press.

Miller, John. 2006. 'Role Playing Games as Interactive Fiction.' *Reconstruction* 6(1). http://reconstruction.eserver.org/061/miller.shtml.
Moore, Christopher Luke. 2009. 'Digital Games Distribution: The Presence of the Past and the Future of Obsolescence.' *M/C Journal* 12, no.3 (July 16). http://journal.media-culture.org.au/index.php/mcjournal/article/viewArticle/166/0.
'New *Facebook* Statistics – Geographic Regions and Country.' 2010. Internet World Stats. September 26, 2010. http://www.internetworldstats.com/stats25.htm.
Newman, James. 2002. 'The Myth of the Ergodic Videogame.' *Game Studies* 1.2. http://gamestudies.org/0102/newman/.
Nielsen. 2010. 'Facebook Users Average 7 hrs a Month in January as Digital Universe Expands.' *Nielsen Wire*. February 16. http://blog.nielsen.com/nielsenwire/online_mobile/facebook-users-average–7-hrs-a-month-in-january-as-digital-universe-expands/.
Nintendo EAD. *Super Mario Bros 2*. [Nintendo]. Nintendo: Kyoto, 1988.
Origin Systems. *Ultima VII: The Black Gate*. [PC] Origin Systems: Manchester, NH, 1992.
Scholz, Trebor. 2008. 'Market Ideology and the Myths of Web 2.0.' *First Monday* 13, no.3. http://www.uic.edu/htbin/cgiwrap/bin/ojs/index.php/fm/article/view/2138/1945.
Silverman, Mark, and Bart Simon. 2009. 'Discipline and Dragon Kill Points in the Online Power Game.' *Games and Culture* 4(4): 353–78.
Smith, C. Jason. 'Body Matters in Massively Multiplayer Online Role-playing Games.' *Reconstruction* 6, no.1 (Winter 2006). http://reconstruction.eserver.org/061/smith.shtml.
Square. *Secret of Mana*. [Super Nintendo]. Square: Tokyo, 1993.
Townley, Barbara. 1993. 'Foucault, Power/Knowledge, and Its Relevance for Human Resource Management.' *The Academy of Management Review* 18(3): 518–45.
Tronstad, Ragnhild. 2008. 'Character Identification in *World of Warcraft*: the Relationship Between Capacity and Appearance.' In *Digital Culture, Play, and Identity: A World of Warcraft Reader*, ed. Hilde Corneliussen. Cambridge MA: MIT Press.
Tully, James. 2006. 'Communication and Imperialism.' *ctheory.net* td035 (February 22). http://www.ctheory.net/articles.aspx?id=508.
Turkle, Sherry. 1995. *Life on the Screen: Identity in the Age of the Internet*. New York: Simon & Schuster.
Wark, McKenzie. 2007. *Gamer Theory*. Cambridge MA: Harvard University Press.
Williams, Dmitri, Nicolas Ducheneaut, Li Xiong, Yuanyuan Zhang, Nick Yee, and Eric Nickell. 2006. 'From Tree House to Barracks: The Social Life of Guilds in *World of Warcraft*.' *Games and Culture* 1(4): 338–61.
Zuckerberg, Mark et al. Facebook. [Web]. Facebook: Cambridge, MA, 2004.

About the Contributors

Josh Abboud recently received his Ph.D. from Clemson University in the Rhetorics, Communication, and Information Design program, where his research focused on bringing together various disciplines to inform critical approaches to writing and human communication. His academic interest in games studies comes from an early engagement with film and video production and which carries on through his work in digital writing and technologies. Most recently, his dissertation project explored multimodal composition, particularly cinematic expressions, as an ethical context of collaboration. He is currently teaching as a lecturer in the Writing, Rhetoric, and Digital Media Division at the University of Kentucky.

Adele Bealer is a third-year Ph.D. candidate at the University of Utah, pursuing a degree in American Studies with an emphasis in ecocriticism. Drawing on her M.A. in Environmental Humanities, her dissertation develops a radical ecocritical methodology that draws heavily from performance and spatial studies and that can be applied to the close reading (and close playing) of a variety of traditional and nontraditional texts, including graphic novels and videogames. Triangulated with ecocriticism's emphasis on process and holism, performance studies and spatial theory challenge traditional nature writing's celebration of the visibly manifest, its refusal to look beneath the surface. The force of this interruption is to recast environmental scenarios in terms of repetitive performances by multiple human and/Other actors. Performances may repeat, but they can be repeated with a difference. Radical ecocriticism refuses futility, instead infusing its examination of environmental texts with an insistence on possibility.

Andrew Baerg serves as an Assistant Professor in Communication at the University of Houston-Victoria where he teaches a variety of media-related courses. His primary research interest involves the relationship between the sports videogame and its broader social and cultural context. His previous work has examined games like *Fight Night Round 2*, *Fifa Football '09* and *NBA Live '09*. However, as the included chapter suggests, he also enjoys thinking about role-playing games as well. When not working or spending time with his wife, he can usually be found playing the latest iteration of the *Football Manager* series.

Josh Call is an Assistant Professor of English at Grand View University in Des Moines, IA. He has a B.S. in English and Philosophy (2001), an M.A. in English (2003) and a Ph.D in Composition in Rhetoric (2009). He teaches courses in composition, literacy, rhetoric and visual culture, and general humanities. In addition to co-editing *Approaches to Digital Game Studies* he is currently researching the connections between games and pedagogy, focusing on reclaiming play in the classroom for better learning. He lives in Iowa with his wife Nichole, daughter Kairie and son Colin.

Lauren B. Collister is a Ph.D. student in Sociolinguistics at the University of Pittsburgh. She received an M.A. in Linguistics in 2008 from the University of Pittsburgh and B.A.s in Linguistics and Music from The Ohio State University in 2006. Under the name of Skakavaz, the level 85 Draenei holy paladin, she has been conducting a participant-observation ethnography of the *World of Warcraft* community since 2007. Her research interests include linguistic change in online spaces, as well as expressions of identity and group affiliation in digital worlds. Past work includes studies on the role of non-alphabetic symbols (such as *, ^, and <--) in online discourse, and linguistic strategies for the portrayal of self and avatar identities in digital worlds.

Christopher Douglas is Associate Professor of English at the University of Victoria. He is the author of *A Genealogy of Literary Multiculturalism* (Cornell UP, 2009), 'Christian Multiculturalism and Unlearned History in Marilynne Robinson's *Gilead*' (*NOVEL* 44.3 [Fall

2011]), and 'You Have Unleashed a Horde of Barbarians!': Fighting Indians, Playing Games, Forming Disciplines' (*Postmodern Culture* 13.1 [September 2002]). His current research project is titled *If God Meant to Interfere: American Fiction During the Postwar Christian Resurgence*.

Benjamin E. Friedline received his B.A. in History and Spanish from Messiah College in 2004 and his M.A. in Applied Linguistics from the University of Pittsburgh in 2008. He is currently a Ph.D. candidate in the Department of Linguistics at the University of Pittsburgh, where he specializes in Applied Linguistics, Teaching English to Speakers of Other Languages (TESOL), Second Language Acquisition, Sociolinguistics, and Linguistic Theory. His most recent work is within the domain of Applied Linguistics in that it connects theories from Second Language Acquisition and Linguistics with practical classroom applications. More specifically, this work investigates how second language learners of English acquire derivational morphology within English as a Second Language classrooms.

Alice Henton received her B.A. in English and History from the University of California, Davis in 2005 and is currently completing her Ph.D. in English at the University of California, Los Angeles. Her current research interests include archival narratives and constructions of the supernatural.

Trent Hergenrader is a Ph.D. candidate in English with a concentration in Creative Writing at the University of Wisconsin-Milwaukee. His research focuses on creative writing pedagogy and incorporating games and gaming in writing courses. His fiction has been published in *The Magazine of Fantasy & Science Fiction*, *Realms of Fantasy*, and *Best Horror of the Year #1*, among others. He recently received a Teaching Excellence Award from his department and was selected for the 2011–12 Tinsley Helton Dissertation Fellowship.

Zachary McDowell is a Doctoral Candidate in the Department of Communication at the University of Massachusetts, Amherst. The first digital game he ever completed was *Wishbringer*, an interactive fiction game by Infocom, released in 1985. The second was *Wasteland*. He played them on an Apple IIE. In general, his research focuses on how digital technologies shape communicative practices. He is currently writing his dissertation on the role of digital sharing in restructuring cultural hegemony.

Chuk Moran is a Ph.D. candidate in the Department of Communication at UC San Diego. He studies videogames, time, the undo function, and everyday software. His recent publications include 'Playing with Game Time: Auto-Saves and Undoing Despite the "Magic Circle"' in *Fibreculture*, and 'Interactive Time and "Real Time" in Software and Society' in *Spectator*. He can be reached at chuk.edu@gmail.com.

Kathleen Murphy holds an M.A. in Rhetoric and Communication Design at the University of Waterloo. She is currently a user experience researcher and designer for a firm in Waterloo ON. Her games research focuses on character and player interaction, dialogue systems, and the intersections of film, theater, and game.

Neil Randall is an Associate Professor in the Department of English at the University of Waterloo; he is also the director of the university's newly constituted (2011) Games Institute. His many game reviews, columns, and features appeared in various game magazines between 1984 and 2002, and he is a long-time contributing editor to *PC Magazine*, contributing over the years on various computing topics. He has taught game studies and game design at graduate and undergraduate levels. In addition, he has co-designed and developed several boardgame simulations, and he has taught the works of J. R. R. Tolkien throughout his career.

Douglas Schules is an Assistant Professor at Rikkyo University's Department of Business in Tokyo. His current research gravitates towards the intersections between copyright, fan translations, and new media. Broadly, however, he is interested in the practices by which Japanese and American cultures are mediated through new technologies, and his dissertation argued, in part, for critical attention towards the medium itself in the act of translation.

ABOUT THE CONTRIBUTORS 367

Roger Travis is Associate Professor of Classics and Ancient Mediterranean Studies in the Department of Modern and Classical Languages at the University of Connecticut, Storrs. He received his Bachelor's degree in Classics from Harvard College, and his Ph.D. in Comparative Literature from the University of California, Berkeley before arriving at UConn in 1997. He has published on Homeric epic, Greek tragedy, Greek historiography, the 19th-century British novel, *Halo*, the massively-multiplayer online role-playing game, ethics in videogames, and game-based learning in classics journals, gaming magazines, and scholarly volumes. He has been President of the Classical Association of New England and of the Classical Association of Connecticut. He writes the blog *Living Epic,* and is a co-founder and contributing author of the collaborative blog *Play the Past*.

Gerald Voorhees is an Assistant Professor at Oregon State University jointly appointed in Speech Communication and New Media Communication. He teaches classes in media studies, rhetorical studies, and game studies. His research focuses on games and new media as sites for the construction and contestation of identity and culture. He is also interested in public discourse pertaining to games and new media, as well as rhetorics of race and ethnicity in mediated public discourse.

Katie Whitlock is an Associate Professor at California State University, Chico, in the Department of Theater. Her areas of teaching range from theater history to identity performance to theatrical theory, with occasional forays into design, all of which is usually spiced with an interest in technology. Her research is focused on popular culture, specifically on the nature of videogames as connected to performance and other aspects of human experience. She directs and designs productions which pull from her interest in popular culture and media, as well as her interest in digital games. She continues to strive for the ultimate production which will blend theater and videogames into one perfect moment of pop nirvana.

Karen Zook is a Ph.D. candidate in Comparative Literary and Cultural

Studies at the University of Connecticut. She received her B.A. in Classical Languages and Literatures from Dartmouth College and her M.A. in Comparative Literary and Cultural Studies at the University of Connecticut.

Author Index

Aarseth, Espen 1, 5, 8, 31, 49, 68, 89, 90, 184, 309
Alcoff, Linda Martín 295
Althusser, Louis 250
Amato, Joe 306
Andrew, Dudley 116, 129
Anzaldúa, Gloria 292–3, 295
Appadurai, Arjun 28
Apperly, Thomas 5, 8, 92, 359n. 5
Arsenault, Dominic 4, 220
Atkins, Barry 353
Austin, J. L. 89, 90, 100–1

Balibar, Etienne 289–91
Barthes, Roland 184, 220
Bartle, Richard 195
Barton, Matt 13, 91–3, 155–6, 175, 347
Baudrillard, Jean 12, 89, 95, 100, 151n. 3
Bayliss, Peter 186
Beck, Ulrich 154, 157–8, 166
Benjamin, Walter 12
Bennett, Tony 261
Biesecker, Barbara 261
Bishop, Kyle 116, 128
Blanchot, Maurice 61
Boas, Franz 285–6, 290–1
Bogost, Ian 1, 32, 35, 39–42, 46n. 5, 53–4, 61, 88, 239, 252, 262, 273–4, 309, 354
Bots, P. W. G. 305
Burn, Andrew 7–8, 15, 184, 189, 265, 330, 348
Butler, Judith 262

Campbell, Joseph 15, 171
Carlson, Marvin 148
Carr, Diane 7–8, 15, 330
Carruthers, Mary 81
Castronova, Edward 162
Chang, Briankle 180–1
Charles, Alec 186
Chaudhuri, Una 31, 46n. 2
Chin, Frank 293–5
Chomsky, Noam 89
Crawford, Chris 6

de Certeau, Michel 73
Dean, Mitchell 157, 158, 169
Derrida, Jacques 44, 51–2, 71, 177–8, 181, 191, 263
DeSario, Nicole 351
Diamond, Elin 136, 140
Dickey, Michele 164–5
Dresher, Melvin 327, 330, 333
Douglas, Christopher 290
Ducheneaut, Nicolas 300n. 5, 350

Edwards, Ron 329, 331, 332, 340n. 4
Emerson, Ralph Waldo 31, 35, 46n. 7

Fine, Gary Alan 154–5
Fleischer, H. Kassia 306
Ford, Richard T. 297, 299
Foster, Thomas 281, 295, 300n. 4
Foucault, Michel 71, 154, 156–7, 260–3, 353

Frasca, Gonzalo 1, 67, 90, 103, 107
Fuchs, Elinor 31, 46n. 2
Gardner, John 308, 314–15, 317
Gee, James 314, 338–9
Geertz, Clifford 237, 295
Goffman, Erving 33, 205
Gregersen, Andreas 222
Grodal, Torben 222
Gunkel, David 183, 187
Hagström, Charlotte 287
Halavais, Alexander 355
Hallford, Neal 345
Harvey, David 157
Hayse, Mark 166
Heidegger, Martin 55
hooks, bell 263
Howard, Jeff 155, 164–5, 171
Howard, Nigel 327, 333
Huizinga, Johan 219, 220, 221, 233, 326
Hurston, Zora Neale 285–6, 290–2, 294, 296–7
Hutcheon, Linda 120, 128
Hymes, Dell 96

Iser, Wolfgang 73, 336

Jackson, John Brinckerhoff 29–30, 34–5, 37, 38, 46n. 6
Juul, Jesper 1, 48–9, 57–8, 68, 332, 336

Kelly, R. V. 196, 212
Kennedy, Duncan 351
Kenny, Sue 158
Kerman, Judith 116
Kiesling, Scott 195, 197–8, 212, 213, 214, 215
King, Geoff 17
Kittler, Friedrich 51

Klastrup, Lisbeth 353
Konzack, Lars 154, 159
Kövecses, Zoltan 223
Krzywinska, Tanya 17, 53, 57, 286–7

Labov, William 96, 197
Lacan, Jacques 250
Lakoff, George 223
Langer, Jessica 288
Lefebvre, Henri 40–1, 45
Leitch, Thomas 115, 117–18, 120–1, 128–9
Locke, John 136–7
Loftus, G. A. 352
Lord, Albert 219, 235–9, 242, 266
Lyotard, Jean-François 89, 100–1, 104

MacCallum-Stewart, Esther 287, 347
McGahan, Christopher 348
MacKay, Daniel 155–6
McLuhan, Marshall 99, 100, 154, 346
Magnet, Shoshana 28–9, 40, 42, 46n. 2
Manovich, Lev 68–9, 84
Mäyrä, Franz 8
Miller, John 344
Miller, Kiri 66
Miller, Toby 262
Momaday, N. Scott 291, 294
Moore, Sonia 137, 150
Morrison, Toni 292
Mortensen, Torill Elvira 12, 209, 287
Murray, Janet 53, 68, 235, 237
Musolff, Andreas 223, 231
Myers, David 5

Nakamura, Lisa 279–80
Naremore, James 116

Newman, James 5, 62, 186, 265, 348–9

O'Connor, Flannery 308
O'Malley, Pat 159
Omi, Michael 280, 295, 297
Ono, Kent 261

Parry, Adam 235
Parry, Milman 235, 237, 239
Perron, Bernard 220, 233n. 4
Phelan, Peggy 145
Peirce, Charles S. 224

Reed, Ishmael 291–2, 294–5
Roach, Joseph 147
Rose, Nikolas 154, 157, 158

Salen, Katie 4, 262, 326
Schechner, Richard 32–4, 40, 42
Schieffelin, Edward L. 28
Scholz, Trebor 356
Schott, Gareth 265, 348
Schulzke, Marcus 319
Schut, Kevin 122, 127
Searle, John Rogers 90
Shannon, C. E. and Weaver, W. 179–80
Sicart, Miguel 244
Sloop, John 261
Smith, C. Jason 348

Steinkuehler, Constance 195, 196

Taylor, Diana 42, 44–5, 85n. 7
Taylor, Laurie 51
Taylor, T. L. 195
Townley, Barbara 353
Travis, Roger 219–20
Tronstad, Ragnhild 216n. 3, 266, 348
Turkle, Sherry 186, 348

Wagner, Geoffrey 116, 129
Wallin, Mark Rowell 128
Wark, McKenzie 353
Werber, Niels 281
Whalen, Zach 8
Whitehead, Anne 139, 144
Whitlock, Katherine Lynne 39
Williams, Dmitri 195, 350
Winant, Howard 280, 295, 297
Wolf, Mark J. P. 5–7, 13, 32, 91
Wolford, Lisa 149

Venuti, Lawrence 89,
Virilio, Paul 60
Voorhees, Gerald 266, 271, 274

Zimmerman, Eric 4, 262, 326
Žižek, Slavoj 186–7, 262

Game Index

Arc the Lad: Twilight of the Spirits (Sony) 36–45, 147

Bethesda 239, 249, 252–3
  see also Fallout; Elder Scrolls
BioWare 221, 232, 236, 238–9, 242–3, 246–53, 333, 338
  see also Dragon Age: Origins; Mass Effect; Star Wars: Knights of the Old Republic
Blizzard 56, 58–9, 279, 282, 286–9, 291, 298–9
  see also World of Warcraft

DC Universe Online (Sony Online Entertainment) 54,
Doom (id Software) 57–8
Dragon Age (series) 67, 137, 274, 333, 338, 340
  Dragon Age: Origins (BioWare) 67, 72–84, 189, 221–33, 239–52,
Dungeons & Dragons (Gygax and Arneson) 153–5, 159–60, 280, 328, 344–6

Elder Scrolls (series)
  Elder Scrolls II: Daggerfall (Bethesda) 12
  Elder Scrolls IV: Oblivion (Bethesda) 137, 249, 253

Fallout (series) 175–8, 182, 184–5, 189–91
  Fallout: A Post Nuclear Roleplaying Game (Interplay Entertainment) 175, 185

Fallout 2 (Interplay Entertainment) 175, 185
Fallout 3 (Bethesda Softworks) 175, 185–6, 253, 307–21, 349, 353,
Fallout: New Vegas (Bethesda Softworks) 175, 185–6
Final Fantasy (series) 142, 271, 274
Final Fantasy VII (Square Co. Ltd) 138, 142–5
Final Fantasy X (Square Co. Ltd) 138, 145–8
Freedom Force vs. The 3rd Reich (Irrational Games) 349–50

God of War (Sony Computer Entertainment) 4
Guild Wars (Arena Net) 54

Halo: Combat Evolved (Bungie) 238

Icewind Dale (Black Isle Studios) 12

Lineage II (NC Interactive) 195–6
The Lord of the Rings: Battle for Middle Earth II (Electronic Arts) 122
The Lord of the Rings Online (Turbine, Inc.) 113–15, 118–30, 239 280–1
The Lord of the Rings: War of the Rings (Sierra Entertainment)
Lost Odyssey (Mistwalker and feelplus, Inc.) 138–42, 148

Lux-Pain (Killaware) 89–109

Mass Effect (series) 22, 137, 333, 338
 Mass Effect (BioWare) 15, 67, 160, 239–52, 259–60, 262–74, 275, 330
 Mass Effect 2 (BioWare) 275

Neverwinter Nights 2 (Obsidian Entertainment) 153–4, 159–70

Rift (Trion Worlds) 54

Secret of Mana (Square) 352
Star Wars: Knights of the Old Republic (BioWare) 238–52
Suikoden 2 (Konami) 332–9
Super Mario Brothers (Nintendo) 4

Super Mario Brothers 2 (Nintendo) 349

Tales of Vesperia (Namco Tales Studio) 13

Ultima (series) 14, 91, 347
 Ultima VII: The Black Gate (Origin Studios)

Wasteland (Electronic Arts) 175–7, 185, 189–91
World of Warcraft (Blizzard Entertainment) 55–63, 195–6, 200–15, 278–99, 350

Zero Wing (Toaplan) 113

Subject Index

adaptation
 cultural 291, 295, 298
 media 113–30, 293
aesthetics 93, 103, 105–9, 163, 168, 284, 288, 305, 345–7, 355–7
affinity spaces 338–9
affordance 329–30, 338, 343
agency 23, 33, 53, 222, 227, 267, 340n. 4, 343–4, 347, 355
anthropology 237, 290–1, 293, 295
archive 66–78, 81–4
Aristotle 140
avatar *see also* player
 character 30–40, 53, 62–3, 161, 176, 200, 250, 265, 314
 abilities 31, 33, 161, 166, 196, 201, 214, 265, 272–3, 312, 347–51, 357
 appearance 126, 137, 215, 224, 310–12, 348
 attributes 70, 85n. 5, 137, 160–1, 272, 282, 307, 312, 347, 350
 class 124–6, 160, 201, 204, 208, 265, 272, 280, 282, 296
 creation 137, 150, 159–61, 306, 310–11, 344
 customization 145, 311–12, 358
 race 125, 160–1, 224
 relation to player 31, 34, 49, 142, 182–91

biopolitics 154, 156–9
Brown v. Board of Education 285

capacity *see* avatar, ability
Civil Rights 291, 299
 codex 71–81
combat 53, 119, 125, 153, 155, 166–70, 185, 200, 239, 271, 274, 346
communication 29, 116, 176–7, 179–83, 188, 220
community 29–30, 34, 39, 58–9, 195–8, 213–14, 354, 357
culture 38, 79–81, 147–8, 154, 190, 262, 266, 279, 282, 283–99, 333, 338, 339

Dada *see* Tzara, Tristan
database 66–7, 69–73, 83–4

ecocriticism 27–8, 44–5
embodiment 27, 183, 186, 223, 230, 233, 314, 347
epic 219, 221, 235–9, 245–6, 252
equipment 33, 161–3, 166–7, 168, 200–9, 212–14
ethnography 199

Facebook 355–8
feedback 51, 62–3, 185, 262, 274
fidelity 115–18, 128–9

gamemaster 155, 347
gameplay 5, 8, 17–18, 28–32, 37, 40, 42, 51, 53–4, 58–9, 63, 68, 71, 73–4, 83–4, 91, 95–9, 104–5, 109, 148–50,

163, 166, 185–6, 203, 220–4, 245, 265, 267–8, 271–4, 281, 287, 310–12, 328, 344, 348–9
gamescape 28–36, 40–5, 46n. 2
gameworld 49, 54, 57, 60–1
gear *see* equipment
gender 108–9, 160, 201, 214–15
genre 3–8, 12–13, 17–18, 50, 129, 239, 346, 354
  functional 7
  ludic 8, 18
  thematic 7–8
gestus 149
governmentality 154, 156–9, 260–3
GNS Theory 329–32, 340
Grutter v. Bollinger 297
Gygax, Gary 159, 169–70
  see also Dungeons & Dragons

Huntington, Samuel 279

identification 63, 128, 220, 232–3, 236, 250–1, 328
identity 49, 55, 107, 137–43, 186, 221–2, 229–32, 344, 347–51, 355–7
  construction 33, 37, 194–216, 250–3, 283
  group 39, 272, 284, 286, 288, 292, 294
  narrative 265, 332, 344, 348
  performed 39, 262, 264–71, 273
ideology 28, 69, 105–8, 156–7, 247–9, 268
imagination 139, 345–8
immersion 28, 70–2, 90, 93, 95, 96, 99, 103–6, 121–2, 146, 184–7, 220–1, 330, 332–3, 356
inventory 161–3,
Iowa Writers Workshop 304–6

Jackson, Peter 113–15, 118, 120, 126–9
Japanese Role-playing Game 92–3, 138, 142, 147, 189, 359n. 1

language 34, 79, 88–110, 139, 195–9, 202–15, 284, 288, 292, 294, 299
language game 89, 99
leadership 196, 208–9, 212,
localization 89, 94–5, 98, 105–6, 109
ludology 67–9

magic circle 326
massively multiplayer online role-playing game (MMORPG) 49–64, 119–29, 164, 170, 194–5, 214, 282, 346–8
meritocracy 351–4
metagaming 325–32, 337–9
metaphor 29, 39, 43, 221–3, 231–3, 295, 307
multiculturalism 279, 290
  literary 290, 291–9
  neo-liberal 262–3, 273–5

narrative 35–40, 41, 49–53, 57–8, 60, 67, 90, 95, 110, 149–50, 220, 233, 247, 266–7, 306–22
  effects on play 33, 69, 84, 137–8, 155, 232, 270
  structures 69–73, 164–9, 237
narratology 67–9
neo-liberalism 156–9, 161–3, 169–71, 259–63, 268, 273–4

party 15, 18, 161, 169, 205–7, 240, 271–4

performance 27–45, 68, 70, 103, 135–8, 149–50, 219, 236–54, 260, 262, 268–74
performance studies 27, 32
player character *see* avatar
possibility space 262
postal principle 181–2
postcolonialism 279, 288
power 51, 85n. 5, 163, 195–216, 261–2
procedural rhetoric 54, 57, 60, 63, 239, 253, 273–4
procedurality 53–5, 60–3, 273–4

quests 53, 58–61, 119–20, 163, 164–6, 184, 287, 318

race 250, 264–6, 272, 280, 283–99, 310, 311
 biological concepts of 223, 288–9, 295
 online 279–80, 282–3
 social construction of 280–1, 285, 295–6
raid 207–9, 212
rhetoric 53, 62, 327
risk 157–9
role-playing game
 fantasy 7, 18, 118–19, 155–6, 224–5, 265, 280–2, 345–7
 genre 11–18, 70, 90–3, 128–9, 170–1, 307, 344–7

history 13–14, 154–6, 345–6
rules 68, 71, 90, 161, 184, 220, 233, 260, 263–4, 273–4, 324–5, 328, 332, 345

space 27–45, 49, 51, 60–4, 287, 326
spamming 209–11
Stance Dancing 330, 337, 339
statistics *see* avatar: attributes
subject 62, 136–8, 156–9, 180–2, 250–2, 260–3
 formation 53, 62, 262
 position 136, 344
subjectivity 49, 51, 186, 253, 332
system operations 35–7, 40, 307

telepresence 51–2, 58–9, 63
theme 225, 230–1, 236–9, 242, 245–6
time 48–63, 140, 150, 177–9, 189–91
translation 89, 110, 116–17, 181
truth game 260–3, 271, 273–4
Tolkien, J. R. R. 113–15, 118–29
Tzara, Tristan 106–8

unit operations 35–6, 39–41, 239, 309, 320

web 2.0 355–6, 358
win conditions 330–1, 333, 337

Lightning Source UK Ltd.
Milton Keynes UK
UKHW02f0135210618
324573UK00008B/75/P